Critical Essays on
SHAKESPEARE'S
Measure for Measure

CRITICAL ESSAYS
ON
BRITISH LITERATURE

Zack Bowen, General Editor
University of Miami

Critical Essays on SHAKESPEARE'S *Measure for Measure*

edited by

RICHARD P. WHEELER

G. K. Hall & Co.
New York

G. K. Hall & Co.
1633 Broadway
New York, NY 10019

Library of Congress Cataloging-in-Publication Data

Critical essays on Shakespeare's Measure for measure / edited by Richard P. Wheeler.
p. cm. — (Critical essays on British literature)
Includes bibliographical references and index.
ISBN 0-7838-0428-8 (alk. paper)
1. Shakespeare, William, 1564–1616. Measure for measure. 2. Brothers and sisters in literature. 3. Chastity in literature. 4. Comedy. I. Wheeler, Richard P. (Richard Paul), 1943– . II. Title: Shakespeare's Measure for measure. III. Series.
PR2824.C75 1999
822.3'3—dc21 99–27396
CIP

This paper meets the requirements of ANSI/NISO Z3948-1992 (Permanence of Paper).

10 9 8 7 6 5 4 3 2 1

Printed in the United States of America

Contents

General Editor's Note

◆

The Critical Essays on British Literature series provides a variety of approaches to both classical and contemporary writers of Britain and Ireland. The formats of the volumes in the series vary with the thematic designs of individual editors and with the amount and nature of existing reviews and criticism, augmented, where appropriate, by original essays by recognized authorities. It is hoped that each volume will be unique in developing a new overall perspective on its particular subject.

Richard Wheeler's introduction calls to attention the ambiguities engendered by the tragic/comic ambivalence of *Measure for Measure's* plot. Its status as a "problem play" has a long life. Wheeler traces the debate through 200 years to the present. It is a "play about sexuality, power, and corruption; about repression, irony, and betrayal; about lies, secrets, and exposures . . ." But from these serious plot elements a happy ending ensues. Whether or not this represents Shakespeare's realistic outcome of tragic complications or a flawed plot structure with a forced ending continues to be fascinating to audiences and scholars alike.

All selected essays were published within the last 20 years and represent a range of contemporary approaches such as psychoanalytic concepts, the effects of cultural materialism, new historicism, and the representation of sexuality and gender in power politics.

ZACK BOWEN
University of Miami

Publisher's Note

Producing a volume that contains both newly commissioned and reprinted material presents the publisher with the challenge of balancing the desire to achieve stylistic consistency with the need to preserve the integrity of works first published elsewhere. In the Critical Essays series, essays commissioned especially for a particular volume are edited to be consistent with G. K. Hall's house style; reprinted essays appear in the style in which they were first published, with only typographical errors corrected. Consequently, shifts in style from one essay to another are the result of our efforts to be faithful to each text as it was originally published.

Introduction

◆

RICHARD P. WHEELER

A thorough history of Shakespearean criticism, Stanley Cavell once wrote, "would be part of a full description of Western cultural history since the Renaissance."[1] Criticism of *Measure for Measure* would make a peculiar—but certainly instructive and fascinating—contribution to that history, demonstrating just how crowded with vexed issues at the heart of Western culture a single play can be. *Measure for Measure* is, among many other things, a play about love, power, and justice; about sexuality, authority, and freedom; about procreation and birth and life and death; about community and communication; about public law and individual conscience; about morality and ethics, good and evil, crime and sin, secrets and lies; about the sacred and the secular; about the Old Testament and the New, religion and religiosity; about representation and theatricality; about self-knowledge and self-deception; about forgiveness and the unforgivable, sameness and difference, means and ends, what changes and what remains the same. But what does the play have to say about all this? And from what vantage point? To what ends? With what success? *Measure for Measure* has been generating impassioned and often wildly conflicting responses to questions like these since interpretive comments on this play began to be recorded.

L. C. Knights began his 1942 essay on the play by identifying "*Measure for Measure* as that play of Shakespeare's that has caused most readers the greatest sense of strain and mental discomfort."[2] His observation reflects remarks made more than a century earlier by Samuel Taylor Coleridge: "This play, which is Shakespeare's throughout, is to me the most painful—say rather, the only painful—part of his genuine works."[3] Coleridge's judgments on "the comic and tragic parts" of *Measure for Measure*—he found "the one disgusting, the other horrible"—in turn call to mind Charlotte Lennox's distaste for the play in the eighteenth century. Lennox believed that in the potentially tragic situation dramatized in *Measure for Measure,* Shakespeare had "made a wrong Choice of his Subject" but was "resolved to torture it into a Comedy," as is evident in "the low Contrivance, absurd Intrigue, and improbable

Incidents, he was obliged to introduce, in order to bring about three or four weddings, instead of one good Beheading, which was the Consequence naturally expected."[4] In the century before that, within a lifetime of the play's first performance, poet, playwright, and critic John Dryden saw *Measure for Measure* as one of Shakespeare's lame-plotted plays, "which were either grounded on impossibilities, or at least, so meanly written that the comedy neither caus'd your mirth, nor the serious part your concernment."[5]

We have no record of what Shakespeare's contemporaries thought of *Measure for Measure*—whether they grumbled about its supposed flaws like Dryden and Lennox some decades later, or admired it as a masterpiece, as many have since. But we know that in 1662, 10 years prior to Dryden's complaint, Samuel Pepys found *The Law against Lovers,* William Davenant's revised and retitled version of *Measure for Measure* for the Restoration stage, to be "a good play, and well performed."[6] John Upton, writing just before Charlotte Lennox found *Measure for Measure* to be disordered and ethically incoherent, praised its "unity of action" and its just morality: "How knowing in the characters of men is our poet, to make the severe and inexorable Angelo incur the penalty of that sanguinary law, which he was so forward to revive."[7] Coleridge's great contemporary William Hazlitt found the play to be "as full of genius as it is of wisdom."[8] And in 1934, a few years before Knights identified *Measure for Measure* as the play of Shakespeare that had most troubled the minds of its readers, C. J. Sisson mocked modern critics for projecting their own troubled minds on to it: "[B]y a process of queer logic they attribute to Shakespeare their own distress and so conclude that it expresses a spirit of cynical revolt." Only "a pseudo-romantic sentimentalism," anachronistic in the extreme, could account for such a drastic misreading, wrote Sisson, for "the play is sound to the core, and profoundly Christian in spirit."[9]

The dense, packed quality of this play partly reflects the time when it came into being. Early in 1603, the London theaters closed in deference to what would be the final illness of Elizabeth I, last of the Tudor monarchs, who had been Queen of England since 1558. After her death on March 24, the theaters remained closed until at least the following February because of a severe outbreak of the plague; *Measure for Measure* appears to have been written during that interim, in the spring or summer of 1603.[10] When the theaters reopened, King James VI of Scotland had become James I of England, and the new Stuart era had begun. In December of 1604, the play was performed at court for the new king, who had recently provided royal patronage for Shakespeare's acting company, making them the King's Men. The contrasting images thus evoked—a tense, disease-ridden city struggling to cope with the Queen's death, an uncertain royal succession, and a debilitating return of the plague; a gala royal entertainment celebrating the Christmas revels in Whitehall Chapel early in the reign of the first Stuart king—provide a convenient frame for beginning to bring this elusive play, and its remarkably varied critical history, into focus.

But this frame (like others) has been as much a trap as an aid—something of a Scylla and Charybdis for critics attempting to navigate what have proved to be troubled interpretive waters. Does the play resonate with hopes associated with the new temporal reign, hopes of a renewed triumph of redemptive Christian law that tempers justice with mercy? The last Tudor ruler had died, and the reign of James I was bringing with it a new ruling family, a new style of rule. A vigorous younger man had replaced the long-dying old woman, who had become queen at the age of 25, six years before Shakespeare was born, and whose childless condition had long unnerved a kingdom fearful of an uncertain succession. With the play's key role of Duke Vincentio plainly "modeled on the King's own account of his principles of government,"[11] there is ample reason to think that *Measure for Measure* celebrates James's ascendance and the hopes the nation brought to it.

Or should we say that *Measure for Measure* was written after the gusto and optimism of the great Elizabethan Age—the reign of Elizabeth, the Virgin Queen, Gloriana—had passed, giving way to "a state of affairs so unstable that great or sustained effort was suspended for a time and a sense of the futility of man's achievement set in"?[12] Should we see this resigned fatalism lurking behind what many have felt to be the superficial resolution brought by the Duke's contrivances to the deep problems that the play dramatizes? Does the play dramatize the helplessness of an unnerved community imperiled by ancient, recurring evils that seem to ramify with efforts to quell them?

Few recent critics have been as inclined to align *Measure for Measure* to a unified historical mood or spirit—whether of optimism or gloom—as many influential critics have been in the past. But the play is deeply and necessarily marked by the social, political, religious, and economic conditions of its time, and critical attentiveness to these conditions has shaped our reading of it in myriad ways. It is important to remember, however, that the play's historical moment itself provokes widely conflicting readings and poses considerable interpretive challenges. History does not provide a static background of stable meanings that can be mapped onto the play. Often the richest historically inflected readings of *Measure for Measure* study complex interrelationships that link the action of the play with social and political practices distinctive to its time—whether on the grand scale of the court or in the textured cultural record that has survived from the everyday social, political, and religious life of early-seventeenth-century England.

Efforts to place the play within a larger view of Shakespeare's work as a dramatist provide a context partly subsumed by the broad historical context for understanding *Measure for Measure* and partly independent of it. *Measure for Measure* is 1 of 37 surviving plays Shakespeare is thought to have been entirely, largely, or significantly responsible for writing. Written and first performed in a span that reaches from about 1590 to about 1613, they include plays in several genres and subgenres, chief among them comedies, history plays, and tragedies.

The surviving evidence is not strong enough to establish with certainty the precise order in which these plays were written, but years of scholarly research have produced an increasingly refined, if still imperfect, chronology.

The range of possible dates for *Measure for Measure* is fairly narrow. The play could not, of course, have been written after its 1604 performance (though it certainly could have undergone significant modifications between its early performances and its first publication in the 1623 Folio—of this, nothing is known). It was probably performed on the public stage before reaching its royal audience at Whitehall, but few scholars now date it earlier than the theater closings in 1603. As for genre, the play is a comedy, or at least its plot is shaped by considerations basic to the usual movement in Shakespearean comedy; that is, nobody quite dies as a direct result of its action, and it ends in the prospect of marriage—indeed, no fewer than four marriages—having addressed en route considerable obstacles obstructing the movement toward marriage.

Efforts to place *Measure for Measure* within the long line of Shakespeare's comedies and efforts to understand it in relation to other plays written at about the same time have tended to produce different interpretive results. Shakespeare wrote more comedies than any other kind of play, and they reach from his very earliest efforts to the variant of comic form that characterizes the last phase of his works, those plays now often called the late romances. To assimilate *Measure for Measure* to this thread of comic development is to stress its affinities with earlier "festive" comedies like *As You Like It,* which also culminates in four marriages, and with late romances like *The Winter's Tale,* where last-act disclosures enable both the wedding of a young couple and the restoration of a marriage that appeared to have been shattered a generation earlier. To associate *Measure for Measure* with other plays written at about the same time, however, is to recognize its kinship with plays like *Hamlet* (1600–1601), *Troilus and Cressida* (1602), *Othello* (1603–1604), *All's Well That Ends Well* (1604–1605), *Timon of Athens* (1605), or even *King Lear* (1605–1606).[13] Of these plays, only the action of *All's Well That Ends Well* follows anything like the ordinary contours of Shakespearean comic form, and it follows them in a peculiar enough way that its interpretive history is marked by many of the same complications that have shaped the critical heritage of *Measure for Measure.*

Northrop Frye is an extreme and eloquent example of critics who stress the place of *Measure for Measure* within the enduring continuities of Shakespeare's preoccupation with comic form. For Frye, both *Measure for Measure* and *All's Well That Ends Well* "are simply romantic comedies where the chief magical device used is the bed trick instead of enchanted forests or identical twins."[14] A key purpose of comedy for Frye is to free us from the stagnating limitations of ordinary society by releasing "a vision of deliverance or expanded energy or freedom" (14). *Measure for Measure* may show a "larger infusion of irony" (61) than most Shakespearean comedies, Frye argues, but at the core of the play is a thoroughly comic "rite of passage from death to new life" (27) that is completed in the marriages of the last act.

By contrast, those who have looked chiefly at the chronological company *Measure for Measure* keeps in Shakespeare's works have tended to see preoccupations that the play shares with tragedies written at about the same time. E. K. Chambers, who found "the limits of comedy . . . sorely strained" in this play, believed that "a narrower spiritual gulf divided *Measure for Measure* from the tragedy of *King Lear* than from the comedy of *As You Like It*."[15] Linking *Measure for Measure* to plays written within a few years of it, in particular to *All's Well That Ends Well* and *Troilus and Cressida,* Chambers saw a record of "the poet's shifting outlook upon humanity": "They are all unpleasant plays, the utterances of a puzzled and disturbed spirit, full of questionings, sceptical of its own ideals, looking with new misgivings into the ambiguous shadows of a world over which a cloud has passed and made a goblin of the sun" (Chambers, 210). For Chambers, *Measure for Measure* at once exemplifies a period in which Shakespeare's outlook on life darkened and anticipates, in its elusiveness to criticism, "certain modern plays, to which its affinities are perhaps closer than to anything in its own age" (Chambers, 211).

In emphasizing "the ferment of doubt and bitterness of disillusion" he found in the plays of this period, Chambers was extending a mode of criticism shaped most decisively, and influentially, by Edward Dowden, who believed that the goal of interpretation was to read the individual works as part of an effort "to come into close and living relation with the individuality"[16] of the writer. Chambers's emphasis on the affinity of *Measure for Measure* for "certain modern plays," however, pointed to another critical vantage point, itself more modern that Dowden's late-Victorian preoccupation with the author as transcendent genius. In 1896, F. S. Boas grouped *Measure for Measure* with *Troilus and Cressida, Hamlet,* and *All's Well That Ends Well* as "problem plays." For Boas, "the general temper and atmosphere"[17] of these plays anticipates the modern problem plays of Henrik Ibsen and George Bernard Shaw, who used drama to identify, isolate, and explore disquieting social problems.

Nearly all later critics have believed that Boas overstated the resemblance of Shakespeare's problem plays to the drama of Ibsen and Shaw. Even the adequacy of the term *problem plays* as a meaningful identification has been assessed differently by those who use it: For E. M. W. Tillyard, it is "anything but a satisfactory term, and I wish I knew a better."[18] The grouping of these works as problem plays or problem comedies has, however, proved to be durable, if not entirely stable. In his 1931 book on *The Problem Comedies,* W. W. Lawrence dropped *Hamlet* from the group.[19] E. M. W. Tillyard and William B. Toole[20] restored *Hamlet* as a problem play; Peter Ure[21] added a fifth play, *Timon of Athens;* and A. P. Rossiter and Carol Thomas Neely have both included *Othello.*[22] *Measure for Measure,* however, seems to be the one play that always shows up in that group—even according to Ernest Schanzer, for whom the other problem plays are *Julius Caesar* and *Antony and Cleopatra.*[23]

Often the meaning of the term *problem plays* has oscillated between what Neely sees as "two poles of definition—that the plays anatomize problems and that they have them" (Neely, 60). The perception that *Measure for Measure* as a play has problems, or is a problem, reaches back to its earliest critics like Dryden or Charlotte Lennox. In twentieth-century criticism, the problem is usually identified as a failure of the ending to address effectively the issues and conflicts that the play has dramatized with such stark dramatic intensity. *Measure for Measure* becomes, in a characteristic formulation of this view by M. M. Mahood, "a great but unsatisfactory play": "Shakespeare is emotionally too involved in the situation to achieve a dramatic clarification of its issues."[24] L. C. Knights saw the last two acts as "little more than a drawing out and resolution of the plot," with the result that "the process of clarification is incomplete" (Knights, 232–33). Tillyard found the shift to allegory in the last half of the play inadequate to the intensely human drama of the first two and a half acts: "[H]owever much the tone changes in the second half, nothing in the play can make an allegorical interpretation poetically valid throughout" (Tillyard, 123). Perhaps A. P. Rossiter, whose lecture-essay on *Measure for Measure* is a landmark of mid-century criticism of the play, formulated this view most compellingly: "There is a solution there: but the 'problem' is on one plane, the 'solution' on quite another. It is like a wish-fulfilment. . . . It ought to apply to existence absolutely: it does *not* apply to experience-as-observed" (Rossiter, 169).

As with everything else with this play, critics have found many ways to take the perceived inadequacy of its ending. Harriet Hawkins found that "the kinds of solutions offered by the Duke—whether Shakespeare intended them to or not—seem hopelessly inadequate in the face of the psychological, sexual, and moral conflicts they are supposed to have resolved." But for Hawkins, these solutions are the "least significant" part of the play: "What seems most significant are the open questions posed along the way."[25] Considerations of structural unity or formal integrity, that is to say, are insignificant in comparison with the play's astonishing power to locate its characters—and its audience—in dramatic situations for which "no single option or argument can possibly be deemed acceptable to all of the individuals concerned" (Hawkins, 65).

Other critics, however, seek another level of dramatic significance in what Anne Barton has called the play's "long and notoriously difficult last scene." For Barton, the Duke's struggle to wrap up the play's supercharged legal, ethical, spiritual, and sexual conflicts with the last-act pardons and marriages parallels Shakespeare's own effort as a dramatist working to establish a comic ending for his dramatic action. "There is something forced and blatantly fictional" in both the Duke's and Shakespeare's role in bringing this play to an end, but Barton sees Shakespeare separating himself from his protagonist: "The Duke refuses to admit failure, but Shakespeare seems perversely to stress the hollowness, in a sense the falsehood, of the happy ending of this comedy."[26] The Duke's facile disposition of the play's problems in the last scene becomes a kind of metacommentary on the inadequacy of comic form by a Shakespeare "now seemingly disillusioned with the art of comedy which, in the past, had served him so well" (Barton, 549).

Perhaps the longevity of the critical grouping of *Measure for Measure* with other plays as problem plays has less to do with the claim that brought it into being—that these plays closely resembled, even anticipated, the dramas of Ibsen and Shaw—than with its malleability, even its conceptual disunity. The designation appears to recognize variously, if not coherently, considerations of genre that link these plays both to each other and to a more modern form of drama; considerations of "general temper and atmosphere" associating these plays with a phase of Shakespeare's work dominated by attitudes and themes expressed most fully in the great tragedies; and considerations of the plays as themselves problems, or at least as problematic. But many critics have vigorously challenged efforts to associate *Measure for Measure* with a modern ironical spirit, to place it in a group of plays that show a dark or pessimistic or disillusioned spirit, to link it to some perturbation in the mental life of its creator, or to see it as structurally or aesthetically flawed.

Five years before C. J. Sisson's eloquent effort to rescue *Measure for Measure* from the "mythical sorrows" he saw dispirited modern critics imposing on Shakespeare's vigorous Christianity, G. Wilson Knight had published his remarkable essay, "*Measure for Measure* and the Gospels." In Knight's reading, the play is a visionary dramatization of "the Gospel ethic" of forgiveness, and the Duke, "like Jesus, is the prophet of a new order of ethics."[27] We must read the play, Knight insisted, "not as a picture of normal human affairs, but as a parable, like the parables of Jesus." He concluded:

> Much has been said about the difficulties of *Measure for Measure*. But, in truth, no play of Shakespeare shows more thoughtful care, more deliberate purpose, more consummate skill in structural technique, and, finally, more penetrating ethical and psychological insight. None shows a more exquisitely inwoven pattern. And, if ever the thought at first seems strange, or the action unreasonable, it will be found to reflect the sublime strangeness and unreason of Jesus' teaching. (Knight, 96)

The visionary Christianity of Knights's essay and the robust Christianity of Sisson's, joined by R. W. Chambers's impassioned 1937 Royal Academy lecture, "The Jacobean Shakespeare and *Measure for Measure,*" initiated the principal interpretive alternative to the problem-play tradition in twentieth-century criticism of the play.

Unlike E. K. Chambers, who believed that in *Measure for Measure* "the searchlight of irony is thrown up the paths of Providence itself,"[28] R. W. Chambers saw the Duke as "an earthly providence" and the play as a dramatization of a Christianity centered in Shakespeare's "belief in forgiveness as the virtue by which human goodness draws nearest to the divine." He believed it was "the depth of [Shakespeare's] belief in forgiveness which has puzzled, in their judgement of that play, so many of his greatest critics, from Coleridge and Hazlitt and Swinburne, down to the present day."[29] In this tradition, *Measure for Measure* is less likely to point forward to Ibsen and Shaw than back to medieval morality play traditions, as in M. C. Bradbrook's allegorical reading in "Authority, Truth, and Justice in *Measure for Measure*"[30] or in Robert G. Hunter's partial secularization of the forgiveness motif as the core of a distinct group of plays that he saw as Shakespeare's comedies of forgiveness.[31] In another influential essay, Neville Coghill grounded the play in deep medieval assumptions about comedy that Shakespeare shared with Dante, in which "comic form was cosmic form." The action of comedy dramatized the paradox of the fortunate fall, which "has always been the mainstay of Christian imagination; we live in a fallen world and yet have hope of salvation,"[32] a hope confirmed by the comic ending of *Measure for Measure.*

"It cannot be objected," Coghill wrote, "that I have imposed an unwarrantably religious pattern upon [*Measure for Measure*], for it is Isabella and the Friar-Duke who import religion into the play, not I" (Coghill, 25). It is undeniable, certainly, that the speech of the play is saturated with Biblical language, much of it clustered around passages from the Gospels that call for forgiveness and tolerance: "Judge not that ye be not judged. For with what judgment ye judge, ye shall be judged: and with what measure ye mete it shall be measured to you again" (Matthew 7:1–2 AV). Where critics disagree is in how to understand this Biblical pattern in relation to the action of the play.

Darryl Gless, for instance, looked at the "extravagance" of the multiple pardons at the end and saw in it a reflection of God's grace to men, who, measured by their sins, "deserve eternal damnation": "The Duke is imitating this divine extravagance, furthermore, in precisely the way that the Sermon on the Mount demands when it sets out God's gentleness toward the sinful as a pattern for all men to imitate in their charity."[33] By contrast, William Empson looked at the same behavior and saw a Duke who throughout has been "playing at being God": [H]aving treated "his subjects as puppets for the fun of making them twitch," his final "flippancy about justice corresponds to a deeper and more desperate feeling in the author, elaborated throughout the action and insisted upon in the title, that the whole business of public justice is fatuous and hideous, whether compared to the mercy of Christ or the humanity of private life."[34] For Empson, there is abundant "Christian symbolism in the play" to support a redemptive, providential interpretation, but "the play simply did not work out like that" (Empson, 285).

For all the profound disagreements among critics of *Measure for Measure,* there is much agreement about the stature of the play, its astonishing complexity, the remarkable power in its drama and poetry, and its "greatness" or "genius." At times that recognition has come almost grudgingly. "*Measure for Measure* is a great play," Sir Arthur Quiller-Couch wrote, introducing the New

Cambridge edition, but great "in parts, and despite that its parts do not fit. It arrests—it impresses while it puzzles—every reader. . . . No play of Shakespeare's carries a stronger conviction that, although the good may be 'mixed', we are trafficking with genius."[35] F. R. Leavis, by contrast, had little patience with qualified views of the play's achievement; he thought the parts fitted just fine and found *Measure for Measure* to be "one of the very greatest of the plays, and most consummate and convincing of Shakespeare's achievements."[36] David L. Stevenson, in *The Achievement of Shakespeare's* Measure for Measure, found the play to be Shakespeare's "greatest comedy," a play that "unlocks our most profound awareness of the nature of an ineluctable evil in man."[37]

The imaginative power of *Measure for Measure* has been recognized by the modern theater as well as by its critics—though again, not without some hesitation. Certainly William Winter, in 1913, did not see much of a future on the stage for this "grim and painful play." Although "powerful, pathetic, and wonderfully eloquent . . . abounding in knowledge of human nature" and "felicitious in its searching inspection of the human heart," this play was "one that might well be spared from the Stage" because, Winter believed, its performances have "always been gloomy and depressing, and if acquaintance is to be made with it at all, it is better to be read than to be seen, for it is unfit for the modern Theatre."[38]

Modern theater, however, has thought otherwise. Set almost prophetically in the Vienna where three centuries later Freud would write *The Psychopathology of Everyday Life* and *Civilization and Its Discontents,* this play about sexuality, power, and corruption, about repression, irony, and betrayal, about lies, secrets, and exposures, came into its own as theater in the post-Victorian cultural world and has held its place since. Imaginative directors have found ways to let the play mirror the twentieth century back to itself again and again, and it has become a staple of contemporary Shakespearean theater in the United Kingdom and America and well beyond. The theater, in turn, has made itself imaginatively present in the criticism of *Measure for Measure,* as in Philip McGuire's *Speechless Dialect: Shakespeare's Open Silences* or David McCandless's *Gender and Performance in Shakespeare's Problem Comedies.* Drawing on representative productions of the play, McGuire explores the implications for theatrical performance in the "open silences" that follow key declarations by the Duke in the last scene—Angelo's silence on his pardon, for instance, and Isabella's in response to the Duke's proposals of marriage to her.[39] McCandless brings his own theatrical experience and imagination—as a director of *Measure for Measure* as well as a spectator at several productions of it—to bear on his interpretation of the text.[40]

The play has thrived among critics in this century. Michael Jameison began a 1972 survey of commentary on the problem plays by stating that the "bulk of criticism on *Measure for Measure* since 1930 almost rivals that on *Hamlet.*"[41] The critical output certainly has not slowed since Jameison's review. My original intention for this volume was to select representative critical statements from the last three centuries, reaching at least back to Doctor Johnson, who thought that "there is perhaps not one of Shakespeare's plays more darkened than this by the peculiarities of its authour."[42] Recent examination of *Measure for Measure* extends, and has much to learn from, a rich critical conversation that reaches back through the centuries, and I have tried to represent some major strands of it in this introduction. But the more recent interpretive encounter with *Measure for Measure* demands a volume of its own if the selections are to provide any indication of its breadth and complexity and underscore what is distinctive to its efforts to find critical vantage points that are responsive to the play, its historical moment, and ours. All the essays that follow were first published in the last two decades.

My own contribution to this group of essays focuses on anxieties about sexuality expressed variously in *Measure for Measure,* from Claudio's disgust with the sexual impulses that led to his being sentenced to death and his apparent acquiescence in the Duke's counsel that he withdraw himself from any investment in life processes at all to his fear of an afterlife conceived as an eternity of sensual overstimulation. In its reliance on some basic psychoanalytic concepts, this excerpt from *Shakespeare's Development and the Problem Comedies* employs a critical method that entered into Shakespearean criticism when Freud decided Hamlet had an Oedipus complex and that has played a significant role in recent criticism of *Measure for Measure.* Janet Adelman develops an imaginative and rigorous psychoanalytic perspective on *Measure for Measure* in "Marriage and the Maternal Body," which explores the psychological roots of the play's resistance to the usual comic resolution in marriage. In Adelman's reading, *Measure for Measure* addresses a powerful unconscious fantasy of maternal origin in which sexual desire is inseparable from desire for, and the desire of, a mother's body, and from a still deeper fear of maternal dominance that reaches back to the conditions of infancy. The action plays out a series of failed (and punished) efforts to escape the contaminating force of a sexuality so experienced, most notably in the retreats from sexual desire that initially structure the characters Angelo and Isabella. The Duke's efforts to bring comic closure is problematic because it rests on an assertion of purified paternal control that itself represents a fantasy of escape from sexuality and maternal dominance—the comic solution reinstates the problem at the heart of the play.

A great deal of recent criticism of *Measure for Measure* has reflected ambitious rethinkings of the relationship between literary texts and the historical culture in which they were produced. Cultural materialism and the new historicism have probably been the most extensive methodological influences on Shakespearean criticism since the appearance of Stephen Greenblatt's *Renaissance Self-Fashioning* (Chicago: University of Chicago Press, 1980). Both of these closely related critical approaches are deeply indebted to the work of Michel Foucault, who stressed the systematic, synchronic networks of power that shape and limit human experience and knowledge at any one historical moment. What holds together one historical moment estranges it from preceding and succeeding ones: Foucault emphasized historical discontinuities both over any continuity presumed to derive from a stable, universal human nature and over narratives of historical progress that attribute rational or organic development to historical change. Cultural materialism has involved a kind of graft of Foucault's work onto traditions of British Marxism that emphasize political engagement and the uses of criticism to further political ends. The new historicism, associated more with a group of highly influential American critics, has stressed the effort to articulate what Greenblatt has called a "poetics of culture," in which a play's significance is explored in the links between its "representational mode" and "the complex network of institutions, practices, and beliefs that constitute the culture as a whole."[43] Both cultural materialism and the new historicism are concerned to blur the boundaries between literary works and other products of a culture and to disrupt older forms of historical criticism that often sought "answers" to questions raised by literary or dramatic texts in authoritative statements drawn from the prescriptive literature of the time.

Jonathan Goldberg's exploration of representation—as it functions in the action of *Measure for Measure* and as it shaped the royal mode of absolutist power to which James I aspired—exemplifies the sort of sophistication that new historicist criticism has brought to Shakespeare studies. For Goldberg, the Duke should not be seen as a character whose pronouncements and actions either approvingly express the king's political philosophy or critically expose his shortcomings. What the play represents in the Duke's speech and practice is representation as a mode of absolutist rule, of power made present through absence, so that the Duke—now present in his own person, now withdrawn behind but active through his deputies and through his disguise—represents both the playwright and the king by way of performing the principle of representation they share. In "Transgression and Surveillance in *Measure for Measure*," Jonathan Dollimore sees a different kind of political legitimation at work. For Dollimore, the play stages a political process in which the state stabilizes its authority by displacing corruption—away from the ruling elite, down the social scale, and onto sexual offenses. The demonization of sexuality is an ideological construction in the service of the state; state suppression of sexual offenders in turn legitimates the authority responsible for the ideological construction. The wayward sexuality identified as a threat to state authority is reunderstood as the means by which power manifests itself as legitimate. Dollimore finds little in the play that opposes this legitimation process, though at the end he gestures toward a later historical moment when the outlaw sexuality vilified in this play will provide the base for a critique of exploitation.

The influence of contemporary feminism has brought heightened attention to the dynamics of gender in Shakespeare. Several recent studies of

Measure for Measure have borrowed from both historicist and psychoanalytic criticism to bring the play's complex presentation of gender into focus. In "Assaying the Power of Chastity," Barbara J. Baines identifies chastity as the value that confers identity on both women and men but then notes the special, somewhat paradoxical place of woman's chastity in the play's male-dominated social world. Because security about the legitimacy of bloodline is crucial to the perpetuation of patriarchal society, chastity confers a power on women that men struggle to control by subordinating female sexuality to husbands in marriage. Isabella's effort to take control of her own body by embracing the chastity of sexual renunciation thus makes her a power center in the play, attacked first by Angelo, who is feminized by her arousal and refusal of him, and then appropriated by the Duke in the last act, when he declares his intention to marry her. Mario DiGangi, in "Pleasure and Danger: Measuring Female Sexuality in *Measure for Measure,*" sees male anxiety about female agency driving the play's preoccupation with defining and controlling female sexuality. DiGangi sets beside the play's articulated categories of marital status (a woman must be a maid, wife, or widow) an implicit corresponding measure of sexual status (a woman must be a virgin, wife, or whore). He then tracks the resistance that meets efforts to confine female desire, agency, and pleasure within those categories, notably in the failed courtroom investigation to determine what happened in Mistress Elbow's quest for the pleasure of stewed prunes.

In "London," from *Puzzling Shakespeare,* an imaginative experiment in topical reading, Leah Marcus explores connections that Shakespeare's contemporaries are likely to have made between *Measure for Measure* and events in their lives. Emphasizing the likenesses of this Vienna to Shakespearean London in 1604,[44] Marcus finds several connections that point in one direction to the different styles of rule in the Duke and his deputy Angelo and in the other to ongoing, always disputed relations between London's autonomy and monarchical power, recently refigured by James I. Although many of these connections seem to favor James, others point to his royal rule as a threat to London's self-governance. The impetus for extravagantly conflicting interpretations, which has shown itself in centuries of criticism, is built into the play, and it would have divided its original London audiences as well. In "Performing Social Practice: The Example of *Measure for Measure,*" Victoria Hayne uses the social history of communal, ecclesiastical, and legal regulation of sexuality and marriage in Shakespeare's England to bring the play's pervasive concern with the relation of sexuality to authority into focus. Angelo's rigid enforcement of the law condemning Claudio to death recalls the demands of contemporary Puritans for draconian criminal penalties to replace the ecclesiastical court system, which relied on public penance and on finely tuned community-based distinctions between, say, a Claudio, eager to complete his marriage to the pregnant Juliet, and a Lucio, who abandoned Kate Keepdown, mother of his child. The play takes its audience through a theatrical extrapolation from the community-based process, inviting identification with the Duke's improvisational theatrical authority as it subdues Angelo's authoritarian determination to punish Claudio's crime with death.

Katherine Eisaman Maus reads *Measure for Measure* in the context of her larger study, *Inwardness and Theater in the English Renaissance*—an inwardness closely linked with sexuality in this play and manifested variously in Angelo, who wishes to be identical with the ideal he publicly declares, or Isabella, who recognizes in herself only what she believes is visible to divine omniscience, or the Duke, who conceals himself to gain access to the secret motivations of others. As on-stage dramatist, the Duke must negotiate a resolution that reconciles the idiosyncratic private motives that drive his subjects with the demands of a public legal system indifferent to individual differences. The ultimate intractability of that task is indicated at play's end when the distinctive instances of inwardness that have shaped the dramatic action throughout recede from view in the Duke's dispensation of pardons and marriages. According to Robert N. Watson, in "False Immortality in *Measure for Measure:* Comic Means, Tragic Ends," the play's ironies corrode the efforts of individuals to find transcendent meanings in conventional routes to immortality—through one's heirs, through one's personal salvation, or through undying fame. The play's tragicomic action intensifies the typical comic movement through obstacles toward marriage as the institution ordained to perpetuate both the species and the social order, but denial and death so extensively shadow the desire driving this action that any ordinary sense of comic victory and celebration is lost. The Duke's plot manipulations hold death in abeyance, averting tragedy, but they cannot recuperate the failed efforts of the principals to find consoling transcendence for mortal limitations.

Like many critics, among them Graham Bradshaw, Harry Berger Jr. finds the Duke's dramatic resolution for the ending of *Measure for Measure* morally and politically unsatisfying. Rather than see the Duke's failure as the play's or Shakespeare's failure, Bradshaw argues that we should see the play as an ironic exposé of the Duke, who brings to the difficult problem of reconciling the rule of law with the Sermon on the Mount his own special mix of ineptitude, cowardliness, vanity, and moral laziness.[45] Berger, accepting Bradshaw's claim that *Measure for Measure* subjects Duke Vincentio's character, practices, and judgments to severe, ironic scrutiny, finds in the Duke a multifaceted determination to exculpate himself from his responsibility for the mess in Vienna that just keeps getting worse, dragging more and more people into it, during much of the play. Because his scurrilous on-stage detractor is a product of the 14 years of the Duke's lenient governance credited with fostering this situation, the Duke is particularly vulnerable to Lucio's scandalous accounts of his past, which force him toward an awareness of his complicity in this situation and release the anger and frustration latent in his efforts to ward off self-knowledge. When Lucio unmasks the Friar, revealing the Duke beneath the disguise, Vincentio's fear of a deeper unmasking of himself to himself is played out in the conflict between his impulse to punish Lucio severely and his need to validate a fantasy of himself as wise justice.

Half of the sentences in Berger's last two paragraphs, which conclude his long chapter on *Measure for Measure* in *Making Trifles of Terrors: Redistributing Complicities in Shakespeare,* are questions opening toward further answers that themselves beget still further questions. Fittingly, these are also the last two paragraphs of this book. The interrogatory mode of Berger's conclusion can serve to return us to the qualities of *Measure for Measure* that provide the impetus driving all these essays. Our experience of *Measure for Measure* grows in complexity with our rigorous questioning of it, and the most subtle and apt and imaginative answers we can bring to those questions generate new questions in turn—or reanimate old ones that had only appeared to go away. This interpretive process has been going on for much of the nearly four centuries since *Measure for Measure* was first staged. The essays in this volume present a small part of that process over a very short period of time. I hope that they represent effectively the energy and ingenuity critics have brought to this work over the last two decades, and that in turn the interpretive work of these decades has enriched the long, ongoing critical conversation about this elusive and powerful play.

Notes

1. Stanley Cavell, *Must We Mean What We Say: A Book of Essays* (New York: Charles Scribner's Sons, 1969), 268.
2. L. C. Knights, "The Ambiguity of *Measure for Measure,*" *Scrutiny* 10:3 (1942): 222.
3. Samuel Taylor Coleridge, *Coleridge's Writings on Shakespeare,* ed. Terrance Hawkes (New York: G. P. Putnam's Sons, 1959), 249.
4. Charlotte Ramsey Lennox, *Shakespeare Illustrated,* vol. 1 (London: 1753), 28. Quoted in Mark Eccles, ed., *Measure for Measure, New Variorum Edition of Shakespeare* (New York: Modern Language Association of American, 1980), 394.
5. John Dryden, "Defence of the Epilogue. Or, An Essay on the Dramatique Poetry of the Last Age," *The Conquest of Granada by the Spaniards* (London: 1672), 163. Quoted in Eccles, *Variorum,* 394.
6. Samuel Pepys, *Diary* entry for February 18, 1662. Quoted in Eccles, *Variorum,* 468.
7. John Upton, *Critical Observations on Shakespeare,* 2d ed. (1748; reprint, New York: AMS, 1973), 72. Quoted in Eccles, *Variorum,* 394.
8. William Hazlitt, *Characters of Shakespeare's Plays,* Everyman's Library (1817; reprint, London: J. M. Dent, n.d.), 245.
9. C. J. Sisson, "The Mythical Sorrows of Shakespeare," *Studies in Shakespeare: British Academy Lectures,* ed. Peter Alexander (London: Oxford University Press, 1964), 21, 22.
10. Alice Walker, "The Text of *Measure for Measure,*" *The Review of English Studies* 34:133 (February 1983): 20.
11. Josephine Waters Bennett, Measure for Measure *as Royal Entertainment* (New York & London, Columbia University Press, 1966), 11.

12. Una Ellis-Fermor, *The Jacobean Drama: An Interpretation,* 4th ed. (1957; New York: Vintage Books, 1964), 2. First edition was published in 1935.

13. I give dates provided by Stanley Wells and Gary Taylor in *William Shakespeare: A Textual Companion* (Oxford: Clarendon Press, 1987), 122–28.

14. Northrop Frye, *The Myth of Deliverance: Reflections on Shakespeare's Problem Plays* (Toronto and Buffalo: University of Toronto Press, 1983), 63.

15. E. K. Chambers, *Shakespeare: A Survey* (London: Macmillan, 1925), 211, 216.

16. Edward Dowden, *Shakespeare: A Critical Study of His Mind and Art* (New York and London: Harper and Brothers, 1881), 2. First edition was published in 1875.

17. F. S. Boas, *Shakspere and his Predecessors* (New York: Charles Scribner's Sons, 1896), 345.

18. E. W. M. Tillyard, *Shakespeare's Problem Plays* (London: Chatto and Windus, 1950).

19. W. W. Lawrence, *Shakespeare's Problem Comedies* (New York: Macmillan, 1931).

20. William B. Toole, *Shakespeare's Problem Plays* (The Hague: Mouton, 1966).

21. Peter Ure, *Shakespeare: The Problem Plays* (London: Longmans, Green, 1964).

22. A. P. Rossiter, *Angel With Horns* (London: Longman, Green & Co. Ltd., 1961); Carol Thomas Neely, *Shakespeare's Broken Nuptials* (New Haven: Yale University Press, 1985).

23. Ernest Schanzer, *The Problem Plays of Shakespeare* (New York: Schocken Books, 1963).

24. M. M. Mahood, *Shakespeare's Wordplay* (London: Methuen, 1957), 99.

25. Harriet Hawkins, *The Devil's Party: Critical Counter-interpretations of Shakespearian Drama* (Oxford: Clarendon Press, 1985), 72.

26. Anne Barton, Introduction to *Measure for Measure,* in *The Riverside Shakespeare,* ed. G. Blakemore Evans (Boston: Houghton, Mifflin, 1974), 547.

27. G. Wilson Knight, *The Wheel of Fire: Interpretations of Shakespearean Tragedy,* 5th ed. (New York: Meridian Books, 1957). The first edition of *The Wheel of Fire* was published by Oxford University Press in 1930; "*Measure for Measure* and the Gospels" was first published in the *London Quarterly Review,* 1929.

28. E. K. Chambers, *Encyclopaedia Britannica,* 11th ed., S. V. "Shakespeare," 785.

29. R. W. Chambers, "The Jacobean Shakespeare and *Measure for Measure,*" *Proceedings of the British Academy* 23 (Oxford: Oxford University Press, 1937): 52, 60.

30. M. C. Bradbrook, "Authority, Truth, and Justice in *Measure for Measure,*" *Review of English Studies* 17 (1941): 385–99.

31. Robert G. Hunter, *Shakespeare and the Comedy of Forgiveness* (New York: Columbia University Press, 1965).

32. Neville Coghill, "Comic Form in *Measure for Measure,*" *Shakespeare Survey* 8 (1955): 18, 26.

33. Darryl J. Gless, Measure for Measure, *the Law, and the Convent* (Princeton: Princeton University Press, 1979), 228.

34. William Empson, "Sense in *Measure for Measure,*" in *The Structure of Complex Words* (London: Chatto & Windus, 1951), 283, 284. First published in *Southern Review* 4 (1938): 340–50.

35. Arthur Quiller-Couch, Introduction to *Measure for Measure,* ed. Arthur Quiller-Couch and John Dover Wilson (Cambridge: Cambridge University Press, 1922), xli.

36. F. R. Leavis, *The Common Pursuit* (London: Chatto & Windux, 1952), 160. Leavis's essay was first published under the title "The Greatness of *Measure for Measure*" in *Scrutiny* 10 (1942): 234–47, in response to Knights, "The Ambiguity of *Measure for Measure.*"

37. David L. Stevenson, *The Achievement of Shakespeare's* Measure for Measure (Ithaca: Cornell University Press, 1966), 128, 133.

38. William Winter, *The Wallet of Time,* vol. 1 (New York: Moffet, Yard and Company), 389.

39. Philip C. McGuire, *Speechless Dialect: Shakespeare's Open Silences* (Berkeley: University of California Press, 1985).

40. David McCandless, *Gender and Performance in Shakespeare's Problem Comedies* (Bloomington: Indiana University Press, 1997).

41. Michael Jameison, "The Problem Plays, 1920–1970: A Retrospect," *Shakespeare Survey* 25 (1970): 4.

42. *Johnson on Shakespeare,* ed. Arthur Sherbo, in *The Works of Samuel Johnson,* vol. 7 (New Haven: Yale University Press, 1968), 174.

43. Stephen Greenblatt, Introduction to *The Power of Forms in the English Renaissance,* ed. Stephen Greenblatt (Norman, OK: University of Oklahoma Press, 1982), 6.

44. In the section of this chapter not reprinted here, Marcus explores the resonance of setting the play in Vienna, a Catholic, Hapsburg monarchy, part of the Holy Roman Empire, and thus associated with long-term international threats to England's peace and autonomy.

45. Drawing on a distinction between true mercy and "vain pity" carefully developed by Sir Thomas Elyot in *The Boke named the Governor* (London, 1531), Bradshaw establishes a contemporary vantage point from which the Duke's earlier permissiveness and his last-act dispensations of pardons are equally clear instances of vain pity—indulgent, negligent exercises in pseudomercy that render the rule of law incoherent. "Tempering Mercy with Justice: *Measure for Measure,*" in *Shakespeare's Scepticism* (New York: St. Martin's Press, 1987), 164–80.

Sexuality, Life, and Death in *Measure for Measure*

RICHARD P. WHEELER

DUKE Reason thus with life:
If I do lose thee, I do lose a thing
That none but fools would keep.
(III.i.6–8)

Claudio, sentenced to die, is eager to defend himself on legal, moral, and practical grounds:

upon a true contract
I got possession of Julietta's bed.
You know the lady, she is fast my wife. . . .
(I.ii.140–42)

But at a deeper level than self-justification, and along with his anger toward Angelo, is a disgust he has come to feel for the "most mutual entertainment" that "with character too gross is writ on Juliet" (II.i.149–50). Explaining to Lucio why he is imprisoned, Claudio records his fate in lines that recall, like Angelo's lust, the "swallowed bait . . . A bliss in proof, and proved a very woe" of Sonnet 129:

From too much liberty, my Lucio, liberty.
As surfeit is the father of much fast,
So every scope by the immoderate use
Turns to restraint. Our natures do pursue,
Like rats that ravin down their proper bane,
A thirsty evil, and when we drink we die.
(I.ii.121–26)

Reprinted from Richard P. Wheeler, *Shakespeare's Development and the Problem Comedies: Turn and Counter-Turn* (Berkeley and London: University of California Press, 1981), by permission of the author.

Of course, it is not surprising that being sentenced to death for any activity should affect one's attitude toward it for the worse. Claudio's lines nonetheless suggest the almost infectious quality in the debased imaging of sexual activity in *Measure for Measure.* Once his activity is forcibly called to his attention as sinful and self-debasing, he cannot help acquiescing in that perspective. Claudio's image of sexuality as a "thirsty evil" shares common ground with Angelo's longing for the "sweet uncleanness" of bedding Isabella. Each sees himself as having taken sexual bait and been contaminated by it. However vigorously Claudio may resent Angelo's law, an element of guilty self-accusation clearly colors his response to it; the rat poison metaphor compromises the very intimacy he is otherwise concerned to justify.

Claudio's association of sexuality with inner contamination through ingestion reflects anxieties shaped by infantile levels of the psyche. In the earliest stage of infantile development, taking nourishment is the paradigmatic mode of sexual gratification as well as survival. The deepest threats to the emerging psyche result from stresses on the bond to the mother, which for the infant is organized chiefly around the rhythms of seeking and taking nurture, of desire that culminates in satiation. Disturbances of these rhythms may lead to crises of various sorts. Violent rage against the source of frustration may lead to attacks of biting and to fantasies of destroying the maternal world by devouring it. When such aggression in turn begets fear of retaliation in kind from a source of greater power, the infant may turn this rage against itself, internalizing the attack on the external world in order to preserve a relation to it. The shattering of psychic equilibrium in this infantile battleground may lead to a fear of being overwhelmed by the very impulses that keep the child alive or to a deep distrust of what may be offered to it for ingestion by the external world. The overriding threat is that impulses originating within the emerging self may lead to abandonment by a nurturing environment gradually recognized as separate from the self but essential to its survival. In extreme instances, when such disturbances are not contained within an environment that encourages the development of basic trust, these crises can become prototypes for disorders that radically inhibit or even preclude further development. But such disturbances are inevitable within the ordinary processes of infantile maturation and leave behind in the psyche what Erik Erikson describes as a permanent residue of basic mistrust.

In earlier comedies, where that residue of mistrust in instinctual impulses is carefully held in check, image patterns often establish benign associations between the processes of loving and feeding, as in *As You Like It,* where "the sight of lovers feedeth those in love" (III.iv.52). In *Twelfth Night,* where festive comic poise regarding sexuality wavers before the swerve into the darker regions of the problem comedies and the tragedies, a more ambivalent attitude to desire is expressed in the food imagery of Orsino's first speech:

If music be the food of love, play on,
Give me excess of it, that, surfeiting,
The appetite may sicken, and so die.
(I.i.1–3)

It is hard to tell from Orsino's lines if he longs more to release sexual desire or to be released from it, though he clearly finds in both notions a source of self-indulgent pleasure. His entire speech is framed by the tension between the "spirit of love" as something "quick and fresh" and as a vast sea that devours and devalues the energies it releases:

Nought enters there,
Of what validity and pitch soe'er,
But falls into abatement and low price
Even in a minute.
(I.i.9, 11–14)

The action of *Twelfth Night* is a search for a way of understanding love that can avoid this fall into "abatement and low price" that Orsino at first seems half to fear, half to crave.

Little of what is "quick and fresh" in love survives in *Measure for Measure,* a play in which mistrust has taken over the dramatized attitudes toward sexuality. Its imagery repeatedly connects debased sexual desire with eating, as when Lucio explains to the disguised Duke: "Yes, in good sooth, the vice is of a great kindred; it is well allied, but it is impossible to extirp it quite, friar, till eating and drinking be put down" (III.ii.95–97). Lucio would, indeed, put himself on a severe diet as the only way to curb his own lechery: "I am fain to dine and sup with water and bran; I dare not for my head fill my belly; one fruitful meal would set me to't" (IV.iii.150–52). In Lucio's imagination, good food leads to debasing sexuality, which for Claudio is in turn imagined as a taking in of poisonous food. To feed on love in *Measure for Measure* is to experience it as an internally corrupting agency, like Claudio's "proper bane," or even to be eaten by it: "Thy bones are hollow; impiety has made a feast of thee" (I.ii.53–54), Lucio observes of the first gentleman, who is being devoured by venereal disease.

Viennese authority counters the threat posed by self-devouring and self-contaminating inner impulses with the aggressive imposition of external controls. Appropriately, Vincentio uses the image of a child attacking its source of nurture to describe the chaos into which civil order has been driven:

And Liberty plucks Justice by the nose;
The baby beats the nurse, and quite athwart
Goes all decorum.
(I.iii.29–31)

To check such unrestrained appetites, the Duke explains to Friar Thomas, requires the renewed enforcement of brutal laws long unused, "Even like an o'ergrown lion in a cave, / That goes not out to prey" (I.iii.22–23). Vincentio's image of the stilled but potentially ferocious lion is restated by Lucio, who notes that sexual offenses "have long run by the hideous law, / As mice by lions" (I.iv.63–64). Later the disguised Duke will complain that "the strong statutes / Stand like the forfeits {extracted teeth} in a barber's shop, / As much in mock as mark" (V.i.318–20). Psychologically, the effort to send the lion after its prey, to put teeth back into the old law that will devour sexual offenders, renews an unconscious threat of retaliation against aggressive sexual impulses; it turns back against the source of desire the aggressive component within it that leads to its being perceived as threatening. This turning back is conveyed tersely in Vincentio's conviction that Vienna must enforce "most biting laws" that will provide "the needful bits and curbs to headstrong jades" (I.iii.19–20).

Angelo exercises these "needful bits and curbs" on Claudio, then goes on to give his own "sensual race the rein." Indeed, Angelo's degradation of sexuality can be charted through images that intensify its connections with both insatiable eating and aggressive, external coercion. "We must not make a scarecrow of the law," he argues in defense of Claudio's death sentence,

> Setting it up to fear the birds of prey,
> And let it keep one shape, till custom make it
> Their perch and not their terror.
>
> (II.i.1–4)

But in response to Isabella, Angelo quickly becomes one of these birds of prey, whose travesty of the law is a source of terror for his victim. After he takes the hook baited with Isabella, Angelo longs to "feast upon her eyes" (II.ii.179). He imagines sexual activity as "saucy sweetness" and as "sweet uncleanness," and would force Isabella to "fit thy consent to my sharp appetite" (II.iv.161).

When Angelo's assault prompts Isabella to condemn those who make the law pawn to their lust, she associates the treacherous mouth of corrupt authority with willful sexual appetite:

> O perilous mouths,
> That bear in them one and the selfsame tongue,
> Either of condemnation or approof,
> Bidding the law make curtsy to their will,
> Hooking both right and wrong to th' appetite,
> To follow as it draws.
>
> (II.iv.172–77)

But Angelo's soliloquy before Isabella enters in this scene reveals the emptiness created in him when his bond to sacred authority is sacrificed to his appetite for sexual satiation:

> When I would pray and think, I think and pray
> To several subjects: heaven hath my empty words,
> Whilst my invention, hearing not my tongue,
> Anchors on Isabel: heaven in my mouth,
> As if I did but only chew his name,
> And in my heart the strong and swelling evil
> Of my conception.
>
> (II.iv.1–7)

For Angelo, to succumb to the "swelling evil" of phallic sexuality is to lose the nourishment he seeks in prayer; he can only "chew" the name of God in spiritual impotence, without partaking of its sacred substance. Lever notes in the Arden edition "the suggestion of a sacreligious communion" in these lines, but the essence of this communion is sterility not blasphemy. For Angelo, neither the "empty words" of prayer nor the conquest of sexual prey will lead to peace or fulfillment.

The mistrust of sexual impulses expressed most directly in the complex of images that link them to eating or biting extends to other image patterns as well, which recapitulate and intermingle the oral, anal, and phallic stages of infantile sexual development. Sexuality in *Measure for Measure* is an appetite that must be checked by a law that devours sexual offenders, but it is also a "filthy vice," an "abhorred pollution," a source of "shame," and, in Pompey's words: "Indeed, it does stink in some sort . . ." (III.ii.26). The release of sexual drives in phallic activity, Lucio would like to think, is intrinsically as harmless as "filling a bottle with a tun-dish" (III.ii.161), but in *Measure for Measure* phallic sexuality, as I will try to show, typically leads to self-alienation and emasculation. Phallic sexuality carries the burden of deeper levels of conflict expressed both through the play's imagery and through its action. The familial contexts out of which these layers of conflict emerge become apparent in the relations among characters brought into crisis by that action.

Isabella relies on the purity of family bonds to relieve her of the burden of Angelo's sexual attack: "I'll to my brother" (II.iv.177). When Claudio seems adamant in his resolve to face death—before he knows the conditions for reprieve Angelo has offered—Isabella sees his resolution as an expression of ideal, patriarchal family bonds: "Thus spake my brother; there my father's grave / Did utter forth a voice" (III.i.86–87). But when Claudio pleads that his life be saved by the only means possible, Isabella responds, as Rossiter has aptly observed, with a terror that matches her brother's fear of death, "and with an analogous cry of the reluctant flesh" (*Angel with Horns,* p. 160):

> Wilt thou be made a man out of my vice?
> Is't not a kind of incest, to take life
> From thine own sister's shame?
> (III.i.138–40)

The anatomical pun on "vice"[1] (Shakespeare's, I assume, and not, at least by conscious intention, Isabella's) catches exactly Isabella's deep physical revulsion from Angelo's sexual design, and assimilates her brother to the crime. It is a "kind of incest" that would allow Claudio to be reborn—fathered and mothered anew—through Isabella's intercourse with Angelo.

Isabella gives voice to an association of sexuality and incest implicit in Angelo as well. This association informs not only their direct responses to sexuality, but also their attempts to evade or control it. Initially for both of them, sexual drives are active only behind a barrier of repression that, when it functions effectively, not only prohibits direct release of sexual desire, but also makes alternative activity serve as disguised metaphor for repressed longings. In serving his severe superego, Angelo serves internalized paternal prohibitions against incestuous sexual desires. Like Angelo's self-imposed chastity, Isabella's desire to enter the convent perpetuates an infantile resolution of the oedipal situation. Isabella, about to join a religious sisterhood that institutionalizes the familial taboo on sexuality, would make a gift of her virginity, her sexual potentiality exalted and desexualized as worship, to God. But everything desexualized for these characters at one level is resexualized at another. Angelo falls prey to his own erotic nature precisely through the appeal of Isabella's saintliness. Isabella's repudiation of Angelo's advances is in turn strangely, masochistically eroticized in a vivid fantasy that expresses her own tormented image of sexual contact:

> were I under the terms of death,
> Th' impression of keen whips I'ld wear as rubies,
> And strip myself to death as to a bed
> That longing had been sick for, ere I'ld yield
> My body up to shame.
> (II.iv.100–104)

Angelo's enforcement of the law against fornication projects and transforms an unconscious stricture that punishes incestuous sexuality with castration into a legal stricture that punishes illicit sexuality with beheading. "Beheading," Freud observed, is "well-known to us as a symbolic substitute for castrating."[2] Isabella implicity accepts and extends the psychological basis for that law when she decides that Claudio, to pay for one sexual crime and to redeem family heritage by preventing a worse one explicitly associated with incest, should go willingly to the chopping block:

> Though he hath fall'n by prompture of the blood,
> Yet hath he in him such a mind of honor
> That, had he twenty heads to tender down
> On twenty bloody blocks, he'ld yield them up,
> Before his sister should her body stoop
> To such abhorred pollution.
>
> (II.iv.178–83)

Claudio is expected to prove himself a worthy son, to redeem paternal honor and heritage, by embracing a fatal extension of the paternal threat of castration.

Claudio casts his resolve to accomplish this in a way that further develops the paradox by sexualizing his own death:

> Think you I can a resolution fetch
> From flow'ry tenderness? If I must die,
> I will encounter darkness as a bride,
> And hug it in mine arms.
>
> (III.i.82–85)

When that element of his resolution that derives from his will to live leads him to choose life and the violation of family bonds over death, the pressure of conflict shifts squarely back onto Isabella. So long as Claudio is ready to die, Isabella finds that "there my father's grave / Did utter forth a voice." But in her outraged reaction to his broken resolution, Isabella calls her mother's reputation into doubt to preserve an image of a father too good to have produced a Claudio:

> What should I think?
> Heaven shield my mother played my father fair,
> For such a warpèd slip of wilderness
> Ne'er issued from his blood.
>
> (III.i.140–43)

Rather than the honorable son of the honored father, Claudio becomes in Isabella's mind the contaminated son of a wayward mother.

As Janet Adelman observes, in a fine introduction written to accompany the telecast of *Measure for Measure* in the BBC/PBS series of Shakespeare productions, "Isabella seems to believe that her nature as a woman ties her to sexuality, particularly sexual misbehavior," a " 'destined livery' " that she "hopes to escape by putting on the robes of a nun."[3] Isabella shares in the deep distrust of women, of female sexuality, diffused throughout the entire play in much the way it permeates *Hamlet* and *Othello.* As she responds to Claudio's plea, she also participates in the defense against sexual contamination through the ideal of male honor. Isabella calls for Claudio's death with a logic like that of Othello:[4]

> Yet she must die, else she'll betray more men.
> (*Oth.* V.ii.6)

> Thy sin's not accidental, but a trade;
> Mercy to thee would prove itself a bawd,
> 'Tis best that thou diest quickly.
> (III.i.150–52)

She resorts to a violence of feeling similar to Othello's:

> Take my defiance,
> Die, perish. Might but my bending down
> Reprieve thee from thy fate, it should proceed.
> I'll pray a thousand prayers for thy death,
> No word to save thee.
> (III.i.143–47)

The unbending rigidity of her moral stance extends to her bodily self-consciousness, reflected in lines that clearly call for Isabella to hold herself stiff and erect in outraged defiance. Having repudiated the sexual heritage she associates with her mother, Isabella, energized with outrage, becomes a metaphor for phallic uprightness; she embodies the potency of paternal heritage Claudio has forfeited.

But Isabella's angry appropriation of a paternal legacy denied by Claudio parallels precisely the precarious resolution of conflict between sexual drives and paternal authority presented by the chaste and tyrannous Angelo. Angelo is the "ungenitured agent" (III.ii.162–63)[5] Lucio finds in him to the extent that he imposes upon his sexual self the psychic equivalent of castration. But Angelo had embraced such "continency" in order to embody desexualized phallic authority. In the oedipal phase, "idealization of the parents . . . becomes focused on their phallic attributes,"[6] attributes internalized in the moral force of Angelo's superego. In denying himself direct sexual expression, Angelo displaces onto an authoritarian moral style rigid, hard, upright qualities that metaphorically extend repressed phallic drives. When desexualization fails, Angelo's whole person becomes subject to the threat of castration that earlier held his sexual impulses in check.

Freud, speculating about the interconnections of castration anxiety and the "dread of women" as reflected in primitive taboos of virginity, wondered if "the effect which coitus has of discharging tensions and causing flaccidity may be the prototype of what the man fears . . ." ("Virginity," p. 199). This pattern of erectness, discharge, and flaccidity describes exactly the curve of Angelo's development as his moral resolution dissolves in its sexual base. His phallic character structure is suddenly charged with repressed sexual content: when the sexual tension of that "swelling evil" is discharged in the night he thinks he spends with Isabella, the "deed unshapes me quite" (IV.iv.18), makes him "unpregnant"—emptied of his strength, his virility—and "dull" (compare Hamlet to Ophelia: "It would cost you a groaning to take off my edge" [III.ii.240]). Finally he submits himself, in shame before Vincentio, to his apparent death by beheading.

In the same essay, Freud describes circumstances that suggest that in relations to a woman "the man is afraid of being weakened, infected with her femininity . . ." (p. 199). The paradoxical nature of this fear—men fear the power of women to make them powerless like women—not only helps explain Angelo's fate, but does much to account for the whole psychological orientation of *Measure for Measure.* Shakespeare's reduction of virginal Isabella to a position of tormented, helpless victimization—until the masculine presence of the disguised Duke intervenes—represents a turning away, a recoiling from the power earlier accorded such resourceful young virgins as Portia and Rosalind in the festive comedies, and in particular Helena in *All's Well That Ends Well.* The subordination of Isabella, both to the sexual assault of Angelo and to the masculine protectiveness of Vincentio, expresses a fearful attitude toward female sexuality often dramatized in the tragedies—in Hamlet's paralyzed brooding over his mother's incest, in the failure of Othello's manhood before the fantasy of Desdemona's infidelity, in Roman speculation about the seductive evil of Cleopatra.

Measure for Measure expresses a deep mistrust of impulses within the self that are provoked in men through relations to women. I have discussed various, largely unsuccessful, defenses the play brings to this fear of masculine vulnerability—the generalized degradation of sexuality, the limitations imposed upon the power of the play's women, the idealization of male authority by Angelo and of paternal honor by Isabella, the law that would prevent illicit sexuality by punishing offenders with death. In the most radical strategy for dealing with the dangers of impulses that threaten to exceed the mastery available to the self, fear of sexual drives spreads into a generalized contempt for and repudiation of all life processes. This strategy is offered in the Duke's prison advice to Claudio: "Be absolute for death" (III.i.5).

The counsel Vincentio offers the condemned Claudio does not reflect the Christian context suggested by his disguise as a friar. J. W. Lever has shown that Vincentio's "description of the human condition eliminates its spiritual aspect and is essentially materialist and pagan."[7] Rossiter emphasized that the speech lacks precisely what would be at the center of a Christian homily on death:

> there is no hint of redemption, no hint of immortality in the whole. The only certainties are existence, uncertainty, disappointment, frustration, old age, and death. It mentions values only as delusions.[8]

Nor does the speech make any explicit effort to put the condemned man into relation with the sin he has committed and for which he has been sentenced to die. Despite the nature of Claudio's crime, Vincentio avoids any emphasis on the place of sexuality in life. "Be absolute for death," Vincentio begins: "either death or life / Shall thereby be the sweeter" (III.i.5–6). There is little in what follows, however, that could conceivably sweeten the experience of living. The Duke proceeds to a somber celebration of death as welcome relief from a life fraught with misery and discontent:

What's yet in this
That bears the name of life? Yet in this life
Lie hid moe thousands deaths; yet death we fear,
That makes these odds all even.

(III.i.38–41)

Vincentio offers an inventory, more fully developed than Hamlet's, of "the heartache, and the thousand natural shocks / That flesh is heir to" (*Ham.* III.i.62–63). His speech expresses a revulsion from life as it is enslaved to processes never halted, which make all experience subject to debasing contingencies, violating even the capacity to be oneself:

Thou art not thyself,
For thou exists on many a thousand grains
That issue out of dust.

(III.i.19–21)

All relations—to property, to the various stages of life, to the quest for happiness, to other people—obliterate solidarity, none more than relations to family:

Friends hast thou none,
For thine own bowels, which do call thee sire,
The mere effusion of thy proper loins,
Do curse the gout, serpigo, and the rheum
For ending thee no sooner.

(III.i.28–32)

The contemptuous reference to procreation in these lines conveys a disgust with the physical dimension of life implicit throughout the entire speech; the cynical summation of parental relations conveys the oedipal hatred that goes with the taboo on sexuality. The fear the Duke associates with the "soft and tender fork / Of a poor worm" (III.i.16–17), whether it refers explicitly to worms that devour the body after death or to the bite of a poisonous snake that would end life, carries a suggestion of impotence that links fear of death to sexual anxiety.

Nothing that urges the self toward gratification brings with it satisfaction, even when apparent aims are accomplished:

> Happy thou art not,
> For what thou hast not, still thou striv'st to get,
> And what thou hast, forget'st.
> (III.i.21–23)

Vincentio's evocation here of impotent striving, like Angelo's and Claudio's earlier reflections on their own sexual drivenness, recalls Sonnet 129:

> Mad in pursuit, and in possession so;
> Had, having, and in quest to have, extreme;
> A bliss in proof, and proved, a very woe;
> Before, a joy proposed; behind a dream.

But in Vincentio's meditation, even the "joy proposed" has lost its lustre; his speech is a movement through and beyond the lament of the sonnet for the "expense of spirit" to a spirit that has nothing to expend. The speech would break the lure of "the heaven that leads men to this hell" (*Son.* 129) by self-willed oblivion. Even death is presented not so much as desirable in itself as simply negation of intolerable life, which in all its "accommodations" is "nursed by baseness" (III.i.14–15).

Vincentio's homily is an elegant refutation of hope, the expectation that desire will lead to gratification, which he sees not, like Claudio, as medicine for the miserable, but as the disease itself. In *Measure for Measure,* impulses that obey the pleasure principle—which seek gratification through a relation with the external world—invariably lead to conditions of heightened inner stress; Vincentio here offers the strategy of withdrawing oneself from those impulses altogether.[9] Shakespeare taps—and momentarily masters through the nihilistic dignity of the Duke's utterance, which accepts annihilation willingly and passively rather than encounter it as a danger—a reservoir of basic mistrust in which the self is so vulnerable to being overwhelmed by its own mixed and unmasterable demands that its only defense is to draw away from the sources of energy that keep it alive.[10] Vincentio's meditation, within its serenity, reveals an estrangement as thorough as Macbeth's chilling account of life as a "walking shadow, a poor player / That struts and frets his hour upon the stage / And then is heard no more" (V.v.24–26).

As advice to the condemned man, however, its usefulness is quickly exhausted. When, in the same scene, Claudio enthusiastically resolves before Isabella to "encounter darkness as a bride," he already speaks from a psychological orientation very different from the passive resignation to death counseled by Vincentio. A few moments later, when Claudio perceives death as a "fearful thing," the situation of traumatic helplessness that Vincentio's speech attempts to short-circuit surfaces with astonishing power. In contrast to death as complete stasis as imagined by Vincentio, Claudio regards his impending death as the initiation of sustained, intolerable process, a savage, perpetual, and thoroughly sensual assault against the spirit:

> Ay, but to die, and go we know not where,
> To lie in cold obstruction and to rot,
> This sensible warm motion to become
> A kneaded clod; and the delighted spirit
> To bathe in fiery floods, or to reside
> In thrilling region of thick-ribbèd ice,
> To be imprisoned in the viewless winds
> And blown with restless violence round about
> The pendent world; or to be worse than worst
> Of those that lawless and incertain thought
> Imagine howling, 'tis too horrible.
> (III.i.118–28)

Claudio fears a death so terrifying that "the weariest and most loathèd worldly life . . . is a paradise" (III.i.129–31) in comparison. His horror of death elaborates a fantasy of eternal torments with the unchecked, "lawless" extremes of the infantile imagination. Although he knows that "this sensible warm motion" will rot in "cold obstruction," his imagination of death, flooded with fears of overwhelming sensual stimuli, extends his sensuality into the fate of the "delighted spirit." Claudio envisions an afterlife in which the howling spirit is passively subjected to extremes of physical torture—submerged in "fiery floods," lodged in ice, both imprisoned and blown violently about in "viewless winds." Death for Claudio is an eternity of traumatic helplessness and terror, a sensational extension of what Vincentio, in his meditation on death, fears in life. This imagination of "what we fear of death" exceeds in intensity even Hamlet's "dread of something after death." Claudio sketches a vivid map of that "undiscovered country" that "puzzles the will / And makes us rather bear those ills we have / Than fly to others that we know not of" (*Ham.* III.i.78–82). Together with the longing for release from shameful urgencies of life counseled by Vincentio (and later embraced by Angelo), Claudio's horror completes the divided relation to death expressed in Hamlet's "to be or not to be" soliloquy. The longing for death Vincentio articulates includes the wish to be ultimately released from tensions that provoke intolerable anxiety and threaten to overwhelm the self's precarious mastery of its own impulses. Claudio projects these tensions into a fate of eternal torment, a terrifyingly passive recasting of his earlier brave resolve to "encounter darkness as a bride." The movement from the Duke's meditation on death as a release from sensuality to Claudio's fear of death as perpetual sensual torture is the most extreme form of an inescapable antagonism, worked out repeatedly in *Measure for Measure,* between intolerable instinctual demands and various unsuccessful strategies that oppose them. Vincentio imagines in death a region beyond the reach of disruptive impulses, but Claudio's imagination of an afterlife redramatizes the impasse of the entire play.

Notes

1. Eric Partridge cites *Ado* V.ii.18–24 to connect *vice* with *pudend and closed thighs* (*Shakespeare's Bawdy,* 2nd ed. [New York: E. E. Dutton, 1995]).

2. "The Taboo of Virginity," in *The Standard Edition of the Complete Psychological Works of Sigmund Freud,* ed. James Strachey, vol. 11 (London: Hogarth Press, 1957), p. 207. There is, perhaps, behind Isabella's initial encouragement to Claudio to face death bravely, a kind of dream logic that sets up there the analogy of beheading with castrating:

> O, I do fear thee, Claudio, and I *quake,*
> Lest thou a *feverous* life shouldst *entertain,*
> And six or seven *winters* more respect
> Than a *perpetual* honor. Dar'st thou *die?*
> The *sense* of death is most in apprehension,
> And the poor *beetle* that we tread upon
> In *corporal sufferance* finds a *pang* as great
> As when a *giant* dies. (III.i.74–81)

I have italicized the words that suggest unconscious sexual content: *quake* suggests bodily excitation as well as the fearfulness Isabella associates with sexuality; *feverous* often, especially in the *Sonnets* (cf. 147: "My love is as a fever, longing still, / For that which longer nurseth the disease"), carries a sexual meaning for Shakespeare; *entertain* is opposed to *winters* as Claudio's sexual indulgence is opposed to Isabella's own chilly response by denial of her sexuality. Against these terms is set *perpetual honor,* which desexualizes, idealizes, and stabilizes the impulsiveness of phallic sexuality. *Sense* here, as elsewhere, suggests sensuality (see William Empson, "Sense in *Measure for Measure,*" *The Structure of Complex Words* [London: Chatto & Windus, 1951], pp. 270–88), a suggestion confirmed by *die,* which often carries the meaning of sexual consummation. The link of *beetle* to *giant* through *corporal sufferance* and *pang* gives a particularly sexual resonance to dying; *beetle* and *giant* suggest both the relation of the penis to the entire body (the equation essential to the symbolic identity of castration and beheading) and the relation of a boy's smallness to a father's largeness as perceived by a boy facing the paternal obstacle to his own sexual ambitions.

3. "Mortality and Mercy in *Measure for Measure,*" in *The Shakespeare Plays: A Study Guide* (Delmar, Ca.: University Extension, University of California, San Diego, and Coast Community College District, 1978), pp. 104–14.

4. I am grateful to C. L. Barber for pointing out to me this resemblance.

5. J. W. Lever's gloss for *ungenitured* in the Arden ed. of *Measure for Measure* (London: Methuen, 1965) is "sterile, seedless; or without genitals."

6. John E. Gedo and Arnold Goldberg, *Models of the Mind: A Psychoanalytic Theory* (Chicago: University of Chicago Press, 1973), p. 85.

7. Introduction to Arden ed. of *Measure for Measure,* p. lxxxvii.

8. A. P. Rossiter, *Angel With Horns* (London: Longman, Green & Co. Ltd., 1961), p. 166.

9. Psychoanalysis has shown that the "avoidance of the unpleasurable . . . is characteristic of the primary mental processes" that govern the actions of the self in its very early stages and that are only gradually modified in the course of development. "The decathexis of endogenous stimuli [withdrawal of psychic investment from inner impulses] which produce unplea-

sure is the mechanism of primary repression." Gedo and Goldberg, the authors I am quoting, observe that primary repression, "passively experienced and unavoidable," is the typical adaptive strategy of early infancy, but "continues to be the defense which becomes operative in case of traumatic overstimulation throughout the life span . . ." (*Models of the Mind,* pp. 95–98). The danger averted by this defense is the direct experience of complete helplessness, of being overwhelmed or annihilated by impulses that exceed the reach of ego mastery. Within the sophisticated, artful advice offered by Vincentio, a process analogous to this primitive defensive response seems to be at work.

10. Erik Erikson associates basic mistrust, the necessary, negative counterpart to the establishment of basic trust in early experience, with "impressions of having been deprived, of having been divided, of having been abandoned . . ." (*Identity: Youth and Crisis* [New York: Norton, 1968], p. 101).

Social Texts, Royal Measures

JONATHAN GOLDBERG

With Shakespeare, instrumentality, or, as Stephen Greenblatt calls it, improvisation, is everything.[1] Shakespeare's relation to his culture remains difficult to summarize, not because he is apart from it but because he assumes no fixed relationship to it. This has often made it possible to act as if Shakespeare was some timeless figure, a man for all times and yet of none. This is, palpably, erroneous. Yet, opposing attempts, for instance E.M.W. Tillyard's,[2] to moor his political and historical attitudes in a morass of Elizabethan commonplaces, have foundered. As Greenblatt says, it seems untrue to characterize Shakespeare as a Tudor propagandist, but equally unconvincing to speak of him as a Marlovian rebel; it is false, too, to locate him (with Jonson) on some *via media.* The space of Shakespearean representation is, Greenblatt concludes, radically unstable, a place of improvisation where all the beliefs of the culture are trotted out, tried on, but where none is ultimately adopted. This is not Keatsian negative capability exactly; rather, Shakespeare occupies a thoroughly theatrical space. But, we must add, his theatrical space is inscribed in a cultural theater. James, we need hardly recall, viewed himself as an exemplary performer onstage. Shakespearean improvisation partakes of the royal mode; it achieves the show of transparency, the heart of inscrutability, to which the king's double language aspired.

Unlike Jonson or Donne, Shakespeare appears to have had no firsthand dealings with the king. Yet their paths crossed significantly. When James came to the throne, his first act in the literary realm was to take the theaters under his patronage. Shakespeare's company, as we all know, became the King's Men. As part of his entertainment, James demanded court performances of plays; the King's Men were favored, and many plays by their leading playwright were performed at court. This is about as far as one can faithfully state the relationship between Shakespeare and the king. Many critics have gone further and have supposed that royal patronage circumscribed the subject matter and attitudes expressed in plays, or involved commissioning plays for court performance. This does not seem to have been the case. Plays

Reprinted from Jonathan Goldberg, *James I and the Politics of Literature: Jonson, Shakespeare, Donne and Their Contemporaries,* 230–39, 286–87. © 1983. The Johns Hopkins University Press.

performed by the King's Men, like *Sejanus,* could be suspected of sedition and atheism. Plays performed at court were always drawn from the public repertory, and there is no example of a play written for court. Even the plays chosen for court performance need not have been overtly adulatory or even topically suitable, *Othello,* for instance, being one play chosen for the marriage celebrations of Princess Elizabeth, nor were the companies performing always in good standing with the court. To take one example, Marston's *The Dutch Courtesan,* performed several times before the king, derives some of its humor from dialects, and the Scots—and thus James and his favorites—are not immune.[3] Cocledemoy, the witty knave and parodist, determining that he "must dissemble, must disguise" takes first the identity of "a Northerne Barbar" (2:1, lines 205–7) named Andrew Sharke (2:2, line 3). The name combines the patron saint of Scotland with Scottish rapacity. Yet, presumably, the play pleased the king for much the same reasons that Jonson's antimasques succeeded. James countenanced what he would not have tolerated behind his back.

In the canon of Shakespeare's works, one play that has induced frequent speculation about the relationship of playwright and king is *Measure for Measure.*[4] We have been assured that it was written for court performance in 1604 (it seems clear that it was performed before the king on Christmas that year), or, at the very least, that the text we have is one revised for that performance.[5] And we have been told that the Duke mouths James's opinions and apes his actions. These claims are as easily answered: no plays were written for court performance; we know too little about the status of Shakespeare's texts to be able to determine that the one we have is a court revision; the opinions that the Duke and James share can be found readily in many political treatises of the time; much as some of the Duke's acts may recall James's, more do not—for instance, his crucial disguise as a monk has no literal counterpart in James's career. Yet criticism is no doubt correct in feeling that *Measure for Measure* has some special relationship to the king. In the pages that follow, that relationship, and with it, Shakespeare's relationship to his culture, are explored through the crucial notion that links theater and culture in James's time: representation. Perhaps one hardly need say more than this, that *Measure for Measure* is a play about substitution, replacement—and thus, representation.[6] In it, the power of theater bears a royal stamp. Hence, it is not surprising to find Josephine Waters Bennett spinning out this fantasy about the play:

> If the author himself acted the part of the Duke, then there could be no suggestion that the Duke was, or represented, King James. He *is* Shakespeare, acting a play which exemplifies what King James had written about kingcraft (that is, he is the King's puppet), and, in the last act, producing a play he has created (as the Duke) to resolve all difficulties and make everything come out

> right in the end. Shakespeare as actor and playwright is the "God on earth" of his play, manipulating the other characters like puppets, and creating Lucio, the puppet who talks back to his creator. He is the God-Ruler in his world of make-believe, as King James thought himself to be in the real world.[7]

Se non è vero (and there is not a shred of evidence for any of the suppositions here) *è ben trovato.*

Not even the vagaries of stage tradition support Bennett's supposition that Shakespeare took the Duke's part. Yet her literalistic fantasy is based on an inchoate insight. The Duke plays two roles that overlap: as a monarch he has powers so extensive that Angelo can say that "your grace, like power divine / Hath looked upon my passes" (5:1, lines 365–66)—like James he rules by Divine Right. Hence, he is also responsible for Angelo's "passes" as well as those of other characters in the play. He authorizes and authors their actions, and Angelo's career, in the seat of government and in bed with Mariana, is entirely scripted by the Duke. In the Duke, Shakespeare has written a role that represents his powers as playwright as coincident with the powers of the sovereign. This is more than the analogical statement that dramatist and king rule their realms, for the Duke reigns in both; dramatist and monarch represent each other, a doubleness housed in his single person. In her study of *Measure for Measure,* Bennett wavers in identifying the Duke with James; without realizing why, she is nonetheless correct; the play of representation does not invite exact identification. The Duke plays his part in two costumes, as ruler and as friar.[8] He is split, and he casts the characters into doubling, substitutive roles as well. In these re-presentational procedures, the play offers an image of its relation to sovereign power.

The play opens in a manner that characterizes its proceedings throughout. The Duke starts a disquisition on the nature of rule, "Of government the properties to unfold" (1:1, line 3), but gets no further than this opening clause. Instead of words, the Duke points to Escalus, to whom he speaks, as the embodiment of the words about government he would have spoken. Although the dramatic procedure is not absolutely clear, its representational force is: as exemplar, Escalus doubles and embodies the Duke's learning and knowledge of government, and the Duke has "unfolded" himself in Escalus. Since Escalus embodies the words, an audience might presume that the Duke is resigning his powers to him, since his "commission" (line 13) embraces "our city's institutions, and the terms / For common justice" (lines 10–11). This supposition proves false immediately. Instead, the reins of power are handed to Angelo. The Duke thus puts two commissioners in his place as his representatives. Escalus seconds the Duke's choice of Angelo, but Angelo does not. The doubling thus produces division, too. "Let there be some more test made of my mettle / Before so noble and so great a figure / Be stamped upon it" (lines 48–50), Angelo asks. "No more evasion" is the Duke's evasive reply.

The Duke has "unfolded" himself in Angelo, who wishes, like the Duke, to refuse to play his part. Yet we cannot know how far Angelo represents the Duke, for we do not know why the Duke has chosen Angelo, or even if he knows why. When, later, it seems that Angelo's refusal to play his part stems from an incipient awareness of his unworthiness to administer a law he himself would violate, we do not know whether this is the Duke's case as well, although Lucio suggests that it is. Lucio exists to suggest that such analogies are identities and that the "Duke of dark corners" (4:3, lines 154–55) "had some feeling of the sport" (3:2, line 112). "The Duke yet would have dark deeds darkly answered" (3:2, lines 165–66). Yet there is no reason to believe Lucio. What we can know is that the exercise of sovereign power and dramatic power as the play opens depends upon the enactment of substitutions whose analogical force remains mysterious. "Do you call, sir, your occupation a mystery?" (4:2, line 30), Pompey the bawd turned executioner asks the hangman Abhorson, whose name at least suggests that he is an alter ego. His avowal of the mystery of his occupation echoes in a play where "though you change your place, you need not change your trade" (1:2, lines 104–5), as Pompey counsels Mistress Overdone, Madam Mitigation as he also calls her. The same places are forever reoccupied. Hence the whorehouse becomes a prison, a bawd an executioner, men's heads pay for maidenheads. Substitution is the law of the play and inherent in justice, the law of society as well. The "mystery" in these multiple replacements and substitutions centers on the Duke, sovereign in both realms.

"What figure of us think you he will bear" (1:1, line 16), the Duke asks Escalus about Angelo, a central question throughout the play. How does Angelo represent the Duke and how far does such representation go? Angelo's pun on *mettle* in the first scene suggests that he is a coin stamped with the Duke's figure. Sovereign power, real and stamped, sustains the exchange system of society, the endless refiguration of the king in representative acts of substitution. At the end of *Measure for Measure,* the Duke replays the opening scene anew, departing and reinvesting himself in Angelo and Escalus. "The Duke's in us" (5:1, line 293), Escalus says. Interior inhabitation there matches Angelo's condition; the Duke has "lent him our terror, dressed him with our love" (1:1, line 19). Similarly, the absent Duke dons a friar's habit and is dressed with love. Thus, the Duke's language of figuration, supplementation ("Elected him our absence to supply" [line 18]), and investiture for his deputy predicts his own form in the play that follows. Angelo may well be called the Duke's "motion generative" (3:2, line 104), his puppet. The substitute occupies the seat of power. But if "the body politic be / A horse whereon the governor doth ride" (1:2, lines 154–55), then public rule has private—and sexual—implications. The law of Vienna connects these two spheres, enforcing the fact that the private sphere is realized in public. The properties of government unfolded from the opening line of the play onward continually catch individual desire within the web of the body politic. This is "the state, whereon [Angelo] . . . studied" (2:4, line 7).[9]

Thus the substitutions within the play are not exactly duplicative, but a series of analogies in which differences are crucial though unfathomable. Hence, at the end of the play, Angelo is in Claudio's position, having repeated his crime (so, too, have Lucio and Elbow, both virgin violators), and the Duke appears to be in Angelo's place, offering redemption to Isabella in exchange for sexual favors. Yet Angelo's crime seems monstrous whereas Claudio's seemed no crime at all, and the Duke's wooing of Isabella, even though he offers marriage, seems at least as much an assault upon her integrity as Angelo's proposition.

The final unsettling refigurations of *Measure for Measure* return the play to its initial premise, the unfolding of individual and communal government, and provide a mirror for the cultural situation of the play. No exact replay of James at all, the play yet manages to catch at central concerns: in the disguised Duke, the king's divided self; in the relations between privacy and the public, the play between internal and external theaters of conscience; in the Duke's actions, the combination of absence and presence through which James claimed authority. More specifically, commentators have felt that the Duke's initial decision to sneak away from Vienna reflects upon James and his aversion to crowds.

> I'll privily away; I love the people,
> But do not like to stage me to their eyes;
> Though it do well, I do not relish well
> Their loud applause and aves vehement,
> Nor do I think the man of safe discretion
> That does affect it.
> (1:1, lines 67–72)

What genuinely seems to reflect James's government in this decision is the function of the Duke's retirement. Although, like James, the Duke could be accused (and is, by Lucio) of having little interest in running the government, delegating all responsibility to others, he does not retire to country pleasures; rather, he rules in absence, through others and in disguise. His presence-in-absence figures a mode of power. James claimed it; Tiberius exemplifies it. Power-in-absence is the central stance of absolutism necessary to maintain prerogatives and the secrets of state. The complexity of the relationship of *Measure for Measure* to this absolutist mode, and to its cultural situation, lies in the fact that the Duke, who professes complete power and control, is not in fact all-powerful. Lucio's accusations have force; the Duke's plots cause us discomfort and strain our credulity, too. Yet the Duke even asserts control over what he cannot control. His withdrawal figures his inability and his disinclination to enact his powers; yet his power lies in withdrawing.

The two Dukes—absolute and absent—meet in act 5 when the two Dukes of the play—Vincentio and Friar Lodowick—confront each other. The Duke, having returned, disappears once again to return disguised anew. He faces his delegates, Escalus and Angelo, dispensing the Duke's justice ("The Duke's in us" [5:1, line 293]). They unfold him. Responding to their attempt to send him to prison—the place where virtually everyone in the play arrives so that it reconstitutes the world and erases the margin between the world outside the prison walls and that within—he protests that the Duke has no power over him:

> The Duke
> Dare no more stretch this finger of mine than he
> Dare rack his own: his subject am I not,
> Nor here provincial. My business in this state
> Made me a looker-on here in Vienna.
> (5:1, lines 311–15)

The Duke's double entendres stem from a doubleness that runs throughout the play (notably present in Angelo's second scene with Isabella where his *sense* fails to meet hers).[10] Self-referentiality is self-divisive: "His subject am I not." More crucially, these double entendres point to the nature of the absolutist ruler—"nor here provincial"—his separateness from the state he rules. Only he is not subject in such a state, and it is his special status—his aloneness, the fact that he is *sui generis*—that makes him no "provincial" even at home, and always a "looker-on," observing, a divine status. The Duke assumes this stance repeatedly, as did James, modeling himself on God in his lieutenancy, standing in place of God. The Duke represents James's Divine Right claims; as a divine—a friar—he claims the right not to be subject to the Duke.

From this stance, the Duke enacts his power, dispensing grace. The return of "royal grace" (5:1, line 3) in the final act recasts the Duke's divine actions throughout; but the point about grace is made best by Lucio: "Grace is grace, despite of all controversy: as, for example, thou thyself art a wicked villain, despite of all grace" (1:2, lines 24–26). As he explains, grace is and is not grace. The wit of Lucio's statement lies in the way a tautology and identification ("grace is grace") becomes exclusionary and self-divisive. That which refers to itself cannot be contained. This explains the Duke's inexplicable behavior. Grace is grace despite the law; it lies beyond the boundaries. Just as Pompey can rename Mistress Overdone and call her Madame Mitigation, so bawdry—the Duke's bed trick, for instance—becomes grace in this play. In the exchanges that lead up to Lucio's definition of grace, this situation is epitomized by the pirate who stole the commandment "thou shalt not steal" and thus remained pious, breaking no commandment, yet remained a pirate, too. These equivocations are suspended in the figure of the Duke and in his various deputies in the play—in Angelo, of course, and even in Elbow, the elbow of the law if not its right hand.

EL. Bless you, good father friar.
DU. And you, good brother father. What offense hath this man made you, sir?
EL. Marry, sir, he hath offended the law; and sir, we take him to be a thief too, sir.
(3:2, lines 10–14)

The Duke's parodic greeting scores a reflective point, as does Elbow's bumbling doubling of Pompey's offenses—for in the play one could offend the law and yet be innocent. The Duke does—and his extension of grace makes it true for Angelo as well as Claudio. They are measured by his own measure. The pirate's loophole is extended to them, in the form of Ragozin the pirate's head. Even Barnardine, who resists the Duke's attempts to manipulate the plot through representative, substitutive acts, is also reprieved at the end. Nothing and nobody escapes the Duke's grasp. He makes the strongest opposing themes of the play, restraint and liberty, one. By a principle like the allophanic extension of Donne's poem on the Somerset wedding, all the characters reflect the Duke and become engaged in his schemes. "The doubleness of the benefit defends the deceit from reproof" (3:1, lines 250–51), the Duke-as-friar tells Isabella, recommending her lying to Angelo and Mariana's lying in her place. The benefit may be double, yet it also leads Isabella to experience the reported death of Claudio, her accusation of unchastity, and imprisonment. All this, the Duke affirms, is for her good, as is, presumably, his final grace—wooing her, and presenting—re-presenting—Claudio as a double of himself, "as like almost to Claudio as himself" (5:1, line 485). In the play, tautology is the Duke's truth, and with it all's good, all's one, reflecting him, serving his ends.

We know that we will never know his ends, that the Duke's motives, unrepresented, can never be known. We see a play of representation in which the rule of doubleness is, from the Duke's perspective, endlessly to his credit, representing multiple mirrors of his powers. Yet representation maintains, from the start, its opacity precisely because the principle of substitution opens up unfathomable differences, making it unclear whether we should read grace-as-grace or grace-despite-grace. We see this when Isabella cannot hear what Angelo says to her, and he assumes that she either is ignorant or pretending to be (2:4, lines 74–75). And we see it uproariously when Escalus attempts to determine what was done to Elbow's wife (2:1). This, of course, will be a vital question later in the play, when it turns out that Angelo has done nothing more than sleep with his betrothed. "Do you hear how he misplaces?" (2:1, line 84), Escalus's question about Elbow's speech—the speech of a constable of the Duke's, an administrator of his justice—applies to all who are replaced in the play—from the Duke in his habit, to Angelo in his.

"O place, O form, / How often dost thou with thy case, thy habit, / Wrench awe from fools, and tie the wiser souls / To thy false seeming" (2:4, lines 12–15).

The enactment of justice is always a scene of representation, putting into language what has occurred, doubling an event in words. In *Measure for Measure,* both events and words share a doubleness, and language when it is most accurate unspeaks itself. Thus, Angelo speaks "empty words" (2:4, line 2) and would have "good Angel" inscribed on the devil's horn (2:4, line 16), a duplicitous autonomy that follows from a tautology—"Blood, thou art blood" (line 15). Such is the language of things and the nature of events. Claudio's deed "with character too gross is writ on Juliet" (1:2, line 150), and Angelo tells Isabella, "I do arrest your words" (2:4, line 134), demanding that she put her body where her mouth was. Instead, she repeats herself. The play operates within language, Claudio apprehended "for a name . . . 'tis surely for a name" (1:2, lines 164, 166). He knows the double nature of "the demigod Authority": "on whom it will, it will; / On whom it will not, so: yet still 'tis just" (1:2, lines 116, 118–19). Authority speaks a language—the Duke's—in which what is and what is not remain the same, always just. The power of authority takes root in language itself, endlessly reduplicative, endlessly re-presenting. "I hope here be truths," Pompey affirms in his first dealing with the law (2:1, line 120); and this character, who has more names than any other character in the play—Thomas Tapster, bawd, caitiff, varlet, Hannibal, Pompey Bum—and whose change in "mysteries" mirrors the Duke's transformation, tells a central truth no matter how much he lies.

Es. How would you live, Pompey? By being a bawd? What do you think of the trade, Pompey? Is it a lawful trade?
Po. If the law would allow it, sir.

(2:1, lines 211–14)

The law to which Pompey refers is the law of Vienna: the law of representation. Representation includes acts of restatement and of interpretation as well as the dramatic act of renaming.

Shakespeare's Vienna is a curious locale, a landscape of Italianate vice (and with a cast of characters whose names are largely Italian) with its leader, the Duke, bearing an Italian title. It is a dramatic domain as another mirror for princes suggests: "This play is the image of a murder done in Vienna. Gonzago is the duke's name; his wife, Baptista" (*Ham.* 3:2, lines 30–31).[11] The dominant trope of *Measure for Measure* is the unfolding of government, the revelation of the politicization of the body, of the single cloth that links public and private spheres. No one is free from another's construction, everyone does himself wrong "whether thou art tainted or free" (1:2, lines 40–41), for "every true man's apparel fits your thief" (4:2, line 42). All men are clothed similarly, free or restrained, innocent or criminal. All are subject to the Duke and his endless scheming and mysterious plotting. All: even the Duke; he, too, is caught within the web, part of the vice he wishes to separate himself from, and, in the last act, caught in his own dramatic manipulations. It is not merely that Lucio "makes" the Duke (5:1, lines 352, 511); his act of revelation and unmasking suggests the contained subversion that deconstructs what the Duke constructs. Lucio's claims that he "spoke . . . according to the trick" (5:1, lines 499–500) deny autonomy in his act; his lie tells a truth. For, although he pretends that his words were given him by the Duke and form part of his play, they do form part of the play, one in which he and the Duke have parts, actuating each other, operating as bound antagonists, linked as firmly as main masque and antimasque in a courtly entertainment. These are the measures of *Measure for Measure,* the principle of representation that prescribes a single law for the state and the theater. In this elusive relationship, the king, the author, and the text of the play all have a part.

Measure for Measure suggests that the essential question that links politics and literature in the Jacobean period is representation. By representing representation, Shakespeare contributes to the discourse of his society and to its most pressing questions about prerogative, power, and authority. These questions also affect him, and his meditation on the nature of rule is inevitably self-scrutinizing as well. Although neither the dramatist nor the king is onstage, the Duke in *Measure for Measure* represents them both, the clearest emblem for the relationship of literature and politics in the Jacobean period. As the careers of Jonson and Donne, and their more explicit confrontation with royal power, suggest,[12] the dilemma of representation that Shakespeare takes as his subject is at the heart of the relationship of literature to royal power, of the words of the poet to the king's language. For Donne, words came from the king directly; for Jonson, double language provided a reflecting glass; for Shakespeare, re-presenting assured autonomy. It was his law, and the king's.

Notes

1. *Renaissance Self-Fashioning: From More to Shakespeare* (Chicago: University of Chicago Press, 1980), pp. 222 ff., esp. pp. 227–28, 252–54.

2. In, for example, *Shakespeare's History Plays* (1944; reprint, New York: Collier Books, 1962). Perhaps the most useful account of Shakespeare's relation to the political and social beliefs of his time is W. Gordon Zeeveld's *The Temper of Shakespeare's Thought* (New Haven: Yale University Press, 1974).

3. Citations from Marston's *The Dutch Courtesan,* ed. Peter Davison (Berkeley and Los Angeles: University of California Press, 1968).

4. Citations from the Penguin edition, ed. R. C. Bald (Baltimore, 1956). The topicality of *Measure for Measure* is the burden of Josephine Waters Bennet's *Measure for Measure as Royal Entertainment* (New York: Columbia University Press, 1966) and an appendix to David Lloyd Stevenson, *The Achievement of Shakespeare's Measure for Measure* (Ithaca: Cornell University

Press, 1966). Occasional arguments are the subject of Richard Levin's attack, "The King James Version of *Measure for Measure,*" *Clio* 3 (1974): 129–96 (reprinted in his *New Readings vs. Old Plays* [Chicago: University of Chicago Press, 1979]) and his debate over Roy Battenhouse's "*Measure for Measure* and King James," *Clio* 7 (1977): 193–215, in *Clio* 7 (1977): 217–26. Levin characteristically attacks straw men; Battenhouse's predictably theological reading (in which James is lectured by Shakespeare for not being a Catholic) is easily answered, as are the literalisms of much topical criticism. Still, as Battenhouse says ("*Measure for Measure* and King James," p. 221), Levin is merely a skeptic, and he sidesteps any real confrontation with the play. It is surely incontrovertible that Shakespeare is of his time; the question is how to describe that relation accurately, not to dismiss it out of hand.

5. This point is made by J. Dover Wilson in the New Cambridge edition, and by John Wasson in "*Measure for Measure:* A Text for Court Performance?," *Shakespeare Quarterly* 21 (1970): 17–24. J. W. Lever in the Arden edition points to many of the limits in this argument about the text.

6. The most cogent treatment of this point is Nancy S. Leonard's, "Substitution in Shakespeare's Problem Comedies," *English Literary Renaissance* 9 (1979): 281–301.

7. *Measure for Measure as Royal Entertainment,* p. 137.

8. The Duke's double form leads to a particularly breathtaking display of power when he consigns Mariana to Angelo: "I have confessed her and I know her virtue" (5:1, line 522). This seems to be an ultimate violation of privacy, and a demonstration of the confluence of sovereign power with the confessional. It is comprehended in the argument of Michel Foucault's *The History of Sexuality,* trans. Robert Hurley (New York: Pantheon Books, 1978). Foucault argues that the law that maintains sovereignty is entangled with the law that constitutes desire (see e.g., pp. 81, 113); the confession is the form of discourse in which sex is made to speak, and the history of sexuality is the history of its being put into discourse. Sexuality is not, for Foucault, a natural phenomenon but "a historical construct" (p. 105, cf. pp. 155–57), and in sexuality one has a "dense transfer point for relations of power" (p. 103). In *Measure for Measure,* the Duke's two forms—as Angelo and as friar—are forms of the virtues upon which government rests, justice and religion. Both meet in sexuality in the play, the underlying privacy dragged into public.

9. In *Shakespeare and Society* (New York: Schocken Books, 1967), Terence Eagleton sees the crime of Claudio and Julietta as their attempt to keep sexual union private; "Personal action, to be real, must be available for social verification" (p. 67).

10. On the meanings of *sense* and for a reading of the play that emphasizes much that is unsettling in it, see William Empson's "Sense in *Measure for Measure*" in *The Structure of Complex Words* (Ann Arbor: University of Michigan Press, 1967). For a reading of the play in which theatricality casts doubt upon the Duke's powers and virtues, see Ann Righter [Barton], *Shakespeare and the Idea of the Play* (London: Chatto & Windus, 1962; Harmondsworth: Penguin, 1967), pp. 158–62.

11. *Hamlet,* ed. Willard Farnham (Baltimore: Penguin, 1957).

12. For Jonson and Donne, see "Social Texts, Royal Measures: Donne, Jonson, and *Measure for Measure,*" the chapter from which this selection is taken, in Jonathan Goldberg, *James I and the Politics of Literature: Jonson, Shakespeare, Donne and Their Contemporaries* (Baltimore: The John Hopkins University Press, 1983), pp. 210–39.

Transgression and surveillance in *Measure for Measure*

JONATHAN DOLLIMORE

In the Vienna of *Measure for Measure,* unrestrained sexuality is ostensibly subverting social order; anarchy threatens to engulf the State unless sexuality is subjected to renewed and severe regulation. Such at least is the claim of those in power. Surprisingly critics have generally taken them at their word even while dissociating themselves from the punitive zeal of Angelo. There are those who have found in the play only a near tragic conflict between anarchy and order, averted in the end it is true, but unconvincingly so. Others, of a liberal persuasion and with a definite preference for humane rather than authoritarian restraint, have found at least in the play's "vision," if not precisely its ending an ethical sense near enough to their own. But both kinds of critic have apparently accepted that sexual transgression in *Measure for Measure*—and in the world—represents a real force of social disorder intrinsic to human nature and that the play at least is about how this force is—must be—restrained.

J. W. Lever, in an analysis of the play noted for its reasonableness,[1] draws a comparison with Shakespeare's romantic comedies where disorders in both society and individual, especially those caused by "the excesses of sentiment and desire" are resolved: "not only the problems of lovers, but psychic tensions and social usurpations or abuses, found their resolution through the exercise of reason, often in the form of an adjudication by the representatives of authority." In *Measure for Measure* the same process occurs but more extremely: "Not only are the tensions and discords wrought up to an extreme pitch, threatening the dissolution of all human values, but a corresponding and extraordinary emphasis is laid upon the role of true authority, whose intervention alone supplies the equipoise needed to counter the forces of negation." Lever draws a further contrast with *Troilus and Cressida* where "no supreme authority exists; age and wisdom can only warn, without stemming the inevitable tide of war and lechery." On this view then unruly desire is extremely subversive and has to be countered by "true" and "supreme authority," "age and wisdom," all of which qualities are possessed by the Duke in *Measure for Measure* and used by him to redeem the State (pp.lx and lxxi). Only these virtues, this man, can retrieve the State from anarchy.[2]

But consider now a very different view of the problem. With the considerable attention recently devoted to Bakhtin and his truly important analysis of the subversive carnivalesque, the time is right for a radical reading of *Measure for Measure,* one which insists on the oppressiveness of the Viennese State and which interprets low-life transgression as *positively* anarchic, ludic, carnivalesque—a subversion from below of a repressive official ideology of order. What follows aims (if it is not too late) to forestall such a reading as scarcely less inappropriate than that which privileged "true" authority over anarchic desire. Indeed, such a reading, if executed within the parameters of some recent appropriations of Bakhtin, would simply remain within the same problematic, only reversing the polarities of the binary opposition which structures it (order / chaos). I offer a different reading of the play, one which, perhaps paradoxically, seeks to identify its absent characters and the history which it contains yet does not represent.

Transgression

Whatever subversive identity the sexual offenders in this play possess is a construction put upon them by the authority which wants to control them; moreover control is exercised through that construction. Diverse and only loosely associated sexual offenders are brought into renewed surveillance by the State; identified in law as a category of offender (the lecherous, the iniquitous) they are thereby demonised as a threat to law. Like many apparent threats to authority this one in fact legitimates it: control of the threat becomes the rationale of authoritarian reaction in a time of apparent crisis. Prostitution and lechery are identified as the causes of crisis yet we learn increasingly of a corruption more political than sexual (see especially V.i.316ff). Arguably then the play discloses corruption to be an effect less of desire than authority itself. It also shows how corruption is downwardly identified—that is, focused and placed with reference to low-life "licence"; in effect, and especially in the figure of Angelo, corruption is displaced from authority to desire and by implication from the rulers to the ruled. The Duke tells Pompey:

> Fie, sirrah, a bawd, a wicked bawd;
> The evil that thou causest to be done,
> That is thy means to live. Do thou but think

> What 'tis to cram a maw or clothe a back
> From such a filthy vice. Say to thyself,
> From their abominable and beastly touches
> I drink, I eat, array myself, and live.
> Canst thou believe thy living is a life,
> So stinkingly depending?
>
> (III.ii.18–26)

This is in response to Pompey's observation that such exploitation not only exists at other levels of society but is actually protected "by order of law" (1.8). This is just what the Duke's diatribe ignores—cannot acknowledge—fixating instead on the "filthy vice" and its agents in a way which occludes the fact that it is Angelo, not Pompey, who, unchecked, and in virtue of his social position, will cause most "evil . . . to be done." But, because Angelo's transgression is represented as growing from his desire rather than his authority, his is a crime which can be construed as a lapse into the corruption of a lower humanity, a descent of the ruler into the sins of the ruled. Provocatively, his crime is obscurely theirs.

If we can indeed discern in the demonising of sexuality a relegitimation of authority we should not then conclude that this is due simply to an ideological conspiracy; or rather it may indeed be conspiratorial but it is also ideological in another, more complex sense: through a process of displacement an imaginary—and punitive—resolution of real social tension and conflict is attempted.

The authoritarian demonising of deviant behaviour was common in the period, and displacement and condensation—to and around low life—were crucial to this process.[3] But what made displacement and condensation possible was a prior construction of deviancy itself. So, for example, diatribes against promiscuity, female self-assertion, cross-dressing and homosexuality construed these behaviours as symptomatic of an impending dissolution of social hierarchy and so, in effect, of civilisation.[4] This was partly because transgression was conceived in public and even cosmic terms; it would not then have made sense to see it in, say, psychological or subjective terms—a maladjustment of the individual who, with professional assistance, could be "normalised." On the one hand then homosexuality was not considered to be the "defect" of a particular personality type since "the temptation to debauchery, from which homosexuality was not clearly distinguished, was accepted as part of the common lot, be it never so abhorred. For the Puritan writer John Rainolds homosexuality was a sin to which 'men's natural corruption and viciousness is prone.' " And this was because homosexuality "was not a sexuality in its own right, but existed as a potential for confusion and disorder in one undivided sexuality" (Alan Bray, *Homosexuality in Renaissance England,* pp. 16–17, 25). On the other hand it was distinguished sufficiently to be associated with other cardinal sins like religious and political heresy and witchcraft.

This association of sexual deviance with religious and political deviance—made of course in relation to Marlowe by the informer Richard Baines[5] and rather more recently by the British tabloid press in relation to Peter Tatchell[6]—facilitates the move from specific to general subversion: the individual transgressive act sent reverberations throughout the whole and maybe even brought down God's vengeance on the whole.

Stuart Clark has shown how the disorder which witches and other deviants symbolised, even as it was represented as a threat to order, was also a presupposition of it. Contrariety, he argues, was "a universal principle of intelligibility as well as a statement about how the world was actually constituted" and "the characterisation of disorder by inversion, even in relatively minor texts or on ephemeral occasions, may therefore be taken to exemplify an entire metaphysic" ("Inversion, Misrule and Witchraft," pp. 110–12). On this view then the attack on deviancy was not just a diversionary strategy of authority in times of crisis but an elementary and permanent principle of rule. Nevertheless, we might expect that it is in times of crisis that this principle is specially operative. The work of Lawrence Stone would seem to confirm this. He argues that in the early seventeenth century the family household becomes, at least in contemporary propaganda, "responsible for, and the symbol of, the whole social system, which was thought to be based on the God-given principle of hierarchy, deference and obedience." Such propaganda was stimulated in part by the experienced instability of rapid change, change which was interpreted by some as impending collapse.[7] According to Stone then, "the authoritarian family and the authoritarian nationstate were the solutions to an intolerable sense of anxiety, and a deep yearning for order" and the corollary was a ruthless persecution of dissidents and deviants. Sexuality became subject to intensified surveillance working in terms of both an enforced and an internalised discipline.[8] *Measure for Measure,* I want to argue, is about both kinds of discipline, the enforced and the internalised. Their coexistence made for a complex social moment as well as a complex play.

J. A. Sharpe's recent and scrupulous study of crime in seventeenth-century England confirms this discrepancy between the official depiction of moral collapse among the lower orders and their actual behaviour. Sharpe also confirms that the suppression of sexuality was only "one aspect of a wider desire to achieve a disciplined society. Fornication, like idleness, pilfering, swearing and drunkenness, was one of the distinguishing activities of the disorderly." Further, the Elizabethan and early Stuart period marked an historical highpoint in an authoritarian preoccupation with the disorderly and their efficient prosecution.[9] Nevertheless, many of those concerned with this prosecution really did believe standards were declining and the social fabric disintegrating. Puritan extremists like Stubbes saw prostitution as so abhorrent they advocated the death penalty for offenders (Lever, p. xlvi). But if, as Stone and others argue, this fervour is the result of insecurity in the face of change, then, even if that fervour was "sincere," the immorality which incited it was not at all its real cause. This is one sense in which the discourse of blame involved displacement; but there was another: while the authorities who actually suppressed the brothels often exploited the language of moral revulsion it was not the sexual vice that worried them so much as the meeting together of those who used the brothels. George Whetstone was only warning the authorities of what they already feared when he told them to beware of "haunts . . . in Allies, gardens and other obscure corners out of the common walks of the Magistrate" whose guests are "masterless men, needy shifters, thieves, cutpurses, unthrifty servants, both serving men and prentices."[10] Suppression was an attempt to regulate not the vice, nor, apparently, even the spread of venereal disease, but the criminal underworld.[11] Similarly, in *Measure for Measure,* the more we attend to the supposed subversiveness of sexual licence, and the authoritarian response to it, the more we are led away from the vice itself towards social tensions which intersect with it—led also to retrace several distinct but related processes of displacement.

The play addresses several social problems which had their counterparts in Jacobean London. Mistress Overdone declares: 'Thus, what with the war, what with the sweat, what with the gallows, and what with poverty, I am custom shrunk' (I.ii.75–7). Lever points out that this passage links several issues in the winter of 1603–4: "the continuance of the war with Spain; the plague in London; the treason trials and executions at Winchester in connection with the plots of Raleigh and others; the slackness of trade in the deserted capital" (p. xxxii). Significantly, all but the first of these, the war, are domestic problems. But even the war was in prospect of becoming such: if peace negotiations then under way (and also alluded to in the play—at I.ii.1–17) proved successful it would lead to a return home of "the multitude of pretended gallants, banck-routs, and unruly youths who weare at this time settled in pyracie" (Lever, p. xxxii). In this political climate even peace could exacerbate domestic ills.

This play's plague references are especially revealing. Both here and at I.ii.85–9, where Pompey refers to a proclamation that "All houses in the suburbs of Vienna must be plucked down" there is a probable allusion to the proclamation of 1603 which provided for the demolition of property in the London suburbs in order to control the plague. But the same proclamation also refers to the "excessive numbers of idle, indigent, dissolute and dangerous persons, and the pestering of many of them in small and strait room."[12] Here, as with the suppression of prostitution, plague control legitimates other kinds of political control. (Enemies of the theatre often used the plague threat as a reason to have them closed.) As this proclamation indicates, there was a constant fear among those in charge of Elizabethan and Jacobean England that disaffection might escalate into organised resistance. This anxiety surfaces repeatedly in official discourse: any circumstance, institution or occasion which might unite the vagabonds and masterless men—for example famine, the theatres, congregations of the unemployed—was the object of almost paranoid surveillance. Yet, if anything, *Measure for Measure* emphasises the lack of any coherent opposition among the subordinate and the marginalised. Thus Pompey, "Servant to Mistress Overdone" (list of characters), once imprisoned and with the promise of remission, becomes, with no sense of betrayal, servant to the State in no less a capacity than that of hangman.

Yet those in power are sincerely convinced there is a threat to order. At the very outset of the play Escalus, described in the list of characters as an "ancient" Lord, is praised excessively by the Duke only to be subordinated to Angelo, the new man. The traditional political "art and practice" (I.i.12) of Escalus is not able to cope with the crisis. Later, the Duke, speaking to the Friar, acknowledges that this crisis stems from a failure on the part of the rulers yet at the same time displaces responsibility on to the ruled: like disobedient children they have taken advantage of their "fond fathers" (I.iii.23). Hence the need for a counter-subversive attack on the "liberty" of the low-life. Yet even as we witness that attack we see also that the possibilities for actual subversion seem to come from quite another quarter. Thus when Angelo resorts to the claim that the State is being subverted (in order to discredit charges of corruption against himself) the way he renders that claim plausible is most revealing:

> These poor informal women are no more
> But instruments of some more mightier member
> That sets them on. Let me have way, my lord,
> To find this practice out.
>
> (V.i.235–7)

Earlier the Duke, pretending ignorance of Angelo's guilt, publicly denounces Isabella's charge against Angelo in similar terms:

> thou knowest not what thou speak'st
> Or else thou art suborn'd against his honour
> In hateful practice . . .
> . . . Someone hath set you on.
>
> (V.i.108–10; 115)

The predisposition of Escalus to credit all this gives us an insight into how the scapegoat mentality works: just as the low-life have hitherto been demonised as the destructive element at the heart (or rather bottom) of the State, now it is the apparently alien Friar (he who is "Not of this country," III.ii.211) who is to blame. The kind old Escalus charges the Friar (the Duke in disguise) with "Slander to th'state!" and cannot wait to torture him into confession (V.i.320, 309–10). That he is in fact accusing the Duke ironically underpins the point at issue: disorder generated by misrule and unjust law (III.ii.6–8) is ideologically displaced on to the ruled—"ideologically" because Angelo's lying displacement is insignificant compared with the way that Escalus really believes it is the subordinate and the outsider who are to blame. Yet even as he believes this he is prepared to torture his way to "the more mightier member" behind the plot; again there is the implication, and certainly the fear, that the origin of the problem is not intrinsic to the low-life but a hostile fraction of the ruling order.

Oddly the slander for which Escalus wants to have this outsider tortured, and behind which he perceives an insurrectionary plot, is only the same assessment of the situation which he, Angelo and the Duke made together at the outset. What does this suggest: is his violent reaction to slander paranoid, or rather a strategy of *realpolitik?* Perhaps the latter—after all, it is not only, as Isabella reminds Angelo (II.ii.135–7) that rulers have the power to efface their own corruption, but that they need to do this to remain in power. And within the terms of *realpolitik* the threat of exposure is justification enough for authoritarian reaction. But the problem with the concept of *realpolitik* is that it tends to discount the non-rational though still effective dimensions of power which make it difficult to determine whether crisis is due to paranoia generating an imaginary threat or whether a real threat is intensifying paranoia. And, of course, even if the threat is imaginary this can still act as the "real" cause of ensuing conflict. Conversely, terms like paranoia applied to a ruling class or fraction, while useful in suggesting the extent to which that class's discourse produces its own truth and apprehends that truth through blame, can also mislead with regard to the class's power to rationalise its own position and displace responsibility for disorder. Put another way, *realpolitik* and paranoia, in so far as they are present, should be seen to coexist more at a social rather than an individual level. An interesting case in point is George Whetstone's *A Mirror for Magistrates* (1584), a possible source for Shakespeare's play. This work related the story of how the Roman emperor, Alexander Severus, re-establishes order in the State by setting up a system of sophisticated surveillance and social regulation which includes himself going disguised among his subjects and observing their transgressions at first hand. These are denounced with moral fervour and the implication of course is that they are condemned just because they are sinful. But as Whetstone's retelling of the story develops we can see a pragmatic underside to his blameful discourse. In fact, as so often in this period, political strategy and moral imperative openly coexist. The focus of Whetstone's reforming zeal are the "Dicing-houses, taverns and common stews"—"sanctuaries of iniquity." But what gives him most cause for concern is not the behaviour of the low but that of the landed gentry who are attracted to them: "Dice, Drunkenness and Harlots, had consumed the wealth of a great number of ancient Gentlemen, whose Purses were in the possession of vile persons, and their Lands at mortgage with the Merchants . . . The Gentlemen had made this exchange with vile persons: they were attired with the Gentlemen's bravery, and the Gentlemen disgraced with their beastly manners" (Izard, *George Whetstone,* p. 135).

Here, apparently, hierarchy is subverted from above and those most culpable the gentlemen themselves. Yet in Whetstone's account the low are to blame; they are held responsible for the laxity of the high, much as a man might (then as now) blame a woman for tempting him sexually whereas in fact he has coerced her. The gentlemen are "mildly" reproached and restored to that which they have transacted away while the low are disciplined. Whetstone believed that the survival of England depended on its landed gentry; in rescuing them from the low-life he is rescuing the State from chaos and restoring it to its "ancient and most laudable orders" (Izard, *George Whetstone,* p. 136). A reactionary programme is accomplished at the expense of the low, while those who benefit are those responsible for precipitating "decline" in the first place. The same process of displacement occurs throughout discourses of power in this period. One further example: one of the many royal proclamations attempting to bring vagabonds under martial law asserts that "there can grow no account of disturbance of our peace and quiet but from such refuse and vagabond people" (*Tudor Royal Proclamations,* III, 233)—and this despite the fact that the proclamation immediately preceeding this one (just six days before) announced the abortive Essex rebellion. The failure of the rebellion is interpreted by the second proclamation as proof of the loyalty of all other subjects with the exception of that "great multitude of base and loose people" who "lie privily in corners and bad houses, listening after news and stirs, and spreading rumours and tales, being of likelihood ready to lay hold of any occasion to enter into any tumult or disorder" (p. 232). For the authoritarian perspective as articulated here, the unregulated are by definition the ungoverned and always thereby potentially subversive of government. At the same time it is a perspective which confirms what has been inferred from *Measure for Measure:* in so far as the socially deprived were a threat to government this was only when they were mobilised by powerful elements much higher up the social scale. Moreover the low who were likely to be so mobilised were only a small part of the "base and loose people" hounded by authority. In fact we need to distinguish, as Christopher Hill does, between this mob element, little influenced by religious or political ideology but up for hire, and the "rogues, vagabonds and beggars" who, although they "caused considerable panic in ruling circles . . . were incapable of concerted revolt" (*The World Turned Upside Down,* pp. 40–1). Of course there were real social problems and "naturally" the deprived were at the centre of them. Moreover, if we recall that there *were* riots, that fornication *did* produce charity dependent bastards, that drunkenness *did* lead to fecklessness, it becomes apparent that, in their own terms there were also real grounds for anxiety on the part of those who administered deprivation. At the same time we can read in that anxiety—in its very surplus, its imaginative intensity, its punitive ingenuity—an ideological displacement (and hence misrecognition) of much deeper fears of the uncontrollable, of being out of control, themselves corresponding to more fundamental social problems.[13]

SURVEILLANCE

In II.i. we glimpse briefly the State's difficulties in ensuring the levels of policing which the rulers think is required. Escalus discreetly inquires of Elbow whether there are any more officers in his locality more competent than he. Elbow replies that even those others who have been chosen happily delegate their responsibility to him.

A similar anxiety about the ungovernability of his subjects leads the Duke to put those of them he encounters under a much more sophisticated and effective mode of surveillance; though remaining coercive, it seeks additionally to get subjects to reposition themselves. First though, a word about the Duke's use of disguise. The genre of the disguised ruler generally presented him in a favourable light. But in Jacobean England we might expect there to have been an ambivalent attitude towards it. In Jonson's *Sejanus,* contemporary with *Measure for Measure,* it is a strategy of tyrannical repression; Jonson himself was subjected to it while in jail, apparently with the intention of getting him to incriminate himself.[14] Next there is the question of the Duke's choice of *religious* disguise. As I've argued elsewhere, there was considerable debate at this time over the "Machiavellian" proposition that religion was a form of ideological control which worked in terms of internalised submission.[15] Even as he opposes it, Richard Hooker cogently summarises this view; it represents religion as "a mere politic devise" and whereas State law has "power over our outward actions only," religion works upon men's "inward cogitations . . . the privy intents and motions of their heart." Armed with this knowledge "politic devisers" are "able to create God in man by art."[16]

The Duke, disguised as a friar, tries to reinstate this kind of subjection. Barnardine is the least amenable; "He wants advice," remarks the Duke grimly (IV.ii.144) and is infuriated when the offer is refused. Barnardine is especially recalcitrant in that he admits guilt yet is unrepentant and even disinclined to escape; he thus offers no response on which the Duke might work to return him to a position of dutiful submission. But the Duke does not give up and resolves to "Persuade this rude wretch willingly to die" (IV.iii.80; cf. II.i.35). A similar idea seems to be behind his determination to send Pompey to prison—not just to rot but for "Correction and instruction" (III.ii.31). Earlier the Duke had been rather more successful with Claudio. His long "Be absolute for death" speech (III.i.5ff) does initially return Claudio to a state of spiritual renunciation, but Claudio has not long been in conversation with

Isabella before he desires to live again. Isabella, herself positioned in a state of intended renunciation, struggles to restore Claudio to his. She fails but the Duke intervenes again and Claudio capitulates.

The Duke makes of Mariana a model of dutiful subjection. Predictably, he is most successful with those who are least powerful and so most socially dependent. He tells Angelo to love Mariana, adding: "I have confess'd her, and I know her virtue" (V.i.524). He has indeed, and earlier Mariana confirms his success in this confessional positioning of her as an acquiescent even abject subject (IV.i.8–20); for her he is one "whose advice / Hath often still'd my brawling discontent" (IV.i.8–9). His exploitation of her—"The maid will I frame, and make fit for his attempt" (III.i.256–7)—is of course just what she as confessed subject must not know, and the Duke confirms that she does not by eliciting from her a testimony:

DUKE: Do you persuade yourself that I respect you?
MARIANA: Good friar, I know you do, and so have found it.
(IV.i.53–4)

Thus is her exploitation recast and indeed experienced by Mariana, as voluntary allegiance to disinterested virtue.

The Duke's strategy with Isabella is somewhat different. Some critics of the play, liking their women chaste, have praised Isabella for her integrity; others have reproached her for being too absolute for virtue.[17] Another assessment, ostensibly more sympathetic than either of these because psychological rather than overtly moralistic, is summarised by Lever. He finds Isabella ignorant, hysterical and suffering from "psychic confusion," and he apparently approves the fact that "through four . . . acts" she undergoes "a process of moral education designed to reshape her character" (pp. lxxx, lxxvii, lxxix, xci). Here, under the guise of normative categories of psychosexual development, whose objective is 'maturity,' moralistic and patriarchal values are reinstated the more insidiously for being ostensibly "caring" rather than openly coercive. But in the play the coercive thrust of such values suggests that perhaps Isabella has recourse to renunciation as a way of escaping them. When we first encounter her in the nunnery it is her impending separation from men that is stressed by the nun, Francisca. The same priority is registered by Isabella herself when she affirms the prayers from "preserved souls, / From fasting maids, whose minds are dedicate / To nothing temporal' (II.ii.154–6). She seeks in fact to be preserved specifically from men:

Women?—Help, heaven! Men their creation mar
In profiting by them. Nay, call us ten times frail;
For we are soft as our complexions are,
And credulous to false prints.
(II.iv.126–9)

If we remember that in the play the stamp metaphor signifies the formative and coercive power of authority, we see that Isabella speaks a vulnerability freed in part from its own ideological misrecognition; she conceives her weakness half in terms of women's supposed intrinsic "frailness," half in terms of exploitative male coercion. Further, we see in Isabella's subjection a conflict within the patriarchal order which subjects: the renunciation which the Church sanctions, secular authority refuses. The latter wins and it is Isabella's fate to be coerced back into her socially and sexually subordinate position—at first illicitly by Angelo, then legitimately by the Duke who "takes" her in marriage.

His subjects' public recognition of his own integrity is important in the Duke's attempt to reposition them in obedience. Yet the play can be read to disclose integrity as a strategy of authority rather than the disinterested virtue of the leader. The Duke speaks frequently of the integrity of rulers but the very circumstances in which he does so disclose a pragmatic and ideological intent; public integrity legitimates authority, and authority takes sufficient priority to lie about integrity when the ends of propaganda and government require it (IV.ii.77–83). And the Duke knows that these same ends require that integrity should be publicly displayed in the form of reputation. Intriguingly then, perhaps the most subversive thing in the play is the most casual, namely Lucio's slurring of the Duke's reputation. Unawares and carelessly, Lucio strikes at the heart of the ideological legitimation of power. Along with Barnardine's equally careless refusal of subjection, this is what angers the Duke the most. Still disguised, he insists to Lucio that he, the Duke, "*be but testimonied in his own bringings-forth,* and he shall appear to the envious a scholar, a statesman, and a soldier" (III.ii.140–2, italics added). After Lucio has departed, he laments his inability to ensure his subject's dutiful respect: "What king so strong / Can tie the gall up in the slanderous tongue?" (II. 181–2; cf. IV.i.60–5). If the severity of the law at this time is anything to go by, such slander was a cause of obsessive concern to Elizabethan and Jacobean rulers,[18] just as it is here with the Duke and, as we have already seen, with Escalus.

The ideological representation of integrity can perhaps be judged best at the play's close—itself ideological but not, it seems to me, forced or flawed in the way critics have often claimed. By means of the Duke's personal intervention and integrity, authoritarian reaction is put into abeyance but not discredited: the corrupt deputy is unmasked but no law is repealed and the mercy exercised remains the prerogative of the same ruler who initiated reaction. The Duke also embodies a public reconciliation of law and morality. An omniscience, inseparable from seeming integrity, permits him to close the gulf between the two, one which was opening wide enough to demystify the one (law) and enfeeble the other (morality). Again, this is not a cancelling of authoritarianism so much as a fantasy resolution of the very fears from which authoritarianism partly grows—a fear of escalating disorder among the ruled which in turn intensifies a fear of impotence in the rulers. If so it is a reactionary fantasy, neither radical nor liberating (as fantasy may indeed be) but rather conservative and constraining; the very disclosure of social realities which make progress seem imperative is recuperated in comedic closure, a redemptive wish-fulfilment of the status quo.

In conclusion then the transgressors in *Measure for Measure* signify neither the unregeneracy of the flesh, nor the ludic subversive carnivalesque. Rather, as the spectre of unregulated desire, they are exploited to legitimate an exercise in authoritarian repression. And of course it is a spectre: desire, culturally manifested, is never unregulated, perhaps least of all in Jacobean London. Apart from their own brutally exploitative sub-cultural codes, the stews were controlled from above. This took several forms, including one of the most subtly coercive of all: economic investment. Some time between 1599 and 1602 the Queen's Lord Chamberlain, Lord Hunsdon, appears to have leased property for the establishing of an especially notorious brothel in Paris Gardens, while Thomas Nashe declared in 1598 that "whoredom (the next doore to the Magistrates)" was set up and maintained through bribery, and Gāmini Salgādo informs us that "Most theatre owners . . . were brothel owners too."[19]

At the same time in this period, in its laws, statutes, proclamations and moralistic tracts, the marginalised and the deviant are, as it were, endlessly recast in a complex ideological process whereby authority is ever anxiously relegitimating itself. *Measure for Measure,* unlike the proclamation or the statute, gives the marginalised a voice, one which may confront authority directly but which more often speaks of and partially reveals the strategies of power which summon it into visibility. Even the mildly transgressive Claudio who, were it not for the law, was all set to become law-abiding, becomes briefly that "warped slip of wilderness" (III.i.141). But if Claudio's desire to live is momentarily transgressive it becomes so only at the potential expense of his sister. The same is true of Pompey and Lucio who, once put under surveillance or interrogation by authority voice a critique of authority itself (III.ii.6–8; 89–175), yet remain willing to exploit others in their position by serving that same authority when the opportunity arises. Ironically though, it is Angelo's transgressive desire which is potentially the most subversive; he more than anyone else threatens to discredit authority. At the same time his transgression is also, potentially, the most brutally exploitative. This is an example of something which those who celebrate transgression often overlook: even as it offers a challenge to authority, transgression ever runs the risk of re-enacting elsewhere the very exploitation which it is resisting immediately.

What Foucault has said of sexuality in the nineteenth and twentieth centuries seems appropriate also to sexuality as a subcategory of sin in earlier periods: it *appears* to be that which power is afraid of but in actuality is that which power works through. Sin, especially when internalised as guilt, has produced the subjects of authority as surely as any ideology. At the same time it may be that not everyone, indeed not even the majority, has fallen for this. The "sin" of promiscuity, for example, has always been defended from a naturalistic perspective as no sin at all—as indeed we find in *Measure for Measure.* But those like Lucio who cheerfully celebrate instinctual desire simultaneously reify as natural the (in fact) highly *social* relations of exploitation through which instinct finds its expression, social relations which, we might say, determine the nature of instinct far more than nature itself:

LUCIO. How doth my dear morsel, thy mistress? Procures she still, ha?
PROMPEY. Troth sir, she hath eaten up all her beef, and she is herself in the tub.
LUCIO. Why, 'tis good: it is the right of it: it must be so. Ever your fresh whore, and your powdered bawd; an unshunned consequence; it must be so.

(III.ii.52–8)

And Pompey, whom he refuses to bail, Lucio perceives as "bawd born" (III.ii.66). Mistress Overdone, her plight as described here notwithstanding, was one of the lucky ones; after all, the life of most prostitutes outside the exclusive brothels was abject. Overdone is at least a procuress, a brothel keeper. For most of the rest poverty drove them to the brothels and after a relatively short stay in which they had to run the hazards of disease, violence and contempt, most were driven back to it.

In pursuing the authority–subversion question, this chapter has tried to exemplify two complementary modes of materialist criticism. Both are concerned to recover the text's history. The one looks directly for history in the text including the historical conditions of its production which, even if not addressed directly by the text can nevertheless still be said to be within it, informing it. Yet there is a limit to which the text can be said to incorporate those aspects of its historical moment of which it never speaks. At that limit, rather than constructing this history as the text's unconscious, we might instead address it directly. Then at any rate we have to recognise the obvious: the prostitutes, the most exploited group in the society which the play represents, are absent from it. Virtually everything that happens presupposes them yet they have no voice, no presence. And those who speak for them do so as exploitatively as those who want to eliminate them. Looking for evidence of resistance we find rather further evidence of exploitation. There comes a time of course when the demonising of deviant sexuality meets with cultural and political resistance. From the very terms of its oppression deviancy generates a challenging counter-discourse and eventually a far-reaching critique of exploitation. That is another and later story.

Notes

1. *Measure for Measure,* ed. J. W. Lever (London: Methuen, 1965).

2. For another kind of critic sexuality in *Measure for Measure* continues to be seen as something deeply disruptive though now it is the individual psyche rather than the social order which is under threat. Thus for Marilyn French this is a play which "confronts directly Shakespeare's own most elemental fears"—hence its "sexual obsessiveness, mixed guilt, abhorrence." She writes further of "the hideous and repellent quality sex has throughout the play. It is, it remains, evil, filthy, disgusting, diseased" (*Shakespeare's Division of Experience* [London: Jonathan Cape, 1982], pp. 195–7).

3. See also Paul Brown's analysis along these lines in " 'This thing of darkness I acknowledge mine': *The Tempest* and the discourse of colonialism," in *Political Shakespeare: New Essays in Cultural Materialism,* ed. Jonathan Dollimore and Alan Sinfield (Manchester: Manchester University Press, 1985), 48–71.

4. Alan Bray, *Homosexuality in Renaissance England* (London: Gay Men's Press, 1982); Stuart Clark, "Inversion, Misrule and the Meaning of Witchcraft," *Past and Present,* 87 (1980), 98–127; Christopher Hill, *The World Turned Upside Down: Radical Ideas During the English Revolution* (Harmondsworth: Penguin, 1975).

5. For the Baines document see C. F. Tucker Brooke, *The Life of Marlowe and the Tragedy of Dido Queen of Carthage* (London: Methuen, 1930), pp. 98–100.

6. Peter Tatchell, *The Battle for Bermondsey,* preface by Tony Benn (London: Heretic Books, 1983).

7. For Stone's summary of this, see *The Family, Sex and Marriage in England 1500–1800* (London: Weidenfield and Nicolson, 1977), 653–54.

8. Lawrence Stone, *The Family Sex and Marriage in England 1500–1800* (London: Weidenfeld and Nicolson, 1977), pp. 653, 217, 654, 623–4; and F. G. Emmison has estimated that in the county of Essex around 15,000 people were summoned on sexual charges in the forty-five years up to 1603 (*Elizabethan Life: Morals and the Church Courts* [Chelmsford: Essex County Council, 1973], p. 1). Commenting on these figures Stone remarks that "in an adult lifespan of 30 years, an Elizabethan inhabitant of Essex . . . had more than a one-in-four chance of being accused of fornication, adultery, buggery, incest, bestiality or bigamy" (*The Family,* p. 519).

9. J. A. Sharpe, *Crime in Seventeenth-Century England: a County Study* (Cambridge University Press, 1983), pp. 57, 70, 215–16.

10. *A Mirror for Magistrates* quoted from Thomas C. Izard's helpful study, *George Whetstone: Mid-Elizabethan Gentleman of Letters* (New York: Columbia University Press, 1942; reprinted New York: AMS Press, 1966), p. 140.

11. See the Proclamation of 1546 ordering London brothels to be closed, in *Tudor Royal Proclamations* (3 vols.), ed. Paul L. Hughes and James L. Larkin (New Haven: Yale University Press, 1964–9), I, 365–6; also Wallace Shugg, "Prostitution in Shakespeare's London," *Shakespeare Studies* 10 (1977), 291–313, especially p. 306.

12. *Stuart Royal Proclamations* (vol. I), ed. James F. Larkin and Paul L. Hughes (Oxford: Clarendon, 1973), p. 47.

13. See especially Leonard Tennenhouse, "Representing Power: *Measure for Measure* in its Time," in *The Power of Forms in the English Renaissance,* ed. Stephen Greenblatt (Norman: Pilgrim Books, 1982), pp. 139–56; David Sundelson, "Misogyny and Rule in *Measure for Measure,*" *Women's Studies,* vol. 9, no. 1 (1981), 83–91.

14. Ben Jonson, *Works,* ed. C. H. Herford and P. Simpson, 11 vols. (Oxford: Clarendon, 1922–52), I, 19, 139.

15. Jonathan Dollimore, *Radical Tragedy: Religion Ideology and Power in the Drama of Shakespeare and His Contemporaries* (Brighton: Harvester, 1984; University of Chicago Press, 1984), pp. 9–17.

16. Richard Hooker, *Of the Laws of Ecclesiastical Polity,* 2 vols., introduction by C. Morris (London: Dent, 1969), II, 19.

17. In the nineteenth century for example A. W. Schlegel praised "the heavenly purity of her mind . . . not even stained with one unholy thought" and Edward Dowden her "pure zeal" and "virgin sanctity." By contrast, Coleridge found her "unamiable" and Hazlitt reproved her "rigid chastity." These other passages from earlier critics are conveniently collected in C. K. Stead, ed., *Shakespeare: Measure for Measure, a Casebook* (London: Macmillan, 1971); see especially pp. 43–5, 59–62, 45–7, 47–9.

18. See especially Joel Samaha, "Gleanings from Local Criminal Court Records: Sedition among the inarticulate in Elizabethan Essex," *Journal of Social History,* 8 (1975), 61–79.

19. E. J. Burford, *Queen of the Bawds* (London: Neville Spearman, 1974); Thomas Nashe, *The Unfortunate Traveller and Other Works,* ed. J. B. Steane (Harmondsworth: Penguin, 1972), p. 483; Gāmini Salgādo, *The Elizabethan Underworld* (London: Dent, 1977), p. 58.

London

LEAH MARCUS

To treat of the great and notable franchises, liberties, and customs of the City of London, would require a whole volume of itself.

Edward Coke's *Fourth Institute*

Modern editions of Shakespeare obligingly provide readers with labels at the head of each play specifying the locus of the action. The First Folio was less solicitous. What sense of place it does offer generally comes via internal stage directions or dialogue, or through the play's title—*The Merchant of Venice, The Merry Wives of Windsor, Timon of Athens, The Two Gentlemen of Verona.* We may be tempted to include the folio's reticence about place among the devices by which it sloughs off particularizing details—details which might subvert its claim to universality by anchoring a given play too obviously in a specific milieu. Unlike the First Folio, Ben Jonson's folio *Workes* gives the place of the action for all but one of his plays in large block capitals preceding the text. But Jonson's meticulous labeling can scarcely be said to have established an ironclad precedent. The word *localization* dates, we will recall, only from the nineteenth century. We cannot assume that a Renaissance audience of readers or viewers would have felt the same disorientation we are likely to feel, conditioned as we are by more recent classificatory procedures and their reflection in editorial practice, over a failure to specify place.

In Shakespeare, place is often left mysterious, or at least undefined, until well into the play. If we are reading a text like *Twelfth Night, or What You Will* in the 1623 folio version, we can locate the action immediately because the first speaker is announced by title in the initial stage direction: "Enter Orsino Duke of Illyria" (TLN 2). But if we miss that written cue, it is not until scene 2 —after we have been introduced to the lovesick duke and his court, then to a completely different set of characters—that Illyria is designated as the locus of the action. In performance, before that point, a theatrical audience not provided with the modern amenity of a printed program might well have been in fecund limbo—not knowing where the stage events were taking

Reprinted from Leah Marcus, *Puzzling Shakespeare: Local Reading and Its Discontents* (University of California Press, 1988), by permission of the Regents of the University of California.

place or whether that information was important. Would such an audience have listened in wary uncertainty to hear the place named, asking, along with Viola in scene 2, "What Country (Friends) is this?" Or would the naming of the locale have been a matter of indifference?

In either case, Illyria was scarcely familiar territory, more significant, perhaps, for its evocation of like-sounding exotica—Elysium, delirium—than for concrete geopolitical associations. But place in other plays can operate in more topographically specific ways. Our project for localization in the larger sense of the term needs to take into account the matter of internal "localization"—the degree to which and the means by which a given play sets itself apart from its contemporary London audience through an evocation of place which is clearly alien, somewhere else, with its own idiosyncratic geographic and cultural features. Given the Renaissance penchant for topical speculation, no locus could be said to be inviolate; no amount of topographical distancing could insulate a play entirely from the contemporary rage for finding homologies with events and people about London. But the kinds of topical speculation which a given play was able to provoke could be strongly influenced by its particular locus of action. Place in Shakespeare is more highly charged, more elusive, sometimes more downright deceptive than the reassuring advance labels provided by modern editors allow us to perceive.

There are two plays in the First Folio for which extratextual place names *are* provided—not helpfully at the top of a text as they are in Jonson's *Workes* and would be in a modern edition, but at the end of the text, just before "The names of all the Actors." The fact that the folio does not usually offer such information makes more curious and provocative the two cases in which it does: for *The Tempest,* "The Scene, an vn-inhabited Island"; and for *Measure for Measure,* "The Scene Vienna." This uncharacteristic specificity has been accounted for as the idiosyncrasy of the copyist Ralph Crane, who seems to have liked to add such information when it had not already been supplied.[1] But that explanation leaves interesting questions unasked. What effect might the anomalous specificity as to place have had on folio readers of these particular plays? "An vn-inhabited Island" is a rather odd description given that Prospero's domain is never quite unpopulated, at least in the audience's experience of it. But the label which will concern us here is the one affixed to *Measure for Measure:* "The Scene Vienna." An unidentified island is potentially neutral territory; Vienna, most emphatically, was not. It was one of the capitals of the Holy Roman Empire, much in the news in the year 1604 as the traditional seat of the Hapsburg dynasty, the administrative hub of a vast and shifting Catholic alliance with which the English had been on hostile terms for decades.

There is, to be sure, little specific evocation of Vienna as a city in *Measure for Measure,* only a handful of references to people and places surrounding it—to the Hapsburg "Dukes," to Bohemia, and to "the King of Hungaries" peace (TLN 100–101). But those are precisely the local references that contemporary Londoners, unacquainted with Viennese topography but avid for the latest news about the fate of continental Protestantism, would have been most likely to pick up. In near-contemporary plays like Shakespeare's *King John* or Anthony Munday's *Downfall* and *Death of Robert, Earl of Huntington* "Vienna" and "Austria" are clearly enemy territory. (And in *Hamlet* the "Murder of Gonzago" takes place in Vienna.) How are we to interpret the folio's uncharacteristic insistence upon place in the case of *Measure for Measure?* And why is "The Scene Vienna"? That is only one of several interesting irregularities in the folio presentation of the playtext that we will want to consider.

The easiest answer to the question Why Vienna? has been to take the name as nothing but smokescreen. Vienna is not actually Vienna; it is London, or at least a place which can easily be taken for London. As numerous historical treatments of the play have pointed out, there are extremely close connections between the Vienna of Duke Vincentio and the London of James I. Mistress Overdone complains about conditions in Vienna, "Thus, what with the war, what with the sweat, what with the gallowes, and what with pouerty, I am Custom-shrunke" (TLN 172–74). All of these local misfortunes can be correlated with matters of public concern in the disease-ridden London of 1604: "The continuance of the war with Spain; the plague in London; the treason trials and executions at Winchester in connection with the plots of Raleigh and others; the slackness of trade in the deserted capital."[2] There are other resemblances as well. In London of 1604, as in Vienna, the "howses in the Suburbs" had been ordered to be "pluck'd downe" by a 1603 proclamation. In London, as in Shakespeare's Vienna, there had been a recent heating-up of efforts to stamp out prostitution. According to one contemporary, "the Lord Cheife Justice . . . hath plaide rex of late among whoores and bawdes and persecutes poore pretty wenches out of all pittie and mercy." Notorious brothel owners and employees from the suburbs were ostentatiously carted and whipped about London, then thrown into Newgate Prison, where they could form a reconstituted "house" like the one Pompey discovers in the Viennese jail, teeming with all his old customers.[3] London, unlike Shakespeare's Vienna, did not punish sexual incontinence with death, but there were numerous "precise" and vocal Londoners who argued, like Angelo, that it should. They made their case for more rigorous laws on the basis of Mosaic precept (in Old Testament law, the penalty for fornication *was* death) and the example of "reformed" cities on the Continent.[4] In London, finally, as in Vienna, there was an overriding "imperial" presence—that of King James I—whose coronation pageant earlier in that same year (1604) had been orchestrated as a Roman triumph over the city very much in the manner of the Holy Roman Empire, of the public pageantry of a Maximilian I or a Charles V.[5] Like Shakespeare's duke of Vienna and like the actual Holy Roman emperors, whose mythos of power James I adopted for himself, the English king frequently provoked, but also tested and challenged, sudden eruptions of local judicial severity within the "empire" of Great Britain.

The only early version of *Measure for Measure* we have is the text of 1623—nearly two decades after the period of its composition and performance. According to the Revels accounts, a play called "Mesur for Mesur" by "Shaxberd" was acted in the Banqueting Hall at Whitehall on St. Stephen's Night, 1604.[6] This may have been the play's inaugural performance and King James was almost certainly present. Again, as in *Cymbeline,* we are confronted with a text which can easily be understood as setting forth a "Jacobean line"—mirroring the king and his most cherished principles by displaying his ideas about equitable government (familiar to contemporaries through the just published *Basilikon Doron,* which was selling like hotcakes in London, and through other royal pronouncements) in triumph over harsher, more limited codes. According to what Richard Levin has derisively termed the "King James Version" of *Measure for Measure,* Shakespeare's intent in writing the play was to appeal to a courtly audience and curry favor with James I in the halcyon aftermath of the new monarch's accession. The purest and least equivocal form of the "authorized" *Measure for Measure* takes the play's local meaning for King James I as the whole meaning of the play.[7] Discordant elements are automatically excluded from the field of interpretation on grounds that King James would not have allowed them, nor would Shakespeare himself have been so foolhardy as to perpetrate them. Small wonder, perhaps, that the King James Version of *Measure for Measure* so often gets dismissed as impossibly reductive.

But there is a deeper intolerance lurking beneath the charge of reductiveness—the old bugaboo of a Shakespeare tainted with ideology. We can accept Levin's rejection of the King James Version as the only "true" meaning of the play without following him in his efforts to cleanse it (and the name of Shakespeare more generally) from all taint of topical meaning. Like *Cymbeline, Measure for Measure* promulgates a Jacobean line, but is "double written" in a way that allows for other meanings, opens the play out to a range of audience reaction and potential signification. Except that in *Measure for Measure,* the devices which undermine the official line are far more flamboyant and ingeniously disruptive than the equivalent devices in *Cymbeline.* In *Measure for Measure,* there are many parallels between the play's locale and London, between its duke and James I. But there is also the problem of Vienna. If the play was designed to compliment King James I, it seems rather odd that it is set in a place associated for most of its 1604 viewers with fears of Catholic invasion and repression, with the dread specter of Hapsburg rule, a return to the Inquisition and to the bloody persecutions of Philip and Mary.

In local reading of *Measure for Measure,* nearly everything depends upon place. If Vienna is taken to be London, then the play goes a fair distance toward the Jacobean line, displaying a ruler who succeeds in establishing equity and a semblance of social order when his deputy has spectacularly failed. But if Vienna is Vienna, or (worse yet) a London *become* Vienna, then the play's topical resonances turn completely inside out: all of the gestures which seem to praise James in his triumphant mastery over London can become elements in a dark fantasy of alien Catholic domination. The play is like a Möbius strip—a single twist of the fabric in the process of construction, and every surface, every seemingly level plane, is at the same time its own volte-face.

Within the Wall

Let us start with the topicality closest to home—the striking likenesses between Shakespeare's Vienna and Shakespearean London. My heading is not meant to suggest that the burgeoning City of London in 1604, or the wide-ranging issues of concern to it, could be contained within its ancient walls. The city had experienced phenomenal growth in population, trade, and commerce during Elizabethan times, and it was to experience far more. In the half century after 1600 it was to double in size; by 1666, in John Dryden's *Annus Mirabilis,* it was, for the first time in English, called a "metropolis"—no longer to be mistaken for the large town it had been in the late medieval period.[8] London in 1604 was bursting out of its traditional topographical limits. There were city wards outside the old walls and the authority of the London Corporation spilled out in various ways into the populous suburbs beyond. The city, for example, had the right to appoint justices of the peace for surrounding areas like Middlesex.[9] Londoners tended to view the areas outside their jurisdiction as hotbeds of vice and disorder. To some extent, that perception was grounded in actual conditions: the suburbs were expanding faster than the City of London itself, and so were suburban problems. But to some extent, Londoners' perception of the lawlessness all around them registered an inability to conceptualize the changing character of the place they considered home. Seemingly chaotic alterations which could not be comprehended in terms of the London they were accustomed to got projected onto the areas outside it, areas which were more obviously outside their control and therefore more available in psychological terms as repositories for that which was new and alien, incapable of immediate assimilation.

Even within the walls, London was scarcely monolithic, more a patchwork of local differences than a single, uniform political and geographical entity. Within its boundaries there were areas outside the jurisdiction of the Lord Mayor and aldermen—pockets of special privilege like Blackfriars, Whitefriars, the Savoy, and the Liberty of the Minories which enjoyed their own "freedoms" apart from the customs and liberties of London. These areas were a constant thorn in the side of city government because they could serve as havens for all sorts of "lawless" activities—as sanctuaries for those seeking to escape military conscription, for example, or for Nonconformist preachers and congregations who sought to evade some of the prescribed ceremonial practices of the Anglican church, or for the companies of players who perpetrated that particularly "notorious abuse," the London theater.[10] But in the areas directly under the control of the London Corporation, there were also frequent conflicts over jurisdiction between the Lord Mayor and aldermen on the one hand and the organs of national government on the other—the Privy Council and the Crown, the church and ecclesiastical courts. London officials stood on their right to assert the customary privileges and jurisdictions which the city had enjoyed "time out of mind" by Magna Carta, a series of royal charters, and customary law; the Crown and church found ways of imposing their own "higher" authority on London by circumventing or running roughshod over the traditional freedoms of the city.

We are all familiar with the battles over the drama in the 1580s and 1590s both within London and in the liberties, a tug of war between the Lord Mayor and Privy Council which sometimes hinged as much on who was to control the theaters as on how that control would be exercised. The year 1599 provides a provocative illustration. For years, city authorities had been sending the Privy Council a stream of complaints against the "disorder" of the theaters without getting much satisfaction. Finally in 1599, *mirabile dictu,* the royal government finally seemed to lend an ear. The Privy Council ordered that the London theaters be shut down. But then, the tables turned, city officials were reluctant to comply and the theaters were not shut down. There may have been numerous factors in this tug of war of which we are now unaware, but one element of the conflict was clearly the issue of whose authority would dominate London.[11] Similar battles took place over the use of the royal "dispensing power" in other fields of activity: the monarch would issue a proclamation or patent that exempted an individual or group from customary city regulations and barred London justices of the peace from enforcing local ordinances against the holder of the privilege, London authorities would then protest that their laws and jurisdiction had been flouted, sometimes there would be an actual physical clash between the agents of the Crown and local justices of the peace, and the jurisdictional conflict would be joined anew. In the long-term dispute over control of the lands surrounding the Crown Liberty of the Tower of London, for example, Tower officials actually removed the boundary stone that marked the limit of city jurisdiction and encouraged their adherents to repeatedly "invade" the territory claimed by the citizens as a way of demonstrating royal jurisdiction. Debtors claiming the "privilege of the Tower" would take refuge within the liberty; when London justices of the peace tried to apprehend them, the justices themselves were arrested and held in the Tower.[12] In many of these disputes, preserving local liberties "within the wall," preserving local autonomy, was as important to London officials as the relief of the particular "abuse."

To say that London valued its areas of autonomy is not to say that the city was by any means autonomous. There were many ways in which it was firmly and even comfortably under royal control. London was the most important source of revenue for the Crown and of financing for the government and aristocracy. It was the Crown's major supplier of goods and services in peacetime, a prime resource for soldiers and matériel in wartime. The nation could not have functioned without a bedrock of cooperation between the city and the Crown. But in terms of its traditional "liberties," London was proudly and sometimes defiantly its own place, jealously guarding its particular customs and freedoms as a bulwark against engulfment in a larger political and cultural entity. As Richard Helgerson has demonstrated, London, like other areas of the realm, was beginning to display a new interest in chorography—in mapping out its particular topographical features in a way that declared an unprecedented involvement with individual "place" and a concomitant concern with individual identity and autonomy.[13]

This emerging pride in local place is evident in John Stow's *Survay of London* (London, 1603), which traverses the whole city, ward by ward and street by street, in order to commemorate its chief worthies and topographical features, the layers of history preserved in its ancient edifices and monuments. The *Survay* is much more than the creation of a collective city heritage, however. At the end of it Stow includes "An Appendix contayning the examination of such causes as haue heretofore moued the Princes, either to fine and ransome the Citizens of London, or to seize the Liberties of the Citty itself." The appendix is a discreet but spirited celebration of London liberties, arguing that London had never really deserved the indignity of royal encroachment, never been seditious on her own, but only when led on by others: she "neuer led the dance, but euer followed the pipe of the Nobilitie" (565–68). Stow's defense of London argues, in effect, that the deprivation of London's traditional freedoms had usually been the result of royal tyranny. It is a most interesting display of civic pride in which the delineation of London boundaries is inextricable from the assertion of local autonomy.

With the coming of the new monarch in 1603, there was a new opportunity for the city to reaffirm its liberties. A petition from the "Mayor, Aldermen, and Commonalty of the City of London" which was probably initiated that year or in early 1604 complained to James I of "certain persons endeavouring to get a grant from His Majesty of privileges always enjoyed by this City both by Charter and usage."[14] It was the first of a number of protests against Jacobean encroachments. James was to be a far worse offender than Elizabeth had been, if only because he lacked her tact and skillful indirection, when it came to the assertion of royal prerogative against the privileges of the city. When he entered London in triumphant domination as the new Augustus in his coronation pageant in 1604, he was engaged in a different kind of mapping from that practiced by Stow. The city and its multiplicity of local "places" gave way to the single presence of the king. He traversed the streets of London not in order to admire them, but to take possession of them, display his dominance over them. The whole pageant was orchestrated as a symbolic conquest—a "pacification" of the city as the *camera regis,* the submissive bride of the monarch, part of the vast, organic body of empire which James wanted to call Great Britain.[15]

Rival images of the city can be identified through different modes of visual presentation. In John Norden's *Specvlvm Britanniae* (1593), London's streets and buildings are framed by the insignia of her illustrious guilds. The honor of the city is proclaimed through reference to its structuring commercial institutions and their members. In the Londinium Arch of James's coronation pageant, by contrast, the city is upheld by the triumphal arch (inscribed with the message of royal dominance) through which the king passed as he entered the city. The city and its institutions are depicted as less than the king, his mere dwelling chamber or *camera regis.* The prospect of such royal domination and the loss of local authority and identity did not necessarily sit well with Londoners. They were already beginning to suspect that James I's dream of empire allowed scant place for the traditional freedoms of the city.

For a contemporary theatrical audience, I would suggest, part of the fascination of *Measure for Measure* was its engagement of a markedly similar conflict in a place called Vienna. Just as the king of England had ceded his right to govern London directly to the Lord Mayor and aldermen, allowing them by royal charter the privilege of choosing their own Lord Mayor, so the duke of Vienna, acknowledging his inability to govern Vienna himself, confers his "absolute power" by special commission on the new deputy Angelo: he has "Lent him our terror, drest him with our loue, / And giuen his Deputation all the Organs / Of our owne powre" (TLN 22–24). The parallel is not precise: in one case the king's surrogate is elected and in the other he is appointed. But the basic mechanism of delegation is the same in both cases, and sets in motion a set of conflicts over who will maintain public order and what form that order will take. The language of prerogative asserts itself: the duke has stamped Angelo with his own great and noble "figure" much as he would coin new money (as only a ruler was empowered to do). What remains to be seen is whether Angelo will prove true "mettle" (TLN 55). In both Shakespeare's London and Shakespeare's "Vienna," the ruler, having delegated his power, proves unwilling to let it remain securely with those to whom he has entrusted it. He hovers upon the scene incognito, covertly and then overtly asserting his own priorities for government over a city which is paradoxically enslaved both by too much "libertie" and by too much trust in the rigidities of law.

Much has been written about law in *Measure for Measure.* But law in the play is not one single thing, an absolute against which various forms of illicit "liberty" and transgression are played off. In terms of the play's meaning for London, we need to distinguish between different kinds of law: between "local" law, which is inscribed in specific places and bound within their limits, and "unlocalized" law, which operates, sometimes with apparent willfulness, across boundaries, outside the limits of place. London and its environs were a crazy quilt of different legal jurisdictions, some inextricable from topography, others more global, independent of topographical boundaries. The former would include city ordinances and customary laws. London's liberties and franchises were jealously guarded by her citizens and, in general, protected by English common law. But there was another system of law interlayered with the "local" law of the city and increasingly in competition with it during the early Jacobean period: that was the amorphous, pervasive, "unlocalized" jurisdiction associated with ecclesiastical law and the canons of the church, with royal prerogative (increasingly questioned by the advocates of common law, but buttressed by the civil law) and with the royal "dispensing power" to exempt individuals from the provisions of statute law. Common law and the liberties it guaranteed were specific to England, embedded in its particular "places" and history; civil and canon law were outgrowths of the Roman law, which was international, operating across boundaries between peoples and places.

The chief area of jurisdictional conflict in the "Vienna" of *Measure for Measure* is the matter of sexual incontinence—how it is to be defined and how it should be punished. The same matter was also a well-known battle ground between competing legal systems in the London of 1604. Twentieth-century interpreters have taken pains to establish whether, in terms of Renaissance perceptions, the play's various irregular unions would have been understood as fornication or as lawful marriage. But critical consensus on that thorny interpretive issue cannot possibly be reached if only because there *was* no single Renaissance understanding of what constituted valid marriage—at least not in England. Even in terms of the canon law, the line between illegal sexual incontinence and true marriage was very flexible in practice. The ecclesiastical courts did not always operate according to a clear-cut set of invariable principles out of medieval canonists or Justinian. And if their tolerance for exceptions was not complicated enough, there was also the problem that canon law itself had just altered. As a result of the Hampton Court Conference between James I, key bishops, and selected Puritan divines, a new canon revising the definition of lawful marriage took effect in 1604, the same year as *Measure for Measure.*[16]

Moreover, canon law was by no means the only legal code by which contemporaries could measure the validity of marriages. What constituted "true" marriage was a more nebulous matter in the London of 1604 than it had been for decades because of new and competing initiatives on the part of Crown, church, Nonconformist divines, and agents of city government to impose consistency upon an area of human conduct which had traditionally been subject only to sporadic regulation. In *Measure for Measure,* as in London of 1604, the question of whose authority will dominate in an area of uncertainty and conflicting jurisdiction is a question which is at least as important—probably more important—than the actual punishments meted out for incontinence.

In late Elizabethan and early Jacobean England marriage was a long, drawn-out process with a number of steps—from the first private promise of marriage *de futuro* between the two parties themselves, to a public contract and the establishment of a property settlement, to the actual church wedding (if that step was even taken at all), and, finally, to sexual consummation (if that step had not been taken already). Before the new 1604 canon took effect, the point in the process at which the couple could be said to be married was largely a matter of local custom, varying from one place to another. In some areas, particularly rural communities, sexual familiarity before the finalization of marriage was tolerated. Couples, in effect, married themselves through the mutual promise of marriage followed by copulation. If, as in the case of Claudio and Juliet in the play, they became parents before their union was publicly acknowledged, they might get hauled before the local "bawdy court" and required to do perfunctory penance before the congregation or, if they could afford it, charged a fine to commute the punishment.[17]

If they were unlucky, however, such a couple might come to the attention of local justices of the peace, who also had jurisdiction according to a parliamentary statute of 18 Elizabeth over any case of sexual incontinence which produced a child as well as customary jurisdiction over various other sexual offenses. According to the canon law before 1604, clandestine marriage was legal but irregular; in common law, it had no legal status at all. Property settlements under the common law required proof of open, public marriage. By the provisions of the parliamentary statute, two justices of the peace acting together could determine the disposition of a bastardy case and impose "by their discretion" what seemed to them appropriate punishment of the guilty parties.[18] It is easy to see that, given zealous officials, the statute could create a much more severe climate for sexual offenders than the church courts usually did. That, no doubt, was the intent behind the parliamentary initiative. In some areas, justices of the peace and constables actually conducted house-to-house midnight bed checks to scout out illicit sexuality. Offenders could be handed over for trial either to the ecclesiastical or to the secular courts. Some cases of sexual incontinence got bounced from the ecclesiastical to the common law courts and back again, as each legal system tried to assert its jurisdictional predominance over the other.[19]

In addition to that possible double jeopardy, there were other quarters from which correction could come. Puritan ministers often took upon themselves the revelation and punishment of fornicators within their congregations. Their doing so was, strictly speaking, unlawful, since it preempted the jurisdiction of the ecclesiastical courts. But the divines who took such measures were usually markedly hostile toward the church courts to begin with, regarding the whole canon law system as a lamentable survival of pre-Reformation "papal filth" that made "but a jest" of vice. The public shaming Puritan divines imposed upon wayward members of the congregation might be similar to the sentence which would have been imposed by the church courts, but it would probably not involve the exacting of fines, it would be imposed in an atmosphere of greater severity toward individual transgression, and it would proceed from a competing source of spiritual jurisdiction.[20]

Some Puritan divines were also prone (like Oliver Martext in *As You Like It*) to conduct what the official church condemned as invalid marriages outside the parish church and without banns or license. Again, part of the point of creating such unions was to circumvent the official system, which would have required "superstitious ceremonies" like the use of a wedding ring. London liberties with substantial Puritan congregations also tended to be havens for irregular marriage.[21] The new ecclesiastical canons which took effect in 1604 were designed to stamp out such practices by specifying that marriage had to be performed by a duly licensed cleric in the parish church of one of the partners between the hours of eight in the morning and noon, after either the announcement of banns on three consecutive Sundays or festival days, or the procurement of a valid license from the bishop.[22] Since the new regulations had been passed by convocation as early as 1584, people had had the time to become familiar with them. Even before they were formally adopted as ecclesiastical law, several ministers who had conducted irregular marriages had been censured by the church.[23] With formal ratification, many more prosecutions were impending.

As it transpired, however, clandestine marriage between the parties themselves, without the use of a minister, remained a gray area of the ecclesiastical law. England did not go as far as Catholic Europe had after the Council of Trent, banning clandestine marriage entirely. But the continuing tolerance in practice was not specifically allowed by the canon. In 1604, with the new canons in place and new, stricter plans for forcing conformity upon resisting ministers, there was considerable uncertainty about whether clandestine marriages would have any continuing validity. Certainly they were now further from official acceptability in England than they had ever been before. The pattern of empire, by which "unlocalized" canon and civil law reached out to encompass and erase local difference, was brought closer than ever to realization in the area of marriage litigation through the canons of 1604.

In London, as we have noted, there was agitation in some reformist circles for the adoption of the Mosaic code as a basis for civic ordinance. That, if put into practice, would have brought London almost into line with the statutes of Shakespeare's "Vienna." Something very much like the Viennese ordinance was in fact put in place some forty years later, during the Interregnum. Under the Commonwealth government, a second offense of incontinence could be punished by death. In addition, church marriage was abolished and justices of the peace were empowered both to conduct marriages and to dissolve them.[24] But such "root and branch" upheaval of the traditional system was only a theoretical model in the London of 1604. As it was, London's own customary penalties against sexual offenders—whipping, shaving the head, public carting, and jail—were far more draconian than the punishment prescribed in most other places and in the ecclesiastical courts. The City of London also claimed the "freedom" of overriding the ecclesiastical laws regulating sexuality with its own customary restraints. For example, London sometimes punished clerics for incontinence according to its own system of penalties, even though that function was in theory reserved to the ecclesiastical courts.[25] As the crackdown against bawds and whores had made evident, reform was very much in the air in London, 1604. The city was taking on a reputation for exceptional vigor against vice. And this was happening at a time when the Crown and Anglican church were exerting their own competing effort to surmount the crazy quilt of local jurisdictions with one overarching standard governing marriage and sexuality.

If Shakespeare's "Vienna" is a jittery and confused place when it comes to questions of sexual morality, Shakespeare's London could be said to suffer from a similar insecurity. What constituted valid marriage was not some idle legal nicety: it was an issue people had to confront in the most personal terms possible unless they remained totally celibate. Amid the nervous welter of conflicting jurisdictions over the crime of sexual incontinence, contemporaries would have differed sharply in their assessment of the validity of *Measure for Measure's* clandestine marriages. Their opinions—if they were able to come to a clear-cut opinion at all—would vary according to their degree of familiarity with recent changes in secular and canon law, and according to their general ideological bent. At a time when the Anglican church itself had launched a new offensive against the problem of clandestine marriage, intolerance for the practice did not necessarily make one overbearingly "precise." Despite the range of different opinions, however, there was one area in which there would have been substantial unanimity in London, 1604. To anyone who lived from day to day amid the open jurisdictional skirmishes among competing authorities in London, the styles of legal authority played off against each other in Shakespeare's "Vienna" would have been immediately identifiable in terms of the local conflict.

Angelo, as chief governor of Vienna, is in effect the city's Lord Mayor, and as a London Lord Mayor would, he acts with the powers of a justice of the peace to defend and strengthen the city's local ordinances, in this case, the "biting" written statute that requires fornicators to be put to death. The duke initially claims that his own goal is also to restore the integrity of the statute—put teeth back into a local code which has fallen into disregard like "threatning twigs of birch" long unused and therefore "More mock'd, then fear'd" (TLN 314–17). But the duke's secret motive is instead to test Angelo—to probe into the workings of city government and the significance of his own delegation of authority by trying the virtue of a "precise" man whose whole demeanor and life seem dedicated to the rigor of law, specifically to civic government and to the common law. The duke praises Escalus for his knowledge of the "*Cities Institutions,* and the Termes / For Common Iustice" (TLN 13–14). In contemporary parlance, the "Termes for Common Iustice" is a phrase specifically associating Escalus and city government with expertise in the common law.[26] This is the realm of legal discourse within which Angelo, too, will function.

In *Measure for Measure,* Angelo and Escalus follow the basic pattern of London civic authorities or justices of the peace, conducting open, informal interrogations and, in accordance with the parliamentary statute of 18 Elizabeth but unlike any of Shakespeare's sources and analogues, working together as a pair to inquire into cases of sexual incontinence and bastardy. The obscure offense committed in Pompey's unsavory "house" against Elbow's pregnant wife at least potentially falls within the statute, since she is with child by someone, but the exact nature of the allegation Elbow wishes to make is hopelessly lost in tangles of lexical confusion. He, a constable and therefore an agent of city law and order, is an "elbow" indeed, incessantly turning the law and language back upon themselves until all possibility for stable meaning is lost. The fact that such an engine for the decomposition of system can hold public office bodes ill for public order in "Vienna." Angelo to some extent abrogates his role as a justice in dealing with Elbow's case, at least by the standard of the English parliamentary statute, in that he eventually loses patience with the constable's obscurities and leaves Escalus to deal with the matter alone. Usually he is more punctilious. In the bastardy case of Juliet and Claudio, the two justices also confer together to determine appropriate punishment and this time Angelo is the more persistent of the two in following through on the case and applying the full rigor of the law. His insistence on the exact letter of the statute makes him close kin to actual London reformers who grounded their campaigns against vice similarly in the powers of surveillance mandated by the "*Cities Institutions*" and "the Termes for Common Iustice."

Angelo, of course, proves corrupt in office, counterfeit "mettle" rather than true coin. For London theater audiences, part of the game of topicality in "Vienna" would have been the titillating pleasure of measuring the hypocrisy of Angelo against their own civic authorities. One obvious candidate for resemblance would have been Chief Justice Popham, probably the most prominent common law justice of the time, who had spearheaded the initiative against brothels about London and was called "bloody Popham" by his enemies. He was known to be so "precise" in his personal habits that he kept the Sabbath Day meticulously even when he was riding circuit for the provincial assizes. He was also widely suspected of hypocrisy. Another prime candidate might have been Sir Edward Coke, who was already known for his defense of the common law and city "liberties" and for his interest in reviving the rigor of old statutes, but who had recently entered into a scandalously irregular marriage himself despite his ostensible veneration of the law. As usual, the game of topical identification was juicy and potentially endless: other ripe candidates were available from among the ranks of pompous London authorities—aldermen, recent Lord Mayors, sheriffs, and zealous justices of the peace. The city's crackdown on vice was bound to create friction and resistance, even perhaps among those who advocated London "liberties" in theory. Other plays of the period make similar capital out of the unveiling of the secret vices of staid, bourgeois officialdom.[27]

But the figure of the duke was just as vulnerable to the game of topical identification. His various personal likenesses to King James I do not require recapitulation here—they are obvious enough to have struck editors and readers of *Measure for Measure* since at least the eighteenth century.[28] As we will note later on, there are several other contemporary figures whom Shakespeare's duke of Vienna could also be said to resemble. What could perhaps bear more attention at this point, however, is the remarkably Jacobean *style* of the duke's activities in the play in terms of the contemporary conflicts over law. He, like the new king of England, begins by asserting his reverence for local customs and ordinances: they are, he claims, *his* laws, "our Decrees" (TLN 317), and he commits himself to giving them more authority. As it transpires, however, the duke is not at all interested in restoring the rigor of the statute against fornication. Instead, he acts in various ways to mitigate it with flexible principles drawn from the civil law and equity. Like James I in London, he acts indirectly and through intermediaries to assert his own ultimate jurisdiction over the city's customary privilege of policing its territory within the walls.

At the end of the play, despite all the initial talk about the rigid enforcement of law, the Viennese statute punishing fornication with death is forgotten. It disappears almost unnoticed amid the splendid theatrics of the public trial before the city gates. Nobody has been executed for fornication, and no one seems likely to be. In the last act, the duke himself in effect becomes the law, the *lex loquens* or speaking law, as the Roman civil code and the speeches of James I would have it, an independent source of legal authority which transcends the city's ordinance, coming down like universal "power divine" to reveal the defects in a fallible local human system.[29] The pattern was already familiar in the London of 1604; it was to become more familiar with James's continuing intervention in the city's affairs. In *Measure for Measure* local authority is overridden by royal prerogative, by the principles of Roman civil law, which fostered the idea of the monarch as the embodiment of a general, mysterious, ultimate legal authority.

Throughout the play, the duke's style of intervention is associated, not with the common law, but with ecclesiastical jurisdiction in a markedly conservative form. He is garbed as a friar for most of the action, serving as a confessor and spiritual adviser to those in need of his ministrations. He appears and vanishes with mercurial suddenness, operating in hidden ways outside local boundaries and limits. In several instances, his methods correlate with procedure under the Roman law. As was the practice in the canon law courts (in marked contrast to the common law), he gathers testimony by interrogating witnesses in private and in advance of the trial. Given the secret way in which the relevant testimony was obtained, at ecclesiastical trials the truth often emerged with sudden and undeniable éclat once all the evidence was revealed.[30] Much the same effect is achieved in the duke's public exposure of Angelo. The trial scene, with its crowd of unruly onlookers, its attendant "clerics," and its emphasis on shaming and public reputation, has some of the quality of a trial in the contemporary bawdy courts, with their odd mix of the awesome and the carnivalesque.

In the end, when the duke throws off his ecclesiastical garb to act in his own person to confer validity on the play's irregular sexual unions, he is assuming a prerogative like that which James I and the Anglican church had asserted in 1604 as they tightened up the canon law governing valid marriage by insisting upon the proper license. Within the Vienna of the play, there are "outlaw" areas like Angelo's private garden "circummur'd with Bricke" and outlying areas like Mariana's lonely grange which appear analogous to the London suburbs, removed from the regular jurisdiction of the city. The duke's activities penetrate these places apart, redress the anomalous situations which have been tolerated there, and bring them under his authority, much as James I and the church were moving in to bring the London liberties under royal and ecclesiastical control. When the duke commands that Angelo and Mariana be immediately married, he is claiming ultimate authority over the system of ecclesiastical licensing. Ordinarily, by the 1604 canon, Angelo and Mariana would require a license from the bishop in order to be married "instantly," without the publication of banns. In this case, the license emanates not from a bishop but from the ultimate ecclesiastical power above the bishop, the *lex loquens* of the ruler.

There are also resemblances between the duke's style of justice and the English Court of Chancery. Traditionally, the chancellors of England had been clerics and the duke's disguise recalls that connection. Chancery was the final court of appeal in ecclesiastical cases involving matters of property (which often hinged upon the validity of marriage); it frequently reversed the severity of the lower common law courts, just as the duke alleviates the severity of the statute. According to one contemporary description, the chancellor "doth so *cancell* and *shut up* the *rigour* of the generall *Law,* that it shall not breake forth to the hurt of some one singular Case and person."[31] By abrogating a local statute in favor of "mercy" and equity, the duke acts, in effect, as his own Lord Chancellor, overriding local justices in the name of the Roman code and the royal dispensing power. The jurisdictional morass has been cleared away; pockets of secret license have been opened up to surveillance; and the duke has publicly established for himself and for the civil and canon law the ultimate right to adjudicate "Mortallitie and Mercie in *Vienna.*"

In twentieth-century editions and productions of *Measure for Measure,* the trial scene usually takes place inside the city. The First Folio itself offers no such certainty as to place. As the scene begins, the duke is approaching the city gates: "Twice haue the Trumpetes sounded. / The generous, and grauest

Citizens / Haue hent the gates, and very neere vpon / The Duke is entring" (TLN 2340–43). The folio stage directions which follow specify only that the "Duke, Varrius, Lords, Angelo, Esculus, Lucio" and "Citizens" enter "at seuerall doores" (TLN 2346–47). In some of the earliest editions of the play specifying the locus of the public trial which follows, the scene of the trial is described as "a publick Place near the City."[32] That added stage direction is interesting because it suggests that early editors of the play thought of Shakespeare's "Vienna" in terms of a topography very like London's: the City proper is a self-contained, walled unit surrounded by other urban areas, like the London liberties, which are not strictly part of it. What the scene enacts is the traditional public ritual by which civic authorities greet a visiting monarch. They meet the ruler with fanfare just outside the walls—the entry "at seuerall doores" suggesting that the different groups have come from different directions—to formally tender up their authority and accompany him through the gates.[33]

In this case, however, the entry is delayed as a result of the duke's proclamation inviting petitioners to approach him publicly for the redress of grievances. The pleas of Isabella and Mariana turn the usual scene of ceremonial transfer of authority into a forum for inquiring into the conduct of the deputy. The duke establishes his superior claim to govern the city from a location just outside the wall, outside its proper jurisdiction; then, much as James I had entered London in triumph in the year 1604, he enters the gates and proceeds in state to his "Pallace," formally taking possession of the place he has demonstrated a transcendent right to control. That which is merely local has been made to appear small, paltry, and corruptible, by comparison with an authority which partakes of the divine and the universal, which cuts through jurisdictional tangles to establish a single, centralized, yet merciful standard of law.

It is easy to see how James I would have relished the play's depiction of victory for the Roman law with which he felt such sympathy and which, in 1604, he still hoped to use as the basis of a united Britain. There are many ways in which the play seems weighted toward the "Jacobean line." The city's own authorities are an unimpressive lot: even Escalus is too shortsighted to suspect the vice of Angelo. Unless Claudio is played as an unusually repellant character, he tends to generate audience sympathy, at least by comparison with Angelo, just as his plight generates sympathy from onlookers within the play. Insofar as an audience takes the part of Claudio against Angelo and the rigor of the statute, they are being invited to side with the duke against the city—recognize the wisdom of the ruler's timely use of equity to redress a reforming zeal which has gone too far.

There were contemporaries who would have agreed with Angelo that death was not an excessive penalty for fornication, but they were the same zealots who were most vehement against the theater. They would not (it seems safe to say) have been part of the audience for *Measure for Measure.* To the extent that London theatrical audiences resented the reformers' endless campaigns against the public "enormity" of stage plays, they may have found it easy to applaud the duke's exposure of a civic leader who was overly precise. The place of the duke's highly theatrical trial just outside the jurisdiction of the city was, in London, the place of the stage itself. There is a natural topographical alliance between the theatricality of the duke and the institution which brought him to life on stage on the outskirts of London.

But for at least some members of a London audience in 1604, the play's victory over statute may have looked more like defeat. Whether or not the duke's influence is perceived as salutary depends to a marked degree on the audience's evaluation of the duke himself. For good or for ill, his *modus operandi* in the play is made to appear arbitrary, manipulative, imposed from without. In modern performances, he is often idealized as the wise exemplar of overarching authority called for by the play's "Jacobean line," a figure whose arbitrary gestures are justified as desperate counters to the rampant crimes of his surrogate. Almost as frequently in modern productions, however, the duke comes closer to Lucio's description of the "fantastical Duke of darke corners" or Angelo's equally disparaging language: "In most vneuen and distracted manner, his actions show much like to madnesse, pray heauen his wisedome bee not tainted" (TLN 2274–76). In modern productions, the duke can be a *deus ex machina* who descends by means of a whirligig, a shadowy trickster who delights in imposing unnecessary gyrations of misery upon his subjects merely to show his power. Like Jupiter in *Cymbeline,* he exists on a perilous boundary between the sublime and the grotesque.

In London, 1604, there may have been nearly as much potential for variability in the portrayal of the duke as there is in modern performance. Because of the heated conflicts over jurisdictional issues in the city, even relatively small alterations in the nervous balance between the duke and his antagonists could markedly have altered the political complexion of the play. Let us take one "localized" example of the problematics that contemporary performance could—perhaps fleetingly—have exploited. If a London audience saw a parallel between the duke of Vienna and James I as the promulgator of the new ecclesiastical laws regarding marriage, they could easily have been puzzled by his uncanonical behavior earlier in the play. The "bed trick" by which Mariana is substituted for Isabella to satisfy Angelo's lust was *not* lawful according to the church's new definition of marriage. The precipitous wedding ordered by the duke between Mariana and Angelo was also uncanonical unless, by some chance, they happened to be married in the parish church of one of them, or unless the duke's verbal "license" is taken to cancel out the usual rules. These are small details, perhaps: topicality thrives on what is almost too insignificant to notice. But they suggest that the duke, insofar as he is identified with James I, can be trusted to respect his beloved canon law no more than Angelo does the statute. That perception unleashes a potential for contemporary deconstruction of *Measure for Measure's* Jacobean line. Like King James, the duke acts above the law, freely overriding even his own preferred code when it suits his purpose to do so. Contemporary viewers could surmount the seeming contradiction in the duke's position by making a "leap of faith" from the law to Christian mercy, by which all legal codes are confounded. As we will note further later on, *Measure for Measure,* like *King Lear,* is associated with St. Stephen's Day, at least through its performance at court, and therefore with the holiday inversion of law and ordinary hierarchy. But to regard the duke as transcending all law would undermine the play's appeal to the ruler as an alternative and superior source of law. In *Measure for Measure,* the rule of law is overthrown by something that may be divine transcendence but can also look like royal whim, unruly "license," a mere recapitulation of the abuse it purports to rectify.

In London, 1604, one of the things on trial in *Measure for Measure* was the city's jealously guarded autonomy. Under such conditions, a strongly divided reaction to the duke and his triumph could easily have been generated by one and the same performance. Not all theatergoers were Londoners, of course; many were foreigners or visitors from the provinces for whom the conflict over law in its particular London form would have been less than familiar, although the general problem was familiar enough. For such viewers some of the intensity of the play's topicality "within the wall" might have been lost. Then too, even for many Londoners, the "honeymoon" between the new king and his people was not quite over. The reign was young enough that many subjects who would later become disaffected were still willing to grant the monarch the benefit of the doubt. The name of king exerted a powerful emotional pull, particularly when coupled, as in *Measure for Measure's* last act, with evocations of sacred divinity. Yet if, in a given audience, on a given day, the passion for city liberties ran high enough, even a sympathetic portrayal of the duke would probably not have made palatable his conquest over a "Vienna" which looked so uncannily like London.

At the end of the play, there is one slight suggestion that the duke's victory may not be complete. His conquest over the city has also been a conquest of the chaste virgin Isabella, or so, at least, he assumes. Twice he publicly asks her to allow him to possess her as his wife, but both times she remains silent in one of Shakespeare's most intriguing "open silences."[34] What can her silence mean? Traditionally in performance, it has meant that no words are necessary: Isabella gladly gives him her hand. In very recent productions, it has sometimes meant refusal: instead of accepting the duke, Isabella turns her back and walks off. It is difficult for us to know whether or not such a stunning rejection of patriarchy and political authority by a "mere" woman could have been staged in Renaissance England. We know little enough about the conditions of Renaissance performance that we should not automatically discount the possibility. But a more muted version of the same response could easily enough have been acted. We, with our quaint late twentieth-century prejudice in favor of consensual marriage, find the notion of bridal reluctance or coercion profoundly shocking. In the Renaissance, it was all too familiar. Isabella could easily have held back, given evidence that she was being conquered against her wishes, before finally yielding to the duke. The effect would be to cast a shadow, however brief, upon his triumph.

For some modern readers and viewers of *Measure for Measure,* Isabella bears a muted resemblance to the dead Queen Elizabeth.[35] Elizabeth, like Isabella, had been an insistent, sometimes strident virgin who had valued her own inviolability above many other pressing matters. She had had her own set of imperial images—to some extent James I was merely adopting her symbology of power. After her death, however, the image of the queen signified political difference from James; she stood for nationalism and "local" identity. To the extent that the identification between the two virgins carries credence (and carried credence for contemporaries), the duke's conquest over Isabella can be seen as yet another dramatic marginalization of the mythos of Elizabeth, like those we have briefly observed already in several other plays we call Shakespeare. Through Isabella, the dead queen and her cult of virginity and national "intactness" are invaded and dominated by an alternative, Stuart ideology of male dominance and imperial conquest.

Despite the fact that she too had sometimes offended against London liberties, Elizabeth was becoming a powerful political symbol in Jacobean London. In the city, as in Parliament, and in contemporary plays and pamphlets, the figure of the queen was associated with resistance to royal absolutism and the maintenance of customary franchises and liberties. Some years later, the city erected a statue of the queen with hair flowing freely to symbolize her (and its own) celebrated "virgin" freedom and self-containedness. Isabella, Elizabeth, London: in terms of gender encoding, all three were associated with vulnerable boundaries stoutly maintained against violation. In Shakespeare's *Rape of Lucrece,* similarly, the "tyranny" of a "King" and the Tarquins' encroachment upon civic "laws and customs" are associated with sexual conquest.[36] Like the resolute virgin Isabella in *Measure for Measure,* the City of London had been called upon through James's coronation pageant and other royal initiatives to open its gates, become the submissive "bride" of the monarch, throw off its cherished inviolacy to become part of a larger "Union." To the extent that the symbolic parallel holds, Isabella's equivocal silence in the face of imperial conquest can resonate strongly with a parallel silence on the part of the city in the face of its incipient forced "marriage" to King James I.

Notes

1. See Mark Eccles, ed., *A New Variorum Edition of Shakespeare: Measure for Measure* (New York: Modern Language Association, 1980), 292–94. My discussion throughout is strongly indebted to Eccles, also to J. W. Lever, ed., *Measure for Measure* (London: Methuen,

1965), who discusses textual problems on pp. xi–xxxi; and to W. W. Greg, *The Shakespeare First Folio: Its Bibliographical and Textual History* (Oxford: Clarendon Press, 1955), 354–56.

2. See Lever's survey, p. xxxii; I am also indebted to Jonathan Dollimore, "Transgression and Surveillance in *Measure for Measure,*" in *Political Shakespeare: New Essays in Cultural Materialism,* ed. Jonathan Dollimore and Alan Sinfield (Ithaca: Cornell Univ. Press, 1985), 72–87.

3. *The Letters of John Chamberlain,* ed. N. E. McClure, Memoirs of the American Philosophical Society 12 (Philadelphia: Lancashire Press, 1939), 1: 48 (letter of October 20, 1598); *Middlesex County Records* (Old Series), Vol. 1, ed. John Cordy Jeaffreson (1886) (reprinted London: Greater London Council, 1972), 234–35, 263, 270, 287. (These cases date from about 1598 to 1604.)

4. That is not to say that contemporary Puritans would have agreed that Claudio's offense falls within the statute. Angelo's interpretation is extreme, even by contemporary Puritan standards. Here and elsewhere, I use the term *Puritan* as opposed to *Protestant* to delineate that group within contemporary Protestantism which was devoted to thorough liturgical reform and restructuring of the ecclesiastical hierarchy.

See the accounts of contemporary Puritan opinion in John Strype, *The Life and Acts of John Whitgift, D.D.* (Oxford: Clarendon Press, 1822), 2:17; G. B. Harrison, "Extreme Tenets of the Puritans," in *The Elizabethan Journals: Being a Record of Those Things Most Talked of during the Years 1591–1603* (1928–33; reprinted as one volume, New York: Macmillan, 1939), 208–9; and the survey of Reformation legal opinion in Gerald Strauss, *Law, Resistance, and the State: The Opposition to Roman Law in Reformation Germany* (Princeton: Princeton Univ. Press, 1986), 191–239. Reformation planning and ideology on the Continent regularly included the death penalty for adultery, if not for fornication. In practice, such ordinances tended to be fleeting. See Steven E. Ozment, *The Reformation in the Cities: The Appeal of Protestantism to Sixteenth-Century Germany and Switzerland* (New Haven: Yale Univ. Press, 1975), 104–57; and E. William Monter, "Crime and Punishment in Calvin's Geneva, 1562," *Archiv für Reformationsgeschichte* 64 (1973): 281–87.

5. For James's pageant, see Jonathan Goldberg, *James I and the Politics of Literature* (Baltimore: Johns Hopkins Univ. Press, 1983), 31–33 and 50–54; Graham Parry, *The Golden Age Restor'd: The Culture of the Stuart Court, 1603–42* (New York: St. Martin's Press, 1981), 1–9; and my discussion of the Londinium Arch in *The Politics of Mirth: Jonson, Herrick, Milton, Marvell, and the Defense of Old Holiday Pastimes* (Chicago: Univ. of Chicago Press, 1986), 64–67. For imperial analogues, see Roy Strong, *Art and Power: Renaissance Festivals 1450–1650* (1973; reprinted Berkeley: Univ. of California Press, 1984), chap. 2, "Images of Empire: Charles V and the Imperial Progress," 75–97; and Stanley Applebaum, ed., *The Triumph of Maximilian I* (New York: Dover Publications, 1964).

6. Lever, ed., *Measure for Measure,* xxxi.

7. Richard Levin, *New Readings vs. Old Plays: Recent Trends in the Reinterpretation of English Renaissance Drama* (1979; reprinted Chicago: Univ. of Chicago Press, 1982), 171–93. For materials linking James and the duke, see Lever's edition of *Measure for Measure,* xlviii–li; and the interpretations in Josephine Waters Bennett, *Measure for Measure as Royal Entertainment* (New York: Columbia Univ. Press, 1966); David L. Stevenson, *The Achievement of Shakespeare's Measure for Measure* (Ithaca: Cornell Univ. Press, 1966); and more recently, Jonathan Goldberg, *James I and the Politics of Literature,* 231–39; and Leonard Tennenhouse, *Power on Display: The Politics of Shakespeare's Genres* (London: Methuen, 1986), 154–59; along with Tennenhouse's important earlier article "Representing Power: *Measure for Measure* in Its Time," in *The Power of Forms in the English Renaissance,* ed. Stephen Greenblatt (Norman, Okla.: Pilgrim Books, 1982), 139–56.

More generally, I am also indebted to Jacqueline Rose, "Sexuality in the Reading of Shakespeare: *Hamlet* and *Measure for Measure,*" in John Drakakis, ed., *Alternative Shakespeares* (London: Methuen, 1985), 95–118; and to Paul Hammond, "The Argument of *Measure for*

Measure," *English Literary Renaissance* 16 (1986): 496–519. Steven Mullaney's work on "the place of the stage" in Renaissance London has influenced my own analysis throughout the chapter. See his *The Place of the Stage: License, Play, and Power in Renaissance England* (Chicago: Univ. of Chicago Press, 1988). Studies of law in the play will be cited further along.

8. *Annus Mirabilis,* epistle dedicatory, *The Poetical Works of Dryden,* ed. George R. Noyes (Cambridge, Mass.: Riverside Press, 1950), 23. For standard accounts of the growth and development of London, see Roger Finlay, *Population and Metropolis: The Demography of London* (Cambridge: Cambridge Univ. Press, 1981); and Harold Edford Priestley, *London: The Years of Change* (London: Muller, 1966).

9. Alexander Pulling, *The Laws, Customs, Usages, and Regulations of the City and Port of London,* 2d ed. (London: William Henry Bond, 1854), 221–22.

10. See Patrick Collinson, *The Elizabethan Puritan Movement* (Berkeley: Univ. of California Press, 1967), 86–87, 339–41; for the liberties used as sanctuary, G. B. Harrison, *The Elizabethan Journals,* note 4 above, 1:192, 2:327; and on the liberties and the theater, Virginia Crocheron Gildersleeve, *Government Regulation of the Elizabethan Drama* (1908; reprinted New York: Burt Franklin, 1961). See also Gildersleeve's indispensable discussion of the slippery meanings of the phrases "Liberties of London" and "London Liberties," 142–43.

11. See the discussion in Virginia Gildersleeve, *Government Regulation of the Elizabethan Drama,* 193–94.

12. For the conflict over the Tower, see *Analytical Index to the Series of Records Known as the Remembrancia . . . AD 1579–1664* (London: Francis and Co., 1878), 426–35; and *Calendar of State Papers Domestic,* James I, 8:452 (dated Aug. 21, 1608). Other areas of conflict are recorded in the *Analytical Index,* 4–6, 17, 56, 70–71, and 94. Some of the key cases at law are collected in Edward Coke, *The Twelfth Part of the Reports of Sir Edward Coke* (London: for Henry Twyford, 1656), 26–27. For a more general view of the conflict, see Carolyn A. Edie, "Tactics and Strategies: Parliament's Attack upon the Royal Dispensing Power 1597–1689," *American Journal of Legal History* 29 (1985): 197–234; and Derek Hirst, "Court, Country, and Politics before 1629," in *Faction and Parliament: Essays on Early Stuart History,* ed. Kevin Sharpe (Oxford: Clarendon, 1978), 105–37.

13. Richard Helgerson, "The Land Speaks: Cartography, Choreography, and the Representation of Power," *Representations* 16 (1986): 50–85. I am grateful to Mr. Helgerson for graciously giving me access to his work in manuscript.

14. *Analytical Index to the Remembrancia,* 438.

15. See the analyses cited in note 5 above.

16. See the survey of canon law approaches in Jonathan K. Price, "*Measure for Measure* and the Critics: Towards a New Approach," *Shakespeare Quarterly* 20 (1969): 179–204; and for individual studies of the play's use of law, see in addition to the sources in note 7 above Peter Alexander, "*Measure for Measure:* A Case for the Scottish Solomon," *Modern Language Quarterly* 28 (1967): 478–88; James Black, "The Unfolding of 'Measure for Measure,' " *Shakespeare Survey* 26 (1973): 119–28; John W. Dickinson, "Renaissance Equity and *Measure for Measure,*" *Shakespeare Quarterly* 13 (1962): 287–97; Wilbur Dunkel, "Law and Equity in *Measure for Measure,*" *Shakespeare Quarterly* 13 (1962): 275–85; Darryl J. Gless, *Measure for Measure, the Law, and the Convent* (Princeton: Princeton Univ. Press, 1979); George W. Keeton's study of equity in *Shakespeare's Legal and Political Background* (London: Pitman & Sons, 1967); and Margaret Scott's reminder as to differences between canon law on the Continent and in England, " 'Our City's Institutions': Some Further Reflections on the Marriage Contracts in *Measure for Measure,*" ELH 49 (1982): 790–804.

For a lively sense of the ecclesiastical courts' flexibility in terms of legal practice, see R. H. Helmholz, *Marriage Litigation in Medieval England* (Cambridge: Cambridge Univ. Press, 1974); and F. G. Emmison, *Elizabethan Life: Morals and the Church Courts* (Chelmsford: Essex County Council, 1973). The new canons are recorded in Anthony Sparrow, *A Collection of Arti-*

cles, Injunctions, Canons, Orders, Ordinances and Constitutions Ecclesiastical . . . of the Church of England (London: for Robert Cutler and Joseph Clarke, 1671), which reprints the 1604 edition of the canons in English translation. The canons in question are on p. 28 of the 1604 reprint. See also the background material in John Strype, *The Life and Acts of John Whitgift, D.D.* 1:232; 2:377–510, and the Appendix (separately dated 1717) to the 1718 one-volume edition of Strype's *Life of Whitgift,* 222–23.

17. See Lawrence Stone, *The Family, Sex and Marriage in England 1500–1800* (New York: Harper & Row, 1977), 32–35; Christopher Hill, *Society and Puritanism in Pre-Revolutionary England,* 2d ed. (New York: Schocken Books, 1967), 298–343; and Peter Laslett and Richard Wall, eds., *Household and Family in Past Time* (Cambridge: Cambridge Univ. Press, 1972). For examples, see Paul Hair, ed., *Before the Bawdy Court . . . 1300–1800* (London: Elek, 1972); and F. G. Emmison, *Elizabethan Life: Morals and the Church Courts.*.

18. Ferdinando Pulton, *A Collection of all the Statutes Now in Use* (London: for John Bell and Christopher Barker, 1670), 973.

19. Christopher Hill, *Society and Puritanism in Pre-Revolutionary England,* 298–343; John Strype, *Life and Acts of John Whitgift,* 1:266, 2:383–84, 397–99, 428–30; and F. G. Emmison, *Elizabethan Life: Morals and the Church Courts,* 10, 20, 30, 40–41.

20. Patrick Collinson, *The Elizabethan Puritan Movement,* 347–49. The particular characterizations of the church courts are cited from Luther as quoted in Strauss, *Law, Resistance, and the State,* 217; and Phillip Stubbes, *The Anatomie of Abuses* (1583), as cited in Hair, ed., *Before the Bawdy Court,* 57. See also Emmison, 310–13.

There is disagreement among historians about the extent to which city and town reform movements coincided with Puritanism. For the controversy, see the essays in *Order and Disorder in Early Modern England,* ed. Anthony Fletcher and John Stevenson (Cambridge: Cambridge Univ. Press, 1985), especially M. Spufford, "Puritanism and Social Control?" 41–57; and S. D. Amussen, "Gender, Family, and the Social Order, 1560–1725," 196–217. For an amusing account of one "outburst of reforming frenzy," see David Underdown, *Revel, Riot, and Rebellion: Popular Politics and Culture in England 1603–1660* (Oxford: Clarendon Press, 1985), 59.

21. Strype, *Life and Acts of John Whitgift,* 2:376; see also the colorful list of examples, Appendix, 222–24. The abuse was not, apparently, corrected until much later, despite parliamentary and ecclesiastical initiatives. For later and more blatant examples, see Gellert Spencer Alleman, *Matrimonial Law and the Materials of Restoration Comedy* (Philadelphia: Univ. of Pennsylvania Press, 1942), 36–50.

22. See Anthony Sparrow, *A Collection of Articles, Injunctions, Canons, Orders, Ordinances,* reprint of 1604 edition of the canons, 28; Lawrence Stone, *The Family, Sex, and Marriage in England 1500–1800,* 33–35; and the detailed discussion in Gellert Alleman, *Matrimonial Law and the Materials of Restoration Comedy,* 34–35.

23. Hill, *Society and Puritanism in Pre-Revolutionary England,* 298–343; Ronald A. Marchant, *The Puritans and the Church Courts in the Diocese of York 1560–1642* (London: Longmans, 1960), 143.

24. Gellert Alleman, *Matrimonial Law and the Materials of Restoration Comedy,* 58–59; for statutes against fornication, see *An Abstract of the Laws Already in Force against Profaneness, Immorality, & Blasphemy Together with the Laws and Ordinances against the same by the Parliament . . . 1640 to 1656* (London: R. Baldwin, 1698).

25. Alexander Pulling, *The Laws, Customs, Usages, etc. of the City and Port of London,* 253–54, 540; John Stow, *Survay of London* (London, 1603), 190–91. In the Middle Ages, the ecclesiastical punishment had been closer to London's, but with time the church courts relaxed the strictness of punishments for sexual offenses. See R. H. Helmholz, *Marriage Litigation in Medieval England,* 182–83. Other towns asserted similar privileges; see Hill, *Society and Puritanism in Pre-Revolutionary England,* 333; and James A. Brundage, *Law, Sex, and Christian Society in Medieval Europe* (Chicago: Univ. of Chicago Press, 1987), 442–44, 469, 482–87, 491–93.

26. See Lever's edition of *Measure for Measure,* 4n. On the Continent, "the terms for common justice" would imply canon law; in England, the law which collected local laws together into a single body of precedent was the common law.

27. See the *Dictionary of National Biography* under Popham and Coke; for other literary examples of the counterpoising of local law and "Imperia" to the disparagement of local justices, see David Bevington, *Tudor Drama and Politics: A Critical Approach to Topical Meaning* (Cambridge, Mass.: Harvard Univ. Press, 1968), 267–86; Lever, ed., *Measure for Measure,* xlvii; my discussion of Jonson's *Bartholomew Fair* in *The Politics of Mirth,* 38–63; Leonard Tennenhouse, "Representing Power: *Measure for Measure* in Its Time"; and Susan Wells, *The Dialectics of Representation* (Baltimore: Johns Hopkins Univ. Press, 1985), 103–32.

28. Mark Eccles, ed., *A New Variorum Edition of Shakespeare: Measure for Measure,* 299.

29. C. H. McIllwain, ed., *The Political Works of James I* (Cambridge, Mass.: Harvard Univ. Press, 1918), 291; for the idea in Roman law, see, among other similar discussions, Gerald Strauss, *Law, Resistance, and the State,* note 4 above, 71. Strauss's discussion uses another common term for the same idea—the emperor as *lex animata.*

30. R. H. Helmholz, *Marriage Litigation in Medieval England,* 17–22, 127–34; for a corrective to Helmholz's essentially positive view of the system, see the discussion of post-Reformation complaints in Ronald A. Marchant, *The Puritans and the Church Courts;* and Christopher Hill, *Society and Puritanism in Pre-Revolutionary England,* 298–343.

31. Cited in John W. Dickinson, "Renaissance Equity and *Measure for Measure,*" note 16 above, 287–97, from William Lambarde's *Archeion* (before 1591).

32. Mark Eccles, ed., *A New Variorum Edition of Shakespeare: Measure for Measure,* 234.

33. For Elizabethan and Jacobean examples of the ritual, see John Nichols, *The Progresses and Public Processions of Queen Elizabeth* (London: John Nichols, 1823), 2:138–43; and G. B. Harrison, *A Jacobean Journal: Being a Record of Those Things Most Talked of During the Years 1603–6* (London: George Routledge and Sons, 1941), 224–25 (the king's 1605 entry into Oxford). In *Measure for Measure,* there is a minor inconsistency between the duke's order to the officials to meet him a league below the city and the actual place of meeting, nearer the gates; as Escalus has earlier complained, "Euery Letter he hath writ, hath disuouch'd other" (TLN 2273).

34. My discussion is indebted to Philip C. McGuire, *Speechless Dialect: Shakespeare's Open Silences* (Berkeley: Univ. of California Press, 1985), 79–96; and more generally to David Bevington, *Action Is Eloquence: Shakespeare's Language of Gesture* (Cambridge, Mass.: Harvard Univ. Press, 1984).

35. See, for example, Josephine Waters Bennett, *Measure for Measure as Royal Entertainment,* 174n.6. Isabella is the only nonroyal character in Shakespeare besides Caesar to use the royal "we": "More then our Brother, is our Chastitie." See Warren D. Smith, "More Light on *Measure for Measure,*" *Modern Language Quarterly* 23 (1962): 309–22. That usage could link her with Elizabeth, or with some other regal personage.

36. Roy Strong, *Portraits of Queen Elizabeth I* (Oxford: Clarendon Press, 1963), 156. The statue was quickly removed, probably because of court objections to its iconography (the interpretation of which is mine). Strong calls the statue "one of the strangest of the posthumous representations of the Queen."

For civic liberties and *Lucrece,* see the "Argument," cited from *The Complete Works of Shakespeare,* ed. David Bevington, 3d ed. (Glenview, Ill.: Scott, Foresman, 1980), 1545–46; and Clifford Chalmers Huffman, *Coriolanus in Context* (Lewisburg, Pa.: Bucknell Univ. Press, 1971), 34–50.

Assaying the Power of Chastity in *Measure for Measure*

BARBARA J. BAINES

For many readers of *Measure for Measure,* Isabella illustrates better than Angelo the paradox that "Some rise by sin, and some by virtue fall" (II.i.38).[1] Critics have, in fact, argued that the primary question of the play is whether Isabella is an embodiment of Christian virtue or pagan pride.[2] Recently Marcia Riefer has defended Isabella as a victim of sexual subjugation who changes in the course of the play "from an articulate, compassionate, woman during her first encounter with Angelo (II.ii) to a stunned, angry, defensive woman in her later confrontations with Angelo and with her imprisoned brother (II.iv and III.i), to, finally, a shadow of her former articulate self, on her knees before male authority in Act V."[3]

This defense, however, is not altogether convincing because it is predicated upon a "powerlessness"[4] that simply does not square with the language and actions of the character. Furthermore, Riefer's delineation of Isabella's defensive reactions does not account for the priority Isabella places upon her chastity at the expense of her brother's life. Although Madeleine Doran identifies the central issue of Isabella as her "choice between her brother's death and the sacrifice of her chastity," Doran also evades the issue she identifies by simply concluding that "Shakespeare meant to put primary emphasis on the problem of the exercise of power . . . and not on the problem of Isabella's chastity."[5] More important, Doran's pronouncement of the playwright's intention separates what the play clearly aligns: chastity and power. Within the context of the relationship between chastity and power, Isabella's "choice" articulates a complex, culturally determined imperative. Chastity is the definitive virtue precisely because it is a site and mode of secular power.

First of all, the priority Isabella places on chastity reflects the values of the entire society that the play depicts, not simply the values of a young woman about to enter the convent. Whether or not Isabella's choice of her chastity over her brother's life can be justified by Renaissance religious convictions is finally irrelevant because her adherence to scripture, to convent

Reprinted by permission of *SEL Studies in English Literature 1500–1900* 30, 2 (Spring 1990).

vow, and to her conscience does not adequately account for her choice. What does account for her choice is the social and psychological, rather than the religious, construct in which she and the other characters function. Isabella's values, then, are representative, not eccentric; and they are grounded more firmly in the secular than in the religious. Society, not scripture, defines chastity as the definitive virtue that gives identity and place to women and to men. The priority society places upon chastity, in fact, enables the distinctions between God's law and man's law, between the letter and the spirit of both secular and divine law, and between the intent and the deed. A theologically prescribed virtue, chastity is appropriated as the standard upon which the economy of secular power is based. Chastity thus establishes each character in the play as a subject, within a pattern of subjection. Interrelated constructs—social, political, and psychological—within which chastity operates define it as a form of power that radically complicates the meaning of Isabella as its principal agent.

Within the social construct, chastity is the definitive virtue not because scripture mandates it but because secular law prescribes it as a remedy for the diseased state. The play presents a society in which the health of the nation and the authority of its ruler are jeopardized by sexual license. Although Claudio, in defense of his sexual liberty, claims that Juliet is "fast" his wife, he acknowledges through his simile the detrimental effects of his incontinence: "Our natures do pursue, / Like rats that ravin down their proper bane, / A thirsty evil, and when we drink we die" (I.ii.128–30). The Duke's response to the threat incontinence poses is to awaken the law that places a higher priority upon chastity than upon human life and to delegate the enforcement of this law to a man whose temperament and sexual conduct appear to qualify him for that harsh task. That a strict enforcement of the law is the Duke's objective is evidenced by his choice of Angelo over Escalus as his deputy and by his approval of Angelo's strict adherence to the law. When Escalus complains to the disguised Duke about the severity of Angelo's enforcement, the Duke answers, "If his own life answer the straitness of his proceeding, it shall become him well" (III.ii.255–56). The Duke also labels his own failure to enforce the law mandating chastity as "my vice" (III.ii.270). The "strict statutes and most biting laws" are, in the Duke's words, "The needful bits and curbs to headstrong weeds" (I.iii.19, 20).

Within this social construct, the laws mandating chastity constitute a prohibition placed on the individual for the greater good of society as a whole; private freedom is subjected by the disinterested concern for the commonwealth. Chastity is thus the form of power that subjugation assumes.

Through a metaphoric explanation of his failure to enforce chastity, Vincentio supplements this altruistic, social concern with his own political concern as patriarch:

> Now, as fond fathers,
> Having bound up the threat'ning twigs of birch
> Only to stick it in their children's sight
> For terror, not to use, in time the rod
> [Becomes] more mock'd than fear'd; so our decrees,
> Dead to infliction, to themselves are dead,
> And liberty plucks justice by the nose;
> The baby beats the nurse, and quite athwart
> Goes all decorum.
>
> (I.iii.23–31)

Enforcing chastity thus becomes not only a means of restoring societal health, but also the means of retrieving or buttressing patriarchal authority. Strict enforcement of *any* law would strengthen the ruler's authority, but society's disregard for the laws that mandate chastity is critical for the Duke specifically because chastity assures legitimacy, and legitimacy authorizes patriarchy.

For similar political and social reasons, the Duke's deputy justifies his strict enforcement of the law that prioritizes chastity over human life by equating the incontinence that results in bastardy with murder.[6]

> It were as good
> To pardon him that hath from nature stol'n
> A man already made, as to remit
> Their saucy sweetness that do coin heaven's image
> In stamps that are forbid. 'Tis all as easy
> Falsely to take away a life true made
> As to put metal in restrained means
> To make a false one.
>
> (II.iv.42–49)

Angelo's equation and Isabella's response, " 'Tis set down so in heaven, but not in earth," are equally illuminating. It is set down in heaven, in scripture, that fornication and murder are sins, but Angelo's equation of the two is set down so in Viennese law, not in divine law. Samuel Johnson in his textual notes commented on the peculiarity of Isabella's response: "I would have it considered, whether the train of the discourse does not rather require Isabel to say, 'Tis so set down in *earth* but not in *heaven.*' "[7] Johnson was perhaps recalling the place of Mary Magdalene in the life of Christ and Christ's intercession on behalf of the adulteress about to be stoned by the Pharisees. Like English law in Shakespeare's time, Viennese law ignores the example of Christ's compassion for the sexual offender because fornication results in bastardy, and bastardy threatens the social and political privileges of the legitimate male heir within an aristocratic, patrilineal society. In the society this play presents, there is no place for the illegitimate. As Marilyn Williamson has most convincingly demonstrated, bastardy was a major problem of the society for which the play was written. And like Vienna, Renaissance England attempted with little success to check the social and political threat of bastardy with harsh laws.[8]

More effective in the enforcement of chastity than biting laws was the threat of social shame. Honor for all family members resided in the purity of the bloodline, in the legitimacy of birth, and thus in the chastity of the female. In a patriarchal society, men are privileged with authority, yet, somewhat paradoxically, that authority depends upon the chastity of women. Thus chastity becomes for woman a form of power; through it the woman legitimizes the power of the man and preserves the patriarchal social structure. Responsibility for the power inherent in woman's chastity is perhaps what the disguised Duke alludes to when he confesses Juliet. Hearing from her that the sin of premarital intercourse "was mutually committed," Vincentio tells Juliet, "Then was your sin of heavier kind than his" (II.iii.28). The Duke's judgment of Juliet is not simply an expression of a male chauvinist's double standard (as Riefer suggests)[9] but an acknowledgment of a patriarchal society's dependence upon woman's chastity.

In Vienna, as in Shakespeare's England, women are defined and placed on the basis of their chastity. The alternatives to Isabella's strict renunciation of her sexuality are the shame and harassment of Juliet, the sorrow of Mariana, the tavern jokes at the expense of Mistress Elbow, the exploitation of Kate Keepdown, and the overuse of Mistress Overdone. According to her chastity or lack thereof, a woman takes her place in the nunnery, the jail, the moated grange, or the brothel (that other "nunnery"). Although sexual relations can be hazardous for men, they are inevitably so for women in this play. The surest protection against the hazards of sexual relations is renunciation and retreat, the nunnery or the moated grange. The chastity that the nunnery protects is thus a form of freedom, the only form of autonomy left for women in a world where sexuality means submission to men and degradation in that submission. Isabella's freedom from sexual subjugation is, of course, not without a price, for it requires her submission to the patriarchal law, defined best by Theseus in *A Midsummer Night's Dream* (I.i.67–78). Under this law, a woman's control of her body necessitates a form of self-castration. Her chastity is deprived of its social, political, and psychological power through isolation and renunciation.

Freedom within the confines of the nunnery is the subtext of conversation when Isabella first appears in the play. She desires a "more strict restraint" as additional protection from the masculine world locked outside of the convent. Having made her one great concession to the patriarchal law by renouncing her sexuality, Isabella willingly embraces the strictest law of the Mother Superior to escape total subjugation under the law of the patriarch or father, signified by the phallus. Once she has achieved through her vows the status of a nun, she will have the full protection of the sisterhood under the law of the Mother Superior. Francisca explains the terms of this protection to Isabella when Lucio appears at the locked convent gate:

> Turn you the key, and know his business of him;
> You may, I may not; you are yet unsworn.
> When you have vow'd, you must not speak with men
> But in the presence of the prioress;
> Then; if you speak, you must not show your face,
> Or if you show your face, you must not speak.
> (I.iv.8–13)

The law of the convent thus anticipates the danger to chastity inherent in man's gaze and in woman's speech that will become apparent when Isabella and Angelo meet. Standing on the threshold between the worlds of masculine and feminine authority, Isabella turns the key of the convent gate to "assay the pow'r" (line 76) of her chastity within the patriarchal order.

As her chastity entitles her to the freedom of the convent, it also elicits the highest esteem in the world outside the convent. The value society places upon chastity is reflected in Lucio's tribute, mocking or not, to Isabella as novitiate:

> I hold you as a thing enskied, and sainted,
> By your renouncement an immortal spirit,
> And to be talk'd with in sincerity,
> As with a saint.
> (I.iv.34–37)

Even Lucio's somewhat blasphemous salutation, "Hail, virgin," suggests that through her chastity Isabella mirrors heaven's queen, the Virgin Mary. According to the men in the play, chastity inspires charity, operates like grace and is, in turn, protected by grace. Lucio assures Isabella that "When maiden's sue, / Men give like Gods" (I.iv.80–81). The Duke tells her immediately after she has affirmed the value of her chastity over her brother's life, "The hand that hath made you fair hath made you good; the goodness that is cheap in beauty makes beauty brief in goodness; but grace, being the soul of your complexion, shall keep the body of it ever fair" (III.i.180–84).

Isabella's power, place, and value in society are so determined by her chastity that its forfeiture would constitute for her a form of social and psychological suicide. What is ironic about Isabella's commitment to her chastity is her self-righteous assurance that this commitment is governed exclusively by her religious convictions; what her language subversively reveals is that it is psychically and socially determined. In other words, she is ignorant of how she, as subject, is constituted and subjected by her chastity. Like the critics who attack or defend her, she is unconscious of the imperatives that govern her choice of chastity over life. Furthermore, her discourse reveals an appropriation, however inadvertent or unconscious, of religious authority to valorize the psychological, social, and political imperative of chastity. This appropriation, problematic by itself, becomes increasingly suspect as it resembles the calculated appropriation by the Duke, through his disguise, of holy orders—both scripture and sacraments—to manifest his absolute authority. The match (made on earth, not in heaven) between Isabella and the Duke, illuminates the forms of power through which each controls and is, in turn, controlled.

Confronted by Angelo with the choice between her chastity and her brother's life, Isabella defends her chastity through a series of lexical shifts. She first equates her chastity with her soul as she equates Angelo's term for her sexual submission, the giving of her body, with death: "Sir, believe this, / I had rather give my body than my soul" (II.iv.55–56). Angelo tries to retrieve the meaning of the words she has thus appropriated: "I talk not of your soul; our compell'd sins / Stand more for number than for accoumpt." As he redefines her sexual submission as one of the "compell'd sins," he can then ask, "Might there not be a charity in sin / To save this brother's life?" But his efforts to control the meaning of words fail as Isabella shifts the referent of his term "compell'd sins" from her sexual submission to Angelo's granting of mercy to Claudio. Having thus shifted the referent, she then crosses out the signifier: "no sin at all, but charity." Angelo, having lost this first lexical round, tries once more to force his terms upon Isabella. She, however, again refuses his terms by holding fast to her equation of her chastity with her soul, an equation that allows her to privilege her chastity above her own life as well as her brother's. The equation of her chastity with her soul thus protects the self from any kind of sacrifice: "Then, Isabel, live chaste, and, brother, die; / More than our brother is our chastity" (II.iv.184–85). More than an effective linguistic defense, this equation reveals that Isabella is totally subjectified by her chastity. Her language reveals a psychic construct that does not allow for a distinction between her body and her soul.

In her confrontation with Claudio, Isabella's terms and arguments mirror, at first, those in the debate with Angelo; again, forfeiture of her chastity would constitute forfeiture of her soul. Moreover, according to Isabella, Claudio's willingness to extend his life at the expense of his sister's chastity would damn Claudio's soul as well: "There is a devilish mercy in the judge, / If you'll implore it, that will free your life, / But fetter you till death" (III.i.64–66). Again Isabella declares a willingness to give her life but not her chastity for her brother: "O, were it but my life, / I'd throw it down for your deliverance / As frankly as a pin" (III.i.103–105). Once more this offer is highly ironic in that Isabella's life is her chastity.

When religion fails to authorize the priority of her chastity over her brother's life, Isabella is forced to shift the terms of her discourse from the religious to the social. Angelo's "devilish mercy" thus becomes that which "Would bark your honor from that trunk you bear, / And leave you naked" (III.i.71–72). She further urges Claudio not to respect "six or seven winters" more than "perpetual honor" (lines 75–76). Suddenly, the entire family honor is at stake as well. When Claudio speaks of the priority of honor over life, Isabella commends him: "There spake my brother; there my father's grave / Did utter forth a voice" (lines 85–86). Claudio's unforeseen willingness to forfeit his sister's chastity, on the other hand, forfeits not only the honor of mother and father but Claudio's legitimacy as well:

> What should I think?
> Heaven shield my mother play'd my father fair!
> For such a warped slip of wilderness
> Ne'er issu'd from his blood.
>
> (III.i.139–42)

Isabella's language further makes it clear that her religious concerns merely supplement social and psychological concerns when she confidently declares, "I had rather my brother die by the law than my son should be unlawfully born" (lines 189–91).

Isabella's identification of her self exclusively with her chastity not only precludes mercy and compassion for her brother but also blinds her to her own passion, her desire for revenge against perfidious Angelo. To gratify this desire, Isabella is willing to do to herself what Angelo and Claudio could not persuade her to do: to compromise her chastity and subsequently redefine herself as something distinct from it. To expose Angelo, she denies her chastity by claiming that she forfeited her virginity to save her brother's life (V.i.). Having thus "unmaid" herself, she refashions herself in the compassion she shows Mariana and Angelo as she pleads before the Duke for Angelo's life. What enables Isabella's release from absolute subjection by her chastity is her trust in the authority of the holy father, disguised Vincentio; one form of power modifies another as Isabella becomes less the subject of her chastity and more the subject of the Duke.

The change in Isabella is mirrored by a change in the terms of her discourse. Although the Duke's judgment upon Angelo centers again on the issue of incontinence, Isabella does not ground her defense of Angelo in scripture, as she did in the case of Claudio. She does not, in other words, remind the Duke, as she did Angelo, that "all the souls that were were forfeit once, / And He that might the vantage must have took / Found out the remedy" (II.ii.73–75), because such a comparison of Christ's mercy with the Duke's apparent condemnation of Angelo would call the Duke's power into question, precisely as it did Angelo's. Her appeal for Angelo is, instead, pragmatic and social rather than scriptural:

> His act did not o'ertake his bad intent,
> And must be buried but as an intent
> That perish'd by the way. Thoughts are no subjects,
> Intents but merely thoughts.
>
> (V.i.451–54)

In other words, within the social context of man's law, no real harm was done. However, under God's law, according to the Sermon on the Mount, the scriptural subtext for this play, the thought or intent is indeed subject: "whosoever looketh on a woman to lust after her, hath committed adultery there already in his heart" (Matt. 5:28, Geneva). To this divine law that is not invoked but nevertheless intrudes, Isabella might again say, "'Tis so set down in heaven, but not in earth."

Perhaps what is most significant in her appeal for Angelo's life is her willingness to speak for him at her own expense by accepting some responsibility for his fall: "I partly think / A due sincerity governed his deeds, / Till he did look on me" (V.i.445–47). Looking back on her relationship with Angelo, Isabella seems to sense what the language of the play has revealed all along: a subtle duplicity in the power of her chastity and thus in the role she, as the embodiment and agent of chastity, has played.

Isabella's role is, in fact, morally problematized even before she appears on stage. Escalus first makes her role suspect through his own efforts to soften Angelo by reminding him of his sexuality. The supposition is thus established that if Angelo were to acknowledge his own sexual desires he would be obliged to show mercy to Claudio. Escalus, however, lacks the power to soften the icy hardness of the deputy. The dark subtext of Isabella's qualifications for the task is indicated by the sexually suggestive language that Claudio uses[10] as he defines for Lucio his sister's power:

> Implore her, in my voice, that she make friends
> To the strict deputy; bid herself assay him.
> I have great hope in that; for in her youth
> There is a prone and speechless dialect,
> Such as move men; beside, she hath prosperous art
> When she will play with reason and discourse,
> And well she can persuade.
>
> (I.ii.180–86)

Lucio offers Isabella the challenge: "All hope is gone, / Unless you have the grace by your fair prayer / To soften Angelo." He urges her, "Assay the pow'r you have" and describes the triumphs that result "when maidens sue." This appeal to the power of her chastity is irresistible because chastity is the seat of Isabella's identity and pride. Her response, "I'll see what I can do," expresses a willingness to test her power against Angelo's authority. Even the minor characters understand the power of chastity in this contest; the Provost introduces Isabella to Angelo as "a very virtuous maid, / And to be shortly of a sisterhood, / If not already" (II.ii.20–22). The authority of Isabella's chastity is suggested by the fact that at first Angelo does not trouble himself with an address for her, but as she becomes increasingly forceful, he recognizes her with "Maiden" and then "fair maid."

After some hesitation, Isabella goes about the necessary task of putting Angelo in Claudio's place by telling Angelo, "If he [Claudio] had been as you, and you as he, / You would have slipp'd like him, but he, like you, / Would not have been so stern" (II.ii.64–66). The intent of Isabella's substitution of Angelo for Claudio is to force Angelo to accept the imperative of mercy; the effect of the substitution, however, is to allow Angelo to register his own sexual desire as figured in Claudio. And since Isabella urges mercy for Claudio, who has gratified his sexual desire, Angelo takes hope from the substitution that he too will be shown "mercy." Having displaced Angelo by putting him in Claudio's place, Isabella, in her angry response to Angelo's dismissal, reveals her desire to displace Angelo in yet another way: "I would to heaven I had your potency, / And you were Isabel!" Isabella's desire for a reversal of roles is ironically fulfilled as she gains the potency to grant or withhold mercy to Angelo, who in his desire becomes her supplicant. The shift in focus of the debate from Claudio's transgression to "the proud man, Dress'd in a little brief authority" reveals that what is ultimately at issue here is power.

Through her power, Isabella does indeed soften Angelo. As he succumbs to his sexual desire for her, he becomes "ten times frail" and "soft as [women's] complexions are" (II.iv.128–29). Angelo defines his submission to Isabella's power in language that suggests, through the image of conception, gender reversal:

> When I would pray and think, I think and pray
> To several subjects. Heaven hath my empty words,
> Whilst my invention, hearing not my tongue,
> Anchors on Isabel; heaven in my mouth
> As if I did but only chew his name,
> And in my heart the strong and swelling evil
> Of my conception.
>
> (II.iv.1–7)

The implication that his sexual desire has quite unmanned him is as paradoxical as his conviction that Isabella's chastity arouses his desire. Angelo recognizes both his impotence and his submission: "this virtuous maid / Subdues me quite" (II.ii.184–85). But he clearly does not understand the force of Isabella's chastity—"Can it be / That modesty may more betray our sense / Than woman's lightness?"—and can only define it as the work of the devil (lines 167–69). In fact, the operation of Isabella's chastity involves neither supernatural good nor evil. For this society and for Isabella in particular, chastity is a natural form of power; it is the control over the body and thus for woman the control of the self and the means of resisting the political power of men. The attraction of Isabella's chastity is thus the attraction of power, and as politicians (real and fictional) seem inevitably to discover, power is the great aphrodisiac. What Angelo desires most is power; what he fears is being, as he says, "the very cipher of a function" (II.ii.39). By robbing Isabella of her chastity as he robbed Mariana of her reputation (III.i.227), Angelo hopes to regain his position of male dominance—to transfer, that is, the image of feminine subjugation from himself to Isabella.

The reversal of gender roles resulting from the power of Isabella's chastity is emblematically presented in Isabella's account of the tryst with Angelo:

> He hath a garden circummur'd with brick,
> Whose western side is with a vineyard back'd;
> And to that vineyard is a planched gate,
> That makes his opening with this bigger key.
> This other doth command a little door,
> Which from the vineyard to the garden leads;
> There have I made my promise upon the heavy
> Middle of the night to call upon him.
>
> (IV.i.28–35)

As conventional sexual symbols, the key is masculine or phallic; the lock, gate, and garden are feminine. Yet here Isabella possesses the phallic keys that open the locks of Angelo's enclosed garden; she is the caller, he is the one who passively waits.

Despite the real and obvious victimization of Isabella by Angelo, there is a sense in which Isabella has never been passive, never totally innocent of the power-play inherent in her chastity. Her gracious defense of Angelo, "I partly think / A due sincerity governed his deeds, / Till he did look on me," is misleading because it implies a passivity that her speech acts and the nature of her language belie. Angelo experiences desire not when he looks at her but when she speaks to him. Her opening words to Angelo constitute a linguistic ambiguity that mirrors the moral ambiguity of the role she is to play:

> There is a vice that most I do abhor,
> And most desire should meet the blow of justice;
> For which I would not plead, but that I must;
> For which I must not plead, but that I am
> At war 'twixt will and will not.
>
> (II.ii.29–33)

Her intent is to plead not for a vice but for a brother's life, yet her language reveals her equation of the one with the other and inadvertently invites Angelo to make the same equation and subsequently to see Isabella as compromised by her appeal. Her account of herself as "At war 'twixt will and will not" is also duplicitous in that it reflects a dilemma, a degree of moral confusion, and thus a degree of moral vulnerability. The phrase is particularly misleading for Angelo since one meaning of the word "will" is "sexual desire."[11] Because Isabella's first speech presents her as pleading for a vice and caught between desire and prohibition, it invites Angelo to see her as a mirror image of himself as he succumbs to his desire for her. As her words make his desire known, they, in a sense, actively engender desire: "She speaks, and 'tis / Such sense that my sense breeds with it" (II.ii.141–42). The duplicitous operation of Isabella's language is most conspicuous in the closure of her appeal: "Hark how I'll bribe you. Good my lord, turn back" (lines 144–45).[12] Set on by the sexual implication of these words, Angelo is then immediately taken off when the bribe becomes the true prayers of "fasting maids, whose minds are dedicate / To nothing temporal." Isabella's bribe is yet another reminder of the power of chastity that excites as it threatens and of the ambiguity of the language that presents this chastity. Thus to her farewell, "'Save your honor!" Angelo responds, "From thee: even from thy virtue" (line 161).

Isabella's language serves her no better in the second meeting with Angelo. Her salutation, "I am come to know your pleasure" (II.iv.31), initiates a dialogue of double meanings and conflicting purposes, in which Isabella could say as well as Angelo, "I can speak / Against the thing I say" (lines 59–60). Angelo expresses his frustration with the ambiguity of language, with the breach between the speaker's intent and the listener's comprehension: "Your sense pursues not mine: Either you are ignorant, / Or seem so {craftily}; and that's not good" (lines 74–75). When Angelo confronts Isabella with the trap her own language creates—"You seem'd of late to make the law a tyrant, / And rather prov'd the sliding of your brother / A merriment than a vice"—she acknowledges the burden of her ambiguous language: "O, pardon me, my lord, it oft falls out / To have what we would have, we speak not what we mean" (lines 117–18). Her failure to control language, to speak what she means, elicits an acknowledgment of human frailty and sets for Isabella yet another linguistic trap, her pronouncement that women are "ten times frail" (line 128). Operating within the male discourse that equates virtue with chastity, frailty with incontinence, Angelo springs the linguistic trap:

> I do arrest your words. Be that you are,
> That is a woman; if you be more, you're none;
> If you be one (as you are well express'd
> By all external warrants), show it now,
> By putting on the destin'd livery.
>
> (II.iv.134–38)

Within Angelo's linguistic equation, to be woman is to be frail, to be subject to and subjected by the sexual desires of men. This language Isabella refuses to comprehend: "I have no tongue but one; gentle my lord, / Let me entreat you speak the former language" (lines 139–40).

At this point the duplicitous play of her language has so betrayed Isabella that she sees no choice but to submit to the authority of the holy father, disguised Vincentio, whose words promise to do what hers could not: preserve her chastity and save her brother's life. But the Duke's performance depends upon the willingness of Mariana and Isabella to allow him to appropriate and exploit the power that resides in their chastity. The power of the father-ruler is qualified not only by this appropriation and exploitation but by the deceptions within which his power operates: the bed trick and the false testimony of Isabella against Angelo.

Aware of the moral questions his scheme raises, Vincentio assures Isabella that Mariana will not be compromised: "I do make myself believe that you may most uprighteously do a poor wrong'd lady a merited benefit" (III.i.199–201). But an element of doubt persists in the clause, "I do make myself believe," and this doubt is not erased by the differences between *sponsalia per verba de futuro,* the betrothal of Angelo and Mariana, and *sponsalia per verba de presenti,* the betrothal of Claudio and Juliet.[13] What seems to justify the forfeiture of chastity by one couple but not the other is neither a statutory nor a moral difference but simply the Duke's authority, the law of the father. The absence of any substantial difference in the premarital consummations of the two couples validates Claudio's perspective:

> Thus can the demigod, Authority,
> Make us pay down for our offense by weight
> The words of heaven: on whom it will, it will;
> On whom it will not, so; yet still 'tis just.
> (I.ii.120–23)

Chastity acquires importance as the site or context within which authority manifests itself. Derived from woman's chastity, masculine authority asserts itself by the control of woman's chastity. Angelo, likewise, cannot be "scal'd" and found wanting by the Duke until Isabella, in compliance with the Duke's instructions, is willing to claim that her chastity has been forfeited. Isabella voices to Mariana her reservations about this lie:

> To speak so indirectly I am loath.
> I would say the truth, but to accuse him so,
> That is your part. Yet I am advis'd to do it,
> He says, to veil full purpose.
> (IV.vi.1–4)

Mariana's simple reply, "Be rul'd by him," underscores the contextual, contestatorial relationship between feminine chastity and masculine authority.

Masculine authority depends not only upon control of the chastity of women but upon the male's adherence to chastity as well, for chastity determines power and place for men as well as for women. Restraint comes "from too much liberty" (I.ii.125) as Claudio, Angelo, and Lucio discover. Even the prince is subject to the rule of chastity. In fact, Vincentio's right to rule others is directly associated with his self-governance, his chastity. He assures Friar Thomas, "Believe not that the dribbling dart of love / Can pierce a complete bosom" (I.iii.2–3). Disguised as the friar, Vincentio takes great solace in Escalus's pronouncement that the Duke is "a gentleman of all temperance" (III.ii.237). Because chastity authorizes authority, nothing, not even the perfidy of Angelo, seems to evoke the ire of Vincentio as much as Lucio's depiction of him as incontinent (III.ii.114–88). The Duke's anger over Lucio's slander threatens for a moment the comic resolution of the play as the Duke twice pronounces the death sentence upon Lucio: "Let him be whipt and hang'd" (V.i.513). The conventions of comedy prevail, however, as the Duke reduces Lucio's sentence from death to marriage.

Shakespeare's adherence to the conventions of comedy goes too far, according to many critics,[14] in the proposal of marriage by the Duke to Isabella. This proposal is not only precipitous but contextually problematic, for it is spoken to one who has already chosen to be a bride of Christ and spoken within the Duke's display of absolute authority. The Duke's proposal is precipitous because the dramatist is trapped by the chastity essential to the characterization of the Duke. One whose "complete bosom" is safe from "the dribbling dart of love," whose chastity allows him to wear the robes of a holy friar, can hardly acknowledge that he has fallen in love. His proposal of marriage must, likewise, be couched not in terms of the fulfillment of his desire but as a benefit to Isabella: "I have a motion much imports your good" (V.i.535). Darryl Gless argues that a Protestant audience would see the offer of chaste marriage to the Duke as preferable to the celibacy of the convent and thus something that, indeed, imports Isabella's good.[15] This argument is, of course, predicated on the dubious assumption that the audience (uniformly reconciled to Protestantism) would share the Duke's perspective, not Isabella's, or would not even register a difference in the perspectives of these two characters.

If the Duke's desire is written out as Isabella's "good" is written in, wherein lies the good of this match for the Duke? Perhaps the answer lies in the terms of his offer. Somewhat inept at asking for anything, he begins with the wrong, but nevertheless telling, terms: "Give me your hand, and say you will be mine" (line 492). He then corrects his egocentric orientation and authoritarian language:

> I have a motion much imports your good,
> Whereto if you'll a willing ear incline,
> What's mine is yours, and what is yours is mine.
> (V.i.535–37)

What the Duke has to offer in this exchange is his authority, his power; what Isabel has to offer is her autonomy, forfeited as she gives her body in marriage. At first glance the Duke's terms of exchange seem an ideal resolution of the power conflict between masculine authority and feminine chastity. But such an offer coming from a prince whose identity is his absolute authority can hardly be taken literally. Furthermore, since marriage institutionalizes the authority of the husband over the wife, the Duke, in fact, has everything to gain and nothing to lose through Isabella's acceptance. Marriage is thus not only the Duke's solution to all forms of sexual liberty but also his solution to the resistance against patriarchy inherent in Isabel's sexual renunciation. By making Isabella his chaste wife, the Duke appropriates the power of her chastity and closes off the one avenue of her resistance to masculine authority. Her probation complete, he takes this prospective bride of Christ as his own in the ultimate act of appropriation that asserts his power as indeed "like pow'r divine" (V.i.369).

To the Duke's twice-offered proposal of marriage, Isabella responds with a perfect silence that challenges the interpretive skills of readers and directors alike. Isabella's silence is usually interpreted in performances as happy compliance and gratitude. Smiling and taking the hand of the Duke, she speaks with her body a submission to marriage in keeping with the conventions of comedy and the ideology of patriarchy. To stage Isabella's silence in this manner, however, is to see it through the Duke's eyes; woman's silence is her submission to the "natural," patriarchal ordering of things. Marcia Riefer offers a different gendered reading of Isabella's silence: "She remains speechless, a baffled actress who has run out of lines. The gradual loss of her personal voice during the course of the play has become, finally, a literal loss of voice. In this sense, *Measure for Measure* is Isabella's tragedy. Like Lavinia in *Titus Andronicus* the eloquent Isabella is left with no tongue."[16]

To these readings of Isabella's silence as either cheerful compliance or tragic defeat, I wish to offer two alternative interpretations. The first is that Isabella does not lose, but only holds, her tongue; she is not silenced but, instead, chooses silence as a form of resistance to the patriarchal authority and to the male discourse within which this authority operates.[17] In her silence to the Duke's proposal, Isabella thus adheres to the rules of the sisters of St. Clare: she shows her face but remains silent, perhaps with the key to the convent still in her pocket.

Appealing as this reading of Isabella's silence might have been to recusant Catholics in Shakespeare's audience or might be to feminist readers today, it is, perhaps, improbable, given that the silence occurs within the context of the Duke's intimidating display of power. But the proposal, itself, attests, paradoxically, to the fact that the Duke's power requires a supplement. His proposal, "What's mine is yours" has validity as an abbreviated and thus coded acknowledgment that can be decoded: "My sexuality and thus my identity as patriarch is yours to validate by your affirmation of your sexuality through your acceptance of me as your husband." Isabella's sexual renunciation, a form of self-castration, would thus, if perpetuated, constitute a form of castration for the Duke as well. Given the significance of Isabella's acceptance of the Duke, the freedom to refuse him seems highly improbable. But the absence of choice for Isabella does not constitute for her the absence of power; the power of chastity operates through and upon the Duke and Isabella alike. The play's depiction of the relationship of the Duke's authority and Isabella's chastity thus confirms Foucault's assertion that

> Power is employed or exercised through a net-like organisation. And not only do individuals circulate between its threads; they are always in the position of simultaneously undergoing and exercising this power. They are not only its inert or consenting target; they are always also the elements of its articulation. In other words, individuals are the vehicles of power, not its points of application.[18]

The Duke is correct in the sense that "What's yours is mine and what's mine is yours" already and inevitably, for authority privileges chastity and depends in turn upon chastity to authorize authority. Whether or not Isabella is free to keep the convent key, she clearly holds the Duke's "key" in her pocket.

Notes

1. All quotations are from *The Riverside Shakespeare,* ed. G. Blakemore Evans (Boston: Houghton Mifflin, 1974).

2. Marcia Riefer, " 'Instruments of Some More Mightier Member': The Constriction of Female Power in *Measure for Measure*" *SQ* 35 (1984): 157–69, provides a brief survey of the conflicting responses to Isabella. For a more detailed survey, see George L. Geckle, "Shakespeare's Isabella," *SQ* 22 (1971):163–68. In defense of Isabella, Raymond Wilson Chambers (*Man's Unconquerable Mind* [London: Jonathan Cape, 1939], p. 288) asserts that "Christianity could never have lived through its first three hundred years of persecution, if its ranks had not been stiffened by men and women who never hesitated in the choice between righteousness and the ties to their kinsfolk." Chambers argues that Isabella's adherence to her chastity must be seen in light of her identity as a votarist of St. Clare: "Whether she remains in the Convent or no, one who is contemplating such a life can no more be expected to sell herself into mortal sin, than a good soldier can be expected to sell a stronghold entrusted to him" (p. 292). J. W. Lever refutes Chambers by arguing that Isabella's stance "is occasioned by no true principle. If lay heroines in previous versions of the story were commended for setting aside the thought of shame in order to save a brother's or a husband's life, the novice of a spiritual order might also overcome the fear of disgrace in the world's eyes and manifest true grace by a sacrifice made in self-oblivious charity. Chastity was essentially a condition of the spirit; to see it in merely physical terms was to reduce the concept to a mere pagan scruple" (Introduction to the Arden Edition of *Measure for Measure* [London: Methuen, 1965], p. lxxviii).

3. Riefer, p. 158.

4. Riefer, pp. 158, 161–62.

5. Madeleine Doran, *The Endeavors of Art* (Madison: Univ. of Wisconsin Press, 1954), pp. 368–69.

6. Angelo's equation reverses, but with the same sophistry, Parolles's equation of virginity with suicide: "He that hangs himself is a virgin; virginity murthers itself, and should be buried in highways out of all sanctified limit, as a desperate offendress against nature" (*All's Well,* I.i.138–41).

7. Quoted from *A New Variorum Edition of Shakespeare: Measure for Measure,* ed. Mark Eccles (New York: Modern Language Association, 1980), p. 109.

8. Marilyn L. Williamson, *The Patriarchy of Shakespeare's Comedies* (Detroit: Wayne State Univ. Press, 1986), pp. 81–99.

9. Riefer, p. 168.

10. David Lloyd Stevenson contends that Claudio "thinks that Angelo's liability to Isabella's attractions as a woman, to the 'prone and speechless dialect' in 'her youth,' to the seductive, feminine qualities he understands so well and has already succumbed to in Juliet, may save his life" (*The Achievement of Shakespeare's* "Measure for Measure" [Ithaca: Cornell Univ. Press, 1966], p. 38).

11. Shakespeare's frequent play on the word "will" is perhaps most evident in the sonnets. See, for example, Joel Fineman, *Shakespeare's Perjured Eye* (Berkeley: Univ. of California Press, 1986), pp. 293–94.

12. Harold C. Goddard, *The Meaning of Shakespeare* (Chicago: Univ. of Chicago Press, 1951), p. 439, describes Isabella's use of "bribe" as "one of those single words on which worlds turn that Shakespeare was growing steadily more fond of." Harriett Hawkins points out that Isabella's speech in her debates with Angelo is "charged with an erotic power that might well envoke a gleam in the eye of the most depraved marquis in the audience, to say nothing of a saint-turned-sensualist like Angelo" (" 'The Devil's Party': Virtues and Vices in Measure for Measure," *ShS* 31 [1978]:107).

13. For a discussion of the two forms of "spousals," see Lever, pp. liii–liv and lxv; also, Darryl F. Gless, *"Measure for Measure," the Law and the Convent* (Princeton: Princeton Univ. Press, 1970), pp. 179–80, 200–201, and 234–35. Gless (p. 200) cites other studies on the subject: Ernest Schanzer, "The Marriage-Contracts in *Measure for Measure,*" *ShS* 13 (1960): 81–89; S. Nagarajan, "*Measure for Measure* and Elizabethan Betrothals," *SQ* 14 (1963): 115–19; and J. Birje-Patil, "Marriage Contracts in Shakespeare's *Measure for Measure,*" *ShakS* 5 (1969):106–11.

14. Most recently, Williamson, pp. 104–105, and Joseph H. Summers, *Dreams of Love and Power* (Oxford: Clarendon Press, 1984), p. 68.

15. Seeing the play as a reflection of the Protestant antimonastic tradition, Gless argues that Isabella's acceptance of the Duke's proposal frees her from "the sterile bondage" of the convent and marks "her entry into a world governed by fruitful, married love" (p. 212).

16. Riefer, p. 167.

17. Williamson supports this interpretation, arguing that "Isabella's silence may be a compound of shock and defiance, and we have other examples in Iago and Hieronimo, where silence after eloquence may signify not acquiescence, but defiance of an urgent authority" (p. 104).

18. Michael Foucault, *Power / Knowledge: Selected Interviews and Other Writings 1972–1977* ed. and trans. Colin Gordon et al. (New York: Pantheon, 1980), p. 98. Although Williamson (p. 11) quotes this passage from Foucault in her introduction, she says nothing in her discussion of *Measure for Measure* about the Duke's "undergoing" or submission to power, but virtually everything about his exercise of power; much, likewise, about Isabella as a point of power's application, but nothing about her as an agent of power.

False Immortality in *Measure for Measure*: Comic Means, Tragic Ends

ROBERT N. WATSON

> All tragedies are finished by a death,
> All comedies are ended by a marriage;
> The future states of both are left to faith,
> For authors fear description might disparage
> The worlds to come of both. . . .
>
> *Don Juan,* Canto 3, stanza 9

Ending with marriage emphasizes the survival of the type through procreation; ending with death emphasizes the extinction of the individual creature. In *Measure for Measure* Shakespeare stops short of explicitly disparaging both "worlds to come," but the abrupt and formulaic comic ending encourages a suspicion that the aftermath of marriage and death alike is merely a biological process with no regard for human consciousness. To expand on Horace Walpole's aphoristic version of the genre distinction, "the world is a comedy to those that think" about the persistent traits of their species, "a tragedy to those that feel" their own mortality and that of the individual things they love. *Measure for Measure* is, from this perspective, a tragicomedy.[1] The play certainly portrays and extols the orderly perpetuation of human life, human society, and human virtue. Yet it also takes the three figurations of immortality to which people most commonly cling—the hope for genetic and spiritual heirs, the hope for divine salvation, and the hope for undying fame and honor—and undermines our faith in each of them, even as it undermines our faith in the comic formula as a whole by the unsatisfying impositions of marriage that conclude this death-filled play. Which is the means, and which the end, between the perpetuation of the species and the experience of individual life? Of these comic and tragic concerns, which one comprises sufficient meaning to expose its counterpart as merely an arbitrary ending? The first part of this essay will offer an abbreviated summary of the play's implicit comic argument for the systematic reproduction of the human race. A longer second part will argue, less conventionally, that the play persistently subverts

Reprinted by permission of *Shakespeare Quarterly.*

the comic promises of immortality, encouraging instead a suspicion that we are each tragically betrayed by the supposedly benevolent biological and political systems to which God has abandoned His human offspring.

COMEDY: THE MORAL AND MORALS OF *MEASURE FOR MEASURE*

Measure for Measure comes closer than any other Shakespeare play to having a schematic, articulable moral. Its primary topic is sexuality, and its primary argument is that neither individuals nor societies can thrive unless license and repression keep each other in balance. Naturally critics are reluctant to admit that sexual morality is what the play is about, because that is what it *seems* to be about.[2] But in this case it may pay to surrender our ingenuity in the face of the obvious. The polar outposts of this play are brothels and convents, its characters are most vivid for their prudery and lechery, and its two crucial actions are bouts of sexual intercourse, one a premarital impregnation, the other a form of attempted rape. From beginning to end, the dominant motive is the need to convert lustful fornication into fruitful married sexuality. Vienna's Sigmund Freud defined as perversion any sexual activity not primarily directed toward heterosexual genital intercourse; Shakespeare's Vienna defines as treason any such intercourse not directed toward legitimate procreation. For the individual, marriage becomes—as in the patristic commonplaces—a way of reconciling unruly sexual desire with necessary sexual restraint; for the state, it becomes a way of maintaining the substance and order of the social fabric. Though *Measure for Measure* is notorious for its strayings from comic sentiment, it thus builds toward the typical comic conclusion far more forcefully and logically than most comedies: by the end, marriage becomes an overdetermined resolution.

Through a series of variations, the thematic argument remains remarkably consistent. The Duke of Vienna—evidently believing that fornication, which creates life, however unlawfully, must be preferable to execution, which destroys life, however lawfully—has allowed sexual license to corrupt his city. This is an understandable error in a humane ruler, all the more understandable to Shakespeare's audience, who, in 1604, were watching the play in a theatre that had again been closed by epidemic plague the previous year, in a city that had lost close to a quarter of its population to the plague over the preceding decade. So, despite some bad harvests in the 1590s and some complaints about the tendency of young people to procreate before they were ready to support a family,[3] population explosion was hardly to be feared; on the contrary, a common measure of a state's health was the growth of its population. Moreover, as the opening of the second scene reminds us, city-states such as Vienna were perpetually on the brink of war, with its voracious appetite for what Falstaff calls "food for powder, mortal men." So there would have been some sociological force to Lucio's warning that Angelo's more severe policy might "unpeople the province," an inverted reminder of the biblical injunction to "Be fruitful and multiply" that Renaissance preachers so often emphasized. Even Puritan figures such as Phillip Stubbes—who laments that "untill every one hath two or three Bastardes a peece, they esteeme him no man" and furiously condemns anyone who argues that "Otherwyse the World wold become barren"—stresses the obligation to multiply *within* marriage and concludes (like Duke Vincentio), "let all men that have put away their honest wyves be forced to take them again, and abandon all whores, or els to taste of the law."[4]

The Duke's problem is that, though his former course may have been understandable, it has not been understood. Lucio says that before the Duke "would have hanged a man for the getting a hundred bastards, he would have paid for the nursing a thousand. He had some feeling of the sport; he knew the service; and that instructed him to mercy" (3.2.113–17). This is intolerable for the Duke, for both the motives and the numbers it claims to reveal. It presents the problem as a disease spreading outward from the Duke's unruly body to his entire body politic rather than as an enlightened choice for healthy growth. It also suggests the threatening multiplication of the problem in a world where even one bastard child is one too many: the villains of Jacobean tragedy are often illegitimate children who necessarily attack the social order that excludes them. So the Duke stages a play for his city, as Shakespeare does for his, an averted tragedy in which all aberrations from married procreation become collaborations with death.

Angelo applies a simplistic system of accounting to this political commodity, the legitimate son; the Duke's calculations are more complex and seemingly humane but perhaps ultimately more cynical as well. According to Angelo, the making of a counterfeit dollar, the forging of that aspect of the state's wealth, is a theft equivalent to the stealing of a real dollar:

> It were as good
> To pardon him that hath from nature stolen
> A man already made, as to remit
> Their saucy sweetness that do coin heaven's image
> In stamps that are forbid. 'Tis all as easy
> Falsely to take away a life true made,
> As to put mettle in restrained means
> To make a false one.
>
> (2.4.42–49)[5]

The comparison is typical of Angelo in being too cold and abstract to be wholly convincing, but given the trends Lucio's speech reveals (however slanderously and hyperbolically), the exchange rate has shifted disastrously, devaluing legitimacy against desire. The Duke is thus obliged to intervene with a temporary didactic choice of order over passion, a morally instructive bit of tragicomic theatre. The laxity of the Duke's own reign leads directly to the excessive restraint promised by Angelo. When Lucio asks the manacled Claudio, "Whence comes this restraint," Claudio replies, "From too much liberty, my Lucio. Liberty, / As surfeit, is the father of much fast; / So every scope by the immoderate use / Turns to restraint" (1.2.116–20). His individual experience is significantly parallel to that of the state, not just the result of it.

Angelo argues that Isabella should be willing to commit fornication in order to save Claudio's life, since she has implicitly asserted that Claudio's fornication was not enough of an evil to merit death: measure for measure. This conundrum allows Shakespeare to offer further proof that unlimited fornication is not the right cure for mortality, because this supposed antidote for Claudio turns out to be poison instead. When Angelo believes he has enjoyed Isabella's body, he orders that the execution be expedited by a few hours. In terms of the moral argument of the play, her supposed yielding only replicates Claudio's crime and therefore can only accelerate his punishment. The real cure, the Duke and his creator seem to suggest, is marriage, and the substitution of Mariana in the bed allows the Duke to achieve the maximum possible number of living and legitimate Viennese.

Sex and death were conventionally associated in the Renaissance, of course, but (as in its emphasis on venereal disease) *Measure for Measure* uses that association in a particularly tendentious way, Lucio's final words—"Marrying a punk, my lord, is pressing to death, / Whipping, and hanging" (5.1.520–21)—are merely the perverse final echo of a thematic association sounded throughout the play. The unholy alliance between these supposed mighty opposites—fornication and repression, conception and execution—surfaces again when the Duke assigns Pompey the bawd to work for Abhorson the executioner. The resulting series of puns and arguments alerts us to the fundamental compatibility of these two professions, even to their moral equivalence. Both men object to the partnership, but Pompey soon concedes, "I have been an unlawful bawd time out of mind, but yet I will be content to be a lawful hangman. I would be glad to receive some instruction from my fellow-partner" (4.2.14–17). The Provost insists that they "weigh equally" in any ethical scale, they promise mutual professional courtesy, and Pompey eventually discovers "many of [his] old customers" from the brothel require his new services at the jail (4.3.1–4). The pun lurking in Abhorson's elided name neatly encapsulates the pattern: the executioner is evidently an abhorred whoreson. Promiscuity again appears to generate its own punishment; the executioner has been created by the fornicator.

If excessive liberty leads to excessive restraint, as the appointment of Angelo demonstrates, then excessive restraint leads to excessive liberty, as the corruption of Angelo demonstrates. The case of Isabella reinforces the same ideas more subtly: that discipline can lead to perversion, that severe rectitude reflects a battle against dangerously powerful appetites and provokes repressed sensuality into a guerrilla war against outward propriety. Angelo insists that Isabella's virgin modesty is what paradoxically inspires his lust; again, extraordinary self-restraint—hers as well as his own—becomes the provocation to an extraordinary self-indulgence. The erotics of Isabella's renunciation could hardly be more lurid:

> . . . were I under the terms of death,
> Th'impression of keen whips I'd wear as rubies,
> And strip myself to death as to a bed
> That longing have been sick for, ere I'd yield
> My body up to shame.
>
> (2.4.100–4)

The erotic undertones of religious flagellation throughout *Measure for Measure,* the ways mortification of the flesh becomes gratification instead, have been thoroughly documented.[6] Furthermore, the death wish Isabella here expresses becomes extended by her, as by Angelo, to virtually everyone: "What a merit were it in death to take this poor maid {Mariana} from the world! What corruption in this life, that it will let this man {Angelo} live!" (3.1.231–33). Her advice to the lovelorn is invariably execution, Robespierre ghostwriting for Ann Landers. The powerful and persistent death wish Angelo and Isabella express, towards themselves and towards others, is almost indistinguishable from their peculiar sexual appetites.

The fate of Isabella and Claudio as a family further emphasizes the deadly alliance of the two extremes, as the sister faces genetic extinction through her implied sexual repression, and the brother faces execution for an excess of sexual liberty. The ascetic and libertine tendencies (though each rather sympathetically represented in this pair) appear as a two-edged sword cutting down a family tree. So *Measure for Measure* is a tragicomedy not only because a convincing threat of barrenness or death appears before sexual desire resolves itself into marriage but also because the play exposes the potentially deadly attributes of sexuality itself. Both fornication and its extreme repression are wastrel expenditures of the bodies natural and politic.

Tragedy: Denying the Denial of Death

Within this rather commonplace moral admonition about physical, social, and psychological decadence, Shakespeare develops a potentially heretical, even blasphemous, meditation about the fate of the human individual. *Measure for Measure* evokes a tragic resistance to comic solutions, not only by emphasizing the destructive potential of sexuality but also by widening our perspective on its creative potential. Valuing procreation as a contribution to demographics and the ecological balance, rather than as individual assertion and gratification, may not sound especially sinister. But the anti-Malthusian conclusion that all is well because the population of Vienna keeps growing does not really answer the fears roused by the various threats of execution and particularly by Claudio's own confused but eloquent terror of death. Claudio evidently finds no consolation in the disguised Duke's argument that, from the standpoint of atomistic philosophy, he really has no self to lose (3.1.19–21); nor is he reconciled to his fate by the idea that he has fathered a child to take his place, which should be thoroughly consoling if genetic survival were truly felt to be an adequate compensation for individual death. As in the more vivid instance of Macbeth, a resolution that is satisfactory for the purposes of the state may not eradicate our terrifying vision of the individual will and consciousness obliterated by nature and mortality.

The comic triumph here belongs not to love or to the hero but instead to a version of what Michel Foucault called "bio-power": specifically, the need of the state, under the guise of personalized benevolence, simply to keep the procreative machine running. Indeed, *Measure for Measure* refutes Foucault's claim that this concern was an invention of the eighteenth century, since the ending of this Jacobean play could be trenchantly described in exactly the terms Foucault used to describe a supposedly post-Enlightenment mode of government: "It is no longer a matter of bringing death into play in the field of sovereignty, but of distributing the living in the domain of value and utility."[7] In *Measure for Measure* domestic bliss is exposed as a euphemism for the domestication of the human animal; it is not only bawds (as Elbow supposes) who "buy and sell men and women like beasts" (3.2.2). Men have commonly blamed women for such Circean transformations, but that is hardly surprising, since (through the figure of Eve) men have long blamed women (who issue mortal bodies and rouse decadent lusts) for death itself. But even Angelo recognizes that Isabella is not really a "tempter" culpable for his own descent into "carrion"; that process is merely the dark side of biology (2.2.162–68). The comic dance of marriage is, measure for measure, also a Dance of Death, and the disguised ruler in the black cowl may carry a sickle as well as a pardon. The state has reached an accommodation with the jealous god Death, and as we play out our biological roles, each of us becomes a propitiary sacrifice. No wonder statecraft is so oddly associated with pregnancy in Vienna (e.g. 1.1.11, 4.4.18). Against the ongoing decimations of the Grim Reaper, *Measure for Measure* pits a Duke who might be called the Grim Breeder, hardly more appealing in his ways of creating people than the Reaper is in destroying them. Vienna is left without eternals, with only maternals and paternals to take their place.

While thus questioning the adequacy of procreation as a response to human mortality, *Measure for Measure* also subjects honor and piety to similarly cynical psychological and political perspectives. These virtues, and the hopes commonly attached to them, stand exposed in Freudian and Machiavellian ways as merely illusory forms of personal redemption. This devastating interrogation of all the "heroic" modes in which individuals attempt to perpetuate their individuality brings me, at last, to my declared main topic: false immortality. *Measure for Measure* resists its genre by undermining the three modes in which comedy usually promises immortality—fame, salvation, and procreation—and by replacing them with an emphasis on the destruction of the individual, an emphasis that is typical of tragedy. Whether or not we accept the pseudo-biographical impression that Shakespeare here vandalizes his own comic form in deference to the great tragedies he had recently begun to write, we can hardly deny the inadequacies of the comic resolution of *Measure for Measure,* the darkness it fails to dispel. It is tragicomic not only because death is strongly present prior to the resolution but, more crucially, because mortality remains imperfectly refuted at the center of that resolution.

"One can see *Measure for Measure* as a play that opens with the law being invoked to punish fornication by death and that closes with the law being utilized to punish fornication by marriage."[8] This witty observation cuts deep; it opens for inspection the common discomfort with the "comic resolution" of *Measure for Measure:* two marriages tainted by unwilling and unenviable bridegrooms, the other two compromised by their peculiar brides, one arguably reluctant and still in a nun's habit, the other newly out of jail and barely back on her feet after childbirth. Given the fact that even the most promising marriages in Shakespeare's plays often teeter on the brink of tragic collapse, we can hardly foresee great good coming of all these awkward alliances, except in tidying up the bookkeeping of the Viennese bureaucracy.

And yet it is not so cynical or unreasonable for a government to treat marriage as merely another, preferable instrument for controlling desire—which is one plausible definition of punishment. From the normal perspective of the romantic individual or of romantic comedy, the absence of choice and love in such matchmaking may be disturbing, but from the perspective of the state, choice and love are subordinate values. The state cannot finally concern itself with the motivation behind marriage any more than it can condemn citizens for unacted evil desires: "Thoughts are no subjects," Isabella tells the Duke, "Intents, but merely thoughts" (5.1.451–52). The opening lines of the play invite us to recognize what follows as a dramatized treatise on the properties of government, and that is largely what we get. But by presenting that treatise in the form of an impassioned human story, Shakespeare creates a peculiar disturbance in our fantasies of personal significance. Amid the threats of death to characters in this play, which fit it to most definitions of tragicomedy, lurks a threat to the spectators' strategies of immortality, a threat to reveal supposedly transcendent values as mere instruments of state, to reveal the hope for individual survival as a hollow fantasy subserving the survival instincts of the body politic.

The solution is thus achieved only in sociological terms. The resurrection of Claudio and the pardons for Angelo and Barnardine are political tricks that only defer the question of mortality. Claudio was told that Angelo's ill-won pardon would gain him merely "six or seven winters" of sickly life; will the Duke's nobler pardon gain him more? The one gesture toward a truly eternal solution—Isabella's religious vocation—apparently yields to the demands of dynastic survival, and the play does not audibly mourn for it. The essence of the Duke's final triumph (and Shakespeare's comic solution) is marriage—not as individual fulfillment but as a practical, worldly, even legalistic solution to the problem of maintaining the size of the Viennese population, and to the no-more-romantic problem of controlling illegitimacy and venereal disease among the city's many wayward citizens. The question of personal annihilation might thus be neatly avoided—except that the play raises it, indirectly but repeatedly. The focus on government appears to offer some respite from the question of individual death, but that anxiety nonetheless finds ways to break through to the surface.

Measure for Measure starts with the Duke fashioning Angelo into a son and heir to the throne. The diction is relentlessly suggestive:

> I say, bid come before us Angelo.
> What figure of us, think you, he will bear?
> For you must know, we have with special soul
> Elected him our absence to supply;
> Lent him our terror, drest him with our love,
> And given his deputation all the organs
> Of our own power.
>
> (1.1.15–21)

The Duke intends thus to make Angelo "at full ourself." Angelo responds to the suggestion that he is to "bear a figure" of his predecessor when, later in the scene, he expresses his anxiety about having "so great a figure . . . stamp'd upon" him (1.1.49–50); in the second act of the play, he will use the same coining metaphor to refer to procreation (2.4.45). The Duke's implicit fantasy of parthenogenesis is common in the struggle of Shakespeare's tragically misguided men (such as Coriolanus and Leontes) against their own mortality.[9] For them to acknowledge either the means or the need to procreate would be to confess the mortally fallen nature of their bodies. Yet to be mere coins in some usurious biological economy can hardly satisfy the desire for transcendent personal significance. The Duke's introductory remarks make the practices of heaven in this regard seem suspiciously congruent with those of nature:

> Heaven doth with us as we with torches do,
> Not light them for themselves; for if our virtues
> Did not go forth of us, 'twere all alike
> As if we had them not. Spirits are not finely touch'd
> But to fine issues; nor nature never lends
> The smallest scruple of her excellence

> But, like a thrifty goddess, she determines
> Herself the glory of a creditor,
> Both thanks and use.
>
> (1.1.32–40)

"Thanks but no thanks" might be the reply of the heroic actor cast as a mere torchbearer. Great creating nature demands back ashes for ashes and dust for dust, and a few pounds more than what we started with. Ben Jonson's epitaph "On My First Son" demonstrates that this loan-shark aspect of God could elicit bitterness, despite all the standard gestures of submission to divine will. When Gertrude remarries so hastily, Hamlet remarks no less bitterly on the way "thrift" has been valued over grief for his dead father. Death tenaciously shadows the procreative process, and the efficiency of the biological economy is an insult to the human spirit, especially when a Ben Jonson is asked to accept the loss of a Ben Jonson, a Hamlet the loss of a Hamlet.[10]

By staging his own miraculous return, in the manner of the disguised-ruler plot so popular on the early Jacobean stage, the Duke fulfills another fantasy familiar from Elizabethan drama: namely, the return of a father from death (or at least from a great distance or great poverty) to remedy the wrongs of the prodigal son who has forgotten him and his ways. King Hamlet and King Lear are grim variations on this theme. The persistent appeal of such stories may reside in their implicit denial of death, in the fantastic defeat of the implacable process whereby children replace rather than reproduce their parents. In the case of *Measure for Measure,* the Duke's purpose in this arrangement is twofold and will be served only to the extent that Angelo stumbles in the footsteps of his paternalistic patron. First, the Duke must show his citizens the dangers of provoking excessive restraint by their false equation of life with mere sensual indulgence. Second, he must prove that even an apparently pure embodiment of his moral law makes a very poor substitute for the Duke's own wit and kindness, for the individual humanity that shines redeemingly even through his disguise. The Duke thus entangles himself in a contradiction: trying to prove to his citizens that replacing oneself procreatively is more important than indulging selfish desires, yet aspiring to do so in a way that will prove himself irreplaceable. Furthermore, the Duke's effort to end illegitimacy in Vienna involves making Angelo, in one sense, the Duke's own bastard son. Angelo's failure as a dynastic heir, precisely by the way it bolsters the Duke's claim to lasting political glory, ruins the Duke's figurative claim to procreative survival.

His lack of a true heir is what the Duke must therefore repair at the end by marrying Isabella. He has evidently viewed his entire citizenry as his figurative children, himself as "the father of their idle dream" (4.1.64)—a complaint about the vulnerability of his fame that links it suggestively to his other immortalizing ploys as a figurative father, a kind of playwright, and a feigned holy "father" (as he is repeatedly called in his disguise). The ending of the play suggests, however, that neither this paternalistic stratgem with Angelo, nor the growth of Vienna's population, nor even his fame-winning masterstrokes in the theatricalized arts of state can adequately substitute for a fruitful marriage. In steering his subjects toward matrimony, the Duke discovers not only a worthy spouse but also the fact of his own mortality that obliges him, too, to marry. If there is any validity to the argument that *Measure for Measure* was written partly in tribute to the accession of King James, it would make sense for the play to contain some endorsement of a monarch who could offer a lineal successor (such as Prince Henry) rather than merely an appointive one, some transformation of the literary legacy that had worshipped a Virgin Queen (though of course Shakespeare would hardly wish to suggest that James's rather indirect accession resembled Angelo's). This is the same promise held out by the mirror portent in *Macbeth:* that James's royal identity will "stretch out to th' crack of doom" (4.1.117), will survive lineally until the Last Judgment revives James himself. Power was intimately bound up with paternity for James,[11] and his legacy to his son Henry was the *Basilikon Doron,* a text on the proper management of a kingdom. The Duke's obsessively paternalistic play, from its very first lines, presents itself as this sort of mixed representation of authority; but power, fatherhood, and authorship all fall short of assuring personal immortality.

The Duke pursues another well-worn path toward immortality in his quest for fame, a category in which I include the putative immortalities of honor and of art. He spreads news of his death (4.2.200) and returns (like Tom Sawyer) to study the reactions, but what he discovers is hardly the canonization he had hoped for. Of course, the Duke claims to be indifferent to fame, even to dislike it:

> I'll privily away. I love the people,
> But do not like to stage me to their eyes:
> Though it do well, I do not relish well
> Their loud applause and *Aves* vehement;
> Nor do I think the man of safe discretion
> That does affect it.
>
> (1.1.67–72)

He doth protest too much, methinks. His nagging resentment of Lucio's casual slanders suggests he cares very much about his audience and about his reviews (the excellent BBC-TV "Shakespeare Plays" production emphasizes this trait when the Duke triumphantly stages himself to the people's eyes in the final scene). He is vainly determined to convince Lucio what a splendid man the Duke actually is, he soliloquizes bitterly about the injuries that await even the most carefully built public reputation, and he promptly begins fishing shamelessly for compliments from Escalus (3.2.137–45, 179–82, 254–75, 224–31). Though it might be something King James would be pleased to hear,[12] the Duke's assertion that "slandering a prince" deserves "pressing to death, / Whipping, and hanging" (5.1.520–21) seems revealingly severe.

When he reappears as himself at the start of the fifth act, the Duke seems to mock his own quest for a glorious place in future Mirrors for Magistrates. He extols Angelo's reign, which he intends soon to expose as mortally corrupt, with the same equivocal puns on "character" and uneasy suggestions of coining used earlier to conflate the immortalities of honor, art, and progeny: Angelo's conduct in office "deserves with characters of brass / A forted residence 'gainst the tooth of time / And razure of oblivion" (5.1.12–14). The Duke's irony presses uncomfortably on Shakespeare's earlier explorations of the quest for immortality in *Love's Labor's Lost* and the sonnets. The facts of fallen flesh and blood have already overthrown this immortalizing project before time and nature can even begin to erode gilded monuments.

The Duke's disguise and return also keep the doctrine of the monarch's two bodies active in the minds of the audience: "The Duke's in us," Escalus announces authoritatively to his disguised and unrecognized sovereign (5.1.293). In a play so concerned with the paradoxical quest for personal immortality, this doctrinal echo (like Hamlet's "the body is with the King . . ." at 4.2.27–30) invites our attention but finally offers no reassurance. When Angelo's corruption of the law renders him instant "carrion" (2.2.167), it may serve to warn the Duke against relying on his official role to immortalize him in any meaningful way. The royal self is hardly the metal stamp of divine justice envisioned earlier; it becomes indistinguishable from the sinful flesh. Angelo describes Isabella as "deflower'd . . . by an eminent body, that enforc'd / The law against it!" (4.4.19–21). This phallic body politic becomes a source of corruption and death, rather than symbolic immortality, to its citizens.

The Duke's immortal longings also lead him to experiment with piety, with the abjuration of the things of this world in hope of a place in the next. There are repeated suggestions that the Duke is so inclined, ranging from his claim to have always "lov'd the life remov'd" (1.3.8), to his request for reassurance of his reputation for preferring contemplation over pleasure (3.2.224–31), to the peculiar evidence that he has long served as a holy confessor to Mariana (4.1.8–9, 5.1.524). But he uses his monkish traits finally as a ploy to effect the civil education and earthly salvation of Claudio and to lure Isabella away from her own such choice, away from her betrothal to Christ and into his own earthly marital embrace. Furthermore, the essentially hollow tone and ulterior motivation of his monkish lessons to Claudio serve to undermine the entire belief-system—both onstage and off—that views death as a blessing. Within the play-world these all prove to be ploys of state, designed to foster stability or at least dynamic equilibrium.

The Duke's speech to Claudio at the start of the third act is essentially a compilation of *contemptus mundi* and *ars moriendi* commonplaces. These commonplaces are marked as clichés by their role in a theatrical performance (Duke as monk) that aims at civic reform through pietistic deception, rather than at any pious conversion that would mitigate the state's punitive power. It is clear that the Duke is not, in reality, scornful of this world and this life; his whole mission in the play is the augmentation of both those things, and here he sedulously avoids any mention of the afterlife that might lead Claudio to value it above his imminent fatherhood.[13] It is also clear that Claudio accepts these formulaic assurances only formally, only superficially. Such pragmatic, even hypocritical, uses of the consolation ritual—making Last Things the means to a worldly end—place the audience in a similarly skeptical position toward the standard assurances of immortality offered by the church, and not only by the church.[14] The pious function of the Last Confessor becomes merely one more strategic role in a game of practical survival, reminiscent of the pious fraud Edgar perpetrates on Gloucester at the cliffs of Dover. Hearing it done so well by these dissemblers only heightens our awareness that the most compelling consolatory arguments might prove to be fraudulent if we could see the real faces and motives behind them. *Measure for Measure* thus accords with the views reportedly held by the boldest of Jacobean blasphemers: centuries before Karl Marx criticized religion as the opiate of an oppressed populace, these radicals suggested that priest and preacher were merely dummies for the Machiavellian ventriloquists who held material power.[15]

In comforting Isabella for the supposed death of her brother, the unveiled Duke reverts to some of his monkish commonplaces, in a form that again suggests their hollowness:

> That life is better life, past fearing death,
> Than that which lives to fear. Make it your comfort,
> So happy is your brother.
>
> (5.1.395–97)

Editors do their best with this, but the statement verges on mere double-talk. If Claudio has overcome his fear of dying, it is only by no longer having any life to lose; he has become (supposedly) a corpse, not a philosopher. The Duke's remark can be taken as a simple endorsement of the afterlife, but (absurdly) the sole virtue it identifies in that consoling afterlife is that it lacks the fear of death; immortality consists only of non-mortality. In its brittle piety the Duke's consolation for Claudio's supposed death echoes the pregnant Juliet's bitter complaint about Claudio's scheduled execution:

> Must die to-morrow! O injurious love,
> That respites me a life, whose very comfort
> Is still a dying horror!
>
> (2.3.40–42)

"'Tis pity of him," the Provost replies, but it is also pity of all consciously mortal beings enlisted in the Sisyphean struggle of procreation to defeat death. The soon-to-be-born child will likely someday voice the same complaint, even if it is not so soon to be fatherless.

Arguably the Duke is mimicking good Christian practice by encouraging penance through mortification in Claudio, his sister, and his fiancée; and one reward of pious daily dying is the seeming daily demonstration of Resurrection. But the theatre of God's judgments begins to look like an ordinary stage fiction. Claudio's supposed demise is made acceptable to the tragicomic form because we learn that the death, no less than the consolation, is merely a piece of play-acting; but that evasion prepares us very poorly for the instances where the death of those we love is real and the offered consolations sound all too similar, where (like Lear over the body of Cordelia) we wait bewildered for the comic resurrection that never comes.

The standard complaint against the marriages of *Measure for Measure*—that the comic solution seems a forced, unconvincing, insufficient answer or counterweight to the tragic elements and atmosphere of the story—applies to the threatened deaths as well. Death is not refuted any more wholeheartedly than marriage is affirmed. Furthermore, death is assigned rather arbitrarily (in Claudio's condemnation and Ragozine's illness) and avoided the same way (in the pardons of Barnardine and Angelo); we are given no compelling justification for these deaths, any more than for the marriages, beyond the mere mechanisms of biology and statecraft. (Indeed, the use of Ragozine invites us to ask a question that our culture, abetted by its newscasts, fiercely resists: is death by disease any less arbitrary or important than death by accident or execution?) Perhaps it is not merely marriage that is undermined as a comic resolution in this play: all the strategies of secular immortality, all the fantasies (religious, artistic, familial) of resurrection (by miracle or statue or progeny), all the ordinary lines of comic consolation for the central and implacably tragic fact of individual annihilation lie mortally wounded amid the formulaic resurrections of the final scene.

Terrible deaths have been averted, but in a way that provokes a modern suspicion that ordinary deaths are the most terrible of all. As Phoebe Spinrad writes, "Death, far from being the glorious martyrdom of Isabella's dreams, the comfortable sleep of the Duke's dreams, the nuisance of Barnardine's, the punishment of Angelo's, or the horror of Claudio's, is in fact simply a part of life, to be accepted on its own terms, and neither fled from nor sought after."[16] Not everyone will agree that this is good news; otherwise we would all agree that *Measure for Measure* is an exemplary comedy and would never turn from it to revenge tragedies, detective novels, war stories, or religious texts for assurances that death is an unnatural event and an ideal occasion for heroism.

Faced with a city that was becoming infamous, impious, and sexually diseased, Duke Vincentio has experimentally revived the three main modes of secular immortality, using his disguise to increase his worldly fame, to appropriate the redemptive mysteries of the clergy, and to establish himself in the genetic future. But even at the end the Duke's fame is under attack from Lucio's slanders, those nagging interruptions from the lower stratum of body and body politic that mar Shakespeare's artistic resolution as well as the Duke's conclusive statecraft. If the Duke's glorious return from supposed death echoes the story of Christ's Resurrection, it does so parodically: it is an illusion manipulated by a fake holy man for his own aggrandizement. Furthermore, this reappearance compromises the principal Christian arguments (which the Duke stressed to Claudio) for the willing surrender of earthly life: that death is certain and that true happiness and justice exist only beyond it. The play alludes to the commonplace that the entire world is a prison from which death is the only true escape, yet several characters are eventually released from death row into worldly pleasures. The pardons constitute a happy ending, but one which (precisely because it *is* happy) subverts a crucial metaphor frequently employed in the Renaissance, within and beyond this play, to reconcile human beings to mortality. Furthermore, the two pleas we hear for bail from this prison are hardly reassuring models of redemptive prayer: Claudio's becomes a solicitation of his sister to fornication—a striking perversion of the prayer to the Virgin for salvation—and Pompey's is met only by diabolical jeering (3.2.40 ff.). We cannot know whether such veiled but persistent blasphemies were the reason, but it is interesting to note that when an English Jesuit censored Shakespeare's works for the Inquisition in the mid-seventeenth century, *Measure for Measure* was the only play he cut out entirely.[17]

The Duke's complex plot serves to remind us that the procreative impulse can be seen as essentially a mechanism of biology manipulated as a ploy of the state, a way of preserving social structures rather than individual consciousness. The state is merely doing its best to harness, rationalize, even sentimentalize, the relentless directionless march of nature. With Isabella apparently about to surrender her virginity, Mariana (by the convention of such stories) probably newly impregnated, Juliet newly delivered, and Lucio's whore the mother of his young child, the self-perpetuating natural system seems to be far more in control than the vagaries of individual human will. Angelo presses Isabella to show that she is a woman "By putting on the destin'd livery" (2.4.137); this equation of her identity as a woman with her sexual submission earns Angelo the jeers of even the most mildly feminist audience, yet the very play that thus makes him the villain suggests that the procreative sheets—and the swaddling clothes, and the burial shroud—are indeed the destined livery of each human being, for all our protestations of free will. One feminist critic rightly complains about the lack in *Measure for Measure* "of women's personal autonomy—her right to control her body,"[18] but men hardly seem to fare better in that category, whether in bed or in prison. It is not only social hierarchy, as some political critics assume, that the state must mystify to sustain itself: reproductive biology seems to demand and receive a similar disguise.

Isabella, in her determination to abjure the procreative mode of immortality, provides an occasion for inspecting the promises of salvation in a seemingly more authentic instance. Yet from the very start her dedication as a spiritual Bride of Christ is subverted and even parodied by her conversion into a procreative bride for the body politic. Isabella's name proclaims her devoted to God, but Vienna, through an ingenious translation of that devotion, enforces its claim on her womb. For fifteen lines she is allowed to profess asceticism; then Lucio rings the bell at the convent and says, "Hail virgin, if you be" (1.4.1–16). This might be an unremarkable greeting under the circumstances, except that it awakens some truly remarkable echoes. Lucio's salutation translates the beginning of the primary prayer to the Virgin Mary, and then questions whether Isabella is actually suited to the role.[19] Furthermore, that hailing of the Virgin (in a Roman Catholic society such as the play depicts) immediately follows the ringing of a bell, a bell that (even under Elizabethan Protestantism) was known as the Angelus bell. Lucio arrives to lure her out of the convent, and arrives as both an agent of Angelo (who wants to turn her into a sexual object) and of the Duke (who then wants to turn her into a procreative agent). Furthermore, "*Ave virgo*" recurs as the opening of the Annunciation, which is precisely what the Angelus prayer celebrates: the summoning of the Virgin into the task of bearing the son of the Lord as a means of redeeming human mortality. Theologians of course stressed that the Annunciation was by no means an angelic rape but instead the occasion of the Virgin's free consent to the patriarchal Lord of whom the angel was merely a deputy (and Angelo is called Vincentio's "deputy" a dozen times in the play). The process of Isabella's seduction reduces the decorum of the Annunciation to a "good cop, bad cop" tactic employed by the interrogating figures of Angelo and the Duke.

The setting Angelo chooses for his tryst with Isabella is heavily marked as a version of the *hortus conclusus* that is the iconographic home of the Virgin Mary. Isabella reports that Angelo

> . . . hath a garden circummur'd with brick,
> Whose western side is with a vineyard back'd;
> And to that vineyard is a planched gate,
> That makes his opening with this bigger key.
> This other doth command a little door
> Which from the vineyard to the garden leads;
> There have I made my promise
> Upon the heavy middle of the night
> To call upon him.
>
> (4.1.28–36)

Medieval depictions of the Annunciation often place Mary in front of a garden surrounded by walls and vineyards; sometimes the descended angel holds the key to its portal.[20] But Angelo's markedly virginal garden—nowhere evident in Shakespeare's sources—is also strikingly similar to the trysting places of the Elizabethan fornicators whom Phillip Stubbes reviles:

> . . . they have gardens, either polled or walled round about very high, with their harbers and bowers fit for the purpose. . . . And for that their gardens are locked, some of them have three or four keyes a peece, whereof one they keepe for themselves, the other their paramours have to goe in before them . . . to receive the guerdon of their paines. . . .[21]

Isabella is positioned as a holy virgin only to be displaced into an object of sexual and reproductive desire, her symbols degradingly recontextualized.

So the course of Isabella's enlistment into the reproductive economy is marked from the start as a queasy burlesque of her religious mission. When Lucio tells Isabella in this initial exchange, "I hold you as a thing enskied and sainted / By your renouncement, an immortal spirit," she replies, "You do blaspheme the good, in mocking me" (1.4.34–35, 38). It is not clear whether Lucio is indeed mocking Isabella as he here calls her back to the earthly business of the body; but it does seem clear that Shakespeare is making a mockery of the pious notion that virginity is a plausible or even permissible way to pursue immortality. Isabella turns the immediate task of bearing Angelo's burden over to Mariana—another refraction of Mary, with a moated grange for her *hortus conclusus*—but soon enough the bells will ring for Isabella as well. Presumably she surrenders her quest for immortalizing chastity by taking the Duke's hand in the final silence of the play, much as Coriolanus surrenders his own heroic immortality strategy to the silent generational panorama by taking the hand of his mother. In silence, and by the body, our shared mortal natures reassert themselves.

The condemnation of Claudio forces Isabella to confront the conflict between (on the one hand) the instincts that resist physical death and (on the other) the daily death at the heart of her religious vocation, with its strident rejection of this world and its confident anticipation of another. In her first confrontation with Angelo, Isabella interprets her brother's threatened execution as a sacrificial preparation for heaven. The proprieties of slaughter seem quite clear to her: as other animals become merely food after death, so human beings become purely souls (2.2.85–88). The fact that she can offer so comfortably this grotesque analogy demonstrates her facile confidence in the scheme of salvation (it may also remind us how deeply Western culture depends, for its spiritual complacency as well as its food supply, on the same absolute distinction). Death to her is merely the tiny unpleasant fraction of human experience shared with a crushed beetle; understandably, she cannot imagine sacrificing "a perpetual honor" for "six or seven winters" of "feverous life" (3.1.73–80).[22] Members of the audience may wince at this reminder of the corrupt bargains they have made with fallen angels for those few extra years of survival. But is honor necessarily any more perpetual than bodies are, than souls might be? When Isabella tells Angelo that she would "rather give my body than my soul" to save her brother, Angelo replies curtly, "I talk not of your soul" (2.4.56–57). Throughout the play, Isabella is thus steadily drawn into the marketplace of the physical, into a mentality that thinks more about desire than about religion; more about the threat of death than about the hope of immortality; more about bodily confinement (a jail or a grave) than about spiritual injury (disgrace or damnation), about the wounded honor that would be a "restraint / Though all the world's vastidity you had" (3.1.68). Both siblings are worried about the "pollution" of their bodies, but they have virtually opposite definitions of the term, Isabella associating it with sexual reproduction and Claudio with mortal decay. When Claudio thinks the alternative to instant death is "perpetual durance," he means imprisonment of his body for the duration of its life—a characteristic misreading of the word "perpetual" as Isabella understands it. By disallowing her orthodox reference to eternals that would easily resolve the dilemma, the play disables the same simplifying reflex in the audience. No wonder critics alternately condemn her declaration that "More than our brother is our chastity" (2.4.184) as mean-spirited hysteria and defend it as correct Renaissance theology. This stubbornly socio-biological play is as subversive to more recent humanistic pietisms as it is to medieval Christian ones, and there seems to be no defensible middle ground.

Claudio finally tells his sister that "If I must die, / I will encounter darkness as a bride / And hug it in my arms" (3.1.83–85). This is an otherworldly resolution with some symptoms of weakness. He is making the afterworld into an image of his earthly desires and deeds—this death sounds like another imperfect marriage prematurely embraced—and equating that afterworld with pure darkness, a plausible symptom of annihilationism. Isabella nonetheless congratulates him—not surprisingly if we remember that she herself had conceived of death as an erotic spouse (2.4.102). The peculiar terms of her congratulation show how the various strategies of immortality mingle together in the desperately denying minds of these characters. To salvation and honor she now adds a ghost of procreation. "There spake my brother: there my father's grave / Did utter forth a voice. Yes, thou must die" (3.1.85–86). The last three words are a standard and starkly unconsoling message from the grave, but the first sentence implies more subtly that by dying properly (and in defense of his sister's procreative purity) Claudio will become eligible for this kind of procreative, not to say paganish, resurrection.[23] The likeness of a son, he is reminded, means that the father does not really die into a rest of silence. When Claudio weakens again some fifty lines later, she turns the same set of assumptions against him. "Is't not a kind of incest, to take life / From thine own sister's shame?" (3.1.138–39), she asks accusingly, as if the life he would save by escaping execution were virtually indistinguishable from the life he would make by procreating within his own genetic field.

When the revenant Duke suggests that Isabella accuses Angelo "in th'infirmity of sense," she replies,

> O Prince, I conjure thee, as thou believ'st
> There is another comfort than this world,
> That thou neglect me not with that opinion
> That I am touch'd with madness.
> (5.1.51–54)

This conjuration makes it all the more interesting that her sanity—and thereby, implicitly, all faith in that otherworldly comfort—is repeatedly called into question as the scene goes on, not only by Angelo but by the Duke as well: her complaint against Angelo is "somewhat madly spoken" (5.1.92), and her plea to spare his worldly life runs "against all sense" (5.1.431). The connection between her faith and her possible psychological infirmities may strike the audience as far less casual than she seems to intend it, especially given the lurid symptomology of her sexual repression. Hers is therefore no random oath of affirmation. It reminds us that belief in an afterlife can be interrogated precisely because it is so necessary a comfort, just as romantic sentiment and the institution of marriage can be analyzed as by-products of biological and political imperatives. To vary Voltaire's famous dictum about God, if there were not conjugal desire, it would be necessary to invent it. Indeed, the Duke seems desperate to simulate both marital love and divine justice precisely because his city seems to have lost track of the original models. As soon as one begins to look behind these necessities, to doubt these comforts—as *Measure for Measure* subtly but persistently invites us to do—the immortality strategies of Isabella and the others may indeed appear insane. A culture of religious faith (such as the Renaissance) commonly diagnoses atheism as a form of insanity;[24] an atheistic culture will doubtless (following Freud) interpret faith as a neurotic symptom. *Measure for Measure* hovers uneasily between those two worlds, leaving Isabella to make a bewildering shift from a religious to a procreative model of immortality.

Angelo studiously rejects the allure of procreation (1.4.57–61) in favor of an immortality strategy based on fame, honor, and purity. The willingness to die for these things by war, duel, or suicide is no less rational an answer to mortality than our modern determination to delay death briefly by health care; but if the denial of death is indeed fundamental to the psychic viability of a society, we will necessarily again diagnose a kind of insanity in any conflicting version. *Measure for Measure* seems determined to reduce Angelo's motives, as well as Isabella's, to psychopathological symptoms. Lucio claims that "Angelo was not made by man and woman, after this downright way of creation" and is therefore "a motion ungenerative" (3.2.100–8). In his sensual restraint and his reluctance to consummate the marriage to Mariana, Angelo refuses to become merely another link in the long chain of mortal human flesh, which transmitted Original Sin (and therefore mortality) through the concupiscence of the generative act. He seeks to be otherworldly here on earth; the coining metaphors suggest that he is ready to be stamped into an "angel," a suggestion that again conflates his official stature with holy transcendence. But—like Coriolanus in search of a similar transcendence[25]—Angelo cannot finally redeem the coining metaphor from its conventional reference to procreation; the Duke converts him back into a marker of the fleshly aspect of the state's usuriously breeding wealth.

As soon as Angelo is forced to face the collapse of his immortality strategy (what the psychological philosopher Ernest Becker would call the denial of death by heroic purity[26]), he compares his moral failure to the rotting of dead flesh in the sun (2.2.167). This is the same macabre view of mortality, the emphasis on the merely decaying body, that haunts Claudio and (as Philippe Ariès has shown in his histories of death[27]) apparently haunted Western Europe through the late Middle Ages. At the start of the play, Escalus describes Angelo as worthy of the "ample grace" for which he has been "elected" (1.1.18–24); the vocabulary makes public reputation (what Cassio calls "the immortal part of myself" in *Othello* [2.3.263]) an alternative model of eternal salvation. But when the truth about his fleshly failings becomes public as well as private knowledge, Angelo says he feels that "your Grace, like power divine, / Hath looked upon my passes . . . and sequent death / Is all the grace I beg" (5.1.367–72). Equating earthly judges with divine ones, he expects a sentence of death—mortality as annihilation—and reaffirms the association by imagining that oblivion is the best to be hoped for from this visitation of grace. Furthermore, the fact that Angelo presumably knows himself to be hypocritical in his pursuit of moral excellence (since he has already mistreated Mariana) only reinforces our uneasy awareness that, upon closer inspection, we might find we did not really believe in the claims to immortality with which we nonetheless console ourselves.

Angelo is fooled by the substitution of Mariana's maidenhead for Isabella's, and again by the substitution of Ragozine's head for Claudio's. The Duke is doubtless right that "death's a great disguiser" (4.2.174) and that the head of Barnardine might be thereby mistaken for Claudio's. But that reassurance to the Provost must be a disturbance to the audience: however indirectly, it invokes the *transi* figure of medieval tomb sculpture, the stark reminder that in decay all human bodies reveal their horrible sameness. This is the dirty secret that *Measure for Measure* half-reveals in half-concealing it: just as these two women's bodies (even at the moment they are supposedly expressing their most intimate qualities) may be virtually indistinguishable, so are all the rest of us when we fall into the clutches of the omnivorous Angel of Death. More subtly disturbing is the renewed recognition that, from the perspective of nature or the state, in the functions of biology or politics, indifference makes perfect sense. Any body will do. The widely expressed critical discomfort with these two substitutions—the bed-trick as immoral, the head-trick as implausible—may cover a symptomatic resistance to this recognition of indifference. Comedies often encourage that recognition but in a far more pleasant manner, on behalf of communal life; tragedies often exhort us to protest against it, but they do so by offering a prospect of heroic transcendence that *Measure for Measure* stubbornly refuses us. The eagerness of commentators to dismiss these juxtaposed substitutions as merely two proximate moments of inferior dramaturgy may partly reflect an unwillingness to see the play's darker purpose—its tragicomic thrust—which is to challenge the sentimental notion of our individual significance.

While humiliating the transcendent strategies of honor and piety that characterize Angelo and Isabella, the play seems, perversely, to reward and endorse the utter negligence of immortality that characterizes Barnardine. He is a kind of reverse synecdoche, a whole man symbolizing an autonomic nervous system. As Claudio hovers, at "dead midnight," on the brink of the death that will make him "immortal," Barnardine is described as sleeping too soundly to be put to death (4.2.61–66) and as "A man that apprehends death no more dreadfully but as a drunken sleep; careless, reckless, and fearless of what's past, present, or to come: insensible of mortality, and desperately mortal" (4.2.140–43). Aside from making it difficult to distinguish Barnardine's moral idiocy from the ideal posture of Renaissance Stoicism, this description disturbingly elides a comic failing with perhaps the most central consolatory metaphor for death. This elision recurs twice in Pompey's urgings—only half comic, I think, or at least not casually comic—that the slumbering Barnardine "awake till you are executed, and sleep afterwards," and that "he that drinks all night and is hanged betimes in the morning may sleep the sounder all the next day" (4.3.31–46).[28] The absurdity—or is it absurd propriety?—of this suggestion exposes the weakness of the conventional assurance that death is merely another sleep (an assurance repeatedly offered to the unwilling Claudio, who fears that if dreams come at all, they will be nightmares).

Barnardine is pardoned because the state can much better tolerate an unregenerate soul than an unregenerating body, but again the Duke feels obliged to obscure the distinction with his rhetoric:

> Sirrah, thou art said to have a stubborn soul
> That apprehends no further than this world,
> And squar'st thy life according. Thou'rt condemn'd;
> But, for those earthly faults, I quit them all,
> And pray thee take this mercy to provide
> For better times to come.
>
> (5.1.478–83)

Barnardine is spared on earth because there is so little hope for him beyond. Perhaps the same worldly assumption underlies—and therefore undermines—the "resurrection" of Claudio and the pardon of Angelo that follow so quickly. Again—as with Gloucester on Dover Beach—salvation seems to be a fraud engineered by earthly leaders in vague imitation of a myth of grace, because human civilization is really only a confused crowd huddled together on that beach (as Matthew Arnold's poem suggests) against a vast, cold, dark, relentless sea.

The Duke's performance of a Last Judgment at the gates of his city, rather than the gates of heaven, is a culminating instance of the way *Measure for Measure* parodies pious archetypes in asserting the priority of earthly order and human survival. The critics who assert that (for example) "The Duke's ethical attitude is exactly correspondent with Jesus'"[29] fall victim to the same manipulation of pious reflexes by which the Duke controls his citizens. They overlook the fact that the Duke prepares his redemptive intervention by its opposite: this lord turns judgment over to a bad son who insists on the punitive letter of the law rather than the established principle of mercy. The Duke strategically regresses Vienna from the New Testament to the Old so that he can claim credit, as head of state, for reinventing Christian forgiveness. This version of redemption serves to defend, not faith or moral purity, but the public procreative order of Vienna.

Perhaps *Measure for Measure* is a product of the plague year 1603 not only in its emphasis on the replenishment of the population but also in its portrayal of a city abandoned by its benevolent but exasperated Lord to an agency of deadly retribution. The sermons and literature of 1603 predominantly characterize the plague as God's scourge visited on an increasingly immoral nation. At times the Vienna of *Measure for Measure* must seem to its citizens much as the world seems to those who feel (as Reformation theology led many to feel) that God has mysteriously absconded and left his children in a pointless (or at least inscrutable) universe, and in the cold hands of Death:

> The Duke is very strangely gone from hence;
> Bore many gentlemen—myself being one—
> In hand, and hope of action: but we do learn,
> By those that know the very nerves of state,
> His giving out were of an infinite distance
> From his true-meant design. Upon his place,
> And with full line of his authority,
> Governs Lord Angelo; a man whose blood
> Is very snow-broth; one who never feels
> The wanton stings and motions of the sense. . . .
> All hope is gone,
> Unless you have the grace by your fair prayer
> To soften Angelo.
>
> (1.4.50–70)

The resemblance to Prospero's "And my ending is despair, / Unless I be reliev'd by prayer" (Epilogue. 15–16) indicates how strongly Lucio's speech partakes of more eschatological pleas for forgiveness, for relief from the condemnation common to fallen flesh. Lucio is hardly a Job or a Christ, but in this speech he might as well be asking why He has forsaken us, why He has given us thus to the dark fallen angel, the common enemy of man (as Macbeth calls his ultimate foe). Isabella's warning to Angelo about the Last Judgment (2.2.73–79) sounds plausibly like a warning about the promised Death of Death after its temporary merciless reign of terror over humankind. When Claudio complains that a seemingly capricious Authority, armed with a deadly blade, makes a few pay for a widely shared sin, he sounds as if he might be talking as much about mortality punishing Original Sin as about execution punishing fornication. Indeed, from the perspective of biological theory that describes death as a necessary by-product of the invention of reproduction, each of us endures Claudio's sentence. Angelo tells Isabella that though Claudio must die under his sentence. "Yet may he live a while; and, it may be, / As long as you or I" (2.4.35–36).

Let me therefore propose one more imperfect but evocative allegory lurking in a play that has perhaps already been allegorized too often and too ingeniously:[30] the Duke, not simply as *imitatio dei,*[31] but as *imitatio dei absconditi.* Angelo as the Angel of Death, Claudio as Everyman, and Isabella as Faith. In this system, Barnardine may represent the body, the stupid force of heartbeat, survival instinct, physical appetite, that is unwilling to die in the condemned Everyman and is (here) finally spared. Lucio, finally, embodies doubt, baffling every path to immortality in mocking Isabella's pious virginity, the Duke's reputation, and the entire procreative process. The state can order that nagging cynical voice to be pressed to death, whipped, hanged, and married to shame, but it cannot be silenced. Even in the triumphant final scene it persists, ruining any hopes—the Duke's, Shakespeare's, ours—that the tragic facts of life can be dispelled (not just disguised) by the warm glow and consoling figurations of comedy. If life goes on, then so does death. "This news is old enough, yet it is every day's news" (3.2.223–24).

Notes

1. In Measure for Measure, *the Law, and the Convent* ([Princeton, N.J.: Princeton Univ. Press. 1979], pp. 15–60). Darryl J. Gless attempts to locate the genre of the play; see also Mary Lascelles. *Shakespeare's* Measure for Measure (London: Athlone, 1953), which classifies the play as a tragicomedy on a more traditional basis; Gregory W. Lanier, "Physic That's Bitter to Sweet End," *Essays in Literature,* 14 (1987), 15–36; and Arthur C. Kirsch, "The Integrity of *Measure for Measure,*" *Shakespeare Survey,* 28 (1975), 89–105.

2. For example, Paul Hammond's "The Argument of *Measure for Measure,*" *English Literary Renaissance,* 16 (1986), 496–519, resists its own title by asserting that there is finally no moral argument discernible in the play.

3. See, for example, Phillip Stubbes, *The Anatomie of Abuses* (London, 1583), sigs. $G8^v$–$H8^r$.

4. sig. $H4^r$.

5. All references to *Measure for Measure* are based on the Arden edition, J. W. Lever, ed. (London: Methuen, 1965). References to other plays are based on *The Riverside Shakespeare,* G. Blakemore Evans et al. eds. (Boston: Houghton Mifflin; 1974), with Evans's square brackets removed to avoid confusion with my own interpolations.

6. Carolyn E. Brown, "Erotic Religious Flagellation and Shakespeare's *Measure for Measure,*" *ELR,* 16 (1986), 139–65.

7. *The History of Sexuality,* 3 vols., trans. Robert Hurley (New York: Pantheon, 1978–86), Vol. 1, 144. Foucault maintains that

> In the eighteenth century, sex became a "police" matter—in the full and strict sense given the term at the time: not the repression of disorder, but an ordered maximization of collective and individual forces. . . . One of the great innovations in the techniques of power in the eighteenth century was the emergence of "population" as an economic and political problem: population as wealth, population as manpower or labor capacity. . . . At the heart of this economic and political problem of population was sex: it was necessary to analyze the birthrate, the age of marriage, the legitimate and illegitimate births, the precocity and frequency of sexual relations, the ways of making them fertile or sterile, the effects of unmarried life or of the prohibitions. . . . This was the first time that a society had affirmed, in a constant way that its future and its fortune were tied . . . to the manner in which each individual made use of his sex.
>
> (Vol. 1, 25–26)

Surely this description fits the governmental work that propels *Measure for Measure.* Perhaps Shakespeare is once again being prescient—or perhaps Foucault is once again exaggerating the disjunctions in recent human history. On "bio-power" as an eighteenth-century invention, see Vol. 1, 138–45; on its strained relation to the death-penalty—again anticipated by *Measure for Measure*—see Vol. 1, 138.

8. Philip C. McGuire, *Speechless Dialect: Shakespeare's Open Silences* (Los Angeles: Univ. of California Press, 1985), p. 71. Victoria Hayne, in her forthcoming U.C.L.A. dissertation, will argue against this perspective by demonstrating that the reluctant grooms are merely forced to honor the marital commitments they have already made by word or deed.

9. Robert N. Watson, *Shakespeare and the Hazards of Ambition* (Cambridge, Mass.: Harvard Univ. Press, 1984), passim.

10. The argument that Angelo's "virtues" (a word with seminal implications) must go forth in "issues" (1.1.27–43) echoes the commonplace arguments for procreation in Shakespeare's sonnets and in fact throughout Renaissance literature, exhortations not to waste nature's finest models by failing to reproduce them in a new generation. In the same passage, the Duke talks about Angelo's life-story as if it were a stable and legible text to be read, and such writing (again with a pun on "character") becomes another metaphor for procreation at 1.2.144. This further interweaves the procreative and artistic aspects of the Duke's immortality strategy—the same pair of projects linked so persistently in Jonson's epitaph and in Shakespeare's sonnets. Yet as those sonnets demonstrate, Shakespeare remains painfully aware that these modes of immortality are merely figurative and highly vulnerable; see Gillian M. Kendall, "The Quest for Secular Immortality in Shakespeare's Romances," Diss. Harvard University, 1987, which insightfully explores Shakespeare's highly equivocal endorsement of these answers to death. For discussion of the procreative theme in the sonnets, see Robert Crosman,

"Making Love Out of Nothing at All: The Issue of Story in Shakespeare's Procreative Sonnets," *Shakespeare Quarterly* 41:4 (Winter 1990): 470–88.

11. Jonathan Goldberg argues that the paternal metaphor permeates James's assertions of authority ("The Politics of Patriarchy" in *Rewriting the Renaissance: The Discourses of Sexual Difference in Early Modern Europe,* Margaret Ferguson, Maureen Quilligan, and Nancy Vickers, eds. [Chicago: Univ. of Chicago Press, 1986], pp. 3–32).

12. Gless compares the Duke's complaints about slander with those of King James (pp. 161–62); others, notably Josephine Waters Bennett, in Measure for Measure *as Royal Entertainment* (New York: Columbia Univ. Press, 1966), pursue the connection more extensively. However, Richard Levin forcefully refutes this instance of "occasionalist" interpretation in *New Readings vs. Old Plays* ([Chicago: Univ. of Chicago Press, 1979], pp. 167–93).

13. Brown, summarizing an observation several critics have made, comments that the consolations the disguised Duke offers are "conspicuously devoid of the promise of a Christian afterlife" (p. 151). Lever characterizes the Duke's argument as "essentially materialist" (p. lxxxvii).

14. Stephen Greenblatt skilfully explores the notion that in improvising cynically on the belief systems of Native Americans, English colonists might have compromised their own Christian confidence ("Invisible Bullets" in *Shakespeare's "Rough Magic": Renaissance Essays in Honor of C. L. Barber, Peter Erickson and Coppélia Kahn,* eds. [Newark: Univ. of Delaware Press 1985], pp. 276–302).

15. This Marxist / Machiavellian perspective on religion is most obvious in the writings of the radical Reformers, though traces of it may be found in canonical figures such as Marlowe, Montaigne, and Hobbes as well.

16. "*Measure for Measure* and the Art of Not Dying," *Texas Studies in Literature and Language,* 26 (1984), 74–94, esp. p. 91. She also analyzes Claudio as an anticipation of the modern "quasi-solipsist who in his own demise sees the disappearance of the universe" (p. 82).

17. Roland M. Frye records this censorship in *Shakespeare and Christian Doctrine* ([Princeton, N.J.: Princeton Univ. Press, 1963], pp. 291–92).

18. Irene G. Dash, *Wooing, Wedding, and Power: Women in Shakespeare's Plays* (New York: Columbia Univ. Press, 1981), p. 251.

19. Gless notes the echo by which Lucio's "salutation mocks Catholic devotion to the Blessed Virgin" (p. 103) but overlooks the further resonances of the Annunciation, which make it much harder safely to isolate the blasphemy as merely anti-monasticism in the mouth of a profane scoundrel. Virtually the entire Annunciation text, which the Book of Common Prayer takes directly from Luke 1:28–35, offers suggestive parallels to Isabella's experience, from the initial novitiate's unease at Lucio's apparently mocking greeting, and embarrassment at the sexual implications of his message, to the submission to shadowy powers that will make her the prospective mother of her lord's son:

> And the Angel went in vnto her, & said, Haile . . . And when she sawe *him* she was troubled at his saying, & thoght what maner of salutacion that shulde be. . . . [Her child] shalbe great, & shalbe called the Sonne of the moste High. . . . Then said Marie vnto the Angel, How shal this be, seing, I know no man? And the Angel answered, and said vnto her. The holie Gost shal come vpon thee, & the power of the most High shal ouershadowe thee. . . .
>
> (quoted from the Geneva Bible)

An eerie futurist echo of Shakespeare's twist on the Annunciation story occurs in Margaret Atwood's recently filmed novel, *The Handmaid's Tale* (New York: Random House, 1985), in which the few women still fertile are dressed in red nuns' habits and forced to bear the children of the ruling men to perpetuate the society.

20. Stanley Stewart, *The Enclosed Garden: The Tradition and the Image in Seventeenth-Century Poetry* (Madison: Univ. of Wisconsin Press, 1966), pp. 40–41.

21. Stubbes, in the version of *The Anatomie of Abuses* edited by William B.D.D. Turnbull (Edinburgh: W. and D. Laing, 1836), pp. 87–88; this passage does not appear in the 1583 first edition but was included well before the time of *Measure for Measure.*

22. This effort to turn the bodily discomforts of both wintry cold and feverous heat against Claudio's prospective nostalgia for the earthly life of the senses backfires when both extremes reappear less than fifty lines later as part of his terror of death.

23. Later the Duke similarly warns that Claudio's "ghost his paved bed would break,/ And take her hence in horror" if Isabella were to forgive Angelo (5.1.433–34). Again the prospect of a posthumous voice is used to extort an earthly response, demanding sacrifices (as sociobiology would predict) in defense of close genetic kin.

24. G. E. Aylmer, "Unbelief in Seventeenth-Century England" in *Puritans and Revolutionaries,* Donald Pennington and Keith Thomas, eds. (Oxford: Clarendon Press, 1978), pp. 22–46, esp. pp. 33–34.

25. In the book cited in note 9, above, I have argued that Coriolanus' effort to extricate himself from the mortal flesh he shares with his fellow Romans obliges him to define his "coining" as a mechanical rather than a procreative process; see pp. 145–61, 169–70, 178, 183, 188.

26. *The Denial of Death* (New York: Free Press, 1973).

27. *The Hour of Our Death,* trans. Helen Weaver (New York: Random House, 1982).

28. Compare Angelo's assertion at 2.2.91 that"The law hath not been dead, though it hath slept." He is resurrecting, by a standard consolatory metaphor, the moral laws by which he has defined his own immortality.

29. G. Wilson Knight, *The Wheel of Fire* (1930; rev. ed. London: Methuen, 1949), p. 82.

30. Lever cites the various Christian allegories that have been applied (p. lvii). Gless also comments on the oversupply of "personification allegory" concerning *Measure for Measure,* then offers a different way of allegorizing the play (pp. 4–5 and 53–60). On pages 247–50, Gless discusses the possibility of identifying the Duke with the Christian God. See also Knight, p. 74; Roy W. Battenhouse, "*Measure for Measure* and Christian Doctrine of the Atonement," *PMLA,* 61 (1946), 1029–59; and Robert G. Hunter, *Shakespeare and the Comedy of Forgiveness* (New York: Columbia Univ. Press, 1965), pp. 204–26.

31. Louise Schleiner, "Providential Improvisation in *Measure for Measure,*" *PMLA,* 97 (1982), 227–36, characterizes the Duke's actions as an *imitatio dei.*

Marriage and the Maternal Body: On Marriage as the End of Comedy in *Measure for Measure*

Janet Adelman

In the midst of Hamlet's attack on Ophelia, he cries out to Ophelia, "I say we will have no mo marriage" (*Hamlet,* 3.1.149). Fusing mother with beloved in his diatribe, he proclaims an end to the institution of marriage itself, giving us a graphic emblem for the need to come to terms with the sexualized maternal body before embarking on the establishment of a new family through marriage. In their own ways, *Troilus and Cressida* and *Othello* play out the end to marriage proclaimed by Hamlet: both record the impossibility of return to the mother's body through sexual union. But patriarchal society nonetheless demands this return: before the son can take his place in that society, he must remake himself as a father; patriarchal authority itself passes from fathers to sons only through the problematic medium of the mother's body. The problem comedies—written roughly at the same time as *Troilus and Cressida* and *Othello*—seem to me ways of attempting to deal with this necessity: through the separations and recombinations recorded in their plots, they figure both the recoil from sexual union and the desperate remedies that might make marriage possible again.

Like Troilus and Othello, Bertram and Angelo are presented as virgins, facing what is in effect their first sexual experience; and that experience again takes the shape of a morning-after fantasy, in which a virgin is violated and then abandoned, psychically transformed into a whore. The morning-after fantasy of contamination and abandonment embedded in each play marks what makes these comedies problematic *as comedies:* under the aegis of this fantasy, marriage—and with it, comedy—becomes impossible. This is in fact the situation at the beginning of both problem comedies, where both protagonists rush out of wedlock toward illegitimate union, desiring only where they do not wed, wedding where they do not desire. And in an extraordinary move, Shakespeare enables marriage again not by evading but by following out the logic of the morning-after fantasy, in effect enshrining it in the plot. In these plays the psychological splittings that govern the fates of Cressida and Desdemona are literalized and enacted: whereas Troilus and then Othello split one woman in two—Troilus finding both his own and Diomed's Cressida in the one body of Cressida, Othello seeing in Desdemona "the cunning whore of Venice, / That married with Othello" (4.2.91–92)—Bertram and Angelo negotiate their sexual desire between two women, one of whom (Diana / Isabella) is apparently violated and shamed, becoming the repository of sexual soiling, the other of whom (Helena / Mariana) mysteriously remains unsoiled and hence—eventually—available for marriage. Split apart and then violently yoked together through the device of the bed trick, the women in *All's Well* and *Measure for Measure* simultaneously illustrate the fundamental incompatibility between marriage and male desire and provide a magical solution to it: the final scenes of both plays depend on something akin to a theatrical exorcism, where sexual contamination is first attached to the supposedly violated virgins and then banished as the virtual wives return and the truth is revealed. And through this two-body accommodation to the morning-after fantasy, Shakespeare is able to turn the tragic endings of *Troilus and Cressida* and *Othello* toward comedy, though comedy of a problematic sort.

In both plays, the bed trick is thus the primary device through which desire is regulated, both legitimized and relocated in the socially sanctioned bond of marriage. Through a version of homeopathic cure,[1] the two bodies of the bed trick allow both Bertram and Angelo to enact fantasies in which a virgin is soiled—one nearly a nun, the other a Diana—only to find out that their sexual acts have in fact been legitimate, that the soiling has taken place only in fantasy. The bed tricks thus offer to save Bertram and Angelo from their own fantasies: presented with legitimate sexuality as a *fait accompli,* they might go on to accept the possibility that they have been tricked into, the possibility of desire within marriage. So much, at least, is promised by Helena's brief glance at the kindness with which Bertram unknowingly used her (*All's Well,* 5.3.304) and by Mariana's wistful "They say best men are moulded out of faults" (*Measure,* 5.1.437). But given the status of the bed tricks as tricks and the unwilling husbands' failure to give much evidence that they have in fact been transformed, that promise seems frail indeed. And insofar as the bed tricks betray the desires of the male protagonists in curing them, they tend to become less a vehicle for the working out of impediments to marriage than a forced and conspicuous emblem for what needs working out. As such, their comic solutions suggest why it is that marriage has become for Shakespeare literally the end of comedy.

The bed tricks thus stand at the center of what is problematic about sexual relations in these plays. Comparison with Shakespeare's source for the bed trick can help us gauge their peculiar valence. In *The Palace of Pleasure,* William Painter's translation of Boccaccio's *Decameron* (Day 3, Story 9), the bed trick is a rather well-mannered and genial affair, repeated often and with affection. We are specifically told that the count (equivalent to Bertram) "at his uprising in the morning . . . used many courteous and amiable words and gave diverse fair and precious jewels."[2] But all this friendliness has been edited out of Shakespeare's versions; the potentially curative mutuality of Painter's account is entirely absent. In both *All's Well* and *Measure for Measure,* the emphasis on speed and silence (*All's Well,* 4.2.58; *Measure,* 3.1.247–48) transform it utterly, so that it becomes the epitome not only of the dark waywardness of desire but also of its depersonalization, the interchangeability of the bodies with which lust plays (*All's Well,* 4.4.24–25). Moreover, these bed tricks are portrayed as one-night stands that the male protagonists have no desire to repeat, and not only for reasons of dramatic compression. Both Bertram and Angelo recoil immediately from the object of desire, losing interest in their virgins as soon as they are ravished; for both, the fantasied act of despoiling virginity seems to be the only source of sexual desire. Thus transformed, these bed tricks do not bode well as cures. The psychic violence of their proposed solutions merely illustrates the seriousness of the disease: the extent to which sexuality here is a matter of deception on the one side and hit-and-run contamination on the other underscores the deep incompatibility that separates sexuality from marriage.[3]

When Montaigne treats this incompatibility in "Upon Some Verses of Virgil," he names it incest: "Nor is it other then a kinde of incest, in this reverent alliance and sacred bond [of marriage], to employ the effects and extravagant humor of an amorous licentiousness."[4] In so naming the tension between the sacred and the sexual, Montaigne comes close to identifying the psychological dynamic of these plays, in which the soiling potentiality of sexuality is understood within a familial context, associated with the prohibitions surrounding the boychild's first fantasies of soiling a sacred space. These are the terms through which Hamlet understands Claudius's literally incestuous relationship with his mother: under the impact of his new knowledge of maternal sexuality, the enclosed garden-paradise that was his mother's body becomes for him the fallen and unweeded garden, possessed by things rank and gross. Insofar as Troilus and Othello associate Cressida and Desdemona with that maternal body, sexual union is for them as for Hamlet the contamination of a sacred maternal space: the soiling of a mother (*Troilus and Cressida,* 5.2.133), the transformation of the garner into a cistern where toads knot and gender (*Othello,* 4.2.58–63). Between them, *All's Well* and *Measure for Measure* provide a complex exploration of the forces that disrupt union in *Troilus and Cressida* and *Othello;* the central actions of both are exfoliations of Hamlet's dilemma, difficult attempts to clear a space for marriage in the face of his terrible knowledge.

In their own ways, both Bertram and Angelo act out the conflict Montaigne depicts, locating their "amorous licentiousness" in the illicit, far from family bonds; and yet sexual desire brings each of them home, to the problematic maternal body and to its traces in the self. *All's Well* analyzes male flight from a woman who has become nearly indistinguishable from the mother and the desperate measures necessary to render her safe and pure; *Measure for Measure* analyzes sexual desire *per se* as a return to contaminated maternal origins and reinvents the bodiless and all-seeing father who can control its dangers. Both problem comedies attempt in effect to legitimize desire, enabling a diminished version of the marriage Hamlet has lost; but the defensive measures they must undertake to enable marriage remain more striking than the marriages they achieve. The marriages that end these comedies fail to satisfy the desires of either the characters or the audience; and their failure marks the extent to which Hamlet's prohibition remains in force and hence the extent to which comedy is no longer a viable genre for Shakespeare.[5] . . .

. . . There are no mothers in *Measure for Measure;* but there is another pregnant body. It is no accident that the unborn child of *All's Well,* who epitomizes the conflicted attempt to bring sexual desire back into the bonds of the family, reappears at the start of *Measure for Measure* as the product of an illicit union, the sign of sin who condemns its parents by proclaiming their sexuality publicly. The transformation of the pregnant Helena into the pregnant Juliet typifies the relation between the two plays: the sexual queasiness that lies behind Bertram's flight from both Helena and Diana is given much fuller expression in *Measure for Measure* with the consequence that the getting of children is the problem, not the purported solution. Here the bed trick cures nothing; it is written in effect from the point of view of Diana, designed overtly to preserve virginity, not to consummate a potentially saving sexual union. The very distinction between licit and illicit sexuality on which *All's Well* depends has broken down in *Measure,* at least until Mariana appears halfway through the play;[6] as this world is initially presented to us, all sexuality is illicit and enforces its own death sentence, whether through Angelo's restitution of the law condemning fornication or through the disease that seems its inevitable attendant. In this play's literalization of the pun that identifies death and orgasm,[7] sexuality becomes the original sin that brings death into the world; the bawd appropriately becomes the executioner. Even the marriages that traditionally end comedy in festivity have here become the punishment for sexual sin. No wonder Helena must be transformed into Juliet; no wonder the baby Juliet carries is not a hope for the future but "the sin you carry" (2.3.19).

The Duke's identification of the baby as "the sin you carry" confounds the illicit act with the product of the act, making the baby itself the bearer of its parents' sin; its sin is derived from its corrupt origin. And though the Duke addresses a Juliet whose sexual union was not fully legitimate, his terms would not be very different if her baby were the product of a perfectly legitimate union. For the Duke—as for the play—disgust at life is expressed as disgust at the facts of human dependency and the corruption inherited at its source. When the Duke condemns Pompey's life for its dependence on illicit sexual transactions, his language undermines the distinction between legitimacy and illegitimacy, unwittingly evoking the corruptness of all our origins:

> Say to thyself,
> From their abominable and beastly touches
> I drink, I eat, array myself, and live.
> Canst thou believe thy living is a life,
> So stinkingly depending?
> (3.2.22–26)

In this psychic lexicon, there is no room for legitimate sexuality: sexual touch *per se* is abominable and beastly; and since we all live from these touches, we are all stinkingly dependent. Hence the degree to which the Duke's question to Pompey—"Canst thou believe thy living is a life, / So stinkingly depending?"—reiterates the logic of his attempt to dissuade Claudio from life: for both, "all th'accommodations that thou bear'st / Are nurs'd by baseness" (3.1.14–15).[8] Both are stinkingly dependent; and in both instances, the language of sexual origin and maternal dependence carries the weight of the Duke's disgust, as though the facts of conception and maternal nursery were in themselves enough to turn one away from life.

Measure for Measure equivocally attempts to make life livable by simultaneously affirming and denying this origin. On the face of it, the play seems to enforce its acknowledgment: Angelo and Isabella are severely punished for their attempt to claim exemption from ordinary sexual processes. For both these baffled puritans, sexuality becomes the sign of bondage to the sexual family, hence literally the sign of their original sin; violently brought face to face with their own sexuality, both are forced to take their places in the bodily family.[9] Isabella is emphatically made to acknowledge the claims of her biological sisterhood even as she tries to immure herself in a spiritual family of sisters and mothers; both Angelo and Isabella are shamed and manipulated into wedlock in the end. The extremity of their self-exposure and degradation seems to me in part the mark of Shakespeare's strenuous attempt to separate himself from the bearers of the impossible fantasy of escape from the sexual body. But even while the play enforces the claims of the biological family in the persons of Angelo and Isabella, it accords the Duke himself the powers of an all-seeing spiritual father, apparently exempt from bodily needs; even as Isabella and Angelo are vindictively brought to recognize their origins and thus their human natures, a muted version of the fantasy of escape from sexual origins is reiterated and vested in the Duke. As the Duke increasingly puts himself in charge of matters of marriage and generation, in the last scene liberally bestowing new life as though he were a god, social and sexual continuance increasingly comes under male management, and the problematic female body comes to seem merely the pliant material means to male ends[10]—as Mariana herself obligingly turns up only when the Duke needs her body to fill in for Isabella's. If Helena's pregnant body is the site of Bertram's honor and the sign of new life in *All's Well, Measure for Measure* makes male honor and even life itself dependent not on the pregnant female body but on the Duke's machinations; the last scene is constructed to make invisible male power, rather than the visibly pregnant female body, the site of revelation. In the end, the replacement of the bodily female by the spiritual male dispensation seems complete.

But it is not entirely complete. The play's very peculiar treatment of Juliet seems to me the sign of its deep equivocation about origins. Juliet's pregnant body is the originating site for this play's confrontation with sin and death; it itself is the "character too gross" (1.2.144) in which Claudio's sin is written[11] and hence the material cause of his subjection to death. As such, it is a visible reminder of maternal origins and of the danger that is their inheritance. But the body so prominent in the beginning is curiously effaced by the action of the play, as the relationship between Juliet and Claudio is effaced; and this effacement seems to me a sign of the play's uneasy relation to sexuality and to the pregnant female body as the site of origin. Silent, strikingly isolated from the other characters—never acknowledged by Claudio during their two appearances on stage together, virtually unmentioned after her brief encounter with the Duke in 2.3—Juliet functions less as a realized character in the social world of Vienna than as a figure for the problem they would all like to efface, the problem of maternal origins. Originating cause of the play's dilemmas, she is largely forgotten as the Duke increasingly commands center stage; her pregnant body—the visible sign of maternal origin and of female generative power—is replaced by his invisible and bodiless control. But at the end Juliet returns, silently entering with Claudio; and her return qualifies the Duke's control. Displaced but never quite effaced by his machinations, wordlessly present at the end as at the beginning, she haunts the play, her body making legible the origin that can never quite be suppressed, as it makes legible the play's originating sin.

The solution to the dilemma registered in Juliet's body at first seems to be Isabella: the life that one woman has ruined, another can repair—or so Claudio hopes. The relationship between the two women is in fact both curious and elusive; though Isabella apparently never gives Juliet a thought after she is drawn out of the convent by Lucio's news, her initial response stresses the former closeness between them:

ISAB. Someone with child by him? My cousin Juliet?
LUCIO Is she your cousin?
ISAB. Adoptedly, as schoolmaids change their names
By vain though apt affection.

(1.4.45–48)

Though Isabella immediately attempts to disown the connection—*vain* though apt affection—it remains; Juliet's membership in Isabella's family comes first through her relationship with Isabella and only later through marriage to her brother. We glimpse here a bond like that of Hermia and Helena, or Rosalind and Celia: the fusion of identities between women that in the romantic comedies will be ruptured by relationship with men. But here the rupture is caused not by the entry into heterosexuality but by what seems to be the radical difference between the two women: one on the point of entering a convent, the other on the point of giving birth to the child of an illicit union. Isabella's response to Lucio acknowledges the difference, disowning not only Juliet but the whole mode of vain affection to which she belongs; in effect, Juliet becomes a part of the past that Isabella tries to leave behind in entering the convent. Yet the two have exchanged names; their identities remain more closely bound than Isabella knows or can later acknowledge. Juliet's pregnancy calls Isabella out of the convent; and later, Angelo will attempt to force Isabella to undo the distance between herself and Juliet by giving up her "body to such sweet uncleanness / As she that [Claudio] hath stain'd" (2.4.54–55).

How are we to understand the bond between the two women?[12] It seems to me to function less as a fact in Isabella's psyche than as an indication of the act of splitting that has produced these two characters and the act of violence that would undo the split, compelling Isabella once again to exchange names with Juliet, through the machinations either of Angelo or of the Duke. Isabella and the cloister she inhabits initially enter the play as the solution to the problem caused by Juliet and registered in her pregnant body; in effect, Isabella is imagined—by Claudio and by the play—as a response to Juliet. In that sense, the women share a common origin. Both derive from the same anxiety about sexuality and female generativity: the body of one—her presence mediated by Mistress Overdone, the bawd who first introduces her into the play—is the repository for the sense of sexual generation as illicit and dangerous; the body of the other—an unpolluted sanctuary about to be immured within another sanctuary—carries the promise of escape from sexuality and from the consequences of sexuality. But the split that initially promises to heal the sexual fault in fact reinforces it; the embodiment of sanctuary in the person of Isabella awakens the desire it would suppress, and the purported solution becomes the new problem. The play abruptly hurries us away from the relatively benign and mutual desire of Claudio and Juliet, transporting us instead into the dark region of Angelo's desire for Isabella. No longer mutual, desire now turns precisely on the destruction of the sanctuary that had seemed to promise escape. For Angelo's desire requires the presence of Isabella as a nun to be violated; having been created to embody an absolute purity, Isabella must be sacrificed to the split—in Angelo, in the play—that engendered her.

The psychic splitting in the play is, for the most part, localized in Angelo, who replicates and hence defines its psychic geography; his attempt to keep the portions of himself radically separate from one another is reproduced in the play's rigidly separated and confined spaces.[13] The battle within him between fierce repression of sexual desire and equally fierce outbursts of degrading and degraded desire is externalized in Vienna's convent and brothel, this play's version of Hamlet's two nunneries (*Hamlet,* 3.1.121, 130, 141); for Angelo as for Vienna, there is only a region of sexual soil below marriage and a region of absolute purity above it, with no middle ground for legitimate sexuality within marriage, no "moated grange" until the Duke magically calls one up through his dubious machinations. And even when it has been invoked by the Duke, this middle ground—spatially undefined except by its position outside the city—can no more be incorporated into the city than it can be incorporated into Angelo himself; he can neither inhabit it nor allow it to inhabit him. The violence with which Angelo carves himself up into separate spaces and attempts to keep them separate is released in the violence of his desire for Isabella:[14] violently separated, nunnery and brothel must be violently brought together. "Having waste ground enough, / Shall we desire to raze the sanctuary / And pitch our evils there?" (2.2.170–72): Angelo's question suggests the degree to which his desire turns on the confounding of places, the radical unmaking of distinctions. The "strumpet / With all her double vigor, art and nature" (2.2.183–84) could not tempt him because he can experience desire only as the remaking of the sanctuary as brothel / privy, only as the polluting of a sacred space by his own bodily wastes.[15]

In the violence of Angelo's sexual imagination, Shakespeare reworks the terrible paradox of male desire as he had presented it in *Troilus and Cressida* and in *Othello.* There, the fantasy of pollution had been the tragic side effect of desire; but here that fantasy is itself the motive-force of desire. Othello destroys Desdemona and himself because he cannot tolerate the contamination of her sanctified being; Angelo wills just this contamination, experiencing desire only in terms of the split it would vindictively undo. But why does *Measure for Measure* portray desire only thus, only through the exciting image of contaminating a sanctified female space? In part, I think, because this image casts male sexuality as a punitive response to original female betrayal: through intercourse, Angelo would vindictively rewrite the sanctified female body as corrupt as though to punish it for originally betraying him to desire.

From the start, the play vests the fantasy of escape from desire in Angelo and allies that fantasy with escape from the body and from sexual origin, the stinking dependence that governs ordinary human life. Withdrawing from visible authority, the Duke—and the play—set out to test Angelo's refusal to confess that "his blood flows; or that his appetite / Is more to bread than stone" (1.3.52–53), claims exaggerated in Lucio's comic contention that his "blood / Is very snow-broth" (1.4.57–58), his urine "congealed ice"

(3.2.106–7). He is the *locus classicus* in Shakespeare for the fantasy of a body born exempt from appetite; and near the center of the play, Lucio associates his coldness specifically with his exemption from the ordinary means of procreation:

> LUCIO They say this Angelo was not made by man and woman, after this downright way of creation: is it true, think you?
>
> DUKE How should he be made, then?
>
> LUCIO Some report, a sea-maid spawned him. Some, that he was begot between two stockfishes. . . . And he is a motion ungenerative; that's infallible.
>
> (3.2.99–108)

The underground logic of Lucio's joke depends on the assumption that one's sexuality is an inheritance from one's parents: being without appetite, Angelo must not have been conceived in the ordinary way. Angelo is "ungenerative" because he is, as Lucio later says, an "ungenitured agent" (3.2.167–68): not only lacking testicles, but himself unbegotten.[16] The Duke's unusual willingness to participate in Lucio's joke, even to entertain for a moment the possibility of an alternative to the "downright way of creation," marks the centrality of this fantasy in the creation of Angelo. But the play sets out ruthlessly to bring Angelo to the startled recognition that his blood does flow ("Blood, thou art blood" [2.4.15]), and hence to demonstrate the obverse of Lucio's joke: here, as in *Hamlet,* one's own sexual body is the sign of original sin, the sin inherited from one's parents.

The discovery of desire is for Angelo initially equivalent to the discovery that he has a body:

> it is I
> That, lying by the violet in the sun,
> Do as the carrion does, not as the flower,
> Corrupt with virtuous season.
>
> (2.2.165–68)

In answering his own questions ("What's this? . . . who sins most?" [2.2.163–64]), Angelo makes the equation "I am flesh," as though recognizing this about himself—"it is I"—here for the first time. And to have a body is to be bound to death: reiterating Hamlet's image for conception (*Hamlet,* 2.2.181–82), Angelo can speak his bodily desire to himself only as the stirring of maggots in dead flesh. Confronting his own sexuality, that is, he experiences the secular equivalent of original sin and the fall into death: hence the logic by which Angelo is eventually brought to enact his sexual desire in a garden. Entry into this garden—itself carefully described to evoke the double passage of the female genitalia[17]—doubly returns Angelo to the female body, the site of origin from which he had seemed to claim exemption.

When we next see Angelo after 2.2, he seems to be exactly where we had left him; though we know that time has passed, he has apparently been immobilized by the discovery that he has a body. The logic that governs the imagery of the meditation that opens 2.4 follows from this discovery:

> Heaven hath my empty words,
> Whilst my invention, hearing not my tongue,
> Anchors on Isabel: Heaven in my mouth,
> As if I did but only chew his name,
> And in my heart the strong and swelling evil,
> Of my conception.
>
> (2.4.2–7)

His new awareness of his bodily self—his tongue, his mouth, his heart—blocks his access to the spiritual father on whom he has relied,[18] transforming God Himself into empty substance in a cruel parody of transubstantiation. And as in *Hamlet,* Angelo's horrified awareness of himself as body distances him from the idealized father and returns him to the moment of his own conception, the maternal site of his original sin. In place of the heavenly father who could protect him from his body, Angelo finds the overwhelming presence of his bodily parents in "the strong and swelling evil / Of [his] conception"; swollen with this conception, he replicates the swelling both of phallic potency and of pregnancy, hence reproduces within himself the downright way he was conceived. For his desire is the mark of this conception: Angelo can imagine his own sexuality only as a return to this point of origin, the point at which he was made flesh. In his own embodiedness, he becomes the sin his mother carried: idealized and bodiless male presence is lost to him and in him as he becomes equivalent to Juliet, female and soiled,[19] pregnant with his own sexuality. In *Measure for Measure's* elaborately psychologized version of the fall, familiar from *Hamlet* and played out in Angelo, recognition of the fall and hence of original sin in oneself is thus equivalent to the loss of the spiritual father and the discovery of the indissoluble link to the maternal body.

The anger of this recognition is turned on Isabella. Angelo's determination to pollute the sanctuary within her is exciting to him in part because it replays his discovery of maternal corruption within himself. In polluting the sanctuary, he would dirty Isabella as he has been dirtied, punitively recording the discovery of corruption in her body, as though tracing his own corruption to its source,[20] in effect, he excitedly desires to replicate the shaming and exciting discovery of maternal sexuality in her. And if she acquiesces in her own corruption, Isabella can moreover assuage the guilt of his polluting desire: acquiescing, she demonstrates that there never was a sanctuary, that all women are the same, all equally subject to soil. Angelo's attempt to compel Isabella's acquiescence in her own pollution thus takes the form of forcing her to acknowledge her kinship with Juliet (2.4.55), hence her position as woman, where "woman" is no more than the sign of sexual frailty:

> Be that you are,
> That is, a woman; if you be more, you're none.
> If you be one—as you are well express'd
> By all external warrants—show it now,
> By putting on the destin'd livery.
> (2.4.133–37)

"Be that you are": Angelo would make Isabella woman with a vengeance,[21] binding her to the livery of a specifically female flesh and hence marking her as inescapably sexual; Isabella's later invocation of her mother's sexual guilt (3.1.140–41) demonstrates how fully she has understood his drift. In his attempt to seduce Isabella, that is, Angelo turns the horror of his self-recognition back toward her, binding her to her corrupt origin as he is newly bound to his.

If Angelo's confrontation with sexuality forces him back toward his sexual origins, Isabella's literally enmeshes her in family; the encounter between them is so explosive in part because her fantasies mesh so well with his. For Isabella is not merely a counter in Angelo's fantasy; when we first see her, she is vividly and independently alive, portrayed with fantasies of her own. Her initial flight to the nunnery and her desire for more restrictions there (1.4.4–5) suggest that she, like Angelo, wishes to be exempt from ordinary human sexuality and from the ordinary bonds so engendered. When Angelo asks her to embrace female frailty by "putting on the destin'd livery," he allows us to understand that this is precisely the livery Isabella had hoped to escape by putting on the livery of the nun. For the religious community promises to free her both from sexuality and from the bonds of the sexual family, replacing its relationships by those of a spiritual family, in which *sister, brother, mother, father* are freed from the taint of sexuality.[22] But just at the moment of Isabella's apparent escape, the sexuality of her natural family draws her back into the world, forcing its ties upon her appropriately through Lucio, emissary of the brothel.

In bringing her face to face with the conflict between her two kinds of sisterhood, the play binds her at once to family and to her female flesh; characteristically, she feels the temptation of this flesh as an inheritance from what Lucio would call the downright way of creation. She responds to Angelo's claim that women are frail—the preface to his invitation to show herself a woman—with an hysteria that voices her own sense of contaminating origins:

> ANG. Nay, women are frail too.
> ISAB. Ay, as the glasses where they view themselves,
> Which are as easy broke as they make forms.

Women?—Help, heaven! Men their creation mar
In profiting by them. Nay, call us ten times frail;
For we are soft as our complexions are,
And credulous to false prints.[23]

(2.4. 123–29)

In her shift from *they* to *us,* Isabella reenacts in miniature her attempt to escape from the condition of "woman" and her eventual entrapment in it. And that condition is inextricably bound to woman's role in reproduction: like Angelo, Isabella can understand her own potentiality for frailty only as the continuation of her mother's fault. Her bizarre response to Angelo fuses conventional commentary on woman's vanity with anxiety about reproductive sexuality, as the mirror becomes a trope for the woman's body, broken as it makes forms;[24] the impulse that has led her to the nunnery becomes visible here, in her image of the female body broken both in the act of penetration and in the act of giving birth. But Isabella turns the fear and shame of this moment against women, attempting to separate herself from "them" as she identifies with the aggressor, articulating her own version of the misogynistic fantasy of male parthenogenesis. "Men their creation mar / In profiting by them": here, in one more version of the fall, Isabella imagines a purely male creation spoiled by concourse with women. But in wishing, as Posthumus later will, that there might be "some way for men to be" without women as "half-workers" (*Cymbeline,* 2.4.153–54), Isabella in effect wishes herself out of bodily existence; and the failure of the fantasy—the inevitability of the female role in reproduction—brings her back to herself and to her woman's body. Within four words, she conspicuously marks the passage from "them" to "us," for the first time acknowledging her own involvement in the offending category, for the first time feeling woman's frailty as her own.

In the underground logic of Isabella's transition from "them" to "us," hereditary participation in the downright way of creation makes female frailty her inescapable legacy, binding her to her fate as a sexual being. Called out of the nunnery by her bodily family, Isabella is forced to confront her sexual origins and hence her complicity in what the play poses as original sin. The panic engendered by this incipient recognition is voiced in the hysteria with which she responds to Angelo and later to Claudio; the second encounter repeats and intensifies the terms of the first. Faced with the evidence not only of her brother's sexuality but of his desire to live, Isabella traces what she sees as his corruption back to his sexual origin, specifically back to his mother's fault; and Claudio's attempt to replicate that fault in her—to pull her into her mother's sphere—is at the center of her panic:

Wilt thou be made a man out of my vice?
Is't not a kind of incest, to take life
From thine own sister's shame? What should I think?
Heaven shield my mother play'd my father fair:

> For such a warped slip of wilderness
> Ne'er issued from his blood.
>
> (3.1.137–42)

Isabella begins by questioning the dependence of manhood on female shame, but her horror gives her question a particularly vivid anatomical cast: "wilt thou be made a man out of my vice?"[25] If Isabella were willing to rescue Claudio by sexual means, he would in effect be born from her; but this would make Isabella into his mother, the woman out of whose vice Claudio was literally made man. In duplicating the parental act that made Claudio man, intercourse with Angelo would incestuously bind Isabella to her family, replicating in Angelo the father who mars his creation in profiting by woman, and in Isabella the mother who is the site of corruption.[26] And in remaking her incestuously as her brother's mother, the act would cancel out Isabella's difference from her mother; revoking her escape from family, it would seal in her the inheritance that is anatomically the woman's part, identifying her vice as her maternal legacy.[27]

Isabella's desperate search for a means to defend herself against this contaminating identification with her mother is registered in the poignant question—"what should I think?"—that breaks her diatribe, calling our attention both to her inner processes and to the peculiarity of what she decides to think. The urgency of her need is underscored by her bizarrely inverted prayer: she calls on heaven to shield—or forbid—not her mother's infidelity but her fidelity, invoking a heavenly father in effect to guarantee the bastardizing of her brother. The idea of her mother's adultery seems to come to her as a saving remedy, offering her some respite from her panic. But how can it serve her to imagine her mother a whore and her father a cuckold? First of all, the very viciousness with which she turns on her mother serves in part to assuage the terrifying identification with her: here as in her parthenogenesis fantasy of 2.4, she allies herself with the male voices condemning female contamination,[28] as though to distance herself absolutely from the mother she attacks. And in the process, she rescues her father from degradation: by locating responsibility for Claudio's corruption entirely with her mother, she manages to maintain the purity of her father and hence the possibility of protection that she has imagined in him. Her image of her father has in fact functioned thus for her earlier, anticipating the logic of this moment. In 2.4, Isabella defends herself against Angelo's proposal in part by imagining in her brother a "mind of honour" that would gladly prefer his own death to his sister's pollution (2.4.178–82). When Claudio in fact speaks with the voice that she imagines there, she sees him as fully his father's son, speaking with his father's voice: "There spake my brother: there my father's grave / Did utter forth a voice" (3.1.85–86). For Isabella, he is his father's son and speaks with his father's voice insofar as he is willing to die to protect her from sexual contamination, allying himself with her against the female body and its frailty.

When that protection fails—when his desire for life threatens her exemption from sexuality—Isabella reinvents his familial relationship, making him radically his mother's son rather than his father's: if Claudio is vicious, then her father had no part in his making. "Such a warped slip of wilderness / Ne'er issued from his blood": her brother's vice, like her own, is purely a maternal inheritance.[29] In response to Claudio's attempt to ally her with female frailty, that is, she rewrites the failed parthenogenesis fantasy of her earlier encounter with Angelo, rationalizing it and hence keeping it within the limits of the possible: once again, women are the source of corruption and men mar their creation in profiting by them; but Isabella manages to make an exception of her father by removing him bodily from the moment of conception. Exonerating her father at her mother's expense, she leaves her father free to remain an idealized presence, separated from the contaminated sphere of female sexuality and hence still available to protect her from it.

Threatened by identification with the mother who can exist for her only as a site of corruption, Isabella responds by invoking the protective image of a pure father who can serve as a buffer between her and the maternal legacy that both Angelo and Claudio bid her to assume. In her need for a saving father as in her flight from sexuality, Isabella resembles Angelo, who also attempts to invoke the pure father as a bulwark against his new bondage to his body and hence to the sexual family. Like Angelo unsuccessfully calling on heaven as he recoils in horror from his own conception (2.4.2), Isabella calls on a heavenly father both here and earlier, when enforced identification with female frailty had threatened her ("Women?—Help, heaven" [2.4.126]). Both Angelo and Isabella need a bodiless father to protect them from the consequences of their own bodily legacy—and this is the role the play assigns to the Duke, its "ghostly father" (4.3.47;5.1.129). The distant heavenly father whom Angelo cannot reach is realized for him in the figure of the newly returned Duke: hence the ease with which Angelo identifies his unseen observation with that of "power divine" (5.1.367). The Duke's mid-play appearance to Isabella similarly follows out the logic of her need for a sanctified father. When the protection of Claudio and the father embodied in him fails, she attempts to invent a father dissociated from the troubling female region of sexuality; and the Duke appears to her magically as a nonsexual father-protector within ten lines. (Indeed, when Claudio had proclaimed his willingness to die, he had in fact been speaking with the voice of this father: it is of course the Duke who has reconciled him to death.) The congruence of this appearance suggests the degree to which the Duke as Friar is the embodiment of the fantasied asexual father who will protect Isabella from her own sexuality, the vice that is her inheritance from her mother. It is striking that Isabella calls him "good father" (3.1.238, 269) not in response to his appearance as friar *per se* but only after he has offered her a way to avoid the destined livery; he becomes the "good father" for her only insofar as he can take on her dead father's protective role.

Angelo needs the Duke as the heavenly father who comes back to judge him, condemning him to death for his manifold infractions against a sacred space and then forgiving him by demonstrating that the space has not been violated after all; Isabella needs the Duke as the heavenly father who can protect her from female frailty and provide her with a safely asexual family. But the play simultaneously needs the Duke to move these characters away from sexual disgust, to enable the marriages on which both social continuance and comic closure depend. For most audiences, I suspect, this conflict in his roles—and hence the ambivalence about sexuality throughout the play—is focused most clearly in his last-minute marriage proposal. The Duke who has protected Isabella from sexuality now invites, or perhaps coerces, her participation in it; and given both the ease with which the distinction between legitimate and illegitimate sexuality breaks down in this play and the suddenness with which the sainted Duke, like the sainted Angelo, announces his desire, his proposal threatens disturbingly to reiterate Angelo's.[30]

Our uneasiness with the final marriage proposal underscores our uneasiness with the Duke's role throughout; he is on the face of it a very odd person through whom to attempt an accommodation to marriage and the life of the sexually created family. He enters 1.1 announcing his intention to withdraw from civic power and enters 1.3 announcing his disdain for what he calls "the dribbling dart of love" (1.3.2); by escaping into the role of friar, he manages to evade the expectation that he will use the paternal rod (1.3.26) either punitively or generatively, practicing a kind of self-castration in handing both sorts of potency on to Angelo. "Be thou at full ourself" (1.1.43), he tells Angelo: as the Duke becomes a friar, he makes Angelo the duke *in absentia,* in effect splitting himself into two figures—the Angelo whose potency he creates and who enacts the conflicts of carnal paternal power in his stead,[31] and the Friar whose status as an unproblematically ghostly father protects him from those conflicts. Through this device, the Duke—who is fully as fastidious about sexuality as Angelo himself—is spared the sort of testing that Angelo must undergo: the affiliation with "dark corners" (4.3.156) that we might be tempted to see in the Duke's voyeuristic fascination with the corruption that boils around him and in his role as virtual bawd to Angelo and Mariana is in effect dislocated from his psyche, given its locus only in Angelo's actions and in Lucio's treasonable slander; thus relocated, it is exorcised from the person of the Duke, who remains strikingly without bodily desires. In the figure of the Duke, that is, the play pulls in two directions at once: even while Shakespeare apparently uses him to reconcile the others to their own human nature, he reinstates in the Duke a fantasy of escape from that nature, allowing the Duke to become an ungenitured agent just as Angelo is forced to acknowledge his own origins.

This doubleness deeply compromises the play's ostensible attempt at cure; in fact it replicates the very split in Angelo—between sexuality and absolute purity, the brothel and the sanctuary—that the bed trick seems designed to heal. The play has throughout made its meaning through its radical division into separate places—not only nunnery and brothel, but prison, moated grange, Angelo's garden—a division that cannot be canceled by ducal (or authorial) fiat any more than the bed trick can cancel the violence of the splittings that haunt Angelo's imagination, the violence that has split even the Duke himself. Throughout, as the Duke crosses boundaries, moving from monastery to prison and moated grange, apparently psychically in control of nunnery and brothel and the garden in which they meet in the bed trick, he carries the promise of a more fluid psychic geography. But instead of incorporating these locales into himself—hence incorporating the possibility of a renewed city—he remains aloof from them all, maintaining both his own and their separateness intact. In the last scene, Shakespeare (through the Duke) moves the play to the fluid open space outside the city walls, as though to break down the psychic rigidity that has immobilized Vienna's citizens; but instead of enabling the transformation of these places, or any kind of communication between them, the Duke seems only to reconstitute them through his intrusive management, simultaneously transgressing their boundaries and reinforcing their stability. Apparently married in prison (5.1.518–19) to the prostitute he has wronged, Lucio will become in effect a permanent inhabitant of the brothel; instead of redeeming marriage, the Duke's sentence makes it equivalent to the prison—or to a worse sentence—for him. For Angelo too, enforced marriage takes the place of a death sentence, binding him permanently to the fallen garden in which he discovered his mortality; even after he has discovered that he has bedded his virtual wife, he craves "death more willingly than mercy" (5.1.474), and can scarcely be persuaded to give up his new alliance with carrion, his conviction that death is the appropriate punishment for his original sin—a conviction unlikely to be changed by the technicality that Claudio turns out to be alive. Distrust of sexuality remains so much in force that Shakespeare deliberately minimizes his one chance for a conventional happy ending: though Claudio and Juliet enter together, there is no indication that they have noticed one another; they remain as separate at the end as at the beginning, unjoined by the Duke who specializes in joining only those who do not want to be together.[32] Instead of resolving the psychic impasse that has made the bed trick necessary—hence achieving even the half-hearted cure of *All's Well*—*Measure* reiterates that impasse in the Duke's final manipulations, in which the bed trick's coercion of desire seems to become not a momentary aberation but rather the law of marriage itself.

In *Measure for Measure,* the curative role of Helena is in effect shrunk to that of Mariana; Helena's vehement and dangerous love is now contained in her much more manageable person. She alone among the play's characters can express desire without a sense of contamination; she carries the fragile hope not only of reformation but of a healing reconciliation to origins and hence to the sins of the body: "They say best men are moulded out of faults" (5.1.437).[33] Both Shakespeare's habitual use of "moulded" and the play on *fault / foutre* throughout *Measure for Measure* let us hear the fullness of the hope that she expresses: not only that Angelo may be improved by the confrontation with his own specifically sexual faults, not only that he will be able to tolerate his own sexuality as the legacy of the fault / foutre that moulded him, but that the sin of origin will be accepted as the common ground of human goodness.[34] "Best men are moulded out of faults," Mariana implies, because, in the downright way of creation, that is the only way men are moulded at all. But the wistful hope that she expresses here is frail indeed. There is little sign that Angelo has been remade by his confrontation with original sin in the garden of her body, and still less sign that Isabella's surrogate participation in Mariana's sexuality has made her any more willing to put on the destined livery. Moreover, as a vessel of cure, Mariana herself is a relatively unsubstantial character, introduced late in the play and as an obvious *corpus ex machina* to solve an unsolvable dilemma. Though her desires are vehement and her own, her very being in the play seems under the management of the Duke: conveniently forgotten by him early in the play, she turns up only when she is useful to him; in effect invented by his need of her, she serves entirely at his pleasure. In the relationship between them, Shakespeare redoes the problematic relationship between Helena and the King, and hence between male and female sites of authority. Now the male ranges freely while the female is impotent and confined: stuck helplessly in her moated grange, freed only by the Duke's intervention, Mariana epitomizes *Measure for Measure's* restructuring of male / female relation.

In its own way, then, *Measure for Measure* takes back what *All's Well* has given Helena, assuaging the acute anxiety that she creates—"that man should be at woman's command, and yet no hurt done!" (*All's Well.* 1.3.89–90)—by relocating sexual and social power firmly in the male domain. Her bed trick is no longer the sign of female control over generation and hence over the passing on of male honor; it is now under male management, the sign of invisible male control over the work of generation itself.[35] So powerful that she must be dismembered in order to be remembered, Helena is in effect split into three in *Measure for Measure,* the better to be contained. Mariana inherits her active desire and her curative role, both now sternly subordinate to the Duke. Juliet inherits her pregnant body, now the sign of sin rather than the sign of generative power: imprisoned and immobilized by that body, always on the point of giving birth (2.2.15–16) but never reaching that fruition, utterly dependent on the Duke's authority for her release, silenced by Shakespeare as by the Duke, she reinscribes pregnancy as the site of female vulnerability and male control. And Isabella inherits Helena's status as sacred virgin, her virginity now the inciting cause of a sick male desire, not the source of a near-magical restoration: a sanctuary made only to be violated, invaded and shamed as much by the play as by Angelo and the Duke, her threatening power is in the end firmly subordinated to the imperatives of patriarchal marriage.[36] Initially self-enclosed, she becomes increasingly a common thoroughfare, in the imagination of whose body the desires of others meet; initially vividly defined by her own unbending selfhood and her articulate voice, she becomes increasingly unable to say what she wants, increasingly the tool of the Duke. By thus splitting Helena's power and revealing the controlling male presence that will finally put her in her place, *Measure for Measure* undoes the central movement of *All's Well,* enabling marriage by putting it under the aegis not of a sexual woman but of a sternly asexual man.[37]

In the final revelations of *Measure for Measure,* it is the pure father rather than the sexual mother who proves to have been everywhere unseen. Only in the presence of this father can sexuality and marriage be made safe; when he withdraws at the start of the play, sexuality bubbles and boils (5.1.316) like a witches' cauldron (*Macbeth,* 4.1.19) in Vienna, threatening to overwhelm both Angelo and Isabella in what they feel as their maternal legacy. But this is exactly the condition that obtains at the beginning of *Hamlet,* where the disappearance of Hamlet's father immerses Hamlet in the realm defined by his mother's sexuality; and it is the condition of *All's Well,* where a similar disappearance puts Bertram under the combined power of his mother and Helena. No wonder, then, that the Duke returns as a revised version of Hamlet's ghostly father,[38] a version in which that father proves to be all-powerful: the pattern of doing and undoing implicit in *All's Well* and *Measure for Measure,* and most visible in its repeated bed tricks—the one the mother's, the other the father's—responds to the crisis initiated by *Hamlet.* But the bodiless Duke is not finally an adequate solution to this crisis; as the persistence of Juliet reminds us, maternal origin cannot simply be wished away. In *King Lear, Macbeth,* and *Coriolanus,* Shakespeare returns to the vulnerability of the bodily father and hence to the world of paternal absence in which the mother is given full sway.

Notes

1. The term is Arthur Kirsch's (*Shakespeare and the Experience of Love* [Cambridge: Cambridge University Press, 1981], p. 136). Kirsch's account of both plays stresses the centrality of the bed trick as cure (see, for example, pp. 84, 98–99, and 141–42); though he finds the plays more celebratory of sexuality and procreation than I do, his argument anticipates mine at several points. For another reading of the bed trick that minimizes its problematic nature, see Eileen Z. Cohen ("Virtue is Bold": the Bed-Trick and Characterization in *All's Well That Ends Well* and *Measure for Measure,*" *Philological Quarterly* 65 [1986]: 171–86). Both Richard P. Wheeler (*Shakespeare's Development and the Problem Comedies* [Berkeley: University of California Press, 1981], esp. pp. 12–13, 55) and Carol Neely (*Broken Nuptials in Shakespeare's Plays* [New Haven, Conn.: Yale University Press, 1985], esp. pp. 71–74, 78–79, and 92–95) have written on the bed trick as a problematic attempt to recuperate sexuality in these plays;

their understanding of what needs recuperating is very close to mine. I am deeply indebted to them both, not only for many specifics of interpretation in these plays but also for long ago introducing me to the interpretative power of a method that understands the plays comparatively, as developments and redevelopments of the same set of issues; along with C. L. Barber, they liberated me from the constraints of a New Critical practice that tended to think about these texts in isolation from one other.

2. See Geoffrey Bullough, *Narrative and Dramatic Sources of Shakespeare,* vol. 2 (London and New York: Routledge and Kegan Paul, Columbia University Press, 1958), p. 395.

3. Instead of legitimizing desire, the descriptions of the bed trick make even legitimate sexuality illicit in fantasy, a "wicked meaning in a lawful deed," where technically "both not sin" and yet we are left with a "sinful fact" (3.7.45–47). Helena's musings on Bertram's "sweet use" of what he hates (4.4.21–25) similarly work to make defilement and loathing central to the sexual act, whether licit or illicit. Helena's language here both hides and declares the sexual act at the center of the play: in her account, both actors disappear, their bodily relation expressed by the interaction of a series of abstractions ("Saucy trusting of the cozen'd thoughts / Defiles the pitchy night"). One is left only with a sense of disembodied but mutual defilement. In her condensation of night with her own body, Helena perfectly explicates this mutuality: the body in that bed is already defiled, already "pitchy," before Bertram comes to defile it; and as Shakespeare frequently reminds us (see, for example, *Much Ado,* 3.3.57, or *1 Henry IV,* 2.4.394), pitch defiles. In this representation of the bed trick, that is, Bertram defiles a body that is already defiled, and is himself defiled in turn; the act that should incorporate desire into marriage succeeds instead in making the marriage bed itself both defiled and defiling.

4. Michel de Montaigne, *The Essayes of Michael Lord of Montaigne,* trans. John Florio (London, New York: J. M. Dent, E. P. Dutton, 1928), p. 72. Kirsch identifies this essay as a source for *All's Well* (*Shakespeare and the Experience of Love,* pp. 38, 122–27); I am very much indebted to his account. The essay seems to have been central to Shakespeare's imagination during this period; Cavell notes the similarity of its topics to those of *Othello* (*The Claim of Reason* [Oxford: Oxford University Press, 1979], p. 474).

5. For some, the play's failure to satisfy desire is the source of its value. See, for example, Joseph Westlund's argument that the play tempers the dangerous tendency of its characters—and its critics—to idealize ("*All's Well That Ends Well:* Longing, Idealization, and Sadness," *Shakespeare's Reparative Comedies: A Psychoanalytic View of the Middle Plays.* [Chicago: University of Chicago Press, 1984], pp. 121–46) and David Scott Kastan's congruent argument that it exposes the danger (especially to the autonomy of others) inherent in the desire for a comic ending ("*All's Well That Ends Well* and the Limits of Comedy," *ELH* 52 [1985]: 575–89).

6. After we have met Mariana the play works hard to reinforce the distinction that has been obliterated—in effect, to clear a space for legitimate sexuality. Hence the Duke's assurance that the sexual union of Angelo and Mariana is legal and no sin, despite its close resemblance to the sin of Claudio and Juliet. But the very insistence of his assurance—an assurance that he feels compelled to give, although Mariana shows no signs of needing it—should remind us that this apparently crucial distinction would be apt to disappear, and not just in the minds of modern audiences, were it not insisted on. The degree to which modern scholars disagree in assigning degrees of legitimacy to the two relationships suggests the flimsiness of the distinction. See, for example, S. Nagarajan ("*Measure for Measure* and Elizabethan Betrothals," *Shakespeare Quarterly* 14 [1963]: 116–18) and Margaret Loftus Ranald, " 'As Marriage Binds, and Blood Breaks': English Marriage and Shakespeare," *Shakespeare Quarterly* 30 [1979]: 77–79); A. D. Nuttall wisely dissolves the distinction (" 'Measure for Measure': The Bed Trick," *Shakespeare Survey* 28 [1975]: 52–53). Margaret Scott notes that neither *de futuro* nor *de praesenti* contracts would have been held valid under the Tridentine decree of 1563 in force in Catholic Vienna; she sees the difficulty in distinguishing between Claudio's and Angelo's act as

characteristic of a play in which differences often lie only in the eye of the beholder (" 'Our City's Institutions': Some Further Reflections on the Marriage Contracts in *Measure for Measure,*" *ELH* 49 [1982]: 790–804).

7. Critics often comment on Shakespeare's structural use of the pun in *Measure.* See especially Meredith Skura's analysis both of the fantasy linking sexuality and death and of the ways in which the play ultimately counters this fantasy (*The Literary Use of the Psychoanalytic Process* [New Haven, Conn.: Yale University Press, 1981], pp. 260–66), Kirsch's account of Claudio's confrontation with sexuality and hence mortality (*Shakespeare and the Experience of Love,* pp. 90–91), and Neely's discussion of the witty equation of love and death in *All's Well* and the very different valence of the pun in *Measure* (*Broken Nuptials,* pp. 92–93, 99–100). For these critics, and many others, the pun expresses sexual anxiety; for Darryl J. Gless, it expresses the "unconventional *imitatio Christi*" through which Isabella is asked "to 'die' in order to 'redeem' Claudio from the 'law' " (*"Measure for Measure," the Law, and the Convent* [Princeton, N.J.: Princeton University Press, 1979], p. 126).

8. Wheeler tellingly notes not only the congruence between these two speeches—a congruence prior to any considerations of legitimacy or illegitimacy—but also the degree to which the Duke arranges matters so that he speaks his disgust in the first person in both cases ("Reason thus with life: / If I do lose thee . . ."; "Say to thyself . . . I drink, I eat") (*Shakespeare's Development and the Problem Comedies,* pp. 121–22).

9. Many critics understand the play in part as a testing of Isabella and Angelo that is designed to bring them to acknowledge their repressed bodily impulses and hence their places in the human community; see especially Kirsch's sensitive (though in my view overly optimistic) account of the curative process (*Shakespeare and the Experience of Love,* pp. 80–89).

10. This is of course a perfectly orthodox rendering of the Aristotelian position on generation; see Janet Adelman, *Suffocating Mothers: Fantasies of Maternal Origin in Shakespeare's Plays, "Hamlet" to "The Tempest"* (New York and London: Routledge, 1992), p. 6. Angelo's imagery of sexual commerce as coining (2.4.45) reiterates this orthodoxy: in it the male stamps his will—and his image—upon an unresisting female matter. Given the extent to which Angelo feels contaminated by the prospect of sexual exchange, this must be a consoling image for him; in transferring power over generation to the Duke, the play reproduces Angelo's metaphor in another register.

11. In assessing the possibilities of a resisting counter-hegemony in *Measure,* Anthony B. Dawson comments suggestively on the imagery of inscription that makes sex "ambiguously semiotic" throughout and hence foregrounds the dubiousness of the final resolution ("*Measure for Measure,* New Historicism, and Theatrical Power," *Shakespeare Quarterly* 39 [1988]: 336–39).

12. Not many critics bother to try. Ralph Berry specifically notes the alliance only to dismiss it ("Language and Structure in *Measure for Measure,*" *University of Toronto Quarterly* 46 [1976–77]: 156); in an unpublished paper, Maurice Charney implies—without quite stating—a relation between the two women when he notes that Angelo's dismissal of the "fornicatress" is followed immediately by the entrance of the "very virtuous maid" (" 'Be That You Are, / That is, a Woman': The 'Prenzie' Angelo and the 'Enskied' Isabella," ms. pp. 7–8). In her very suggestive analysis of the many splittings and doublings that make the play a "masterly study of repression, and of the repressed, and of its Hydra-headed return," Ruth Nevo reads the relation in terms very close to my own; for her, Juliet is Isabella's "alter ego, . . . the women in Isabella which Isabella . . . has not chosen to be" ("*Measure for Measure:* Mirror for Mirror," *Shakespeare Survey* 40 [1988]: 112, 115).

13. Many note the play's psychic and geographic rigidity; see, for example, Berry's suggestive account of overworld and underworld as fragments both of a body politic and of a single mind ignorant of its separate parts ("Language and Structure in *Measure for Measure,*" pp. 147–49). For Skura, this rigidity is symptomatic of the overly rigid psychic organizations that the play must work through (*The Literary Use of the Psychoanalytic Process,* p. 247); for Gless,

the play's various claustrophobic confinements point to its participation in the tradition of anti-monastic satire (*"Measure for Measure," the Law, and the Convent,* pp. 94–98).

14. See Wheeler (*Shakespeare's Development and the Problem Comedies,* p. 100) for a very similar account of this process.

15. See J. W. Lever's helpful note for the presence of the privy in Angelo's lines (Arden *Measure for Measure,* p. 50). Angelo's shocked recognition here is a tragic reworking of Montaigne's much cooler meditation on the mixture of delight and disgust in sexuality, where "our joyes and filthes" are "pell-mell lodged together" ("On Some Verses of Virgil," p. 105). But what amuses and repels Montaigne attracts Angelo.

16. Lever notes that "ungenitured" is a Shakespearean formation, used only here (Arden *Measure,* p. 89). The word is usually glossed as "sexless" or "without genitals," but "unbegotten" seems equally plausible and follows from Lucio's previous joke on the subject. Among the relevant meanings current for "geniture," *OED* lists (1) "begetting, generation; birth," (3) "that which is generated; offspring, product," and (5) "genitals"; its citation of Fulke (1579) in support of (3)—"he is a geniture, that is a thing begotten"—is particularly germane.

17. The resemblance is often noted; see, for example, Berry ("Language and Structure," p. 151), Rupin W. Desai ("Freudian Undertones in the Isabella-Angelo Relationship of *Measure for Measure,*" *Psychoanalytic Review* 64 [1977]: 490), Neely (*Broken Nuptials,* p. 95), and Nevo (*"Measure for Measure:* Mirror for Mirror," p. 119). The enclosed garden—traditionally associated with the virgin body—is Shakespeare's addition here, not found in the play's sources.

18. For Wheeler, the disappearance of the protective father here reiterates and reveals the consequences of the Duke's earlier disappearance; see his rich discussion of Angelo's reliance on the Duke as externalized father / superego (*Shakespeare's Development,* esp. pp. 93–97, 110).

19. For David Sundelson, anxiety about the precariousness of male identity is at the heart of *Measure;* he notes the pun on "conception" and comments extensively on Angelo's fear both of female potency and of his own feminization (*Shakespeare's Restorations of the Father* [New Brunswick, N.J.: Rutgers University Press, 1983], pp. 91–92).

20. Both Richard A. Levin ("Duke Vincentio and Angelo: Would 'A Feather Turn the Scale'?" *Studies in English Literature, 1500–1900* 22[1982]: 263) and Wheeler (*Shakespeare's Development,* p. 100) understand Angelo's vindictiveness toward Isabella in part as his attempt to replicate his own shame in her. My emphasis on the corrupting of a specifically maternal body here is particularly indebted to Wheeler, who reads Angelo's rigid separation of the ideal and the sexual—and the devastating collapse of that separation when Angelo confronts Isabella—as the consequence of Angelo's imperfect resolution of oedipal desire for the mother (see especially pp. 96–97; see also Stephen A. Reid, "A Psychoanalytic Reading of 'Troilus and Cressida' and 'Measure for Measure,' " *The Psychoanalytic Review* 57 [1970]: 278). One name for Angelo's exciting desire is thus incest. This is in fact the name that Isabella gives to their proposed sexual concourse (3.1.138) in her rage at Claudio; here again, as in *Hamlet* and *All's Well,* the more visible threat of brother-sister incest seems to function partly as a displacement for the threat of mother-son incest. Isabella herself repeatedly asks Angelo to identify his desires with Claudio's (2.2.64–66, 137–42; see also Escalus at 2.1.8–16). It seems to be in response to this proposed identification with Claudio that Angelo first feels desire, signaled by his abruptly telling Isabella to leave (2.2.66) or attempting to leave himself (2.2.143); does Angelo feel desire only insofar as the object of desire is constructed incestuously as a sister / mother?

21. Charney notes the coerciveness of Angelo's attempt but on the whole seems to approve of it; in his view, it is disappointing that the play does not reward Angelo for "educating Isabella and bringing her out" by giving her to him in the end (" 'Be That You Are,' " ms. p. 14).

22. *Measure* frequently plays on the doubleness of these familial terms; the ambiguities coalesce in *sister* (see especially 1.4.19; 2.2.19–21; 2.4.18) because Isabella is most centrally "in probation of a sisterhood" (5.1.75), but they also affect *brother* (the earliest of the play's great many uses of the word refers to the Duke as spiritual brother [1.3.44]; the latest is the Duke's

proposal that Claudio become his brother [5.1.491]), *mother* (1.4.86), and *father* (see p. 98). In his powerful meditation on incest in *Measure for Measure,* Marc Shell notes Isabella's ultimately futile attempt to replace the physical with the spiritual family; in his view, her attempt "merely relocates the problem of incest from the consanguinous family to the Christian Family" (*The End of Kinship: "Measure for Measure," Incest, and the Idea of Universal Siblinghood* [Stanford, Calif.: Stanford University Press, 1988], p. 54). Although Shell is more concerned with the metaphysics and social theory of incest than with its psychological implications, his understanding of the incestuous subtext of the chief relationships in the play is frequently close to mine; see, for example, his discussions of Claudio and Juliet (pp. 37–38), Isabella and Claudio (pp. 51, 61, and 102), Isabella and Angelo (pp. 105–9), and Isabella and the Duke (pp. 92, 163–67).

23. As with so much of Isabella's language, the terms in which she expresses her fear—calling attention both to her softness and to her capacity to conceive—could hardly be more effective in stirring Angelo's desire, particularly since her phrase "false prints" echoes one of Angelo's favorite tropes for generation (2.4.45–46).

24. Lever notes "the traditional association of glass and virginity" (Arden *Measure for Measure,* p. 61).

25. The anatomical cast of "vice" here is often noted; see Reid ("A Psychoanalytic Reading," p. 279), Wheeler (*Shakespeare's Development,* p. 111), and Neely (*Broken Nuptials,* p. 99). The pun is frequently incipient in the play's other uses of "vice"; see especially Lucio's "the vice is of a great kindred" (3.2.97), which immediately precedes his meditation on the alternate means through which Angelo was created, and Isabella's "There is a vice that most I do abhor" (2.2.29), with its evocation of both *whore* and *Abhorson.*

26. Sexual union with Angelo would in effect force Isabella to take her mother's place in a fantasied act of incest with her father, from which union her brother Claudio would be made a man; the Duke's proposal of marriage at the end is so disturbing partly because it replicates the threat of father-daughter incest that shapes Isabella's response here. (See Wheeler, who understands Isabella's desire to become a nun as a perpetuation of her imperfect resolution of oedipal desire [*Shakespeare's Development,* pp. 111–12, 130]; see also Reid, "A Psychoanalytic Reading," p. 278.) But given the intensity of Isabella's response to Claudio, there are undercurrents of brother-sister incest here as well. Isabella has earlier attempted to identify Angelo with her brother (see note 35) as Angelo has attempted to make Isabella into Juliet; and insofar as Juliet and Isabella have exchanged names (1.4.47), Claudio's union with Juliet may carry elements of a fantasied union with Isabella. Isabella's incestuous desire for her brother is central to Nevo's argument that the play, from 3.1 on, is "the replay . . . in Isabella's wishful fantasy, of the traumatic events that are happening to her"; in her view, the sequence of surrogates in the bed trick allows for the satisfaction of Isabella's repressed desire, while Isabella's exposure and repudiation serve as punishment for her guilt ("*Measure for Measure:* Mirror for Mirror," pp. 118–21). I understand Isabella's use of "incest" in this context to signal not only her fear of a specifically incestuous alliance with Claudio as brother or Angelo as father but also her fear of becoming her mother; here, as in *Pericles,* incest threatens to confound all the distinctions that confirm identity. Insofar as Isabella's participation in any sexual act would undermine the distinction between her and her mother, any sexual act is for her potentially incestuous in its collapsing of necessary categories.

27. *All's Well* twice invokes this legacy, when Parolles tells Helena that "to speak on the part of virginity is to accuse your mothers" (1.1.134–35), and when Bertram asks Diana to model herself on her mother ("Now you should be as your mother was / When your sweet self was got" [4.2.9–10]).

28. Wheeler's account of this moment is very close to my own; see especially his analysis of Isabella's participation "in the defense against sexual contamination through the ideal of male honor" as she shifts the blame to her mother (*Shakespeare's Development,* p. 114).

29. Logically, of course, Claudio's bastardy requires the presence of a father, albeit an illegitimate one; but Isabella here elides his role, making Claudio purely his mother's child.

30. This reiteration is by now a critical commonplace, as is more general uneasiness with the Duke's relation to his own sexuality; see, for example, Levin ("Duke Vincentio and Angelo," pp. 259–60), Berry ("Language and Structure," p. 153), Marvin Rosenberg ("Shakespeare's Fantastic Trick: *Measure for Measure,*" *Sewanee Review* 80 [1972]: 64–67), and Sundelson (*Shakespeare's Restorations of the Father,* pp. 98–100). Westlund finds the Duke's value precisely in his distance from the ideal, insofar as his failings–and his acceptance of them–induce tolerance in us and so limit our tendency toward idealization (*Shakespeare's Reparative Comedies,* esp. pp. 153, 156, and 168).

31. Many critics read the opening action of the play as the Duke's substitution of Angelo for an aspect of himself, though they do not always agree on which aspect; see, for example, Berry ("Language and Structure," pp. 153, 159), Nancy S. Leonard ("Substitution in Shakespeare's Problem Comedies," *English Literary Renaissance* 9 [1979]: 296–97), Levin ("Duke Vincentio and Angelo," pp. 259–60), Sundelson (*Shakespeare's Restorations of the Father,* p. 90), Alexander Leggatt ("Substitution in *Measure for Measure,*" *Shakespeare Quarterly* 39 [1988]: 345–46), and Nevo ("*Measure for Measure:* Mirror for Mirror," pp. 111–12). In Bernard J. Paris's Horneyan analysis of the play, the Duke's deputizing of Angelo perfectly serves the Duke's conflicting trends toward perfectionism and self-effacement ("The Inner Conflicts of *Measure for Measure:* A Psychological Approach," *Centennial Review* 25 [1981]: 274); in Jonathan Goldberg's account, it initiates the series of substitutions that represents "the endless refiguration of the king in representative acts of substitution" and hence analyzes James's absolutist mode of "presence-in-absence" (*James I and the Politics of Literature* [Baltimore, Md.: Johns Hopkins University Press, 1983], pp. 234–35). In Wheeler's brilliant argument about the structure of the play, the substitution is Shakespeare's, not the Duke's: Shakespeare preserves Vincentio as an ideal figure by displacing "conflict away from [him] and into the world around him"; "Shakespeare . . . uses Angelo as a scapegoat who suffers in his person the consequences of a conflict Vincentio is thereby spared" (*Shakespeare's Development,* pp. 133, 138).

32. Claudio's image of rat poison (1.2.120–22) suggests that even Claudio and Juliet want to be together only ambivalently. Lever argues that the "thirsty evil" is liberty rather than lust (Arden *Measure,* p. 15); but given the striking resemblance of Claudio's "when we drink, we die" to *The Faerie Queene,* 2.1.55, where Acrasia's poison works on Mordant as soon as he drinks, lust seems the more obvious choice. But the distinction is probably unnecessary, since in this play sexuality is the mark of excess liberty.

33. See Neely's fine discussion of Mariana's potential as the instrument for comic rejuvenations and resolutions that remain largely undramatized (*Broken Nuptials,* pp. 96–98).

34. Shakespeare often associates "mould" and its variants with the shaping of the body in the womb: see, for example, *Richard II,* 1.2.22–23 ("That bed, that womb, / That metal, that self mould that fashioned thee"); *1 Henry IV,* 1.1.23 ("whose arms were moulded in their mother's womb"), and *Pericles* 3. chorus 10–11 ("By the loss of maidenhead, / A babe is moulded"); Coriolanus calls his mother "the honour'd mould / Wherein this trunk was fram'd" (5.3.22–23). Other uses of the term are more broadly associated with generative process; see *King Lear* 3.2.8, *Cymbeline* 5.4.49, and *The Winter's Tale* 2.3.102. For *fault / foutre,* see Chapter 2, note 26. "Fault" in *Measure* often carries the weight of the double meaning; see particularly Escalus's "some condemned for a fault alone" (2.1.40) and Isabella's "ask your heart what it doth know / That's like my brother's fault" (2.2.138–39). Though he does not work with Mariana's series of puns, Lawrence W. Hyman sees the play as an attempt to bring its characters to the sardonic recognition that life "not only can but *must* come out of vice, shame, and dishonor" ("The Unity of *Measure for Measure,*" *Modern Language Quarterly* 36 [1975]: 12).

35. See Marilyn L. Williamson's full discussion of Jacobean attempts to regulate sexual behavior—especially of the poor—through government control; in her view, the play "exposes the limits of public power and the fantasy of intruding power into the personal realm" (*The Patriarchy of Shakespeare's Comedies* [Detroit, Mich.: Wayne State University Press, 1986],

pp. 74–110). Both Wheeler (*Shakespeare's Development,* pp. 12–13) and Neely (*Broken Nuptials,* p. 94) note specifically the shifting of the bed trick from female to male control; my understanding of the relationship between the two plays is very much indebted to theirs.

36. In the context of the other arranged marriages of 5.1, it makes sense to ask what crime in Isabella the Duke proposes to punish through marriage. Though the marriage proposal might be supposed to bring Isabella back to the world, and has usually been interpreted thus, its more fundamental function is to re-contain her dangerous desire to define a self outside the sphere of marriage and hence beyond the reach of male power as it is embodied in the state. (In this formulation—and doubtless elsewhere—I am indebted to a brilliant unpublished paper by Laura Camozzi Berry, written for my graduate Shakespeare seminar in May 1988; she sees the threat of independent female desire—embodied in Isabella and in Juliet's unauthorized pregnancy—as that which the play seeks to control, both through the Duke's appropriation of the powers of generation and through his management of marriage, which encloses and erases women.) Interpretations—and productions—that have Isabella refusing the Duke, even perhaps slapping his face (see Rosenberg, "Shakespeare's Fantastic Trick," p. 71), do a disservice to the play by undermining its portrayal of the impasse to which Isabella has been brought—an impasse that in effect acts out the closing of the nunneries and the loss of that option for women. In her full account of the constricting of Isabella's power—especially in comparison with the earlier comic heroines—as she comes under the Duke's control, Marcia Riefer notes the closing off of this option (" 'Instruments of Some More Mightier Member': The Constriction of Female Power in *Measure for Measure,*" *Shakespeare Quarterly* 35 [1984]: 162); in her view, Shakespeare's concentration of dramaturgical control in the Duke illuminates both the incompatibility between patriarchy and comedy and Shakespeare's tendency to drain life out of the women in the tragedies (pp. 159, 168–69). Wheeler understands the diminishing of Isabella's power as a defensive response to the fear of women that will become rampant in the tragedies (*Shakespeare's Development,* esp. pp. 116, 147–51); for Sundelson, the play repeatedly exposes and then tames the threat of women (*Shakespeare's Restorations of the Father,* pp. 92–96). But Kathleen McLuskie argues in effect that there is no real change: from the start, Isabella is "defined theatrically by the men around her for the men in the audience"; any attempt to see from her point of view "involves refusing the pleasure of the drama and the text" ("The Patriarchal Bard: Feminist Criticism and Shakespeare: *King Lear* and *Measure for Measure,*" in *Political Shakespeare: New Essays In Cultural Materialism,* ed. Jonathan Dollimore and Alan Sinfield [Ithaca, N.Y.: Cornell University Press, 1985], pp. 96–97).

37. Leonard Tennenhouse historicizes the shift from female to male, reading *Measure for Measure* as one of several disguised ruler plays that mark the transitional period between Elizabeth and James by revealing the true king as the idealized patriarch and source of law, hence participating in the "master narrative . . . of a return to origins in which the monarch is restored to a natural position of supremacy as a father over a family" ("Representing Power: *Measure for Measure* in its Time," in *The Forms of Power and the Power of Forms,* ed. Stephen Greenblatt, *Genre* 15 [1982]: 139–56). Despite my disagreement with Tennenhouse's assumption that Shakespeare's representation of women, sexuality, and the family arises from "anxiety in the political realm" (p. 154), this seems to me a brilliant reading of a particular cultural moment; though operative throughout Shakespeare's career—as early as the transition from *Venus and Adonis* to *The Rape of Lucrece* and as late as the transition from *The Winter's Tale* to *The Tempest*—the representation of the shift from female to male control must have had a particular piquancy in 1604. (See Jonathan Dollimore, "Transgression and Surveillance in *Measure for Measure,*" in *Political Shakespeare,* pp. 72–87, for the more general argument that anxiety about sexuality is an ideological displacement in *Measure.*) The particular parents of the new father-king must have made it especially attractive to vest in the male ruler not only control over marriage and generation (see Tennenhouse, p. 153) but also the fantasy of exemption from the woman's part in generation. This fantasy, elaborated and rejected in Angelo, returns in a

muted and disguised form in the Duke and will become very signficant in *Macbeth,* another play associated with James (see Chapter 6, note 39).

38. Both Wheeler (*Shakespeare's Development,* p. 143) and Sundelson (*Shakespeare's Restorations of the Father,* pp. 98, 102) note the incipient pun on Old Hamlet in *Measure's* ghostly father.

Performing Social Practice: The Example of *Measure for Measure*

VICTORIA HAYNE

The Royal Shakespeare Company advertised its 1987 production of *Measure for Measure* with this description:

> *Measure for Measure* is a complex mixture of high principles and questionable actions, exploring sexuality and the abuse of authority by those in power in a corrupt Vienna of dank prisons and seething brothels. The play faces squarely the problems encountered when the state tries to regulate the sexual and emotional lives of individual citizens.[1]

As a piece of advertising, this summary of the play makes some assumptions about the audience it tries to entice into the theater: it assumes, not surprisingly, an audience interested in sex and in power, and it uses its antitheses and adjectives to good effect in appealing to those interests. But it also assumes a social competence on the part of its readers, who are expected to bring from their own experience particular concepts and attitudes evoked by such words as "state," "regulate," "sexual and emotional lives" in order to imagine what the unspecified "problems" the play "faces squarely" might be. As a reader, you will have already brought to mind images of such problems, and the advertising implies that the play addresses the problems you have just imagined.

The critical attention the play has received in recent years is testimony to how powerfully it does speak to the modern imagination about problems no doubt very like those you have in mind. Inevitably, however, at least some of the problems you have imagined are products of your historical position, inhabiting a postindustrial society at the end of the twentieth century. Few of us who are not immersed in the social history of marriage will have immediately imagined, for example, problems of the sort that arose on a midsummer evening in 1549, when a Cheshire clergyman named John Cotgreve and a group of his friends escorted Alice Gidlowe home after a village festivity. Passing an abandoned house, John asked Alice to go inside with him to make

Reprinted by permission of *Shakespeare Quarterly.*

love. She agreed, provided they promise to marry one another. So, on the spot, surrounded by their friends, they exchanged vows, kissed, and retired to the house. When they emerged to catch up with their friends, they were, according to ecclesiastical law, irrevocably married. We know these intimate details about a long-dead couple, however, because their hasty union didn't stick. Though they continued their sexual relationship for some time, they never formally wed in church and later, during John's absence, Alice did formally marry another man. The triangle ended up in the ecclesiastical courts to identify Alice's legal husband; it is John Cotgreve's deposition that preserves these details of their courtship.[2] *Measure for Measure* was written to speak to an audience who could imagine, could experience, such situations and such problems; recent research in social history allows us to see how profoundly—and how concretely and with what particularity—the play is embedded in the social practices of its historical context.

As the dubious marital status of John Cotgreve and Alice Gidlowe suggests, the process of marriage formation in the sixteenth and seventeenth centuries was full of ambiguities and potential conflicts. In representing its culture's social practices for forming marriage, *Measure for Measure* exposes those ambiguities and anatomizes, in the marriages it portrays, the personal and social problems those practices could give rise to, problems ranging from the emotional toll of a ruptured betrothal to the social difficulty of accommodating and caring for illegitimate children. These issues, and how society should respond to them, were matters of active debate when *Measure for Measure* was written; books were published, sermons preached, and bills presented to Parliament defending and attacking the culture's traditional ways of dealing with these problems and proposing alternative responses. The play engages the terms of that debate, scrutinizing the varied connections between sexual license and death, connections deployed by both traditional rituals and reformist polemics. Beginning with a one-dimensional definition of sexual license as crime, the play's developing action differentiates among different kinds of sexual behavior and redefines certain sexual "crimes" as, rather, problems of disrupted relationship. Through its own wedding of social and literary conventions, the play takes up, and implicates its audience's theatrical responses in, its position in the contemporary debate over sexual regulation.

To say the play "does" these things implies that there is some unspecified but existent relationship between the play text (and performance) and the social phenomena of which text and performance are in part built and are in part instances. The kinds of abstract, sometimes metaphorical and prosopopoeic, verbs I have thus far used to characterize that relationship—the play "engages," "is embedded in," "scrutinizes"—are one critical convention for positing that relationship. But it is a further purpose of this essay to foreground and to analyze the particular transactions between aspects of social life and theatrical experience that make up much of *Measure for Measure.* As Stephen Greenblatt argues in the introduction to *Shakespearean Negotia-*

tions, "where we had once seen simple reflection" between social life and literature, historically oriented critics must now recognize "a whole spectrum of representational exchanges. . . . In some exchanges the object or practice mimed onstage seems relatively untouched by the representation; in others, the object or practice is intensified, diminished, or even completely evacuated by its encounter with the theatre; in still others, it is marked as a prize—something 'up for grabs'—in an unresolved struggle between competing representational discourses."[3] Systematic investigation of the mechanisms of exchange between social practice and theatrical representation seems to me indeed a promising alternative to the widely criticized new-historicist reliance on analogy as an analytical and rhetorical tool.[4] Accordingly, my argument proceeds on two levels. I will be arguing that *Measure for Measure* stages certain social practices; at the same time, I will be attempting to articulate the varied representational exchanges by which those practices in the social world are transformed into elements of theatrical meaning in the playhouse.

I. "Neither simply single, nor actually maried"

Amid *Measure for Measure's* proliferating displays of sexuality, the plot hinges on a social question: how should society respond to a betrothed couple who conceive a child before their wedding day? Claudio and Juliet's offense was, in fact, a very common one in Tudor-Stuart social life. It is astonishing—indeed even embarrassing in an era when it is unfashionable to make mimetic claims for literature—to read in ecclesiastical court records case after case in which the testimony, if rendered in iambic pentameter, could pass for Claudio's explanation of his relationship. This close correlation between legal testimony and dramatic dialogue might tempt one to dismiss it as an interesting but essentially trivial instance of social realism on Shakespeare's part. But even in this most apparently direct representation of social practice, the transaction between world and stage is a complex one.

Betrothal itself, as a socially constructed status, consisted entirely in its own representations. In sixteenth- and seventeenth-century social practice, becoming married was "a prolonged transitional process begun by private agreement and only completed by public rites."[5] Couples paired off into personal or sexual relationships only when they could begin thinking of marriage, or so the low rate of illegitimacy in women below the usual age of marriage suggests.[6] After brief courtships (in which the extent of active involvement by family or friends varied with both social class and personal inclination), a couple began the process of becoming married by exchanging a promise to marry. A more-or-less public betrothal, a "contracting" or "handfasting," usually followed; this ceremony, in which the couple's joining hands symbolized their union, may have been the most socially significant part of the process. After exchanging this promise, couples usually regarded and referred to themselves as "husband" and "wife." But they were not yet fully married. Completion of the betrothal in marriage required calling the banns in the parish church on three successive Sundays and, finally, the culmination of the process on the wedding day—the church ceremony, a feast, and the bedding of the couple. Although the peculiarities of ecclesiastical law meant that the moment of legal marriage might occur at any point during the betrothal period, in social terms the couple's commitment began with the first promise and grew gradually more binding as each ritual step was completed.[7] During that transitional process, however, the couple's status was fluid and ambiguous; in the words of one contemporary, "contracted [i.e., betrothed] persons are in a middle degree betwixt single persons, and maried persons: they are neither simply single, nor actually maried."[8]

Measure for Measure's action hinges on three betrothals disrupted in the interval between the "time of the contract and [the] limit of the solemnity"[9] in order to exploit for dramatic purposes the ambiguities and dangers of betrothal's indefinition. Several of the changes Shakespeare made to his source materials—making Claudio and Juliet clearly betrothed, adding the Angelo-Mariana relationship, adding Lucio and his reported involvement with Kate Keep-down—place the problems of marriage formation at the center of the play. Shakespeare captured one principal danger of betrothal in Mariana's situation after she has been to bed with Angelo; betrothed and sexually active, she is "neither maid, widow, nor wife" (5.1.178–79), proverbially an ill-defined and risky status.[10] The church's official position was clear: sex before the wedding ceremony was a sin. But it was also a widespread practice. In the communities whose parish registers have been studied by the Cambridge Group for the History of Population and Social Structure, an average of thirty-one percent of Elizabethan brides were pregnant at the time of their church weddings; the rate of bridal pregnancy ranged as high as forty-four percent in some areas.[11] Since these represented only those couples fertile (or unlucky) enough to conceive in the ordinarily brief months of betrothal, the actual rate of prenuptial intercourse must have been considerably higher.

This evidence of widespread prenuptial intercourse and the records of ecclesiastical court proceedings involving betrothed couples reveal that social attitudes toward prenuptial sexual relations were complex and ambivalent.[12] The term "fornication" and the moral opprobrium it conveyed were applied to any sexual union between an unmarried man and woman; nevertheless, in practice the church courts' punishments clearly distinguished a hierarchy of offenses based on the social context of the sexual act. Although the church officially required abstinence until the wedding day, there is little evidence that betrothed couples were disciplined solely for initiating their sexual relationship unless they flouted public opinion in some exceptional way, such as living together before the wedding ceremony. In normal circumstances, both church and society tended to wink at prenuptial sex as long as it had no permanent socioeconomic consequences in the form of a child. Betrothed couples who conceived a child before their wedding, however, were regularly summoned to the ecclesiastical courts and ordered to solemnize their unions in church as soon as possible; if they were assigned a penance, it was usually a private one involving confession to a small group of fellow parishioners. In contrast, fornication in the absence of a betrothal was regarded much more seriously: like adultery, it merited a full public penance, usually before the assembled parish in church on Sunday or in the marketplace. Although they were sentenced to penance, couples found guilty of fornication were never ordered to marry, even if they had an illegitimate child.[13] Only couples who had previously betrothed themselves and, by consummating their union, created a legally irrevocable marriage would be ordered to complete with public ritual what they had enacted in private, to end betrothal's ambiguity with a representation whose social meaning was incontrovertible.

When a prenuptial pregnancy brought individuals into ecclesiastical courts, a new set of representational conventions was employed. Faced with the ambiguity inherent in their culture's practices, people constructed narratives elaborating the social context of their actions in order to control or at least to guide social and judicial evaluation of their sexual behavior.[14] Thus, in a real-life dilemma much like the fictional one of Claudio, an Essex man in 1591 offered the court this story to answer a charge of fornication, the evidence for which was his betrothed's pregnancy:

> He and his wife were contracted in the presence of their parents half a year before they were married in the face of the church. After the same contract their parents did vary in some points touching their marriage, the solemnization was deferred longer than they did expect, whereby they forgetting themselves had carnal knowledge whereby his wife was begotten with child, desiring the judge in justice to consider of his cause.[15]

In this case, the narrative strategy—constructing a sequence of socially acceptable actions and mitigating circumstances—was successful. Although the pregnancy made a guilty verdict unavoidable, the judge sentenced the couple only "to acknowledge guilt before ten honest parishioners," the mildest variety of penance.

Shakespeare's replicating these narrative strategies to stage his characters' relationships—instead of staging the performative and nonverbal representations, the promise and the handfasting, of the betrothal process itself—creates a specific relationship between the characters and the audience. The audience is not invited to participate imaginatively in the celebratory representations that created the betrothals but is instead invoked as witness or judge to evaluate the narratives that explain how the betrothals went wrong.[16] As Claudio explains to Lucio, he and Juliet were betrothed, having exchanged a private promise to marry. They intended to complete their marriage with the proper "denunciation . . . / Of outward order [i.e., public betrothal and/or marriage ceremony]" (1.2.137–38) but temporarily refrained from doing so in order to gain the consent of Juliet's relatives, who controlled her dowry.[17] In the meantime, they had, all too obviously, begun their sexual relationship. Similarly, later in the play, Shakespeare is equally diligent in having the Duke spell out to Isabella all the ritual steps of betrothal that had been completed between Angelo and Mariana: they were contracted, publicly "affianced," the dowry negotiated, and "the nuptial appointed" (3.1.213–14). At that late moment in the marriage process, when the loss of Mariana's dowry prompted Angelo to renege, he "swallowed his vows whole, pretending in her discoveries of dishonour" (3.1.226–27). These narratives, by virtue of their similarity to those constructed by people in real life, place the fictional relationships squarely within the audience's social experience and guide the audience in using its social competence to evaluate them.

It is less commonly recognized by modern readers and audiences that these two disrupted betrothals are paralleled in the play by a third, that of Lucio and Kate Keep-down. As Mistress Overdone explains:

> Mistress Kate Keep-down was with child by him in the Duke's time, he promised her marriage. His child is a year and a quarter old come Philip and Jacob. I have kept it myself; and see how he goes about to abuse me.
>
> (3.2.193–97)

Mistress Overdone suggests that Lucio and Kate had exchanged a promise of marriage when they initiated their sexual relationship. This implication is reinforced by her odd way of dating the child's age: a child is "a year and a quarter old" on the second anniversary of its conception; the feast day of Saints Philip and James (colloquially Jacob) was May Day, the holiday traditionally associated with courtship and betrothal.[18] Lucio himself admits the relationship:

> LUCIO I was once before him for getting a wench with child.
>
> DUKE Did you such a thing?
>
> LUCIO Yes, marry, did I; but I was fain to forswear it; they would else have married me to the rotten medlar.
>
> (4.3.167–72)

This might seem an admission only of fornication, but in contemporary social practice (which has been so carefully invoked as the standard of evaluation for the other two relationships) the courts would have tried to enforce a marriage *only* if a betrothal existed; had no betrothal existed, Lucio's perjury might have saved him from penance, but it would not have been needed to save him from marriage.[19] In these elliptical fragments of evidence, betrothal is represented at its most ambiguous, the social consequences of that ambiguity most calamitous. And while the marriages that repair these disrupted betrothals bring the play to social and formal closure, the Duke's unanswered proposal to Isabella opens it up again, its indefinition underscoring the fact that in this culture the perilous ambiguity of betrothal lies before every couple, every time a man offers, in the Duke's words, a "motion" and a woman "a willing ear incline[s]" (5.1.532–33).

II. "Shame which bringeth honor"

The widespread incidence of prenuptial pregnancy in Elizabethan and Jacobean England suggests that when the play reiterates, in some ten different speeches, how very common Claudio's crime is—as the Provost says, "All sects, all ages smack of this vice" (2.2.5)—the audience was being asked to recognize in "Vienna" their own familiar London.[20] *Measure for Measure* builds upon this recognition and upon the complex of social attitudes and emotional responses it would have prompted. Victor Turner has postulated that there is "an interdependent, perhaps dialectic, relationship between social dramas [i.e., a culture's characteristic patterns of conflict resolution] and genres of cultural performance" such as theater, in which "the manifest social drama feeds into the *latent* realm of stage drama" and in the process creates "a metacommentary, explicit or implicit, witting or unwitting, on the major social dramas of its social context."[21] Tudor-Stuart culture had, in its ecclesiastical courts, an elaborate system for regulating sexual behavior and resolving conflicts arising from breaches of sexual norms and, indeed, from the fluidity of its betrothal practices. The play alludes only briefly to the overt structures of this system, but, as Turner's formulation suggests, it is possible to see the values and behavior patterns inherent in this system as providing a normative structure that underlies the action of the plot. At the same time, the play's freedom to dismantle and rearrange elements of the penance ritual generates a critique of its symbolic connection between illicit sex and death—a connection at the heart of the period's conflicts over the social dramas enacted in its ecclesiastical courts.

The ecclesiastical courts—the combined administrative and judicial arm of the church—had jurisdiction over a wide range of community life. The courts were certainly an instrument of church authority, but in the regulation of sexual behavior, the courts were, in practice, a site of intersection between authority and popular will. The courts' own procedures of investigation, determination of guilt, and sentencing gave popular will the upper hand. Churchwardens, members of the parish elected for one-year terms, were responsible for presenting to the court any irregularities in the parish, from the church wall in need of repair to the adulterer. In some sexual cases a couple might have been caught in the act, so that the presentment to the court would specify, for example, that the defendants had been seen "tumbling together in a ditch, very unseemly."[22] Most often, however, presentments were based on "bad fame," reasonably widespread public suspicion of immorality. This reliance on public opinion in formulating charges gave the community a very real and practical influence on what offenses and which offenders came to the courts' attention.

Similarly, judgment was, in very practical terms, in the hands of the community. In the majority of sexual cases where no direct evidence was available, an accused person who denied the charge would be given the opportunity to "purge" himself or herself of bad fame by taking an oath of innocence. If the accused could then produce a specified number of "compurgators" (usually four to eight fellow parishioners of the same sex and of good reputation) who would swear on oath that they believed the accused's oath of innocence, the accused was automatically cleared of ill fame and the charge dismissed. As Richard M. Wunderli notes, "Proofs depended on social relationships rather than scrutiny of evidence. . . . Innocence and guilt were arrived at through the personal interplay of neighbors who were willing to act as compurgators."[23] Such a procedure gave the judgments of the community, through the judicial use of fame and of purgation, the decisive vote in determining the standards that would be enforced.

If concord in the community was privileged over fact in arriving at verdicts of innocence and guilt, reconciliation of the offender with the community was the explicit aim in punishing the guilty. The severest penalty the church courts could impose was public penance, a ritual of striking theatricality. As described in an order for a typical penance in the diocese of Ely in 1594, the penitent, wearing a floor-length white sheet and carrying a white wand, was surely the focus of attention, standing in the church porch

> from the second peale to morning praire untill the readinge of the second lesson, dessiringe people that passe by her into the church to pray God for her and to forgive her; at which time the Minister there shall comme downe to this penitent and fetch her into the church with the psalme of *Miserere* in English, and place her in the middle alley there apart from all other people, where she shall penitently kneele untill the reading of the ten commaundementes.

At this point, the penitent was required to confess directly to the congregation, saying,

> Good people I acknowledge and confesse yt I have offended All-mightie God and by my evill example you all, for that I have broken his Divine lawes and commaundementes in committinge yt most shamefull and abhominable sin of adultrie or fornicacion, for which I am most hartily sory, and I aske God and you all most hartily forgiveness for the same, promisinge by Godes helpe never to offend hereafter in the like againe.[24]

This performance was to be repeated on three successive Sundays, followed on the first by a reading of the Homily against Adultery and on the third by the Homily of Repentance.[25] The two homilies structure the ritual, emplotting it as a two-part moral tragicomedy. The Homily against Adultery emphasizes, in the most strident tones, the wickedness of sexual sin, "so filthy and stinking sin, . . . so wicked vice, . . . such detestable abomination." A horrendous catalogue of Biblical and historical punishments for sexual sin—the Flood, the destruction of Sodom and Gomorrah, putting out of eyes, burning, beheading, whippings of a thousand lashes—is recited in graphic detail, bringing the penitent and congregation, if not near to death in actuality, near to death in imagination, to an apprehension of death as the deserved wages of sin.

After this imaginative brush with mortality, the Homily of Repentance offers a reprieve, quoting God's words to Ezekiel, the prophet of vengeance: "I will not the death of the wicked, but that he turn from his wicked ways and live." With this retraction of the threat of death, the sinner is reconciled to the congregation. As the ritual has throughout involved and implicated the congregation in the penitent's moral standing—through their prayers and their forgiveness—the ritual's purpose, this homily explains, has been as much corporate as individual: it allows the congregation "to confess our weakness and infirmities one to another; to the end that, knowing each other's frailness, we may the more earnestly pray together." This ritual of condemnation and reconciliation was a commonplace in Tudor-Stuart life, something witnessed many times by every member of Shakespeare's audience. In the archdeaconries of Essex and Colchester, for example, an estimated 15,000 people were charged with sexual misbehavior during Elizabeth's reign.[26] In Wunderli's words, "public penance became a cosmic—comic—drama of sin and redemption acted openly with all London as a stage. . . . The entire drama was played out weekly in a hundred London parishes."[27] Like many rituals, this one is "ordered by *dramatic* structure, a plot . . . involving an act of sacrifice or self-sacrifice, which energizes and gives emotional coloring to . . . the meaning inherent in the dramatic *leitmotiv*."[28] The first homily's threat of death and torture serves as a metaphor for the penitent's moral and social risk and invests the final reprieve and reconciliation with the triumph, for both penitent and congregation, of mortal danger overcome.

Shakespeare had previously recognized the spectacular quality of this ritual in dramatizing part of the penance of Eleanor Cobham, complete with white sheet and taper, in *2 Henry VI* (2.4.17ff.). In *Measure for Measure* the ritual is not represented directly, but its values and emotional rhythms provide an undergirding coherence to the plot's movement toward its resolution. As soon as the initial premise of the play, the transfer of authority from the Duke to Angelo, has been established, the scene moves to a public place, a site of news and gossip where characters meet in casual comings and goings. In this metaphorical, if not actual, marketplace, the audience first hears of Claudio in

Mistress Overdone's tidbit of scandal: "his head {is} to be chopped off . . . for getting Madam Julietta with child" (1.2.63, 66–67). Into this public arena enter Claudio and Juliet, led in procession by the Provost and officers. Claudio's first words are "Fellow, why dost thou show me thus to th'world?" (1.2.108). The stage is empty. Mistress Overdone and Pompey have just left; Lucio and his friends follow behind the procession. The "world" to whom Claudio is shown is, of course, the audience. Claudio's introduction by way of this moment of theatrical self-reference redefines the relationship of the play and its spectators. The theater audience is re-constituted as congregation, witnessing a sinner's penitential procession. Once that context is invoked, it hovers over the remainder of the scene. Claudio's reluctance to name his sin, "What but to speak of would offend again" (1.2.128), may echo the familiar Homily against Adultery: "the blessed Apostle willeth us to be so pure and free from adultery, *fornication, and all uncleanness, that we not once name them among us.*"[29] Once Claudio has been induced to name his sin, however, the audience learns that, in the context of judgment which has just been invoked theatrically, Claudio's is the mildest of sexual sins, the one least deserving of the punishment he is to suffer. This juxtaposition of incompatible perspectives—the overt events of the plot seeming at this point to endorse a drastically punitive social response to sexual misbehavior while the theatrical experience invokes a more forgiving set of values—creates a tension that prompts the audience to recognize the contradiction and to discriminate between perspectives.

If Claudio's public shaming has focused on identifying and denouncing his sin, "a thirsty evil" (1.2.122), the ritual's other half—confession and reconciliation—is displayed by his betrothed, Juliet, in her repentance scene (2.3).[30] Brief as it is, her repentance scene is quite complex in its effects. At once reverent and bawdy, touching and funny, the scene literally gives voice, through its double and triple entendres, to the culture's paradoxically combined acceptance and censure of sexual relationships during betrothal. The sin Juliet repents is a sin she "carr[ies]" and "bear[s]," puns on her visible pregnancy (ll. 19–20). The apparent sternness of the Duke's rebuke, "Then was your sin of heavier kind than his" (l. 28), is virtually evaporated in the simultaneous and pointedly bawdy reference to both the heaviness of her pregnancy and the weight she bore to get it. In this context of contradictory attitudes, the audience sees Juliet behaving as they would have known neighbors, relatives, perhaps themselves, to behave—confessing and repenting. She does so with an edifying balance: "I do repent me as it is an evil / And take the shame with joy" (ll. 35–36). She repents her sexual love as (because) it is a sin but also as (to the extent that) it is a sin. She welcomes shame as a symbol of repentance, because, as a contemporary writer on the ecclesiastical courts asserts, "in matters *spirituall* . . . there is a *shame* which bringeth honor."[31] She also accepts her shame as mingled with the joys of her love for Claudio and her impending motherhood. Juliet's lapse is thus placed among life's sorrows and joys, accepted among what the Homily of Repentance calls the "daily falls that we, as long as we carry about this body of sin, are subject unto."[32] This perspective on sin comments on the juridical issues raised by the preceding scene, Angelo and Isabella's debate over justice and mercy. The logical rigor of Angelo's concept of justice and the moving eloquence of Isabella's plea for mercy have resulted in a stalemate. Justice and mercy seem irreconcilable. In twenty lines Juliet's repentance demonstrates how they may be reconciled. Repentance, the "shame which bringeth honor," neither excuses sin nor exacts an irrevocable penalty for it.

The peace Juliet achieves is quickly shattered by the reminder of Claudio's impending execution, the avoidance of which motivates the rest of the plot. From this moment until the final resolution, the plot enacts a repeated pattern of threatened death and reprieve, first directed at Claudio and then, in the final act, involving most of the major characters. This mixture of "mirth and killing," as Fletcher defined tragicomedy, would have been very familiar emotional territory in which to explore the consequences of sexual sin, the play recapitulating the emotional pattern of the ritual by which similar problems were resolved in social life. In reproducing that pattern, however, the play adopts a critical distance absent in the ritual, probing and analyzing those responses to the idea and the threat of death, insisting that, within the confines of the play, death must remain a metaphor. Death and sex, death and justice, "Mortality and mercy" (1.1.44) are repeatedly placed in juxtaposition, equation, opposition. The plot twice brings Claudio near to death and then "redeem[s him] from the angry law" (3.1.200–201). In 3.1, death itself is described in vividly conflicting terms—as the welcome end of a life "none but fools would keep" (1.8), as a "most good, most good indeed" passport to heaven (l. 55), as something worse "in apprehension" (l. 77) than in reality, as something so horrible that "the weariest and most loathed worldly life . . . is a paradise / To what we fear of death" (ll. 128–31)—a conflict of perspectives that generates uncertainty about the death that is perhaps too easily, too automatically invoked as a penalty for sin.

Angelo, on the right side of the law, does invoke it easily, knitting sex, death, and justice into a seamless unity. For him, causing a death and creating a bastard are equal as crimes (2.4.42–49); as punishment, death is both justice and pity (2.2.101–5). Angelo's subsequent order, demanding alike the deaths of the dissolute and unrepentant murderer, Barnardine, and Claudio, the repentant lover of his betrothed wife, gives this equation dramatic force. For all her opposition to Angelo, Isabella, when faced with the prospect of sin, adopts a position logically similar to his: "I had rather my brother die by the law, than my son should be unlawfully born" (3.1.188–90). But these equations of sex and death are constantly challenged. Refusing to believe that Claudio is condemned for impregnating Juliet, and faced with Claudio's refusal to name his crime because the word itself would offend, Lucio abruptly demands, "What, is't murder?" (1.2.129). His reaction implies, as a spontaneous and naturalized assumption, a clear hierarchy of crimes, a value system in which causing death is the worst one can do. The absurdity of leveling out such a hierarchy into Angelo's kind of equation is given a devastatingly ironic portrayal in the "rehabilitation" of Pompey. Forced to give up his criminal trade of prostitution, he is offered a respectable occupation, that of executioner. Though Pompey argues that the two trades are unequal as "mysteries," he is forced to admit that being an executioner is the more moral calling—because the executioner asks forgiveness more frequently than the bawd! The "penitent trade" (4.2.48) of hangman requires its practitioner, each time he carries out his duty, to perform the same kind of penitential action the convicted sinner is sentenced to. Pompey's equation of guilt for sex and for death, with its embedded reminder of the forgiveness both executioner and sinner are entitled to, is a disrupting mirror of Angelo's apparently logical position, a mirror that shows the way to escape from such equations. Ultimately the play's scrutiny of death as physical reality and as metaphor works to loosen the connection between death and illicit sex as a consciously arguable proposition. It does so at a time when, in the world outside the theater, death as a penalty for illicit sex was, in fact, a proposition not only arguable but publicly argued.

III. "Every evil in a state is not to be met with in a law"

In associating illicit sex with "death," the standard Christian definition of the wages of sin, various voices in Elizabethan and Jacobean culture were, in fact, using the word in significantly different semantic modes. For the practitioners and proponents of the established church's courts and rituals, "death" was purely symbolic, its potential referentiality to the actual death of the penitent both denied by the ritual context and explicitly disrupted by the ritual's dramatic pattern. When other voices, however, voices critical of the established church and eager for moral reform, invoked death as a penalty for illicit sex, they did so with a difference: they meant it literally.

While some recent critics have seen *Measure for Measure* as interrogating the validity and indeed the possibility of any social regulation of sexual desire, the terms of the debate in 1604 centered not on *whether* sexual behavior should be regulated but on *how:* the alternatives were penance or death. To defend the traditional answer—penance—Richard Cosin, official of the ecclesiastical courts and sometime member of Parliament, was commissioned to write *An Apologie for Sundrie Proceedings by Jurisdiction Ecclesiasticall,* in which he articulates the principles underlying the church's judicial function much as Hooker's *Laws of Ecclesiastical Polity* did for church governance. An incidental part of Cosin's purpose was "to make it more plaine, that all unlawfull companie of man and woman, not being capitall by the lawes of the *Realme,* is subject to the *Jurisdiction ecclesiasticall.*"[33] In the face of criticisms of the church courts' leniency, he acknowledged that criminal "punishments are usually *corporall* and otherwise farre more grievous, then inflicted in any Court *Ecclesiasticall.*" This difference, however, was entirely as it should be: "penancies . . . are not taken in [ecclesiastical] lawe for *poenae,* but *medicinae.*" The public spectacles of both criminal and ecclesiastical punishments—carting, pillorying, public executions, as well as repentance rituals—are likely to seem to modern students of the period similar acts of signification, inscribing the norms of the society and its power to enforce those norms with and on the bodies of the punished.[34] Cosin, however, draws from within those norms a distinction in the potential significance to contemporary audiences of different kinds of penal spectacle:

> in the one of them [criminal punishment], the delinquent is propounded for a publike spectacle of shame and reproch, to be shunned of all men: the other [ecclesiastical penance], by these outward tokens of *humilitie* and *submission,* testifieth his inward sorow and griefe for the sinne, and as it were thereby craveth (in pitie and compassion) to be received againe, into the *Christian* fellowship, as a man (by *repentance*) fully reconciled again unto God, and unto his *Church.*

Cosin's discussion makes clear the explicitly symbolic and rhetorical nature of the penance ritual's threats of death: "the end of those animadversions or chastisements which consist in words, is referred onely to the reformation and amendment of him, upon whom they are used." The rhetorical effect of a punishment that "especially aimeth at . . . bettering" the offender gains its power precisely from being "punishment tempered with mercie," a rhetorical formula of threat and reprieve in which "the partie is in deed punished as an offender, yet the rigour of the penaltie is spared, and he commiserated and pitied as a man, and therefore apt inough to offend through humane frailtie."

Cosin wrote in response to attacks on the church courts by writers and preachers of puritan leaning.[35] Puritan responses to sexual sin stressed not reconciliation of the sinner to his neighbors and to the encompassing embrace of the national church but his separation from the godly community, even to the ultimate separation of death. Phillip Stubbes in *The Anatomie of Abuses* expresses this intention very clearly:

> I would wish that the Man or Woman who are certenlye knowen without all scruple or doubte, to have committed the horryble fact of whordome, adulterie, incest, or fornication, eyther should drinke a full draught of *Moyses* cuppe, that is, tast of present death or els, if it be thought too severe (for in evill, men will be more mercifull, than the Author of mercie him selfe, but in goodness, fare well mercy,) than wold GOD they might be cauterized, and seared with a hote yron on the cheeke, forehead, or some other parte of their bodye that might be seene, to the end the honest and chast Christians might be discerned from the adulterous Children of Sathan.[36]

Several very popular books published in the years immediately before the writing of *Measure for Measure* echo Stubbes's view.[37] Arthur Dent's *The plaine mans Path-way to Heaven,* for example, which ran to four editions between 1601 and 1603 (with some twenty-one more between 1605 and 1640), recounts Biblical precedents of death inflicted as punishment for adultery, concluding that "God . . . bindeth all, upon paine of death, to the obedience of his Commaundements."[38] Similarly, John Dod and Robert Cleaver in *A treatise or exposition upon the ten commaundements* (three editions in 1603–4 and sixteen more before 1635), asserted that "by the law of God the adulterer is as culpable of death as the willful murderer,"[39] the equation that, in *Measure for Measure,* Angelo asserts and other characters insistently question.

For these writers the argument that death was an appropriate penalty for sexual offenses was not merely a literary or theoretical one. It was part of a legislative program. A number of Protestant reformers, English as well as Continental, asserted the contemporary validity of Mosaic judicial law, including the death penalty for adultery. Influenced by such arguments, the *Reformatio Legum Ecclesiasticarum,* a sweeping proposal to replace Catholic canon law in the English church drawn up in the reign of Edward VI, would have punished adultery, albeit not with death but with life imprisonment or exile. The *Reformatio* was never implemented, but the argument over the applicability of Mosaic law in England continued in Elizabeth's reign. Against the official position articulated by Archbishop Whitgift, that the coming of Christ had abrogated Mosaic law, Thomas Cartwright argued that adultery's injuries to God, to the individuals involved, and to the commonwealth demonstrated beyond doubt the "perpetuall equitie off the lawe off God in the revengement off this sinne by death," so that "the punishment off death against adulterers . . . standeth in as full force nowe as ever yt did before the coming of our Sa. Christe."[40] Parliament was urged, by puritans and by reform-minded members of the church hierarchy, to bring English law more closely in line with Mosaic law. In a sermon to Parliament printed in 1585, for example, Edwin Sandys, Bishop of London and subsequently Archbishop of York, exhorted the members to urgent action: "That vile sin of adultery, in God's commonwealth punished with death, so overfloweth the banks of all chastity, that if by sharp laws it be not speedily cut off, God from heaven with fire will consume it. Prevent God's wrath: bridle this outrage: so shall you serve the Lord in truth."[41]

Such exhortations were not without effect. Parliament debated bills to enact criminal penalties for adultery and other sexual offenses in 1543, 1549, 1576, and 1601.[42] In 1604, William Stoughton published *An Assertion for true and Christian Church-policie,* a proposal for an act of Parliament to abolish completely the ecclesiastical court system and replace all canon laws with civil and criminal laws. Among the matters he proposes for incorporation in the criminal law are adultery and fornication.[43] The year 1604 also saw yet another bill, "An Act for the better repressing of the detestable Crime of Adultery," get as far as a second reading in the House of Lords. (Ultimately it was returned from committee with the recommendation that the House not act on it, because the bill was found "rather to concern some particular Persons than the public Good,"[44] a tantalizing suggestion that Angelo's attempt to misuse legislative power was not without its real-life analogues.) Though these bills were not finally passed, they were serious proposals with a near-by precedent: Scotland—in 1604 the recent home of England's new king—had had since 1563 a law punishing adultery with death and fornication with imprisonment on bread and water (and banishment for the third offense). The colony of Virginia was soon to follow suit; the death penalty for adultery was instituted there in 1610.

These bills to punish adultery through the criminal law were part of a larger effort by "a number of Puritan or radical Protestant members of the Commons" to transfer various areas of personal behavior from the jurisdiction of the ecclesiastical courts to the criminal law in order to stiffen the penalties on proscribed behavior.[45] The majority in Parliament, however, resisted imposing criminal penalties for offenses they regarded as primarily moral. This opposition stemmed in part from a conviction that there were limits to how far the state, conceived as separate from the church, should intrude upon the personal and moral lives of subjects. Arguing in Parliament in 1601 against a bill to make swearing a criminal offense, Edward Glascock asserted that "man is made of two parts, a soul and a body; and there are two governments, one imperial, the other sacerdotal; the first belonging to the commonwealth, the other to the church. Swearing is a thing moral and toucheth the soul; and therefore fitter to be spoken of in a pulpit than a Parliament." Other opponents had a keen sense that, however rigorously the state might wish to control its subjects through the mechanism of law, there were real limits to what it could do and that attempting to exceed those limits threatened to undermine the state's authority more than inaction did. John Bond, an outspoken and consistent opponent of social regulation, argued in Parliament against a bill in 1601 to make absence from church a criminal act:

> Every evil in a state is not to be met with in a law. And as it is in the natural, so it is in the politique body, that sometimes the remedy is worse than the disease. And therefore particular laws against particular offenses produce novelty, and in novelty, contempt.[46]

In the context of this public debate about how to regulate moral behavior, the dramatization of a death penalty for fornication in *Measure for Measure* asks its audience to imagine the consequences of the most extreme proposal put forward by puritan reformers and legislators. In doing so, the play associates Angelo with this puritanism in several ways.[47] Given the authority "to enforce or qualify the laws / As to {his} soul seems good" (1.1.65–66), Angelo's first act is to revive and enforce an old law punishing illicit sex with death. This action, with its resonance of puritan legislative proposals, is taken by a character who describes himself as a "saint" (2.2.180), the puritans' own preferred term for a member of the godly elect. By other characters Angelo is called "precise" (1.3.50; 3.1.93, 96) and a "seemer" (1.3.54), the more common Elizabethan pejorative terms for the social type we now label puritan.[48] Though Angelo is a fuller character than the typical stage caricature of the puritan, that fullness derives from the untypical interiority represented in his soliloquies, which develop from his point of view precisely the qualities he shares with the caricature: a superficial rectitude covering intense and unregulated passions and, above all, the hypocrisy to hide that disjunction and dictate morality to others. Such qualities were central to the satiric portrait of the puritan onstage and in print, and at least one puritan moralist felt he had to combat the stereotype among his own readers. Arthur Dent's *The plaine mans Path-way,* written in dialogue form, gives voice to views opposing his own in order to argue with them. When one of his interlocutors asserts that "there be some counterfeits, even amongst the greatest professors," Dent's authorized voice, Theologus, admits that such people exist and calls them hypocrites. Another speaker pursues the issue, arguing that the term applies not to a few exceptions but to all who present an ostentatiously godly face to the world when in fact "they will doe their neighbour a shrewd turne as soone as any body: and therfore in mine opinion, they be but a company of hypocrites, and precise fooles." Theologus does not deny the existence of such people but chides his questioner, "You judge uncharitably. Ful little do you know what they feele," suggesting that below the superficial appearance of hypocrisy is a failed struggle to overcome evil impulses and private suffering for that failure.[49] Angelo's hypocrisy differs in quality, though not in kind, from more superficial portraits of puritan hypocrites because it is an attempt to imagine—and to portray—what they feel.

Costuming may well have added to the identification of Angelo as a puritan. Fulminations against elaborate and ostentatious dress were a regular feature of religious and moral tracts,[50] and puritans were conventionally identified by plain dress. A 1602 play, *How a Man May Chuse a Good Wife from a Bad,* describes the costuming, presumably based on social conventions of dress, which identified a stage character as puritan. In that play a gallant narrates his seduction of a young puritan woman; he was unsuccessful when wearing his own fashionable clothing, but she responded enthusiastically when he approached her as a fellow puritan,

> Seeming to be conformd in looke and speech,
> My shooes were sharpe toed, and my band was plaine,
> Close to my thigh my metamorphis'd breech:
> My cloake was narrow Capte, my hair cut shorter.[51]

In *Measure for Measure,* the several references to Angelo's clothing have been critically regarded as part of a system of iterative imagery symbolizing themes of reality and appearance, being and seeming.[52] But if Angelo is, as the Duke calls him, a "seemer," that quality and the term itself also identify him as a puritan. It seems likely that in performance the clothing references function not solely as verbal imagery but also as part of the system of visual signs deployed onstage to convey dramatic meaning. When Angelo, disgusted with himself for his newly acknowledged passion for Isabella, cries that he might as well change the "gravity" in which he takes a secret pride for an "idle plume" (2.4.9–11), certainly the line can only make sense onstage if he is not already wearing a plume, if the referent of "gravity" includes a costume that presents a visual image significantly different from and opposed to the image and associations of "plume," a gallant's fashionable, extravagant accessory, the sort of thing Lucio would wear. Having thus symbolized the disjunction between his inner impulses and outer appearance in terms of his costume, Angelo goes on to describe his clothing, his "case" and "habit," as a means by which his hypocrisy works: with them, he is able to "Wrench awe from fools, and tie the wiser souls / To [the] false seeming" in his place and form (11.13–15). Similarly, when Claudio reacts in surprise that the "precise Angelo" should be capable of the "filth within" that Isabella describes, she responds "O,'tis the cunning livery of hell / The damnedst body to invest and cover / In precise guards!" (3.1.92–96).[53] In both these speeches the clothing imagery used to characterize Angelo's hypocrisy is combined with terms—"seeming" and "precise"—that are contemporary code-words for puritan. If both Isabella and Angelo himself say, in effect, that his true character is obscured by his puritan dress, it seems likely that the actor playing him wore such dress.

Angelo's position on the law he enforces also allies him with puritan legal views. When Angelo declares that "It is the law, not I," which condemns Claudio and that he both "will not" and "cannot" rescind the sentence (2.2.80, 51–52), he adopts a legal absolutism whose parallels can be found in puritan arguments for the death penalty. Thomas Cartwright, for example, argued against the right of any magistrate to "mitigate" punishments decreed by God, "utterly den[ying] . . . that there is any place, time, or other circumstance, which can lessen these crimes that they should not be worthie of death."[54] This position was expressed even more strongly by the separatist Henry Barrow. In his view the established church had usurped the right to regulate moral behavior, which properly belonged only to the godly elect, the "saints"; of them "it is written, 'lette the highe accts of God be in ther mouthes and a towe [two] edged sword in ther hands, to execut vengance upon the heathen and corrections among the people; such honour have all his saynts.' " For Barrow there was no latitude for intervention in the laws of God by even the highest human authority: "A godly prince is bound to God's lawe. . . . Moses, Joshua, Samuel, David, Hezekiah, made no new lawes, but revived and executed the old lawes which God had made."[55]

David Leverenz has characterized the assault of puritans such as Barrow on the established church as "a war . . . between a fantasy of pure authority and the realities of civil compromise."[56] In Barrow's arguments the fantasy of pure authority is clear: the pure and unalterable authority of God's word becomes the instrument of temporal authority—"pure" in both senses—of the saints whose privilege it is to exercise it. Similarly, Angelo rejects any modification of the law that would lessen its, and thereby his, authority, reducing him to the "cipher of a function" (2.2.39). For Angelo a mercy that rescinds the penalty of death does not create a metaphor with its own healing rhetorical power but merely empties judicial power, leaving a symbol signifying nothing. To be "the voice of the recorded law" (2.4.61) is for Angelo to speak such a transparent, absolutely referential language that he becomes the function itself, "indeed Justice," the personification he wrests from the reluctant Escalus (3.2.248).

The social consequences of Angelo's attempt thus to speak the law become evident in his response to the Provost's request for instructions regarding "the groaning Juliet . . . very near her hour" (2.2.15–16). Angelo replies, "See you the fornicatress be remov'd" (1.23). The Provost's identification of Juliet in terms of her impending motherhood reminds the audience that it already possesses, through Claudio's narrative and Lucio's recapitulation of it to Isabella, a fully adequate social context in which to understand her behavior, a common and relatively minor lapse. For Angelo, however, the label on her sin is all he needs to define her: she is "the fornicatress." In the conflict of these two modes of articulating Juliet's situation, Shakespeare's dramatizing of a threatened execution for betrothal pregnancy reveals a cultural incoherence, a rift between the available categories of definition for such behavior and the actual evaluation of it in social practice.[57] The only word in the contemporary sexual lexicon to describe Claudio and Juliet's behavior was indeed "fornication," despite the fact that social practice made finer distinctions without possessing the terms to articulate them. Speaking only the language of the "recorded law," Angelo, in judging Claudio and Juliet, literally cannot distinguish between a betrothed woman and a prostitute (a position, ironically, that historical change forced later critics to share). In one of Shakespeare's sources, George Whetstone's *Promos and Cassandra,* the heroine explicitly complains that "all is one in this [death sentence for fornication], / The lecher fyerd with lust, is punished no more, / Then he which fel through force of love, whose mariage salves his sore."[58] In *Measure for Measure* the imperative for such social evaluations becomes a part of the play's structure. Displaying onstage the punishment of betrothed couples as a logical consequence of turning the descriptive term "fornication" into a criminal offense would seem potentially to promote the audience's critical awareness of its own culture by bringing into focus the conflict between the two modes of comprehending the significance of sexual behavior.

IV. The Playwright's "Craft against vice"

Seeing Angelo as a representative puritan, R. G. Hunter has suggested that *Measure for Measure* can be read as an "answer to Puritan polemics" on the need for rigorous punishment of sexual offenses.[59] Indeed, the polemical answer to puritan proposals for the death penalty—the concrete arguments put forth by men like Whitgift, Cosin, and Bond—are represented in the play, primarily through Isabella's arguments. Like Whitgift, she asserts that Christ "Found out the remedy" for the law decreeing death (2.2.73–75); like Cosin, she argues that Angelo should commiserate the human frailty shown by Claudio and temper his punishment with mercy; with Bond, she knows the contempt that too-presumptuous authority, "like an angry ape" (1.121), invites. But polemics are, in the world of the play, oddly ineffective: neither Angelo nor Isabella convinces the other; nor does the debate, as such, affect the events that ensue. Rather, those events are shaped to marshall in opposition to what Angelo represents not polemical argument but theatrical power. Robert Weimann has argued that Shakespeare's theater stages forms of authority in two distinct ways. One, the "represented *locus* of authority," exists within the fiction, constructed of verbal and behavioral elements mimetic of socially "sanctioned modes of authorizing political, ecclesiastical, and juridical types of discourse." The second form of authority is theatrical, grounded in the audience's accumulating responses to "the provision of pleasure, . . . the distribution of information and newsvalue, and the functions of social release and collective memory." Thus,

> Authority in this theatre is not something unified or conclusive; it is not given, as it were, at the beginning of the play in performance but is implicated in the process—in the effect of, in the response to, the dramatic production itself. In Shakespeare's theatre the uses of mimesis were remarkably open-ended; they were bound up with a multiplicity of divergent social and cultural functions by which altogether different authorities could quite effectively be negotiated in the very form and pressure of the theatrical performance.[60]

Measure for Measure opens with the construction of Angelo's political and judicial authority in the Duke's formal, public, legally inscribed transfer of rule. But even as that authority is constructed by the play's deployment of the discourses of politics and law, performance questions and dismantles it—beginning, if I am right in my speculation about Angelo's costuming, in that same first scene. Revealing his plan to appoint Angelo deputy, the Duke asks Escalus, "What figure of us, think you, he will bear?" (1.1.16). Angelo enters and the Duke seems to answer his own question: "Angelo: / There is a kind of character in thy life / That to th'observer doth thy history / Fully unfold" (ll. 26–29). As with Angelo's reference to his "gravity," these lines seem to depend for full theatrical meaning on there being something immediate about Angelo's appearance that will in fact unfold his character to the audience: the latent reference to the audience's own status as observers specifically invites their interpretive attention. In a theater that depended heavily on elaborate costuming for its visual spectacle, the sight of a plainly dressed Angelo entering to replace the "figure" of a more lavishly costumed Duke would provide a striking image of what Mistress Overdone will call "a change indeed in the commonwealth" (1.2.96–97). If Angelo is costumed as a puritan, then a whole complex of characteristics would be unfolded in that image, summoning up both attitudes toward real-life puritans and theatrical expectations based on the dramatic tradition of anti-puritan satire. If the audience witnesses the formal discourses of politics and law conferring authority upon a figure whose visual appearance provokes their hostility or even merely skepticism, the opening scene would thus instigate the division between Angelo's represented authority and the authority of the theatrical experience, which comes to be embodied in the disguised Duke.

The Duke's second appearance, in 1.3, makes explicit the divided experience of Angelo's authority. This brief scene articulates the Duke's reasons for appointing Angelo deputy; he offers two. The first reason grants the proposition that sexual regulation is necessary and puts forward the possibility that puritan arguments for rigorous punishment are correct: unenforced, the Duke explains, the threat of death fails to eliminate sexual license. The invocation of a death penalty in the manner of the penance ritual, only "for terror, not to use" (l. 26), loses the desired rhetorical effect through repetition and familiarity. But the Duke presents a second reason as well: "Lord Angelo is precise" (l. 50). The Duke wants to see what will happen when a puritan is given power. This second reason interrogates the first, pitting the connotations of Angelo's "precision" against the argument for the death penalty and raising the question whether such a law enforced by such a person will indeed by either effective or just. The question is underscored by the Duke's concluding couplet, ". . . Hence shall we see / If power change purpose, what our seemers be" (ll. 53–54). This couplet's choric function bridges stage and audience, fiction and social experience. The audience is, perforce, part of the "we" who will see the developing events; what they will see is not simply Angelo as an individual character but the effect of power on him as a sample of the social type he represents—puritans, "our seemers."

In this same scene the Duke also reveals his plan to go into disguise as a friar. With this the play moves to a different mode of fiction-making. Against the "fantasy of pure authority" embodied in Angelo and his powerful associations with the legislative projects of puritan reformers, Shakespeare pits a fantasy of a distinctly theatrical kind, a duke in disguise as a friar, intriguing through bed-trick, substituted head, and theatrical display both to defeat that legislation and to provide an alternate resolution to the play's broken betrothals. Utterly unmimetic of anything in the social world outside the theater, the Duke instead offers the experience of pleasures unique to the playhouse. In a play that does little to invite sustained identification with any of its characters, these pleasures become the central point of audience involvement in the play.

To encourage that involvement, Shakespeare lays the comedy on rather thickly, constructing the role of the Duke by combining two different comic conventions then in vogue, the duke-in-disguise and the intriguing-friar disguise. *Measure for Measure* was written in the middle of a brief and intense fad for a specific disguise convention, the disguised duke, and it works a variation on the convention as established by its predecessors, Marston's *The Malcontent* and Middleton's *The Phoenix.*[61] Like his precursors, the disguised Duke in *Measure for Measure* has a political and social quest, but, unlike them, his is a very specific one: he goes into disguise not to correct social abuses himself but to "behold [Angelo's] sway," to find out "what our seemers be" when they have the power "to enforce or qualify the laws" (1.3.43, 54; 1.1.65). Consistent with this more limited focus, the Duke, unlike the Phoenix and the Malcontent, does not intervene in the purely criminal cases he comes across in disguise—and the play demonstrates that he doesn't have to. Despite the comic inefficiency of Elbow, the disguised Duke eventually sees his law enforcement apparatus working well enough: Pompey and Mistress Overdone, pimp and brothelkeeper, are finally arrested by the ordinary workings of the law. It is only the question still open in Jacobean society—how the sexual behavior of ordinary people, nonprofessionals as it were, should be regulated—that the Duke intervenes in, to make a choice between the alternatives under debate. And when the Duke chooses, when the role of the Duke switches from observer to intriguer, the play becomes a contest between the two authorities: Angelo, determined to inflict the death penalty, and the Duke, improvising to avert it.

As a means to that improvisation, the Duke uses his disguise as a friar, itself a popular novelty at the time. Friars as intriguers and romantic go-betweens have a long history; witness Shakespeare's own use of Friar Lawrence in *Romeo and Juliet* and the friar who, in *Much Ado About Nothing,* arranges the deception by which Hero and another Claudio's disrupted betrothal is resolved. Disguise as a friar or hermit was also a minor plot device of long standing. Between 1602 and 1604, however, dramatists began to use disguise as a friar as a means for central characters to further their own intrigues and romantic plans. The device figures significantly in two plays staged by Shakespeare's company in the year or two before *Measure for Measure* was written, plays that offer an interpretive context for the disguise the Duke adopts, just as the disguised-duke plays provide a context for his ducal role. In 1603 or 1604, Shakespeare's company staged *The Merry Devil of Edmonton,* a very popular play in which a friar disguise is used to repair a disrupted betrothal.[62] Here a love match is threatened by financial difficulties and parental opposition. The woman's father, wishing to end the betrothal because her young man's financial fortunes have declined, invents a ploy to evade the public commitment they had made. He sends his daughter to a nunnery, declaring that she has renounced her betrothal in favor of the spiritual life. Her betrothed appeals for help to his tutor, a semi-legendary magician-academic. The two go into disguise as friar-confessors to gain access to the nunnery. After a mock penance scene laden with erotic overtones, the lovers escape the nunnery and, in a long nocturnal scene of mistaken identities, substitutions, and tricks, the tutor-friar arranges for the lovers to wed; a central device is a kind of inverted bed-trick in which the friar switches inn signs to prevent the pursuing father from discovering the lovers before they can consummate their marriage. Confronted in the morning with the *fait accompli,* the father relents, the lovers ask forgiveness, and all are reconciled.

At about the same time, the King's Men were also performing *The Faire Maide of Bristow.* In this play a central character adopts a friar disguise in order to visit in prison a friend who has been erroneously condemned to death for murdering him. In disguise, he consoles his friend and, unrecognized, elicits a declaration of repentance and readiness for death. The play concludes with a complex trial scene, replete with disguises and substitutions, in which the condemned man's spurned wife pleads for mercy for him, asserting that "Intents are nothing till they come to acts."[63] A happy ending is achieved when the supposed murder victim throws off his friar's hood and is revealed alive. As these brief summaries indicate, a number of very specific plot and thematic elements associated with the friar disguise seem to have been appropriated and transformed to the social and political purposes of *Measure for Measure.*

In *Measure for Measure* the comic connotations of the friar disguise are layered—literally in the robe and cowl the Duke puts on—over the significance of the disguised duke. The audience knows this character is a duke in disguise, but they *see* him in the costume and behavior of an intriguing friar. This composite figure's appeal to specifically theatrical desires and pleasures mobilizes the authority of the audience's response to the unfolding performance in opposition to the authority Angelo represents. As the play unfolds, the theatrical expectation set up by seeing a duke go into disguise—that he will scout out and correct political or social abuses—modulates into an understanding that some of those abuses, the sexual peccadillos of ordinary people, are to be resolved not by defining them as crimes and applying the rigor of the law but by regarding them as relationships to be sorted out and directed toward completion in marriage, a dramatic function appropriate to the friar disguise the Duke assumes.

That redefinition from crime to relationship is accomplished in part through the tricks and substitutions the Duke organizes and in part through the increasingly direct relationship the duke-as-friar establishes with the audience. His very theatricality and conventionality mediates between the representations of social practice in the play and the fact that the audience is experiencing them *as* representations in the social context of theatergoing.

Throughout the long third act, the Duke wanders through an unlocalized space, a mobile observer stepping in and out of the vignettes that pass across the stage. He sees Pompey and Mistress Overdone caught and jailed and learns that Lucio has seduced a woman with a promise of marriage. In all these encounters the Duke first addresses the audience, with asides such as "O heavens, what stuff is here!" (3.2.5) and "Still thus, and thus: still worse!" (l. 51), before he is noticed by the other characters and steps in to interact with them. The Duke's journey ends with a "soliloquy," summing up the action.[64] He reacts to Angelo's malfeasance with an expostulation similar to his earlier ones—"Twice treble shame on Angelo" (l. 262)—and concludes

> Craft against vice I must apply.
> With Angelo tonight shall lie
> His old betrothed, but despised:
> So disguise shall by th'disguised
> Pay with falsehood false exacting,
> And perform an old contracting.
> (ll. 270–75)

That is, he will arrange for an old betrothal to be completed in sexual intercourse and marriage. The otherwise very effective BBC-TV production of *Measure for Measure* demonstrates vividly how poorly these tetrameter couplets work as a meditative soliloquy.[65] In fact this verse form was that traditionally assigned to comic friars and clerics; in *Merry Devil,* for example, both the authentic Prioress and the characters disguised as friars jingle in tetrameter rhymes. As direct address to the audience, the Duke's lines emphasize the comic significance of the intriguing-friar disguise and crown the developing intimacy between the audience and the Duke-friar as a kind of inverted Vice figure, applying the Vice's craft, and inviting complicity, not in opposition to virtue but to vice itself masquerading as law.[66]

In *Merry Devil* it is an abuse of patriarchal authority—the articulated, if inconsistently practiced, right and duty of parents to arrange or consent to their children's marriages—that is contravened by another kind of authority figure, the intellectual, moral, and theatrical authority of the tutor / magician / friar. In *Measure for Measure* the political implications of such theatrical opposition to represented authority are drawn more sharply. Statute law and the authority of legal institutions are abused by Angelo, so it is perhaps a species of political tact that here the subverter of the law imposed by Angelo is, in fact, the legitimate authority in the state. The layering of conventions—duke in disguise, disguise as a friar, friar as mender of troubled relationships—allows the law to be defeated without openly representing such a challenge by any citizen of lower rank than the Duke himself. Though a superficially scandalous plot development is thereby avoided, the disguise device has a paradoxical effect: the fact that the opposition to an oppressive law is engineered by the Duke also gives that opposition a bedrock of legitimacy. Everyone else in the play—including Escalus and the Provost, state officials themselves—voices opposition to the law Angelo enforces, but in the Duke's action the practice of managing matters so as to adapt the law to the actual standards of the community is shown as springing from, and secretly empowered by, the highest authority in the state. This implicit authorization is the more significant because, uniquely among disguised dukes, this Duke depends for success on the willing help of a number of others who do not know his true identity. Though offered the hope by the "friar" that the Duke will be pleased by their actions (3.1.202, 4.2.184–97), Isabella, Mariana, and the Provost must themselves take the risk of authorizing their own acts of resistance to and amelioration of the law. If we accept that Shakespeare's public audience comprised a fairly broad cross section of London's population,[67] then a substantial proportion of the audience must themselves have been actual or eligible participants in the law-enforcement process, serving their turns as members of the watch, headboroughs, constables, members of a jury, justices of the peace, etc. Many members of the audience would thus have had the experience of serving in positions where they too faced a choice between Angelo-like rigor and their own acts of mediation between law and community.

The possibility of such acts of mediation meant that, though it was certainly more violent than the church courts, criminal-law enforcement as it was practiced in Tudor-Stuart England was not quite the rigid and inflexible sword of retribution puritans would have liked it to be. Because it depended so heavily on local participation—prosecution of a felony case, for example, typically involved some three dozen members of the community from beginning to end—law enforcement was, like the moral standards overseen by the ecclesiastical courts, very much open to modification by local community values and judgments.[68] A well-known and widespread example was the action of juries assigning artificially, sometimes ludicrously, low valuations to stolen goods in order to prevent the crime from being classed as a felony and the culprit from being hanged. But even more wholesale modification of the law was easily possible when the law departed significantly from a community's own values. A Cheshire minister's diary records an example in 1651 of his community's response to a recently enacted law imposing a stiff fine for breaking the Sabbath.[69] Most of the village regarded the law as too harsh, so that infringements of it were generally ignored. In one instance, however, a young servant woman was found working on Sunday by some of the more puritanically minded members of the community, who insisted on prosecution. At the urging of his wife and neighbors, the minister instead connived with the local constable to accept the probably untrue assertion that the woman was a minor, so that she could be spared the prohibitive fine and referred to her employer for correction. Charged with the legal responsibility of punishing her, the employer publicly plucked a twig from a nearby bush, tapped it a few times on the girl's clothing, and with this "beating" declared her punished. This performance raised a good laugh from the actors and onlookers alike; John Bond had evidently known what he was talking about when he had argued in 1601 that such laws would invite contempt. But that contempt did not result in rebellion or confrontation. Rather, opposition to the law took the form of a little behind-the-scenes stage management and a public performance that, while satisfying the forms of law, in fact enforced the community's own standards. A law perceived as draconian was gutted by comedy. That is, of course, exactly what *Measure for Measure* does.

In arguing that Shakespeare's use of the comic thus participates in a larger cultural logic of mediation, I am not thereby attempting to recuperate romantic, celebratory, or providentialist readings of the play's conclusion. In fact, each of the three marriages with which it concludes gestures toward a different comic convention. Claudio and Juliet do echo the pattern of romantic comedy, as the blocking figure, Angelo, is defeated in his attempt to obstruct their loving union. Angelo and Mariana's marriage carries at least a suggestion of the errant man redeemed by the love of a good woman, a convention seen, for example, in *The London Prodigal* of 1605. In an entirely different comic tone Lucio is "the biter bit," the manipulator who outwits himself, as his successful exploitation of betrothal's ambiguities is undone by his inability to resist boasting of it to the disguised Duke. The discomfiture meted out, not only to Lucio but to all the characters, suggests that the satisfactions this play offers its audience are closer to those of satire, as it concludes not in celebration but with an altogether more Jonsonian ending than we may usually associate with Shakespeare. Following *The Alchemist's* universal discomfiture of its characters, Face refers the final judgment to the audience, whom he addresses as his "country," that is, his jury. Throughout *Measure for Measure* the audience is repeatedly invoked as witness, compurgator, congregation, jury; all the invitations for specific forms of imaginative participation in the play stress the audience's capacity to evaluate, to discriminate, to judge. The typicality of the social practices the play performs suggests that most members of the audience would recognize that the Duke's orders complete what the couples themselves began; that, Lucio's protests notwithstanding, no one is forced to marry as punishment for crime; that the resolutions, however extraordinary the Duke's methods of achieving them, were the resolutions communities would have expected and the ecclesiastical courts did require of similar relationships in the world outside the play. In pitting theatrical pleasure against puritanical authority, the play has invited its audience to recognize that, as a remedy for sexual misbehavior, marriage—however unromantic—is preferable to death. But the complexity of tones in the final scene, the mix of pain and joy, humiliation and triumph, allows members of the audience a wide range of emotional reaction to these recognitions.

Epilogue: 1650

The play's last joke is Lucio's: "Marrying a punk, my lord, is pressing to death / Whipping, and hanging" (5.1.520–21). In one more bid to escape the culmination of his insincere betrothal, Lucio presents the play's final equation of sex and death. But if the play has worked on its audience as I suggest, if the recognitions of social norms, the judgments of competing social discourses about sexual regulation have been made, his protest becomes a moment of dramatic irony. The joke is on Lucio as he appeals in a transparently dishonorable cause to the by-now thoroughly discredited equation of sex and death; Lucio's variation on his culture's multiple ways of connecting sex and death, in Greenblatt's term, "evacuates" it of any serious meaning. An equation that was initially presented to the audience as the rationale for Angelo's seriously argued social policy has now become merely laughable.

Just how powerful were the social norms *Measure for Measure* asked its audience to pit against the social forces represented by Angelo? To what extent was power in the state dispersed through the various structures of local and popular authority? To what extent did popular judgment and negotiation alter in practice the configurations of authority that we find so confidently inscribed in the various forms of elite discourse? It is not often that life so cooperatively imitates art as to suggest some answers to these questions, but in this case it did. In 1650, Angelo's real-life analogues in the Parliament of the Commonwealth abolished the ecclesiastical courts and enacted a criminal law decreeing adultery punishable by death. By parliamentary order the Act was printed and distributed to every parish in the country. Historians differ on the number of people in England executed under this statute: four, or two, or none. We can hardly conclude that these figures represent the actual incidence of adultery in those years. Rather, in hundreds or thousands of other cases, which in earlier years would have been brought to the ecclesiastical courts, the criminal law was ignored by the citizens whose role it was to enforce it. When charges were brought, juries exercised their prerogative and simply refused to find the defendants guilty.[70] Whatever the law may have decreed, it would seem that, to borrow a few more words from *Measure for Measure's* Duke, "The nature of [the] people," as they played their roles in their villages' and cities' "institutions," continued to authorize, as the people always had done, "the terms / For common justice" (1.1.9–11).

Notes

In writing this essay, I have incurred many debts of gratitude: A. R. Braunmuller's encouragement and comments improved each of its several versions; Coppélia Kahn provided the impetus for the project; and helpful criticism was offered at various stages by David Cressy, Stewart

Eames, R. A. Foakes, Peter Goldstein, Andrew Gurr, Lorraine Helms, Thomas J. Otten, Robert N. Watson, and, at last, this journal's anonymous referees.

1. Royal Shakespeare Company, Stratford-upon-Avon, 1987 season brochure.

2. F. J. Furnivall, *Child-Marriages, Divorces, and Ratifications in the Diocese of Chester, A.D. 1561–6,* Early English Text Society (London: Kegan Paul, 1897), p. li.

3. *Shakespearean Negotiations: The Circulation of Social Energy in Renaissance England* (Berkeley and Los Angeles: Univ. of California Press, 1988), p. 8.

4. For examples of recent analysis and criticism of new historicism, see Leeds Barroll, "A New History for Shakespeare and His Time," *Shakespeare Quarterly,* 39 (1988), 441–64; Jonathan Goldberg, "Recent Studies in the English Renaissance," *Studies in English Literature,* 24 (1984), 157–99; Jean E. Howard, "The New Historicism in Renaissance Studies," *English Literary Renaissance,* 16 (1986), 13–43; Theodore B. Leinwand, "Negotiation and New Historicism," *PMLA,* 105 (1990), 477–90; Richard Levin, "Unthinkable Thoughts in the New Historicizing of English Renaissance Drama," *New Literary History,* 21 (1990), 433–47; Alan Liu, "The Power of Formalism: The New Historicism," *English Literary History,* 56 (1989), 721–71; Edward Pechter, "The New Historicism and Its Discontents: Politicizing Renaissance England," *PMLA,* 102 (1987), 292–303, and the response by Carolyn Porter, "Are We Being Historical Yet?" *South Atlantic Quarterly,* 87 (1988), 743–86; and H. Aram Veeser, ed., *The New Historicism* (New York: Routledge, 1989).

5. Ralph A. Houlbrooke, *The English Family 1450–1700* (London and New York: Longman, 1984), p. 88. For other discussions of the social practices surrounding marriage formation, see John Gillis, *For Better, For Worse: British Marriage, 1600 to the Present* (New York: Oxford Univ. Press, 1985), chaps. 1–3; Martin Ingram, *Church Courts, Sex and Marriage in England, 1570–1640* (Cambridge: Cambridge Univ. Press, 1987), pp. 125–67; R. M. Smith, "Marriage Processes in the English Past: Some Continuities" in *The World We Have Gained,* Lloyd Bonfield, Richard M. Smith, and Keith Wrightson, eds. (Oxford: Blackwell, 1986), pp. 43–99; and Keith Wrightson, *English Society, 1580–1680* (New Brunswick, N.J.: Rutgers Univ. Press, 1982), chap. 3.

6. Karla Oosterveen and Richard M. Smith, "Bastardy and the Family Reconstruction Studies in Colyton, Aldenham, Alcaster and Hawkshead" in *Bastardy and Its Comparative History,* Peter Laslett, Karla Oosterveen, and Richard M. Smith, eds. (London: Edward Arnold, 1980), pp. 96–97, 107.

7. Over the past three decades a series of scholars have attempted to clarify the play's central relationships by applying sixteenth-century ecclesiastical law to the play's marriage "contracts." See Davis P. Harding, "Elizabethan Betrothals and 'Measure for Measure'," *Journal of English and Germanic Philology,* 49 (1950), 139–58; S. Nagarajan, "*Measure for Measure* and Elizabethan Betrothals," *SQ,* 14 (1963), 115–19; Ernest Schanzer, "The Marriage-Contracts in *Measure for Measure,*" *Shakespeare Survey,* 13 (1960), 81–89; Arthur H. Scouten, "An Historical Approach to *Measure for Measure,*" *Philological Quarterly,* 54 (1975), 68–84; Margaret Scott, " 'Our City's Institutions': Some Further Reflections on the Marriage Contracts in *Measure for Measure*" *ELH,* 49 (1982), 790–804; Karl P. Wentersdorf, "The Marriage Contracts in *Measure for Measure:* A Reconsideration," SS, 32 (1979), 129–44. As these scholars establish, legal marriage was accomplished solely by the voluntary consent of the two people involved; therefore, a legally valid and binding marriage was formed *whenever* a man and woman exchanged vows worded in the present tense or when they followed vows worded in the future tense with sexual intercourse. No other conditions were required—not parental consent (after 1604 parental consent was required of minors only), not the presence of witnesses or a priest, nor any specific ritual form to the vows exchanged. For a seventeenth-century discussion of the difficulties arising from this legal definition of marriage, see Henry Swinburne, *A Treatise of Spousals* (1686; London, 1711). Although the bare exchange of vows was the legal basis of marriage, more recent historical investigation has made clear that this fact had little importance in ordinary

social practice. Remarkably, of the many social rituals surrounding betrothal and marriage, none specifically marked the moment when the marriage became legally irrevocable. In this respect ecclesiastical law was not directly prescriptive of ordinary social behavior and was, in fact, generally invoked only after the fact to determine the status of disputed marriages.

8. William Gouge, *Of Domesticall Duties* (London, 1622), p. 199. In this and subsequent old-spelling quotations, I have silently expanded contractions and modernized i / j, u / v, and long s.

9. *Measure for Measure,* ed. J. W. Lever, The Arden Shakespeare (London and New York: Methuen, 1965), 3.1.215–16. ("Limit of the solemnity" means "date set for the wedding ceremony.") Subsequent citations of this edition will appear in the text. Quotations from other Shakespeare plays will be from *The Riverside Shakespeare,* ed. G. Blakemore Evans (Boston: Houghton Mifflin, 1974).

10. See R. W. Dent, *Proverbial Language in English Drama, Exclusive of Shakespeare, 1495–1616* (Berkeley: Univ. of California Press, 1984), M26; and Morris Palmer Tilley, *A Dictionary of the Proverbs in England in the Sixteenth and Seventeenth Centuries* (Ann Arbor: Univ. of Michigan Press, 1950), M26.

11. Peter Laslett, "Introduction" in Laslett et al., eds., p. 23 (Table I.3).

12. For a contemporary analysis and defense of the ecclesiastical courts, see Richard Cosin, *An Apologie for Sundrie Proceedings by Jurisdiction Ecclesiasticall* (London, 1593). For modern discussions of ecclesiastical court procedures and surviving court records, see Jay P. Anglin, "The Essex Puritan Movement and the 'Bawdy' Courts, 1577–1594," *Tudor Men and Institutions,* Arthur J. Slavin, ed. (Baton Rouge: Louisiana State Univ. Press, 1972), pp. 171–204; E.R.C. Brinkworth, *Shakespeare and the Bawdy Court of Stratford* (London: Phillimore, 1972); F. G. Emmison, *Elizabethan Life: Morals & the Church Courts* (Chelmsford: Essex County Council, 1973); Hubert Hall, "Some Elizabethan Penances in the Diocese of Ely," *Transactions of the Royal Historical Society,* 3rd ser., 1 (1907), 263–77; Ralph A. Houlbrooke, *Church Courts and the People During the English Reformation, 1520–1570* (Oxford: Oxford Univ. Press, 1979); Martin Ingram (cited in n. 5, above); Roger B. Manning, *Religion and Society in Elizabethan Sussex* (Leicester: Leicester Univ. Press, 1969); Ronald A. Marchant, *The Church Under the Law: Justice, Administration and Discipline in the Diocese of York, 1560–1640* (Cambridge: Cambridge Univ. Press, 1969), and *The Puritan and the Church Courts in the Diocese of York, 1560–1642.* (London: Longmans, 1960); and Richard M. Wunderli, *London Church Courts and Society on the Eve of the Reformation* (Cambridge, Mass.: Medieval Academy of America, 1981).

13. Bastardy (i.e., the begetting of bastards), alone of sexual offenses, was also a civil crime, punishable by flogging, under an Elizabethan statute of 1576; the law, however, was rarely enforced before the 1620s (Ingram, p. 338). Enforcement did vary geographically and, in some localities where puritan tendencies combined with traditional jurisdictions that permitted some independence from national laws, justices of the peace imposed corporal punishments for lesser sexual offenses as well; for examples, see Patrick Collinson, *The Religion of Protestants: The Church in English Society, 1559–1625* (Oxford: Clarendon, 1982), pp. 158–60.

14. For an analogous examination of the narrative strategies of convicted murderers appealing for royal pardons in France, see Natalie Zemon Davis, *Fiction in the Archives: Pardon Tales and their Tellers in Sixteenth-Century France* (Stanford, Calif.: Stanford Univ. Press, 1987).

15. Emmison, p. 4.

16. As Ann Jennalie Cook notes, in *Making A Match: Courtship in Shakespeare and His Society* (Princeton, N.J.: Princeton Univ. Press, 1991), "Shakespeare's uses of the traditional forms of betrothal and marriage . . . [in] most plays rely on compression, a kind of shorthand, to signify the precise status of a couple" by means of significant details that "link up with a whole set of assumptions that were the ordinary furnishings of an Elizabethan mentality" (p. 183); see pp. 143–45 and 212–14 for her discussions of the influence of money on and the dangers of courtship. Carol Thomas Neely, in *Broken Nuptials in Shakespeare's Plays* (New

Haven: Yale Univ. Press, 1985), also stresses the play's "painfully negative attitude toward marriage" (pp. 92–102, esp. p. 102).

17. "The norm at middling and lower social levels" was for couples to initiate their relationship and begin the first stages of betrothal before involving their families (Ingram, p. 201); Wrightson extends this norm to apply to the lesser gentry as well (*English Society,* p. 73).

18. Lever notes the significance of Mistress Overdone's calculations (p. 91n).

19. *Pace* the numerous critics who have accepted at face value Lucio's later characterization of Kate as a "punk" (5.1.520), that is, a professional prostitute, the logic of his admission here suggests otherwise. Moreover, Kate's association with Mistress Overdone does not necessarily imply she is a prostitute. As Mistress Overdone notes, their association seems to center on the child whom Overdone has "kept": at the time bawdy houses served as "underground maternity home[s] . . . that pregnant girls were often packed off to," so that the man involved could avoid the sanctions the church courts would impose (Houlbrooke, *Courts,* p. 76). Compare what the audience learns about Lucio and Kate to a potentially similar situation in a play generally regarded as a source of or influence on *Measure for Measure,* Marston's *The Malcontent* (ed. G. K. Hunter [London: Methuen, 1975]). At that play's celebratory conclusion, a courtier attempts to seduce a young woman with the promise, "let me enjoy you to-night, and I'll marry you to-morrow fortnight, by my troth" (5.6.93–94). The experienced bawd Maquerelle warns her not to believe him: "promise of matrimony by a young gallant to bring a virgin lady into a fool's paradise, make her a great woman, and then cast her off—'tis as common as natural to a courtier" (5.6.97–100). Interpreting the elliptical fragments that define Lucio and Kate's relationship by forming a narrative sequence similar to Maquerelle's prediction was, at least, one option open to a Stuart audience. By analogy with Tearsheet and Nightwork, the name "Keep-down" does suggest some, although not a clearly explicable, sexual innuendo. While it is hard to resuscitate very fine distinctions in attitudes about so fluid a status as betrothal, it may be that sexual relationships during betrothal were more socially acceptable the more public and close to completion the betrothal. The Folio's designation, on the list of dramatis personae compiled by the scribe Ralph Crane, of Juliet as "beloved of Claudio" and Mariana as "betrothed to Angelo" may reflect such a distinction based on Crane's reaction as a reader or spectator to the play's narrative about each betrothal. Likewise, the indefinite sexual aura surrounding Kate's name may suggest a judgment, not that she is a prostitute but merely a young woman "no better than she should be," eager to engage in sex as soon as a promise of marriage is exchanged and, Lucio fears, perhaps inclined to be equally morally relaxed after marriage. But that implication, if present, does not prevent the Duke, who knows only what the audience knows, from regarding her as a "woman wrong'd" (5.1.507).

20. Leah Marcus discusses the relevance of the Viennese setting and its applicability to contemporary London in *Puzzling Shakespeare: Local Reading and its Discontents* (Berkeley: Univ. of California Press, 1988), pp. 165–202.

21. Victor Turner, *From Ritual to Theatre: The Human Seriousness of Play* (New York: Performing Arts Journal, 1982), pp. 72, 107.

22. Emmison, p. 19.

23. p. 41 (cited in n. 12, above).

24. Hall, p. 268 (cited in n. 12, above). The individual for whom this penance was ordered was a woman. The church courts, however, made no distinction in theory between men and women in either culpability for sexual offenses or the penances decreed for guilty individuals. Most presentments named both parties; and in those less usual cases where an unmarried woman was found to be pregnant without the community having a plausible suspicion as to who the father was, considerable pressure would be placed on the woman to name him, so that he could be charged, assigned penance, and ordered to support the mother in her confinement and the child thereafter. In practice women were somewhat more vulnerable to charges and to guilty verdicts than men because the biological fact of pregnancy made denial

or evasion less possible for women than for men, so that, for example, slightly more than half the charges brought in Essex were against women (Emmison, p. 6; Houlbrooke, *Courts,* p. 76 [both cited in n. 12, above]).

25. G. E. Corrie, ed., *Certain Sermons Appointed by the Queen's Majesty . . .* (Cambridge: Cambridge Univ. Press, 1850). For the Homily against Adultery, see pp. 118–34, esp. p. 122; for the Homily of Repentance, see pp. 525–50, esp. p. 526.

26. Emmison, p. 1.

27. pp. 50–51.

28. Turner, p. 81.

29. Corrie, p. 124.

30. Stephen Greenblatt (cited in n. 3, above) analyzes this scene in *Shakespearean Negotiations* (pp. 138–41) but sees in it the Duke's disapproval of Juliet's "unwelcome doctrinal slippage in the shift from sin to shame" (p. 139). As the penance ritual demonstrates, however, a public display of shame was an integral part of the culturally and institutionally authorized means of correcting and reconciling the sinner to the church and community.

31. Cosin (cited in n. 12, above), Bk. 3, p. 234.

32. Corrie, p. 532.

33. Cosin, Bk. 1, p. 61. Subsequent citations in this paragraph appear on pages 55, 125, and 127 of Book 3 and on page 2 of Book 2.

34. Such analyses derive from Michel Foucault; see *Discipline and Punish: The Birth of the Prison,* trans. Alan Sheridan (New York: Pantheon, 1977), pp. 3–69. For a recent example of a Foucauldian analysis of Renaissance drama, see Karen Cunningham, "Renaissance Execution and Marlovian Elocution: The Drama of Death," *PMLA,* 105 (1990), 209–22.

35. "Puritan" was in the sixteenth and seventeenth centuries and remains for modern historians an imprecise and a contested term. For discussions of contemporary usage of the term, see Marius van Beek, *An Enquiry into Puritan Vocabulary* ([Groningen: Wolters-Noordhoff, 1969] pp. 9–14, 32–35), and Patrick Collinson, *The Puritan Character: Polemics and Polarities in Early Seventeenth-Century English Culture* ([Los Angeles: William Andrews Clark Memorial Library, Univ. of California, Los Angeles, 1989] esp. pp. 19–21). The term "puritan" had meanings in different areas—for example, church policy, theology, politics, morality—which did not necessarily form a consistent platform held by any one individual, who might be labelled "puritan" on the basis of views in any one area. Although the term covered a range of positions and did not in 1604 designate anything that could be regarded as a party or a unified set of principles (and therefore I do not capitalize "puritan"), for the purposes of this essay it is sufficient that puritan views and attitudes were recognized as such by contemporaries and formed an identity coherent enough to be portrayed, for example, in satirical plays and pamphlets. Jacobeans probably used the term "precise" most frequently to describe the particular complex of puritan attitudes I discuss with respect to Angelo, but I will use "puritan" consistently to register the continuum that existed in Tudor-Stuart England between a private, "precise" morality and the public and political incarnations of that morality, which are now contained in the modern usage of "puritan.".

36. (London, 1583), sig. H6.

37. The two works quoted here were particularly popular, judging from the number of editions printed. For other works proposing death or other severe penalties for sexual offenses in the years preceding *Measure for Measure,* see George Estey, *A most sweete and comfortable exposition, upon the tenne commaundements* (London, 1602), sig. Q7v; William Harrison, *The Description of England* (originally published with Holinshed's *Chronicles,* 1577), ed. Georges Edelen (New York: Cornell Univ. Press, 1968), pp. 189ff.; William Segar, *Honor Military and Civil* (1602), ed. Diane Bornstein (Delmar, N.Y.: Scholar's Facsimiles, 1975), fol. 21; and Thomas Tymme, *A plaine discoverie of ten English lepers* (London, 1592), sig. I2.

38. sig. C4v.

39. sig. O1v.

40. *The second replie of Thomas Cartwright* (London, 1575), sigs. N3^{r}–N3^{v}.

41. *The Sermons of Edwin Sandys,* ed. John Ayre (Cambridge: Cambridge Univ. Press, 1841), p. 50. For other examples of sermons or addresses to Parliament urging the enactment of criminal laws for adultery, see Alexander Nowell, *A Catechism,* ed. G. E. Corrie (Cambridge: Cambridge Univ. Press, 1853), p. 226; and W. H. Frere and C. E. Douglas, eds., *Puritan Manifestoes: A Study of the Origin of the Puritan Revolt* (1907; London: Church Historical Society, 1954), pp. 9, 34.

42. Keith Thomas has surveyed the history of proposals for the death penalty for adultery from the Reformation to the Restoration in "The Puritans and Adultery: The Act of 1650 Reconsidered," *Puritans and Revolutionaries: Essays in Seventeenth-Century History presented to Christopher Hill.* Donald Pennington and Keith Thomas, eds. (Oxford: Clarendon, 1978), pp. 257–82.

43. sigs. H2^{v}–H3.

44. *Journal of the House of Lords,* 2:271–73.

45. Joan R. Kent, "Attitudes of Members of the House of Commons to the Regulation of 'Personal Conduct' in Late Elizabethan and Early Stuart England," *Bulletin of the Institute of Historical Research,* 46 (1973), 41–71, esp. p. 42.

46. The quotations from both Glascock and Bond appear in Kent on pages 47 and 61.

47. A number of critics have noted aspects of Angelo's puritanism. See, for example, Harold Fisch, "Shakespeare and the Puritan Dynamic," *SS,* 27 (1974), 81–92; Brian Gibbons, ed., *Measure for Measure.* The New Cambridge Shakespeare (Cambridge: Cambridge Univ. Press, 1991), pp. 1–6; Robert G. Hunter, *Shakespeare and the Comedy of Forgiveness* (New York: Columbia Univ. Press, 1965), pp. 210–13; Donald J. McGinn, "The Precise Angelo," *Joseph Quincy Adams Memorial Studies,* James G. McManaway, Giles E. Dawson, and Edwin E. Willoughby, eds. (Washington, D.C.: Folger Shakespeare Library, 1948), pp. 129–39; and Louise Schleiner, "Providential Improvisation in *Measure for Measure,*" *PMLA,* 97 (1982), 227–36.

48. Van Beek discusses terms used by puritans themselves. See Collinson, *Puritan Character,* and William P. Holden, *Anti-Puritan Satire, 1572–1642* (New Haven: Yale Univ. Press, 1954), for discussion of the varieties of satire and invective against puritans onstage, in print, and in social life.

49. Quotations from Dent in this paragraph appear on signatures C3^{r}–C3^{v} and C4^{v}.

50. E.g., Dent, sigs. D4^{v}–E3^{r}.

51. (London, 1602), sig. G3. This play was extremely popular, at least with the reading public; it was published in seven editions between 1602 and 1634.

52. See, for example, Lever's notes to 1.3.54; 2.4.15, 149; and 3.2.38.

53. The Folio reading in lines 93 and 96 is "prenzie," commonly but not universally emended to "precise." The crux is a difficult one, and my reading may at best offer some contextual support for the emendation. The absence of the word "precise" in these two lines, however, would not materially affect my analysis of the play's varied ways of associating Angelo with puritanism.

54. sig. N4.

55. *The Writings of Henry Barrow, 1587–1590,* ed. Leland H. Carlson (London: Allen and Unwin, 1962), pp. 75, 602.

56. *The Language of Puritan Feeling: An Exploration in Literature, Psychology, and Social History* (New Brunswick, N.J.: Rutgers Univ. Press, 1980), p. 48.

57. David Lloyd Stevenson, in *The Achievement of Shakespeare's* Measure for Measure (Ithaca, N.Y.: Cornell Univ. Press, 1966), argues that the play produces a "slow revelation . . . that a wholly satisfactory evaluation of human actions goes beyond our ability to classify them according to categories of virtue fixed by theologians or by statutory law. . . . [W]e truly evaluate them by the less conditioned, more nearly morally intuitive response of that side of us which operates below the level of conscious dogma" (p. 61). I argue that these two contrasting modes of evaluation have specific correlatives in Tudor-Stuart social practice.

58. (London, 1578), sig. B4.

59. p. 212 (cited in n. 47, above).

60. "Bifold Authority in Shakespeare's Theatre," *SQ*, 39 (1988), 401–17, esp. pp. 402–4, 409.

61. See G. K. Hunter, ed., *The Malcontent* (cited in n. 19, above), pp. xli–xlvi, and John Bradbury Brooks, ed., *The Phoenix* (New York and London: Garland, 1980), pp. 1–24, for dating evidence for these plays. Critical attention to the disguised-duke convention has tended to conflate its various instances to a single paradigm, leading to arguments like Leonard Tennenhouse's, that all the disguised-duke plays of the early 1600s "invoke a regressive and magical—mythic—notion of the monarchy" (*Power on Display: The Politics of Shakespeare's Genres* [New York and London: Methuen, 1986], p. 159), or to arguments that criticize departures from an exemplary model, such as Rosalind Miles's complaint that the Duke is less "vital, spontaneous, and attractive" than Marston's Malevole (*The Problem of "Measure for Measure": A Historical Investigation* [London: Vision, 1976], p. 177), or, as Thomas Pendleton noted, to a general critical disapproval of the Duke's "inefficiency as a civic reformer" compared to the Phoenix ("Shakespeare's Disguised-Duke Play: Middleton, Marston, and the Sources of *Measure for Measure*" in *"Fanned and Winnowed Opinions": Shakespearean Essays Presented to Harold Jenkins,* John W. Mahon and Thomas A. Pendleton, eds. [London and New York: Methuen, 1987], p. 96). Such interpretations tend to grant fixed and unchanging significance to the elements of a dramatic convention. I would suggest, rather, that just as the operative meaning of linguistic units is conditioned by a range of contexts from the sentence to the speech act, significant elements of dramatic conventions are also shaped by the context of the convention's theatrical history and by the specific purposes to which it is put in each work. I argue here that when Shakespeare, in his turn, employed the disguised-duke device, he partially re-directed its political, social, and dramatic functions from the examples of his predecessors.

62. *The Merry Devil of Edmonton,* ed. William A. Abrams (Durham, N.C.: Duke Univ. Press, 1942). See pages 3–13 and 28–36 for dating and performance evidence and for discussion of the numerous allusions in other contemporary works, which suggest the play's popularity.

63. *The Faire Maide of Bristow* (London, 1605), sig. D4^{v}; cf. Isabella's "His act did not o'ertake his bad intent" (5.1.449).

64. Stanley Wells and Gary Taylor, in *William Shakespeare: A Textual Companion* (Oxford: Clarendon, 1987), suggest that the Folio text of *Measure for Measure* includes revisions by another author, possibly Middleton, in the 1620s. They propose that Shakespeare's version lacked the song and opening dialogue of Act 4, resulting in a continuous scene in which the Duke moves from Claudio in prison through the brief episodes with Pompey, Lucio, and Mistress Overdone to his consultation with Isabella and Mariana without ever leaving the stage. As they reconstruct this version, this speech covered the silent discussion between Isabella and Mariana in which they arrange to complete the "old contracting" (pp. 468–69). If this was the case, the continuous action would have underscored the distinction between those incidents the Duke merely observes and the one situation in which he intervenes, and the placing of this speech would have emphasized that the Duke regards his intervention as the repair of a ruptured betrothal.

65. *Measure for Measure* (London: British Broadcasting Corporation, 1979).

66. See Mathew Winston, " 'Craft Against Vice': Morality Play Elements in *Measure for Measure,*" *Shakespeare Studies,* 14 (1981), 229–48, for an argument for the Vice-figure antecedents and resonances of the Duke-friar.

67. Andrew Gurr, *The Shakespearean Stage 1574–1642,* 3rd ed. (Cambridge: Cambridge Univ. Press, 1992), pp. 212–31; and *Playgoing in Shakespeare's London* (Cambridge: Cambridge Univ. Press, 1987), pp. 49–79. The view of Shakespeare's audience as fairly heterogeneous is challenged by Ann Jennalie Cook in *The Privileged Playgoers of Shakespeare's London, 1576–1642* (Princeton, N.J.: Princeton Univ. Press, 1981), where she argues for a largely elite and affluent

audience; her arguments are rebutted in detail in Martin Butler's *Theatre and Crisis 1632–1642* (Cambridge: Cambridge Univ. Press, 1984), Appendix II, pp. 293–306.

68. For discussions of the effects of wide communal participation in the law enforcement process which argue that, as Joel Samaha puts it, "discretion in enforcing the law was a perfectly respectable practice in the sixteenth century," see Cynthia B. Herrup, *The Common Peace: Participation and the Criminal Law in Seventeenth-Century England* (Cambridge: Cambridge Univ. Press, 1987) and "Law and Morality in Seventeenth Century England," *Past and Present,* 106 (1985), 102–23; Joel Samaha, "Hanging for Felony: The Rule of Law in Elizabethan Colchester," *The Historical Journal,* 21 (1978), 763–82, esp. p. 775; Keith Wrightson, "Two Concepts of Order" in *An Ungovernable People: The English and their Law in the Seventeenth and Eighteenth Centuries,* John Brewer and John Styles, eds. (New Brunswick, N.J.: Rutgers Univ. Press, 1980), pp. 21–46, and *English Society* (cited in n. 5, above), pp. 155–59. For a slightly different perspective, arguing that both statute law and selective enforcement practices were guided by and thus made compatible by a "logic of exemplary punishment," see P. G. Lawson, "Lawless Juries? The Composition and Behavior of Hertfordshire Juries, 1573–1624" in *Twelve Good Men and True: The Criminal Trial Jury in England, 1200–1800.* J. S. Cockburn and Thomas A. Green, eds. (Princeton, N.J.: Princeton Univ. Press, 1988), pp. 117–57, esp. p. 157. For an argument that literary analyses of the configurations of power in Renaissance texts should take into consideration the social effects of the law-enforcement process in practice, see Leinwand (cited in n. 4, above).

69. Wrightson, English Society, pp. 158–59.

70. For the legislation, see C. H. Firth and R. S. Rait, eds., *Acts and Ordinances of the Interregnum, 1642–1660,* 3 vols. (London: HMSO, 1911), Vol. 2, p. 388. For its publication, see *Calendar of State Papers, Domestic Series,* 16 May 1650, ed. Mary A. E. Green (London: HMSO, 1876; rpt. 1965), p. 164. Derek Hirst, in *Authority and Conflict: England 1603–1658* (London: Edward Arnold, 1986), states that four executions took place under this law (p. 296). Thomas documents two, noting that the law was framed by Parliament, under the influence of its moderate members and to the unhappiness of militant reformers, to make conviction difficult (pp. 258, 278–80). Lawrence Stone, in *The Family, Sex and Marriage in England, 1500–1800* (New York: Harper and Row, 1977), discusses one case in which there was a conviction but doubts that the sentence was carried out (p. 632). For evidence of juries' refusal to convict, see F. A. Inderwick, *The Interregnum (A.D. 1648–1660)* (London: Simpson, et al., 1891), pp. 33–38.

Pleasure and Danger: Measuring Female Sexuality in *Measure for Measure*

MARIO DIGANGI

Despite its initial promise of equity and levity—a balanced title and a Folio classification as a comedy—*Measure for Measure* delivers what many readers have felt to be a skewed and dismal account of sexual desire. Feminist and psychoanalytic critics, responding to this antifestive comedy's persistent reiteration of the manifold dangers that accompany sexual unions and desires, have usefully considered how female sexuality in particular is linked to "shame" and "contamination"; treated with "disgust" and "deep distrust"; figured as the "original sin that brings death into the world"; reduced to the "bloody associations" of rape and beheading.[1] Ironically, however, feminist responses may also be inhibited by the very centrality of female sexuality to the play's ideology, the unpleasantness of which leads Kathleen McLuskie, in her trenchant essay "The Patriarchal Bard," to deem the play impenetrable to feminist criticism. Although McLuskie demonstrates the inadequacy of monolithic empirical and psychological approaches to an ideologically informed feminist reading of *Measure for Measure,* she curbs those interventions (her own and others') that could provide new theoretical paradigms, insisting that

> feminist criticism of this play is restricted to exposing its own exclusion from the text. It has no point of entry into it, for the dilemmas of the narrative and the sexuality under discussion are constructed in completely male terms.[2]

McLuskie specifically regrets the exclusion of "pleasure" that results from reading the text against its sexist grain: to reject its tendentious construction of female sexuality is to refuse "the pleasure of the drama and the text," which "focuses the spectator's attention and constructs it as male."[3]

Yet, as Jean Howard and Stephen Orgel have persuasively argued, the London theater allowed many women to become desiring spectators despite

Reprinted from *ELH* 60:3(1993): 589–609. © 1993. The Johns Hopkins University Press.

the fact that it ideologically objectified them as desired spectacles and materially excluded them, as McLuskie notes, from being "shareholders, actors, writers, or stage hands."[4] In "Scripts and / versus Playhouses," Howard provocatively asks: "Is it possible that in the theatre women were licensed to look—and in a larger sense to judge what they saw and to exercise autonomy—in ways that problematised women's status as object within patriarchy?"[5] Unravelling Stephen Gosson's prescriptions on the female playgoer, Howard stresses the complications that arise in considering the female spectator not only as an endangered *object* of the male gaze, but as a gazing *subject* who endangers patriarchal control. Orgel briefly surmises in "Nobody's Perfect" that women enjoyed the "liberating theatrical freedom" not only of attending the London playhouses but also of seeing there the enactment of female liberty in the subjects of "love matches and cuckoldry."[6] In his subsequent paper "Call Me Ganymede," Orgel, first questioning the standard notion that women were officially "banned" from the stage, develops this argument regarding the London theaters' pleasurable representations of female power. He finds that "the powerful side of cuckoldry plots from the woman's perspective is the conviction that her sexuality is powerful and attractive, threatening to husbands, and under her own control," and he adduces Portia's and Nerissa's ring trick at the conclusion of *The Merchant of Venice* as an example of a theatrically constructed "fantasy of female sexual power."[7]

If we take into account Howard's and Orgel's historicization of the female spectator's pleasure, might we not find that *Measure for Measure* likewise constructs a position that may elicit a female (or, in our age, feminist) subject's pleasure? Might not that pleasure come precisely from reading oppositionally, with the purpose of discovering the kind of female agency those "male terms" would exclude and restrict? In pursuing such a reading here, I will argue that the relentless definition and manipulation of female sexuality in *Measure for Measure* is the graphic symptom of male anxiety about female agency: to unravel male-constructed meanings for erotic pleasure, pregnancy, and abortion is to discover a fear of the dangers thought to ensue from a woman's control over her own body. Because it measures the perceived cost of a woman's autonomy in marital and reproductive affairs, *Measure for Measure* foregrounds female sexual desire only to deny the desirability of seeking pleasure for pleasure's sake. Paradoxically, the central emblem of this dangerous desire is the pleasure-seeking body of a woman who is excluded both from the *personae* of the drama and from the pages of critical texts: Mistress Elbow.[8]

Mistress Elbow, as one might well not recall, is the only legal wife in the play. In order to understand the significance of her status, we must first determine what is at stake in the play's implicit and explicit allusion to the commonplace Renaissance marital paradigm—maid / wife / widow—whose central space is occupied by Mistress Elbow alone.[9] Mariana, who is "nothing," according to the Duke, because "neither maid, widow, nor wife," frustrates but does not subvert the paradigm, as McLuskie notes, for the logic of comedy ultimately maneuvers her into the central slot.[10] Nevertheless, in privileging the "coherent maleness" of the maid / wife / widow paradigm to which the Duke heavy-handedly directs (male?) attention, McLuskie loses the opportunity to demonstrate the paradigm's failure as an ideological measuring device.[11] As Lucio observes, the Duke's seemingly comprehensive list of female socio-sexual roles is incomplete: "My lord, she may be a punk; for many of them are neither maid, widow nor wife" (5.1.180–81). Likewise, a reading that places pressure on the conventional system can superimpose upon the Duke's tripartite measure of *marital status* a parallel and more problematic measure of *sexuality.* What I am calling the measure of female sexuality would account for the number and kind of a woman's sexual partners: the virgin (none), the wife (one / legal), and the whore (more than one / illicit). Following this line of inquiry allows not only the examination of an early modern discourse surrounding and constructing the barren or pregnant female body but a reexamination, through Mistress Elbow, of the normative category of "wife," the middle term of both systems, as inherently unstable and challenged.

It is crucial to maintain the analytic distinctness of these two "measures," even while noting their areas of overlap or intersection. We then realize that, before her marriage, Mariana threatens order not only because she disrupts the maid / wife / widow paradigm but because she simultaneously and equivocally occupies the sexual position of "wife" in the virgin / wife / whore paradigm. Juliet, before she legally becomes a wife, occupies the sexually charged space between "wife" and "whore." And Isabella occupies the space of resistance and loss between "virgin" and "wife"—a space that is collapsed by the apparently seamless passage from "maid" to "wife." Such ideological gaps between fixed, normative roles and shifting, unruly sexualities are smoothed over by Carol Thomas Neely's argument that "women are defined and contained through their place in the marriage paradigm. . . . These roles are in turn defined by the mode of sexuality appropriate to them: virginity for maidens, marital chastity for wives, and abstinence for widows."[12] Because it attaches an "appropriate" sexuality to the marital roles through which women are always already defined, this formulation does not acknowledge that the marital paradigm, with its chronological progression of essential roles in which the "wife" can never be a "maid" or "widow," itself obscures the resistances that Mariana, Isabella, and Juliet pose to its containing and defining strategies—the resistances posed in the overlapping and contested spaces between virgin and wife, between wife and whore.

As the only wife in the play, Mistress Elbow most powerfully and paradoxically represents the unruly resistance within marital sexuality: the possibility of the wayward wife, who is at once promiscuous (like the stereotypical widow), and, as I hope to show, opposed to fertility (like the maid). The logic of comedy may require that Isabella, Mariana, and Juliet progress from their unstable marital roles and sexualities into the nominally stable marital role and sexuality of the "wife." Yet Mistress Elbow demonstrates that such a resolution is fictive, for she provokes, instead of dispelling, the anxieties that surround and interpret (Juliet's) active sexual desire on the one hand and (Isabella's) virginity on the other. Since female sexuality in *Measure for Measure* is tendentiously "read" through specific bodily characteristics, the "gross characters" inscribed in Juliet's pregnant, ideologically whorish body reveal "all th'effect of love" and incite others volubly to evaluate all the causes. Isabella's virginal body, by contrast, allows others (and herself) only veiled, sublimated, allusions to a deferred sexuality that will blossom with ripe time. I will assess the male anxieties that construct Juliet's and Isabella's bodies before demonstrating how they converge to construct Mistress Elbow's equivocal body, which, absent and silent, is the cipher onto which various meanings for female sexuality are projected, and through which feminist criticism can make the crisis of marriage intelligible. I begin with a reading of Juliet's indelibly pregnant body, the first text from which differently interested readers—the bawds, Claudio, Duke Vincentio, Angelo—disseminate the signifieds of female sexuality.

Preparing us for the dramatic procession in which Claudio and Juliet are publicly humiliated, Mistress Overdone and Pompey initiate a central concern of the play: the observation and classification of the woman through her body, which is "credulous to false prints" (2.4.129). Pregnant, marked with the prints of sexual intercourse, Juliet's excessive body is, appropriately, read cumulatively: male judgments of what her belly reveals—sexual appetite, uxorial docility, ethical and theological shame, legal infraction—amass charges of culpable agency and carnal passivity. When Mistress Overdone asks if Claudio has gotten a "maid with child by him," Pompey deftly responds, "No: but there's a woman with maid by him" (1.2.84–85). Mistress Overdone is sensitive to how sex has altered the (former) maid's body; Pompey insists on naming her new status as the specifically non-maiden, and "woman" is all he has available to him. Juliet's intermediate marital status may confer no fixed name, but her body sufficiently indicates the sexuality which has marred her reputation. Lisa Jardine notes that due to the absence of effective contraception, "sex and pregnancy went hand in hand in the Renaissance imagination"; hence, "the pregnant woman is the Renaissance image of female sexuality."[13] Moreover, the popularity in England of a Galenic view of conception produced, according to Angus McLaren, "a common culture of procreational knowledge in which women's sexual pleasure was seen both by laymen and doctors as necessary for fecundity."[14] The pregnant woman is therefore an image of her own fulfilled sexuality, her belly an eloquent narrative of her illicit desires.[15] Juliet's expressive body, which is both the ritual object of public scrutiny and the subject of Claudio's discourse, explains the silence of her tongue.

Even as he insists that their relationship is "mutual," Claudio reigns in Juliet's expressive and expansive sexuality when he reclaims her body as his personal property. Retaining the liberty of speech denied Juliet, who only later and under the Duke's prompting admits that her sinful act was "mutually" committed (2.3.27), Claudio defends his sexual indiscretion by insisting that "she is fast my wife" (1.2.136). He resents not only the law's regulation of his sexuality but its usurpation of his rights as a true husband who "upon a true contract . . . got possession of Julietta's bed" (1.2.134–35). As a husband, he would indeed have control of his wife's property, including her bed, but his legalistic use of synecdoche reduces Juliet's loose sexual energies to the status of an object that can be bound "fast" to the conjugal bed. Peter Stallybrass observes that "woman" is produced as a property category in early modern England not only in such legal discourse but also in economic discourse, as "the fenced-in enclosure of the landlord."[16] For example, as the spokesman of the conservative aristocracy in Dekker and Middleton's *The Roaring Girl,* Sir Alexander pronounces upon the occasion of his son's marriage that "the best joyes, / That can in worldly shapes to man betide, / Are fertill lands, and a faire fruitfull Bride."[17] Likewise, if Lucio's description of Juliet's impregnation invokes what Marjorie Garber calls a "fruitful and productive value of sexuality" otherwise absent in the play, it also casts Claudio in the role of the laborer who produces fair fruit from fertile lands:[18]

> Your brother and his lover have embrac'd,
> As those that feed grow full, as blossoming time
> That from the seedness the bare fallow brings
> To teeming foison, even so her plenteous womb
> Expresseth his full tilth and husbandry.
> (1.4.40–44)

Though Juliet at first resembles one who satiates herself with food, she is finally shown to provide the "bare" material upon which male sexual labor generates the female labor of childbirth. The pander in *Pericles* clearly exposes the violent overtones of this commonplace view of female passivity when he threatens to rape Marina: "An if she were a thornier piece of ground than she is, she shall be ploughed" (Pericles, 4.6.136–137). Juliet is a less thorny piece of ground and Claudio is a gentler plower, but he similarly considers the female body as the available site of male inscription: "The stealth of our most mutual entertainment / With character too gross is writ on Juliet" (1.2.143–44).[19] While "gross" is relevant in that it means large letters, clear evidence, or ripe fruit, it also associates the woman's reproductive body with the uncontrollably grotesque body of an unruly Falstaff, "a gross fat man" (*1 Henry IV,* 2.4.486).[20] Despite the pleasure, then, that Juliet may have experienced in her sexual "entertainment" with her lover, both Lucio and

Claudio, by stressing her body's compliance to male instrumentality, attempt to control its boundless sexuality.

Given Claudio's putative dominance in erotic agency, it is ironic that the Duke finds Juliet more blameworthy for the couple's sexual indiscretion. Even though Juliet has apparently done no more than passively express Claudio's "husbandry," the Duke requires her to acknowledge a greater share of guilt in the pregnancy. By disguising himself as a religious father and addressing Juliet as a daughter, the Duke can re-establish the authority of the paternal birch-rod, previously "more mock'd than fear'd" (1.3.27). He succeeds in this project by encouraging Juliet to confess her legal infraction as an ethical and theological one: a "most offenceful act" (2.3.26). When he asks, "Repent you . . . of the sin you carry?" (2.3.19), the Duke equates the content of Juliet's protruding belly with the illegal act that caused it; her offending body thereby becomes an index of her moral and spiritual degeneration. She avows her repentance and her willingness to "bear the same most patiently" (2.3.20). As Lisa Jardine astutely remarks, Juliet will "*bear* it—carry it to term, support the shame, and give birth in the pain which is woman's punishment for the concupiscence she acquired at the Fall."[21] And doubtless, she is "groaning" in prison with the pain of her labor (2.2.15).[22] Because both Duke Vincentio and Juliet accept the ideology which posits a woman's chastity as her essential virtue, they agree that Juliet's sin is of "heavier kind" than Claudio's (2.3.28), despite the fact that the law will punish him more severely, with death. Furthermore, Escalus, Lucio, and the Provost all regard Claudio's fornication as a trifle, which merely proves that he has natural masculine instincts. Juliet, however, is always said to have ruined her reputation: she must bear the unequal weight of social censure for the mutual action in which Claudio left his impression on her heavy body.

The Duke's focus on Juliet's unborn child as a "sin" implies that even after their marriage, in which Claudio is instructed to "restore" his wronged wife (5.1.522), her reputation will be stained with a child unlawfully begotten if not unlawfully born. Angelo, legally precise in his categorization, describes Juliet in neither the Provost's class terms as "gentlewoman" nor the Duke's disturbingly physical terms as "fair one" (2.3.10, 19), but as the "fornicatress" (2.2.23), thus investing her far-from-airy nothing with a local habitation and name, (which Pompey was unable to do). The punitive zeal which seeks Claudio's death seeks to over-write Juliet's reputation with gross characters. Therefore, the Provost's claim that Juliet has "blister'd her report" by "falling in the flaws of her own youth" (2.3.11–12) shows more than his mastery of metaphor. His image of a painful imprint on the body aligns Juliet with another "fallen woman": the prostitute who was branded on the forehead by the state or who carried the syphilitic blister.[23] Consequently, Juliet's body shares the "shame" imputed to the common body of the whore (2.3.36), if not the actual mark impressed upon it.

Through the example of Juliet, one sees that patriarchal ideology constructs two positions for active female sexuality: either its confinement within the "outward order" of formal marriage (1.2.138), or its whorish transgressiveness, which threatens marital values. On the other hand, the virgin is threatening for her very lack of sexuality, for her denial of normative sexual functions and gender roles. If Juliet can be identified as a "fornicatress" by the blossoming of her womb, then the true virgin, the unplucked rose, can also be recognized by outward signs. Thus Lucio addresses Isabella: "Hail, virgin, if you be—as those cheek-roses / Proclaim you are no less" (1.4.16–17). While the deceptiveness of appearances is an anxiety which the play—and playing itself—brings sharply into focus, Isabella's unsullied hue convinces Lucio that she indeed is a virgin. But against what standard is Lucio quantifying and measuring her virginity? What would it mean to be proclaimed "less" than a virgin?

Angelo's attempt to define Isabella's sexuality provides a significant answer. In contrast to the corporeal language used to identify Juliet, Angelo's language profits from a rich use of the essential ideological verb "to be," which appears seven times in the first three lines of Angelo's demand that Isabella submit to his desires.[24] In his exasperation at Isabella's refusal to understand the exchange he offers her, Angelo bluntly articulates the burden of her sexual destiny:

ANGELO: Be that you are,
That is, a woman; if you be more, you're none.
If you be one—as you are well express'd
By all external warrants—show it now,
By putting on the destin'd livery.
ISABELLA: I have no tongue but one; gentle my lord,
Let me entreat you speak the former language.

(2.4.133–39)

According to Angelo's logic, being more than a woman is taking womanly chastity to its extreme of virginity, which paradoxically thrusts her past the boundaries of dependent womanhood into the realm of the self-sufficient saint. Angelo's corrective requires that she act more like the "woman" her appearance proves she "is" and less like the virgin that in making her more then a woman, makes her less human.[25] For both Lucio and Angelo, the category "virgin" is more rarified than that of "woman," making the maid an "immortal spirit" instead of an impressionable piece of flesh (1.4.35). David Sundelson argues that in this scene of "female potency" Angelo "fears that Isabella may really be a man."[26] Far from this, however, Angelo's doubt, discovered in his evasive grammar, reveals an anxiety about female autonomy (as the super-feminine virgin) and its threat to male desires for ownership and control.

Isabella tempers this meditation on female ontology by asserting the honesty of her tongue, which metonymically proclaims her sexual "honesty" or chastity. Her simple reply that she has "no tongue but one" further implies that Angelo's slippery discourse reveals more about his own hypocrisy than about her need to "be one" woman. Ending the guessing game, but still hiding his larger meaning in equivocal language, Angelo commands: "Plainly conceive, I love you" (2.4.140). To be "a woman," Isabella must conceive, become pregnant. If she will show her essential femininity "plainly" (or, punning on the French *plein,* "fully"), she needs to exhibit more "external warrants" than mere attire and complexion. In an earlier speech on the nature of justice (2.1.17–31), Angelo uses "pregnant" in its sense of "obvious," a usage deriving from the Latin *premere,* to press. That Juliet's pregnant body registers "pregnant" evidence of pressing makes her subject to the Duke's fornication law. By requiring Isabella to become pregnant, Angelo directs her into a similar position of sexual lucidity he can understand and manipulate.

Unlike Angelo, Duke Vincentio understands Isabella all too well; instead of battering her with essentialist definitions of "woman," he works underhandedly to transform her virginal body into a womanly one. The Duke's ostensible aim in arranging the bed-trick is to have Mariana express "all th'effect of love" (5.1.198), the condition that we see in Juliet, and that Angelo yearns to see in Isabella. But because he conceals his desire more carefully than does Angelo, the language of the Duke's interchange with Isabella is loaded with double entendre that hides personal interest under the cloak of fatherly beneficence:

> DUKE: The maid will I frame, and make fit for his attempt. If you think well to carry this as you may, the doubleness of the benefit defends the deceit from reproof. What think you of it?
>
> ISABELLA: The image of it gives me content already, and I trust it will grow to a most prosperous perfection.
>
> DUKE: It lies much in your holding up.
>
> (3.1.256–62)

Strangely here, but not in light of the Duke's later proposal to Isabella, the language of pregnancy is ascribed to her part in the deceit: if she can "carry" and "hold up" her part, his idea will "grow" to a successful end, its "image" giving her "content," or substance.[27] Impressed by his authority, Isabella reactively takes up the Duke's sexual puns in what may be considered a passive, and therefore "prone and speechless dialect" (1.2.173). What the Duke offers in return for her prone complicity in his plot is a supine sexual position—"Tis well borne up," he later assures her (4.1.48). In the context of this suggestive passage and the later one in which Isabella promises to meet Angelo "[u]pon the heavy middle of the night" (4.1.35), "doubleness" may refer not only to the advantage accruing to each woman's honor, but to the swelling of her belly. Likewise, "benefit" may refer to this double belly's being well made (L. *bene* + *facere*) by the man for whom her frame has been made "fit," producing "perfection" (L. *per* + *facere*). Recalling Elbow's misplacement of his "two notorious benefactors" for "malefactors" (2.1.50–52), the equivocal language of this passage blurs the distinction between the legal malefaction of Claudio and Juliet and the moral benefaction of the Duke, given his intentions to fit Isabella to his own attempt. The Duke himself realizes the suspiciousness if not the culpability of his plan. In asking the provost to leave, the Duke anticipates an accusation of sexual motive and defensively proffers his disguise as a guarantee of his good intentions: "Leave me a while with the maid; my mind promises with my habit no loss shall touch her by my company" (3.1.175–77). No loss, but perhaps a tangible gain.

As the Duke's interpellation of Isabella through metaphors of growth indicates, female sexuality becomes intelligible (hence manageable) not only by the identification of the virginal or the whorish body, but also by the measurement of that body's movement along a temporal scale. Women accomplish a physiological progression through three stages, which are analogous to stages of botanical growth: the young "fresh" virgin becomes the "ripe" wife and / or the old "rotten" whore. In the different but parallel economy of the brothel, the epithet "fresh" is reserved for the healthy and young, "rotten" for the diseased and experienced.[28] Lucio refers to "your fresh whore and your powdered bawd; an unshunned consequence; it must be so" (3.2.57–58). The young prostitute inevitably becomes the old bawd with powdered hair, who soaks in a sweating-tub that resembles the beef-powdering tub. More generally, Shakespeare's whores are punningly called "hoar" or merely "old": Lucio refers to Kate Keepdown as "the rotten medlar," a fruit rotten before ripe (4.3.171–72).[29]

Given the above constructions, the language of "fit time" or "ripeness" which in several of Shakespeare's plays is connected with Christian patience and trust in providence has special figurative relevance in *Measure for Measure,* regarding the age of marriage and term of pregnancy. Ripeness refers to marriageable age for a young woman; Juliet Capulet will be "ripe to be a bride" at sixteen years of age (*Romeo and Juliet,* 1.2.11). When Isabella conventionally addresses the heavens, "Keep me in patience, and with ripen'd time / Unfold the evil which is here wrapt up / In countenance" (5.1.119–21), she is unaware that her words apply to her own ripeness to be plucked by the Duke in his comic finale. Even more problematic, because decidedly anticomic, are the text's images of abortion, the fatal delivery of unripe fruit. In a treatise called *The Byrth of mankynde,* the physician Thomas Raynalde describes abortion (miscarriage) in these terms: "Aborcement or untimely birth is, when the woman is delyvered before due season, and before the fruite be rype."[30] His metaphor of the woman's biological time as a harvest recalls Lucio's ploughing image, in which "blossoming time" brings the "bare fallow" to "teeming foison" (1.4.41–43); the connection is significant since ideology makes biological reproduction and nurturing the woman's "natural" role in the socio-economic system. It is worth noting in this regard that Mariana had a brother who "miscarried" at sea, thus losing her marriage dowry and her opportunity to participate in the processes of marriage and reproduction (3.1.210). The image of Juliet as a ploughed field bursting with life equates the productivity of female generative labor with that of economic labor; conversely, the image of the shipwreck as a miscarriage equates the untimely destruction of the "perished vessel" with that of the fetus in the aborting female vessel (3.1.217).[31]

The play's allusions to abortion repeatedly evoke the unnaturalness of denying or disrupting this reproductive economy. Oddly, however, most of these allusions are associated with men—Angelo and the Duke—whose legal power to kill is linked to women's unique power to abort. The effect of the homology between female and male control over life is not to empower the men (by their appropriation of "the feminine") but to indict them for their association with a monstrously destructive prerogative. Whereas in *Love's Labor's Lost* Berowne compares an "abortive birth" to the unseasonable appearance of a rose in winter or snow in May (*Love's Labor's Lost,* 1.1.104), Angelo goes further in figuring illegitimate children as "evils" that must be aborted before they are "hatch'd." He praises the newly-awakened law which:

> like a prophet
> Looks in a glass that shows what future evils,
> Either new, or by remissness new conceiv'd,
> And so in progress to be hatch'd and born,
> Are now to have no successive degrees,
> But ere they live, to end.
> (2.2.95–100)

Angelo's law will destroy those who "coin heaven's image / In stamps that are forbid" as easily as he could stamp out the life of a fertilized egg (2.4.45–46). Calling the deputy a "motion ungenerative" and an "ungenitured agent" (3.2.108, 167–68), Lucio implies that he has neither *genitor* nor genitals, that he represents a freakish rupture in a procreational chain. Angelo himself articulates in the language of abortion the self-destructive consequences of his supposed rape of Isabella: "This deed unshapes me quite; makes me unpregnant / And dull to all proceedings" (4.4.18–19). Through its corruptness, the act by which he impregnates another is not life-affirming but annihilating: it destroys his honor, his "grace," and his unified subjectivity—"Nothing goes right; we would, and we would not" (4.4.32).

In Angelo's sterile legalism the product of sex is death, but sex and death are conflated in the Duke's original law and in the means for fulfilling it, the executioner Abhorson. David Sundelson, among others, comments on the components of "his highly suggestive name ('abhor,' 'whore,' 'whoreson')," but not on the fact that the entire name is a virtual homonym for "abortion."[32] In his *Breviarie of health,* for instance, Andrew Boord uses the almost identical form "abhorsion."[33] The Renaissance pun on "to die" as the moment of sexual climax is anthropomorphized in *Measure for Measure:* the former bawd who facilitated sexual unions must as executioner's aide destroy "fornicators"; conversely, the executioner himself is symbolically associated with the destruction of the product of sexual union.[34] If the literal execution of the law is figured as abortion, then the Duke's obsession with "fit time" can be seen as a desire to deflect attention away from the abortive, deforming justice of his "most biting laws" onto his theatrically deferred display of mercy (1.3.19). Assuring Mariana that his bed-trick will grow to a prosperous conclusion, the Duke echoes the harvest metaphor with which Lucio announced Juliet's pregnancy: "Our corn's to reap, for yet our tithe's to sow" (4.1.76). By withholding certain information which he then dispenses at carefully engineered moments, the Duke establishes himself not as the guarantor of an evil law "by remissness new-conceiv'd" but as the one figure who can reveal truth in ripe time.

That abortion is figuratively linked in *Measure for Measure* with costly destruction and with an unnaturally harsh law that measures out untimely death for sexual activity indicates what is at stake in a wife's regulation of and responsibility for her "ripe time." Far from being the rational choice of a woman who desires to control her fertility, abortion is intelligible only as the consequence of the dangerous desires of a pregnant wife, Mistress Elbow. Named after a bodily joint, Mistress Elbow is the pivot on which turn the male anxieties directed at the fertility of Juliet's body and the infertility of Isabella's body. Her pregnant body, like Juliet's, is legible as a signifier of sexual desire, but Mistress Elbow's threateningly misplaced sexuality leads her to seek pleasure in a dangerous place promoting "fornication, adultery, and all uncleanliness," including, I would argue, abortion.

The copiousness of the whore and the barrenness of the virgin are presented as ideological counters in *Measure for Measure,* against which the exclusive closure of the chaste wife ("won" by and "one" for the husband) should be posited as the ideal measure. Although the wife's only doubleness should come from the stamp of the single man, the play's only wife generates a crisis of sexual and linguistic doubleness, indeterminacy, and "misplac[ing]" (2.1.87):

ELBOW: My wife, sir, whom I detest before heaven and your honour—

ESCALUS: How? Thy wife?

ELBOW: Ay, sir: whom I thank heaven is an honest woman—

ESCALUS: Dost thou detest her therefore?

ELBOW: I say, sir, I will detest myself also, as well as she, that this house, if it be not a bawd's house, it is pity of her life, for it is a naughty house.

ESCALUS: How dost thou know that, constable?

ELBOW: Marry, sir, by my wife, who, if she had been a woman cardinally given, might have been accused in fornication, adultery, and all uncleanliness there.

ESCALUS: By the woman's means?

ELBOW: Ay, sir, by Mistress Overdone's means; but as she spit in his face, so she defied him.

(2.1.68–83)

Despite his misplaced readings of his wife's misplaced body, Elbow manages to affirm that the "woman's means" is Mistress Overdone's intermediary or bawd, Pompey; but as Frankie Rubinstein notes, Escalus's vague query carries a more general meaning.[35] The "woman's means" may be synonymous with what the Bawd of *Pericles* calls "the way of womenkind" (4.6.141), the inherent feminine wantonness that marital sexuality may actually encourage. For instance, a flustered Isabella deduces from her brother's behavior ("a kind of incest") her mother's infidelity to her father, whose blood could not have produced "such a warped slip of wilderness" (3.1.138, 141). She displaces her disgust at illicit familial sexuality away from both men and onto the untrustworthy mother.[36] The irrational mother is also targeted when Pompey connects Mistress Elbow's being "great with child" with her "longing . . . for stewed prunes," which were commonly served in brothels (2.1.88–89).[37] And his bawdy description of Froth's "cracking the stones" of the two remaining prunes reveals a crude male view of what pregnant women want (2.1.107). In response to the justice's exasperated attempt to determine "what was done to Elbow's wife, once more?" Pompey asserts, "Once, sir? There was nothing done to her once" (2.1.138–40). Elbow may indeed be anxious to know what his wife did with Froth, a name Rubinstein glosses as both "semen," and (from "frot") sexual rubbing, but Pompey answers equivocally, implying that nothing was done to her at all or that nothing was done to her merely once, but rather, repeatedly.[38] Pompey appropriately expresses his innuendo by a grammatical construction known as "negative pregnant," which the *OED* defines as "a negative implying also an affirmative." Seemingly denying that anything was done to Mistress Elbow, he in fact affirms that something was done to her.

In this scene, male suspicion and misunderstanding of female sexuality translates the expansiveness of pregnancy into moral negativity. The wife's being "great-bellied" proves that something was done to her at least once but also makes her susceptible to the charge that nothing was done to her only once: she was either "respected" (that is, suspected) with her husband before marriage (2.1.172), or "overdone" by Froth after marriage. Though the justices' interrogation cannot determine what the wife wanted or what Froth did, Mistress Elbow's presence in a bath-house brothel merely confirms the recklessness imputed to the pregnant woman. Elbow claims that his wife was discovered in a "hot-house" run by Mistress Overdone (2.1.65).[39] J. W. Lever, who believes that Overdone ran a tavern, takes Elbow's claim as "a mere gag." However, Lever concedes that bath-houses "were notoriously blinds for houses of ill fame; hence the word 'stews,' " and he cites Jonson's Epigram 7, "On the New Hot-House," in support of this connection (2.1.65n):

> Where lately harbour'd many a famous whore,
> A purging bill, now fix'd upon the dore,
> Tells you it is a hot-house: So it ma',
> And still be a whore-house. Th'are *Synonima.*

Given this corroboration and Elbow's manifest anxiety, it seems unlikely that Elbow is making a "gag" about the brothel, which is euphemistically described as a "common house" and a "tap-house," but never called a "tavern" (2.1.43, 206). Furthermore, the allusions to stewed prunes and the sweating "tub" (3.2.55), the suggestive names "Overdone" and "Froth," and the Duke's complaint that he has seen "corruption boil and bubble / Till it o'errun the stew" all add weight to the reading of the brothel as a bath-house (5.1.316–17). Mistress Elbow's presence in a hot-house would be especially threatening because, according to Thomas Raynalde, pregnant women should "exchewe much bathing or going to the hot houses in their teemyng, for that may do hurt three wayes": the extreme heat can variously work to force the child out of the womb prematurely.[40] Because of an irrational maternal desire for stewed prunes—a "thirsty evil"?—Mistress Elbow risks not only her and her husband's reputations but the life of their unborn child.

Moreover, another reading could see Mistress Elbow's seemingly reckless visit to the stews as an informed and deliberate decision. In an examination of birth control practices in early modern England, Angus McLaren concludes that married women employed several methods and justifications for abortion: they "were not passive in relation to their fertility; they wanted to control it and were willing to go to considerable lengths to do so."[41] Fearful of such autonomy, Andrew Boord refuses to list certain purgatives in his treatise lest any "light woman" willfully use them to induce abortion.[42] Such light women are the objects of Ben Jonson's satire in *Epicoene,* in which the following exchange takes place between the inquisitive young wife and the leader of the amazonian Collegiates:

> EPICOENE: And have you those excellent receits, madame, to keepe your selves from bearing of children?
>
> HAUGHTY: O yes, Morose. How should we maintayne our youth and beautie, else? Many births of a woman make her old, as many crops make the earth barren.[43]

The passage is striking in that Haughty uses the botanical metaphor of women's time to link ripeness directly to sterility—too much fertility accelerates barren aging—while she blithely articulates the double threat of a self-imposed barrenness: its interminable justification (feminine vanity) and its immediate availability. As long as city wives are vain about their appearance, the passage implies, so long will such "excellent receits" be in demand. Like Jonson's presentation of the domineering Haughty, Shakespeare's presentation of Mistress Elbow, dangerous in either her feverish irrationality or her cold calculation, provides ammunition for male fears about a woman's power in pregnancy.[44]

The sole depiction of conjugal relations within the play, the scene concerning Mistress Elbow adds the wife to the virgin and whore as a focus of male anxiety about female sexuality. The marriage itself, a microcosm of all the marital problems the play treats, violates on several counts the ideology of the Elizabethan "Homily on Matrimony," which held that the "original beginning of matrimony . . . is instituted of God, to the intent that man and woman should live lawfully in a perpetual friendly fellowship, to bring forth fruit, and to avoid fornication."[45] In this marriage, the fruit of the union risks untimely delivery, the wife is implicated in fornication, and the husband's parapraxis that he "detest[s]" his wife reflects ironically on the "friendly fellowship" they are supposed to maintain. If the intermediate position of the betrothed creates confusion, so does the marriage towards which the betrothed, and the logic of comedy, move. Constructed as the scene of a sexual ripeness that must be controlled, marriage becomes the unstable middle term between the self-repressed sexuality of maidenhood and the publicly monitored sexuality of prostitution. The ripe wife is uneasily situated between the rottenness of the oversexed prostitute and the barrenness of the childless maid.

Previous criticism is clearly mistaken, then, in relegating Elbow and his wife to the harmless irrelevancy of a bawdy "subplot." Since this scene of conjugal discord accentuates and epitomizes those issues of female sexuality that permeate the entire play, its concerns significantly inform the four marriages of the comic finale. Because none of the couples which crystallize at the end demonstrate mutual affection and commitment, they are no more the heralds of a renewed, redeemed society than Elbow and his wife. Instead, like the Duke's unanswered matrimonial "motion" to Isabella (5.1.532), the motion of the final scene constitutes a deferment of resolution, a suppression of the dangers of unsanctioned pleasure through an institution which poses dangers of its own.

The four women who become wives at the play's end move from their marginal positions along the virgin (none) / wife (one) / whore (more) spectrum into the central, nominally stable, position. Yet the problems this transition brings are not limited to the lack of compatibility and mutuality the couples demonstrate. The dialogue concerning Mistress Elbow strongly implies that marriage displaces male anxiety about female sexuality away from the virgin and whore figures onto the wife-mother figure itself. Each woman occupying the normative position of "wife" may be economically and legally subject to her husband ("one" / "won"), but her sexuality—as Luce Irigaray would have it, the "sex which is not one"—slips away from his control. It is precisely the play's harsh focus on what Irigaray affirmatively calls the "multiplicity of female desire," the plurality of female sexuality, that opens the way for a feminist reading of female pleasure and the dangers it poses to male rule.[46]

As a result of the unruliness of the wife's sexuality, the "fit time" of comic marriage activates a new measure of sexual suspicion that demonizes women's time. At one pole, the wife, emulating the whore's promiscuity, escapes the husband's control through her excessive pleasure. Here, the ripeness of time becomes the ripe womb that certifies not only the husband's sexual stamp but the wife's sexual pleasure and her likely search for further gratification. The double belly, a double signifier of avaricious gastronomic and libidinal appetites, compels Mistress Elbow to satiate its hunger for "stewed prunes," a signifier of food and sex. In other words, Juliet's pregnant body signifies her ability to satisfy her own desires—"as those who feed grow full," says Lucio—rather than her obligation to express and fulfill Claudio's "husbandry." At the other pole, the wife, emulating the virgin's barrenness, defies the husband's control through her dangerous autonomy. Here, the anticipation of fit time becomes the woman's power to truncate life in abortion. Ignoring the authority of both physician and husband, Mistress Elbow enters a hot-house "before due season," an action which could lead to premature birth. As for the main couple of the comic finale, there's at least reason to surmise that Isabella will be particularly open to suspicions of this nature, given that her history of homosocial independence and cherished virginity suggests her likely resistance to marriage and pregnancy. And the Duke, for his part, is particularly liable to suspect such behavior, considering his past experience in observing and circumventing the abortive deeds of an "unpregnant" subordinate.

Notes

I borrow my title from the collection of essays edited by Carole S. Vance entitled *Pleasure and Danger: Exploring Female Sexuality* (London: Pandora, 1989). The essays arose from the Scholar and the Feminist IX conference, "Towards a Politics of Sexuality," held on 24 April 1982 at Barnard College.

This essay has immeasurably profited from the patient and incisive readings of David Scott Kastan and Jean E. Howard.

1. The quotations come respectively from Carol Thomas Neely, *Broken Nuptials in Shakespeare's Plays* (New Haven: Yale Univ. Press, 1985), 101, and "Constructing Female Sexuality in the Renaissance: Stratford, London, Windsor, Vienna," in *Feminism and Psychoanalysis,* ed. Richard Feldstein and Judith Roof (Ithaca: Cornell Univ. Press, 1989), 225; Richard Wheeler, *Shakespeare's Development and the Problem Comedies: Turn and Counter-Turn* (Berkeley: Univ. of California Press, 1981), 96 and 114; Janet Adelman, *Suffocating Mothers: Fantasies of*

Maternal Origin in Shakespeare's Plays, Hamlet *to* The Tempest (New York: Routledge, 1992), 87; Meredith Skura, "New Interpretations for Interpretation in *Measure for Measure,*" *Boundary 2* 7 (1979): 52. Many psychoanalytic critics of the play have discussed how sexuality is feared, loathed, regulated, and ultimately linked with corruption and death. Skura notes that sex "threatens only the males with death," and "is always a trap" for them (51). Wheeler examines how imagery presents sexual impulses as "self-devouring and self-contaminating" (109). Neely posits that "the first half of the play moves towards the substitution of death for sexuality," until, following the Duke's lecture to Claudio, "sexuality is substituted for death, marriages for executions" (*Broken Nuptials,* 99); in "Constructing Female Sexuality" she finds that the play represents male sexuality as "unrestrainable and degrading," and female sexuality as "paradoxically essential and fatal, voluntary and enforced, central and subordinated" (225 and 229). Adelman, who believes that, to the Duke, "sexual touch *per se* is abominable and beastly," traces characters' effacement of and disgust at "sexual origin and maternal dependence" (87–88). Dollimore, a cultural materialist, argues that the State constructs a negative view of sexuality: "Diverse and only loosely associated sexual offenders are brought into renewed surveillance by the State; identified in law as a category of offender (the lecherous, the iniquitous), they are thereby demonised as a threat to law" ("Transgression and Surveillance in *Measure for Measure,*" in *Political Shakespeare: New Essays in Cultural Materialism,* ed. Jonathan Dollimore and Alan Sinfield [London: Manchester Univ. Press, 1985], 73).

2. Kathleen McLuskie, "The Patriarchal Bard: Feminist Criticism and Shakespeare: *King Lear* and *Measure for Measure,*" in *Political Shakespeare* (note 1), 97.

3. McLuskie (note 2), 97 and 96. My critique here resembles that of Lynda E. Boose: "To be a feminist in McLuskie's terms is to renounce completely one's pleasure in Shakespeare and embrace instead the rigorous comforts of ideological correctness. . . . If Shakespeare can be accused of participating in the reification of patriarchy by his reproduction of it, then surely McLuskie has here likewise participated in the reproduction of—if not the production of—the feminist exclusion upon which she insists" (724). See "The Family in Shakespeare Studies; or—Studies in the Family of Shakespeareans; or—The Politics of Politics," *Renaissance Quarterly* 40 (1987): 707–42.

4. McLuskie, 92.

5. Jean E. Howard, "Scripts and / versus Playhouses: Ideological Production and the Renaissance Public Stage," in *The Matter of Difference: Materialist Feminist Criticism of Shakespeare,* ed. Valerie Wayne (Ithaca: Cornell Univ. Press, 1991), 225.

6. Stephen Orgel, "Nobody's Perfect: Or, Why did the English Stage Take Boys for Women?" in *Displacing Homophobia: Gay Male Perspectives in Literature and Culture,* ed. Ronald R. Butters, John M. Clum, and Michael Moon (Durham: Duke Univ. Press, 1989), 19.

7. Stephen Orgel, "Call Me Ganymede: Shakespeare's Apprentices and the Representation of Women," unpublished conference paper, 13 and 14. I would like to thank Professor Orgel for making this paper available to me.

8. In "*Measure for Measure,* New Historicism, and Theatrical Power," *Shakespeare Quarterly* 39 (1988): 328–41, Anthony B. Dawson accords unusual attention to Mistress Elbow. He notes that she "is defined chiefly by her desire for stewed prunes, but that simple desire leads to a tangle of contradictory and vagrant meanings" (336). I agree with his assessment that Mistress Elbow challenges stable meaning but not with his feeling that her challenges are tonally "comic," as opposed to the "more threatening" epistemological and political challenges offered in the Angelo-Isabella scenes.

9. For a thorough discussion of this paradigm in the literature of the period, see Linda Woodbridge, *Women and the English Renaissance: Literature and the Nature of Womankind, 1540–1620* (Urbana: Univ. of Illinois Press, 1984), especially 84 and chapter 9. Carol Thomas Neely asks "what room for maneuvering there was within these definitions of women" in Shakespeare's society and in *The Merry Wives of Windsor* and *Measure for Measure* ("Constructing Female Sexuality" [note 1], 213).

10. *Measure for Measure,* 5.1.178–79. All references to *Measure for Measure* are from the Arden Edition, ed. J. W. Lever, (New York: Routledge, 1988), and will be subsequently given in the text. References to other plays will be from *William Shakespeare: The Complete Works,* ed. Alfred Harbage (New York: Viking-Penguin, 1977).

11. McLuskie (note 2), 97.

12. Carol Thomas Neely, "Constructing Female Sexuality" (note 1), 213.

13. Lisa Jardine, *Still Harping on Daughters: Women and Drama in the Age of Shakespeare,* 2nd ed. (New York: Columbia Univ. Press-Morningside, 1989), 130–31. Dorothy McLaren ("Marital Fertility and Lactation 1570–1720," in *Women in English Society 1500–1800,* ed. Mary Prior [New York: Methuen, 1985]) shows, however, that women could increase intergenesic intervals by breastfeeding. While prolonged lactation generally leads to lower fertility, the "extent to which this was consciously controlled is not known" (43).

14. Angus McLaren, *Reproductive Rituals: The Perception of Fertility in England from the Sixteenth Century to the Nineteenth Century* (London: Methuen, 1984), 21. In this regard see chapter five ("Sexuality and Conception") of Audrey Eccles, *Obstetrics and Gynaecology in Tudor and Stuart England* (London: Croom Helm, 1982); and Thomas Laqueur, "Orgasm, Generation, and the Politics of Reproductive Biology," *Representations* 14 (1986): 1–41.

15. In a reading of characters, "attempts to make the flesh word" against the "pervasive refusal of the flesh to acquiesce in the imagination's plots and compacts," Ronald R. Macdonald ("*Measure for Measure:* The Flesh Made Word," *Studies in English Literature* 30 [1990]: 265–82) similarly sees the "mute spectacle" of Juliet's pregnant body as "more eloquent finally than any of the sermons and bookish theories offered by other characters in the play" (279).

16. Peter Stallybrass, "Patriarchal Territories: The Body Enclosed," in *Rewriting the Renaissance: The Discourses of Sexual Difference in Early Modern Europe,* ed. Margaret W. Ferguson, Maureen Quilligan, and Nancy J. Vickers (Chicago: Univ. of Chicago Press, 1986), 127.

17. *The Dramatic Works of Thomas Dekker,* ed. Fredson Bowers, 4 vols. (Cambridge: Cambridge Univ. Press, 1958), 3:5.2.202–4.

18. Marjorie Garber, *Coming of Age in Shakespeare* (London: Methuen, 1981), 131.

19. In "The Politics of Style: Discourses of Law and Authority in *Measure for Measure,*" *Style* 16 (1982): 22–37, David Aers and Gunther Kress posit that lower class characters use a kinetic discourse—"verbal, concrete, active, *I*-centered" (33)—to challenge authority, while the language of the powerful is static, "marked by a prevalence of nominal forms," "agentless passives," and synecdoche (32). Aers and Kress consider Claudio's speech heavily static with its nominals ("stealth," "entertainment," "characters") and passives ("is writ on Juliet"). Their conclusion accords with my argument about Claudio's relationship to Juliet: "Here the experience of (sexual) love is pressed into the forms of the static, alienating discourse, with ugly results: human love is presented in terms of *contracts, possession of a bed,* which seem of the same order as *denunciation of outward order,* or *propagation of a dower*" (35).

20. In a psychoanalytic reading of the Henriad, Valerie Traub ("Prince Hal's Falstaff: Positioning Psychoanalysis and the Female Reproductive Body," *Shakespeare Quarterly* 40 [1989]: 456–74) argues that Falstaff "represents to Hal not an alternative paternal image but rather a projected fantasy of the pre-oedipal *maternal* whose rejection is the basis upon which patriarchal subjectivity is predicated" (461). She notes that Falstaff's body, with its "increasingly feminized" belly (463), demonstrates the grotesque corpulence and openness that early modern societies attributed to the maternal body.

21. Jardine (note 13), 133.

22. Keith Wrightson notes in *English Society: 1580–1680* (New Brunswick: Rutgers Univ. Press, 1982) that "death in childbed was common enough. Quite apart from the risk of death, suffering in childbirth could be appalling in an age lacking either anaesthetics or gynecological sophistication, and in which the aid of the village mid-wives could be as much an additional danger as a help" (105).

23. See Frankie Rubinstein, *A Dictionary of Shakespeare's Sexual Puns and Their Significance,* 2nd ed. (London: Macmillan, 1989), 26. Compare Joseph Swetnam, *The Araignment of Lewd, idle, froward and unconstant women; or the vanitie of them; chuse you whether* (London, 1615): "Againe, Lust causeth you to doe such foule deedes, which makes your foreheads for ever afterwards seeme spotted with blacke shame and everlasting infamy, by which meanes, your graves after death are closed up with times scandall" (sig. E1^{v}).

24. I am thinking here of Aers's and Kress's (note 19) claim that in the static discourse of power "the verb *to be* appears frequently, in ideologically prominent speeches" (32).

25. In "Sexuality in the Reading of Shakespeare: *Hamlet* and *Measure for Measure*" (*Alternative Shakespeares,* ed. John Drakakis [New York: Routledge, 1988]), Jacqueline Rose finds in Angelo's statement "the *more* and *less* that the woman becomes when she fails to contain for the man the sexuality which she provokes" (97).

26. David Sundelson, "Misogyny and Rule in *Measure for Measure,*" *Women's Studies* 9 (1981): 83–91, especially 85–86.

27. Elizabeth Sacks also discusses in *Shakespeare's Images of Pregnancy* (London: Macmillan, 1980) the sexual imagery of this and other passages in the play. Her method, however, which depends upon locating "literal" and "figurative" images of pregnancy in Shakespeare, leads to this unhelpful appraisal of *Measure for Measure:* "[It] portrays the world realistically, devoid of illusions, as its equivalent spiritual and physical terminology makes quite clear" (61).

28. See *Pericles,* where "fresh ones" must replace those whores who "with continual action are even as good as rotten" (4.2.10–11). Also, *As You Like It:* "And so, from hour to hour we ripe and ripe, / And then, from hour to hour we rot and rot" (2.7.26–27).

29. See Rubinstein (note 23), 177.

30. Thomas Raynalde, *The Byrth of mankynde, otherwise named the womans booke* (1545; London, 1560), folio 82, sig. N5^{r}.

31. For a discussion of beliefs about and images for pregnancy and miscarriage in early modern Europe (especially France), see Jacques Gélis, *History of Childbirth; Fertility, Pregnancy and Birth in Early Modern Europe,* tran. Rosemary Morris (Boston: Northeastern Univ. Press, 1991). Chapter five, "The Body in Pregnancy," examines botanical metaphors for fetus and womb; chapter sixteen, "The Falling of the Flower," deals with miscarriage, and chapter seventeen, "The Unripe Fruit," with premature birth.

32. Sundelson (note 26), 84.

33. Andrew Boord, *The Breviarie of health: wherin doth folow, remedies, for all maner of sicknesses & diseases . . .* (1547; London, 1598), page 7, sig. A7^{v}.

34. Many critics have noted the play's "literalization of the pun that identifies death and orgasm" (Adelman [note 1], 87). No critic, to my knowledge, has connected this central pun to abortion / Abhorson.

35. Rubinstein (note 23), 156.

36. Jacqueline Rose (note 25) similarly reads Isabella's fantastic reconstruction of her "mother's sexual crime" (108). Adelman (note 1) discusses this scene at length, concluding: "Threatened by identification with the mother who can exist for her only as a site of corruption, Isabella responds by invoking the protective image of a pure father who can serve as a buffer between her and the maternal legacy that both Angelo and Claudio bid her to assume" (97).

37. Jacques Gélis (note 31) describes the dangers that the mother's irrational "cravings and imaginings" were believed to pose to the unborn child (53–58).

38. Rubinstein (note 23), 106.

39. The *OED's* primary sense for "hot house" is "a bathing-house with hot baths, vapour-baths, etc."; the second sense is "a brothel."

40. Raynalde (note 30), folio 85, sig. N8^{r}. On the various precautions recommended for reducing the chances of "spontaneous abortion," see Linda A. Pollock, "Embarking on a

rough passage: the experience of pregnancy in early-modern society," *Women as Mothers in Pre-Industrial England,* ed. Valerie Fildes (New York: Routledge, 1990).

41. McLaren (note 14), 111. See his chapter, "Abortion as birth control," which attempts to demonstrate, "first, that concerns for health and family well-being could have led many to contemplate abortion; second that there existed a wide range of techniques that were believed to be effective in precipitating miscarriages; and third that the concept of 'quickening' permitted women to consider the action as legitimate. For these reasons we have to conclude that abortion played a far more important role in the regulation of fertility in past generations than has usually been believed" (111). Dorothy McLaren (note 13) argues that rich women who desired to breastfeed, perhaps to reduce their fertility, may have had to negotiate or battle their decision with husbands and friends (27–28).

42. Boord (note 33), sig. A8^{r}.

43. *Ben Jonson,* ed. C. H. Herford and Percy Simpson, 11 vols. (Oxford: Clarendon, 1954), 5:4.3.57–61.

44. A striking parallel to the male anxieties inscribed in the mistrust of Mistress Elbow's sexuality appears in Carol Smith-Rosenberg's account of the abortion movement in Victorian America. In their anti-abortion campaign, male physicians of the AMA constructed a mythic figure of the "autonomous bourgeois wife, [who] by rejecting the domestic and maternal role bourgeois men had constructed for her" deceived both husbands and doctors. "The AMA linked doctor and husband as the equally wronged and innocent parties. The aborting wife, in contrast, was unnaturally selfish and ruthless" (236). In the AMA ideology, as in Andrew Boord, "the mother was potentially lethal and insane; only the male physician could protect the male fetus" (242). I thank David Scott Kastan for drawing to my attention Smith-Rosenberg's *Disorderly Conduct: Visions of Gender in Victorian America* (New York: Oxford Univ. Press, 1985).

45. "An Homily on the State of Matrimony," in *Certain Sermons or Homilies Appointed to be Read in Churches* (London: Society for Promoting Christian Knowledge, 1908), 534.

46. Luce Irigaray, *This Sex Which Is Not One,* tran. Catherine Porter with Carolyn Burke (Ithaca: Cornell Univ. Press, 1985), 30.

Sexual Secrecy in *Measure for Measure*

KATHERINE EISAMAN MAUS

Like *Epicoene, Measure for Measure* treats of the public regulation of sexual behavior in a disorderly urban world. Shakespeare's Vienna, like Jonson's London, defies traditional forms of policing, because an enforceable consensus on sexual morality no longer seems possible to attain. Like *Epicoene,* too, *Measure for Measure* reflects contemporary misgivings over the functioning of the ecclesiastical courts. In the early seventeenth century an increasingly influential group of Puritans, disgusted by what they considered the courts' leniency and their preference for mediation over retribution, recommend stiffening punishments imposed for sexual transgressions. Angelo seems zealously to subscribe to the arguments that forty years later, in the Cromwell regime, eventuate in a statute making adultery a capital crime. And Angelo's special animus against Claudio reflects a perennial complaint about the ecclesiastical courts' misplaced priorities, since the courts often fail to deter serious offenders but come down hard on less insolent sinners who are often easier to locate and to embarrass.[1]

These marks of current controversies do not necessarily mean, however, that *Measure for Measure* constitutes an explicit policy recommendation. As Margaret Scott points out, "The law of *Measure for Measure* is . . . story-book law"; and it is not at all clear that English customs with regard to the marital precontract, for instance, are imagined to hold in Roman Catholic Vienna.[2] In fact, I would argue that like Jonson's, Shakespeare's concerns are more general, more profound, and more closely wedded to his theatrical medium. As . . . in the case of *Epicoene,* the ecclesiastical courts' supervision of sexual conduct poses difficult problems about the relationship between truth and public knowledge, between individuals and communities, and between precepts and behavior. These issues matter to Shakespeare, too; but his notion of what is at stake is substantially different from Jonson's.

While Jonson's fascination with the impotence trial recurs in play after play, Shakespeare's emphasis on explicit sanctions in *Measure for Measure* is quite atypical. In Shakespeare's earlier comedies, although the connection between sexual desire and its "fulfilment" in marriage often seems less than automatic, marriage remains a recognizable *telos* as it never is in Jonson's plays. In *As You Like It* Touchstone succinctly describes the alternatives:

Reprinted from Katherine Eisaman Maus, *Inwardness and Theater in the English Renaissance* (Chicago: University of Chicago Press, 1995).

> Come, sweet Audrey,
> We must be married, or we must live in bawdry.
> (3.3.95–96)

In *As You Like It* living in bawdry is not a genuine option, so Audrey and Touchstone march to the altar with the rest of the young couples, despite the implausibility of their union. In *Measure for Measure,* however, any link between desire and marriage seems to have snapped. No one, with the possible and problematic exception of the Duke, weds unless and until compelled to do so. Elbow is the only husband in the play, and his wife, "whom I detest before heaven," risks being debauched in Mistress Overdone's brothel. Once desire comes unhinged from the institution that is meant to contain and direct it, to make it publicly useful, it begins to seem scandalously subversive of personal and social order. Even Claudio, the would-be bridegroom, speaks the language of destructive compulsion:

> As surfeit is the father of much fast,
> So every scope by the immoderate use
> Turns to restraint. Our natures do pursue,
> Like rats that ravin down their proper bane,
> A thirsty evil, and when we drink we die.
> (1.2.126–30)

It is difficult to imagine Lysander or Orlando censuring his own passion so savagely.

When sexual indulgence is imagined to bring with it turmoil, animalism, even suicide, celibacy can seem a positive relief, certainly the only way to maintain self-respect and to retain the respect of others.[3] The three morally ambitious characters in *Measure for Measure*—Isabella, Angelo, and the Duke—differ from the retrospectively self-reproachful Claudio not in their outlook but in the energy and consistency with which they translate their principles into action. All three take it for granted that sexuality is dangerous, that their virtue demands sexual continence, and that such continence in turn sanctions their social power. In *Measure for Measure,* as Barbara Baines writes, "chastity authorizes authority."[4] Even those characters whose behavior strays farthest from the ideal of chaste virtue admire that ideal: Lucio, for instance, tells Isabella that her vow of perpetual virginity renders her "a thing enskied and sainted / By your renouncement an immortal spirit" (1.4.34–35). Julietta, pregnant under indefinite circumstances, admits that her sin is "of heavier kind" than Claudio's, and "take[s] the shame with joy" instead of attempting to make a case for herself (2.3.28, 30). Even Pompey Bum admits that his trade "does stink in some sort, sir" (3.2.28). It occurs to no one in *Measure for Measure* to argue for the social utility of sexual enjoyment. Only Lucio's brief analogy between Julietta's pregnancy and agricultural fecundity even approaches a celebratory tone.

> Your brother and his lover have embraced.
> As those that feed grow full, as blossoming time
> That from the seedness the bare fallow brings
> To teeming foison, even so her plenteous womb
> Expresseth his full tilth and husbandry.
> (1.4.40–44)

In Lucio's formulation, Claudio's desperate "surfeit" becomes the "fullness" of innocent gratification, and appetite not a "ravening down" but a natural impulse that regenerates the abundance upon which it feeds. Attempting to enlist Isabella's support for her brother, Lucio emphasizes the connections between Claudio's behavior and the innocent cycle of bloom and harvest, momentarily recovering the morally less tense and conflicted view of the earlier comedies. Just as a spark intensifies darkness, the effect of these radiant lines in their grim setting is to underscore the prevailing distrust of sexuality by providing a glimpse of a less troubled alternative.

The prevailing idealization of "purity" in Vienna far exceeds communal need. With the important exception of Angelo's harassment of Isabella, the sexual "crimes" the Duke wishes to root out of Vienna are victimless and the city, however seedy, in no real danger of revolution or collapse. Jonathan Dollimore has plausibly argued that the sense of sexual crisis in Vienna, as in Jacobean London, is an ideological screen for an anxiety of a different nature: the real targets of repression are members of the lower classes who might foment rebellion against their "betters."[5] But sexual surveillance in Vienna does not merely oppress the proletariat while letting the elite off scot-free. If anything, rather like its English counterpart, it has more severe consequences for better-off people concerned to protect their "good fame." I would suggest that concepts of restraint and transgression, discipline and capitulation, seem indispensable to the upper-class characters not primarily because they provide an excuse to oppress others (although they may indeed provide that excuse) but rather because those terms so profoundly structure the experience of desire in *Measure for Measure* that in some cases they can come to seem indistinguishable from personality itself.

Once sexual desire is regarded as intrinsically, disgracefully errant, and therefore as subject to public punishment, it becomes by reflex something to hide. The play's numerous enclosures—convent, private study, locked garden, moated grange—are sites congested with sexual desire, actual or rumored, frustrated or enacted. Even the prison is populated by fornicators. Consequently, when Lucio calls Vincentio a duke of dark corners, we recognize instantly that the dark corner metonymizes sexual voracity. Prohibition and concealment, surveillance and inwardness, mutually produce and necessitate one another, in a dialectic that by now ought to seem familiar.

As in *Epicoene,* then, sexuality seems a particularly troublesome issue because it is double-faced, both importantly public and intensely private. We have already seen how the law of early modern England acknowledges this doubleness: on the one hand making marriage the basis of weighty familial and social obligations, and on the other hand permitting valid marriages between two people by verbal promise only, without presence of witnesses or consent of parents. In *Measure for Measure* Claudio and Julietta founder in this legal quagmire.

> Thus stands it with me: upon a true contract
> I got possession of Julietta's bed.
> You know the lady, she is fast my wife
> Save that we do the denunciation lack
> Of outward order.
>
> (1.2.145–49)

What is Claudio claiming here? He might be arguing that the contract is "true" only in the sense that it was faithfully undertaken, or he might be claiming, in the stronger sense, that it ought to be acknowledged as valid. His equivocal word "fast" nicely captures the ambiguity of the lovers' situation. If "fast" means "very nearly," Claudio implies that he and Julietta do not consider themselves married until they have undergone a public ceremony. If "fast" means "securely," Claudio is asserting the binding force of the private contract, beside which "the denunciation . . . of outward order" is a formality that only ratifies what is already the case.

In either case Claudio and Julietta, in "the stealth of our most mutual entertainment," have attempted rather like Jonson's Volpone or Morose to create for themselves an unseen life of bodily pleasure, a life that dispenses with the consent and collaboration of the community. Unlike Jonson's protagonists, however, these lovers do not anticipate keeping their secret indefinitely; they wish only to defer their public commitment until Julietta's kin have come to favor the match. The entirely provisional quality of their clandestine arrangement allows them to remain thoughtless to its implications. Since they have apparently never bothered to justify their conduct to themselves, they are easily brought to repent of their "error" once their union is accidentally made public. Neither Claudio nor Julietta attempts to argue that the existence of a private contract, however "true" or "fast," means that they are innocent of fornication after all.

Angelo's internalization of Vienna's disciplinary regimen is far more complex than Claudio's simple avoidance strategy. Angelo's initial qualification for judicial office is that he possesses, as the Duke says, "a kind of character in thy life, / That to th'observer doth thy history / Fully unfold" (1.1.28–29). "Character" here refers to legible writing, the self made publicly available. Angelo denies himself a private life, apparently everting his entire person to the public gaze. This ambition for transparency seems wholly compatible with the Christian tradition of asceticism. For "we owe to asceticism," as Geoffrey Galt Harpham writes, "the notion that the exemplary self is observable."[6] The ascetic everts his inwardness, holding his self-mortification up for display: even when his struggles, his agonies, his triumphs are undertaken in rigorous isolation, they acquire meaning insofar as they are narrated to or witnessed by others, rendered into patterns for others to emulate.

Nonetheless, Angelo's legalistic identification of the true with the publicly available turns out not to be merely impossible, but morally dangerous. It allows him to muddle the relationship between the realm of intention—acts merely contemplated but not executed—and the realm of the secret, which might include deeds as well as intentions. When Escalus, seeking clemency for Claudio, asks Angelo whether he is not himself subject to the same unruly desires, Angelo replies:

> Tis one thing to be tempted, Escalus,
> Another thing to fall. I not deny,
> The jury passing on the prisoner's life
> May in the sworn twelve have a thief or two
> Guiltier than him they try; what's open made to justice,
> That justice seizes.
>
> (2.1.17–22)

Angelo begins by drawing a distinction between being tempted and actually committing a crime, but his example cuts in another direction, differentiating the known thief in the dock from the unknown thief on the jury. Whereas logic requires him to supply an example of a successfully resisted temptation, Angelo cites a person who really has acted on his temptation, but who merely happens not to have been apprehended. This unintentional but revealing blunder foreshadows the slippage that permits Angelo's sexual harassment of Isabella. His equation of truth with publicity means that the secret act, which is not "open made to justice," may as well never have occurred.

Thus Angelo's pretension to complete visibility turns out to have an escape hatch, as it were, into a hidden room in which he may conceal everything he does not wish to acknowledge to the world. Moreover the secrecy of this hidden place itself arouses Angelo's appetite.

> these black masks
> Proclaim an enshield beauty ten times louder
> Than beauty could, displayed.
>
> (2.4.79–81)

In his imagination, in other words, the ignominious pleasures of sexual abandon require and are abetted by interdiction and concealment. Angelo's yearning for a clandestine union is simply the flip side of his equally intense yearning for rigid containment. Whereas Claudio desires a woman that happens to be denied him and sleeps with her in the expectation that their relationship will eventually be legitimized, Angelo desires a woman because she is forbidden, choosing as the object of his passion the most ostentatiously pristine woman in Vienna.

Angelo's behavior is exactly what one would expect of someone who assumes that all sexual expression is tantamount to moral ruin. "I have begun," he tells Isabella, "And now I give my sensual race the run." Once embarked upon such a "race," he imagines, there is no stopping, no limit, no brake. Angelo's phrase recalls an earlier locution of the Duke's, who speaks of "strict statutes and most biting laws / The needful bits and curbs to headstrong jades." In Plato's ancient metaphor, the appetitive part of the soul is a strong but recalcitrant horse which requires, but often escapes, a rider's firm management. Paradoxically but necessarily, the Duke's emphasis on the importance of control mutates easily into Angelo's excuse for capitulation: for if sexuality is essentially antisocial, it cannot be expected to contain and direct itself any more than a horse could be expected to govern itself without bit or bridle. At the same time, Angelo needs constantly to remind himself that Isabella is taboo, that he is defiling her, that his proposition flagrantly violates the rules he has been entrusted to administer.

> Is this her fault, or mine?
> The tempter or the tempted, who sins most, ha?
> Not she; nor doth she tempt; but it is I
> That, lying by the violet in the sun,
> Do, as the carrion does, not as the flower,
> Corrupt with virtuous season.
>
> (2.2.162–67)

Angelo quite accurately recognizes that the very awareness of merit that ought to foster his excellence in fact precipitates his disintegration. He struggles to remember, even to exaggerate, the prohibition against which he determines to act, because for him prohibition is aphrodisiac. If he were to rationalize his behavior, or blame it on Isabella, the novice of St. Clare would interest him no more than the devoted, licit Mariana. Therefore Angelo's extraordinarily lucid self-condemnation functions not as an impediment but as a spur and leads not to penitence but to an increasing moral recklessness. The importance of what Angelo thinks of as "external" controls can hardly be overestimated, both for the rigidity of his principles and for the peculiar liberties he takes with them.

Isabella's asceticism is more rigorous and consistent than Angelo's, for she does not confuse God's unlimited knowledge with the limited perspective of the courtroom. She possesses the subjectively constitutive sense of divine supervision that, as we have seen, so many Renaissance clerics try to cultivate in themselves and in their followers. A number of consequences follow from this vivid conviction of omniscient witness. The first is that in Isabella's case, the bar against sexual transgression must be absolute. There is no nook or cranny undetectable by God within which she might permit herself release. Nor could she acquiesce to Angelo merely in body, retaining the purity of her mind intact: for the purity of her mind is constituted precisely by her refusal to allow space for anything clandestine. In fact, the clandestine is an almost impossible category for Isabella, since worldly reputation, in relationship to which secrecy acquires its meaning, is insignificant to her compared to what God thinks. As she considers Angelo's proposition, it never even seems to occur to her that she might return to her nunnery after a wild night in the locked garden with her good fame unscathed. For good fame, in this sense, is no concern of hers unless it happens to match up with the truth. Similarly, Isabella cannot countenance compromising her primary supernatural allegiance for the sake of secondary, natural ones. Although, of course, it is Claudio's life rather than her own that she proposes to jettison, it is not entirely absurd that Isabella thinks of herself as a kind of martyr, like those saints who renounce spouses, siblings, offspring in order to be burned at the stake, torn on the wheel, or devoured by savage beasts. Like martyrs in the first century or in the sixteenth, she refuses to define herself in terms of her affection for or duty toward her kin.

Yet Isabella's way of coming to terms with Vienna's disciplinary regimen entangles her, too; and the debate about her among *Measure for Measure* critics reveals how the trap works. Critics who approve of her, like G. Wilson Knight and Muriel Bradbrook, tend to read the play as an allegory in which the function of the characters is iconic. In this scheme Isabella "stands for sainted purity," or "represents both Truth and Mercy."[7] For such critics, Isabella has no "inward truth" at variance from her superficies, for that kind of inwardness would violate what they understand to be the play's generic conventions. They apprehend Isabella much as she would like to apprehend herself, as a woman with nothing to hide whose very limpidity allows her to reflect a truth outside of, and greater than, herself. Critics who disparage Isabella presume that she is a psychologically complex character and use that presumption of complexity to attack her. Anne Barton chastises Isabella for an "irrational terror of sex which she has never admitted to herself"; Carolyn Brown and Harriet Hawkins for "her subliminal attraction to sexual abuse"; J. W. Lever for her "psychic confusion"; Arthur Kirsch for her "unconscious sexual provocation"; Harold Goddard for her "unplumbed sensual element"; Barbara Baines for her ignorance "of how she, as a subject, is constituted and subjected by her chastity."[8]

All these critics believe they can detect something about Isabella that she does not, or will not know. If even guilty intentions, according to the New Testament, are culpable, then one way to escape culpability is scrupulously to renounce those intentions. In Isabella's case this disavowal seems to require, however, a massive screening of herself from herself. It is hard to second-guess Angelo, because in his soliloquies he freely admits what he is. Isabella's more stringent version of the ascetic project, by contrast, seems to demand not merely self-denial, or careful conduct before others, but a repression-into-unconscious. Then her conscience can indeed be clear, but only because it is partial. Many Renaissance Christians, especially those of ascetic leanings, devoted themselves to various forms of introspective discipline designed to protect them from committing this error:[9] which is, in fact, a more subtle, less witting version of Angelo's mistake. If Angelo might be said to construct a hidden garret behind his public facade, Isabella might be said first to devise one and then contrive to forget where the door is, so that she seems to be mere facade even to herself. For many modern critics, psychoanalytic techniques of undoing this disavowal have seemed called for, because Isabella's denial of her own complexity seems precisely the kind of psychic mechanism that psychoanalysis is designed to expose and reverse. The unexamined assumption of the "therapeutic" view, in sixteenth-century writers like William Perkins or Daniel Dyke as much as in Freud, is that self-knowledge despite its painfulness is invariably ameliorative.

Possibly, however, Isabella's dilemma challenges this notion. A favorite term for her in the criticism is "hysterical,"[10] a term for a psychological malady that originally referred to a bodily disorder. A "hyster" is a womb, the secret inner place that, . . . becomes a corporeal analogy for psychological inwardness in the minds of many male writers in the English Renaissance. Perhaps it is possible to see Isabella's furious resistance to Angelo as a way of protecting her mental virginity, refusing to touch the seal upon her inwardness, in which case her critics' attempts to penetrate beyond or behind her "face value" or "virtuous facade" recapitulates Angelo's scandalous importunity. Of course, however, we *cannot help* but see that Isabella, insofar as she can be perceived as more than an allegorical abstraction, is victimized by her own principles. In *Measure for Measure,* then, the ascetic impulse to complete self-display before God or before others ironically but inevitably invites accusations of hypocrisy—not merely, as in *Richard III,* because the appearance of guilelessness can itself be a studied tactic, but because the residue of anarchic secrecy that attaches to sexual desire can never successfully be exorcised.

Like *Epicoene, Measure for Measure* depicts a world in which traditional means of socially specifying what sexual relations take place, and between whom, are no longer trustworthy. At the same time, no other way of indicating the secret life of individuals or couples has taken its place. Thus in both plays, sexuality somehow exceeds the publicly ascertainable. Yet the nature of this excess or evasion is conceived very differently by Jonson and by Shakespeare. In the impotence trial the erect penis serves theoretically as the "absolute insignia of manhood" even while its invisibility and evanescence call that absoluteness into question. Similarly in *Volpone* and *Epicoene,* the genitals that cannot be shown in public become "that within which passeth show." They are a metonymy for a private truth constituted not as an individual essence or an inalienable right, but as the unstable limit beyond which an intense, imperfect scrutiny, whether theatrical or juridical, cannot proceed. The obscene materiality of Jonsonian subjectivity is entirely consistent with the practices of the ecclesiastical courts, which deliberately restricted their definition of marital incompatibility to bodily defectiveness. Jonson is . . . acutely aware of the difficulties of naive materialism both in the courtroom and the playhouse, but he cannot or does not choose to elaborate an alternative to a material standard of truth.

Measure for Measure occasionally makes reference to sheerly corporeal secrets; for instance, in Lucio's speculations that Angelo is an "ungenitured agent" who pisses ice. But significantly, Lucio's speculations are facetious; and the kind of defamation he practices, however it infuriates the Duke, never poses the kind of practical danger it does in Jonson's plays. In general, bodies in *Measure for Measure* are not secretive: they unequivocally publicize sexual behavior. The furtive dalliance between Claudio and Julietta is exposed by pregnancy, which offers exactly the kind of uncontestable proof that Bonario, in *Volpone,* had found so frustratingly elusive.

> The stealth of our most mutual entertainment
> With character too gross is writ on Juliet.
> (1.2.154–55)

As in the Duke's praise of Angelo, the word "character" refers to a publicly legible inscription which betrays any attempt at "stealth." While Jonson's dramatic purposes lead him to the impotence trial, troubled as it is by the difficulty of obtaining material evidence, Shakespeare's lead him to the inquiry into fornication, in which the woman's belly physically obtrudes her culpability. And the paternity of extramaritally conceived children, which might have incited a Jonson-style probe into undecidable physical particulars, is never disputed by anyone in *Measure for Measure;* even Lucio admits, despite his earlier courtroom perjury, that he has fathered a child upon his whore.

Nonetheless, the revelatory bodies of *Measure for Measure* do not settle much. The bed trick drives a wedge between corporeal performance and the intention that the law generally assumes attaches to performance, complicating, for the male protagonist, the relationship between the inner domain of intention and subjective awareness and the "external" behavior of the body. This trick merely poses in a dramatically acute form a more general difficulty that plagues attempts at sexual policing throughout the play: the problem that bodily acts fail to have meaning in themselves, but acquire the significance participants and witnesses attach to them. Angelo compares Claudio's offense to murder and counterfeiting; Lucio thinks it "a game of ticktack." The sex act does not mean the same thing to Isabella and to Mistress Overdone, or even to Isabella and Mariana. The loving union of Juliet and Claudio seems importantly different from the commercial relationship of Lucio to his whore, and likewise from the vexed, covertly legitimate connection between Angelo and Mariana. Motives, outcomes, class position, religious conviction, temperamental imperatives, all complicate what Lucio calls "this downright way of creation." The problem is not merely how strictly the authorities ought to regulate particular sexual behaviors, but how that behavior is to be defined and interpreted.

The ecclesiastical courts' inquiry into sexual privacy, then, actually involves not one kind of problem, but two. The first dilemma, with which Jonson is deeply concerned, involves the epistemological puzzles in ascertaining physical facts to which no disinterested party can possibly be a witness. The other problem—Shakespeare's main concern in *Measure for Measure*—is that the material terms in which the ecclesiastical courts construe sexuality may be entirely inadequate to an accurate understanding and evaluation of erotic desires and behaviors.

A radical response to this sense of inadequacy would entail abolishing the external regulation of sexual behavior altogether. In fact John Milton argues for just such an abolition in *The Doctrine and Discipline of Divorce* several decades after the first performances of *Measure for Measure* and *Epicoene,* when the triumph of Milton's own party has made the enactment of severe laws against sexual transgression more likely than they had been in Shakespeare's time.

> How vain therefore is it, and how preposterous in the canon law to have made such careful provision against the impediment of carnal performance, and to have had no care about the unconversing inability of mind, so defective to the purest and most sacred end of matrimony. . . . Tis read to us in the liturgy, that "we must not marry to satisfy the fleshly appetite, like brute beasts that have no understanding:" but the canon so runs, as if it dreamt of no other matter than such an appetite to be satisfied.[11]

Milton's conception of the relation between body and mind is, . . . anything but settled; still, he is convinced that restricting the truths of marriage to "the mere instrumental body" improperly inverts the superiority of spirit over matter, and of inwardness over externals.

The position Milton advances in the divorce tracts, characterizable as antinomian or extreme casuist,[12] would have it that sexual and marital dilemmas are impossible for third parties to adjudicate. His argument involves three interrelated assumptions. First, individual circumstances are imagined to be highly variable, and those idiosyncrasies weigh more heavily than any apparent similarities among cases. Secondly, the experience of those circumstances "from the inside" is always radically different from its experience "from the outside." Thirdly, the true, "internal" state of affairs, which Milton believes must serve as the basis for moral decision-making, is a mental, not a bodily condition. The body is, in fact, a positive distraction, because its visibility to others, and its similarity to other human bodies, falsely obscures the variability of inward experience, and deceptively suggests that sexuality might be regulated by external precept. In effect, Milton locates the experience of sexuality in that inward realm, disembodied and unavailable to secular jurisdiction, which some of his contemporaries controversially associate with the domain of religious conviction. He argues that no general law can be formulated to encompass the infinite diversity of individual situations; no evidentiary criteria can possibly be established to prove or disprove essentially invisible mental states; no magistrate can possibly acquire the knowledge required to monitor the sexual conduct of others.

I've devoted some time to describing Milton's position in *Doctrine and Discipline of Divorce* because it is one that Shakespeare could conceivably embrace, but seems deliberately to abjure. *Measure for Measure* acknowledges the kind of difficulties Milton adduces, but does not subscribe to Milton's radical solutions. While carefully specifying an extraordinary diversity of attitudes toward sexuality—different kinds of asceticism, various degrees of libertinage, and so forth—*Measure for Measure* is fascinated at the same time by the ways in which human beings resemble one another. Again and again in the play, characters are confused, exchanged, or substituted for one another. Isabella's attitudes to sexuality, and to Angelo, are entirely different from Mariana's, but in the dark, Angelo cannot tell them apart. Claudio is the scion of an honorable family, Ragozine a hardened pirate, but their heads are interchangeable.

A fascination with the substitutability of one body for another is recurrent in Shakespeare. In many of his comedies, it reflects a primary irony of sexual desire: that the lover's vivid conviction—or illusion—of the beloved's uniqueness conflicts with a kind of *eros* perhaps best described as depersonalized genital attraction. The history plays and tragedies make a less specifically sexual assertion of bodily community, when kings in moments of despair insist upon their corporeal equivalence with their subjects.

> Mock not flesh and blood
> With solemn reverence, throw away respect,
> Tradition, form, and ceremonious duty,
> For you have but mistook me all this while.
> (*Richard II* 3.2.171–74)

In all these cases, just as in Milton, the ground of human similarity is imagined to be a bodily ground. It may seem curious to conceive of human beings as corporeally indistinguishable: do persons really differ more mentally than they do physically? Do not social and temperamental differences impress themselves upon the body as well as upon the mind? Surely the patent improbability of the bed-trick is part of what constitutes its charm as a "literary" device. In fact, however, one possible effect of the schematic differentiation between inward and outward . . . is the fantasy, or romance, or fear of a common, unindividuated corporeality, an embodiment that is both part of the self, and outside of or distinct from it.

It may be helpful to summarize at this point a three-way contrast among the attitudes I have called, almost by shorthand, Jonsonian, Miltonic, and Shakespearean.[13] These writers posit three different ways in which the categories body / spirit, outward / inward, and communal / individual might be imagined to interact. In the comedies of Jonson's prime, there is no separate spiritual realm. The routine and the singular, the visible and the secret, the inward and the external: all are conceived to be material effects (Jonson calls the internal materials that produce idiosyncrasy "humours"). In this scheme some facts might be hard to discover, but they are not different in kind from facts that are easy to know. The Milton of the divorce tracts, by contrast, associates particularity and privacy with a mental inwardness qualitatively distinct from the manifest workings of the body, workings associated by contrast with a degraded publicity and lack of differentiation. In *Measure for Measure* Shakespeare endorses Milton's implicitly dualist ontology: whereas in Jonson the body is the ground of truth, but is hard to "get at," in *Measure for Measure* the body is relatively easy to get at but truth seems not to be grounded there. At the same time, Shakespeare does not subscribe to Milton's ethics; the fact that all human beings are embodied seems to remain morally momentous to him, rather than an ethical distraction.

What accounts for this difference—and what are its consequences for *Measure for Measure?* In this play the bed-trick and the sleight-of-heads are only two instances of a pervasive and complex pattern of substitutions, deputations, and interchanges by which one person or thing is "taken for" or made to stand in the place of another.[14] The title of the play itself refers to the principle of talion justice, a principle by which a violation of social order can be undone or wiped out by a *quid pro quo* reversal of the original direction of the transgression: "life for life, eye for eye, tooth for tooth, hand for hand, foot for foot" (Deuteronomy 20.21). Ordinarily a simple restoration of the *status quo ante* is impossible. Because a murderer cannot return his victim's life, an assailant cannot return his victim's damaged limb, he must render up a life, eye, or tooth equivalent to the one he took. "Justice," in other words, involves substitution in kind or in proportion.

It may be less obvious that mercy, the renunciation or apparent opposite of talion justice, likewise operates by a principle of substitution. Shakespeare takes the title of *Measure for Measure* from a passage from the Sermon on the Mount characterized by a rapid alternation of active and passive constructions.

> Judge not, that ye be not judged. For with what judgment ye judge, ye shall be judged: and with what measure ye mete, it shall be measured unto you again. (Matthew 7.1–3)

One refrains from judging because one is capable of imagining oneself as the victim of censure; one is convinced to forbear from punishment by considering that one might, oneself, become the object of such punishment. For a passage often construed as offering hope and renewal, Christ's formulation is remarkably menacing. He reveals that the transcendence of talion law itself turns upon a principle of taliation.

In *Measure for Measure* as in Matthew, appeals for mercy commonly involve similar invitations to occupy, imaginatively, another person's position. Escalus, for instance, attempts to get Angelo to mitigate Claudio's punishment:

> Let but your honor know
> (Whom I believe to be most straight in virtue)
> That, in the working of your own affections,
> Had time cohered with place or place with wishing,
> Or that the resolute acting of your blood
> Could have attained th'effect of your own purpose,
> Whether you had not sometime in your life
> Erred in this point which now you censure him.
> (2.1.8–15)

Isabella attempts to make a similar case:

> If he had been as you, and you as he,
> You would have slipped like him; but he, like you,
> Would not have been so stern.
> (2.2.64–66)

What is the relation between the kind of imaginary taking-of-another's-place invoked by Escalus and Isabella, and the "cruder," bodily substitutions of Mariana for Isabella, Ragozine for Claudio? Angelo, the slow learner who cannot suppose himself capable of Claudio's "slip," is made physically to reenact it. If he were able to put himself in Claudio's place in the conditional, hypothetical way Isabella and Escalus propose, he would not need to do so in actuality. In other words, vicarious or empathetic identification with the wrongdoer constitutes an alternative to bodily reenactment. So conceived, empathy stands in relation to reenactment much as we have seen persuasion stand in relation to coercion in Marlowe's plays: as the less forceful, more voluntary, and therefore morally more attractive mental analogue to a painful corporeal process. Just as persuasion mimics coercion and depends upon its possibility, even while seeming to evade its brutal physicality, so the capacity for vicarious feeling depends upon the possibility of reenactment, even while that possibility remains in the realm of imagination.

Now the theater audience, insofar as it is instructed by the action of *Measure for Measure,* proves itself capable of the kind of imaginative flexibility that Angelo cannot initially manage; for the theater, according to such defenders as Sidney and Heywood, is a place where spectators are supposed to imagine themselves undergoing the events depicted onstage by the actors, so as to acquire the lessons of another's experience without themselves having actually to suffer it. The conditions of apprehending *Measure for Measure* thus recapitulate in some degree the moral problems raised by it. The spectatorial exercise of self-substitution is, however, as we have already seen in the case of *Othello,* highly undependable, subject to misleading analogies between self and other.

How are we to know which substitutions are right? It is possible to see the history of *Measure for Measure's* reception as a series of debates about what kinds of empathetic substitution are appropriate, about which equivalences and cathexes are and are not suitable. Do Mariana and Angelo recapitulate the crime committed by Julietta and Claudio, or is there a significant difference in the kind of precontract by which they are bound?[15] When Isabella recruits Mariana to take her place in bed with Angelo, does she, as David Lloyd Stevenson argues, preserve her chastity only by becoming a bawd, foisting her quandary onto another? Or is it more important to remember, with Bernice Kliman, the "difference in the sex act as an expression of mutual love . . . and the sex act as a humiliating act of violence?"[16] Does the Duke's arrangement of the bed-trick reduce him to the level of the panderer Pompey, as Richard Wheeler believes?[17] Does commercial prostitution seem "comparatively harmless," as Harriet Hawkins argues, "when set beside the diseases of the soul?"[18] Is Angelo, as Marc Shell claims, the Duke's substitute in a sexual as well as a governmental sense, so that his proposition to Isabella acts out the Duke's disowned or repressed desire for her, as eventually revealed in his marriage proposal?[19]

The importance of evaluating comparatively the propriety of various substitutions in *Measure for Measure* has made certain strategies of reading seem especially fruitful or plausible. Allegorical readings, for instance, like G. Wilson Knight's, M. C. Bradbrook's, or Roy Battenhouse's, involve a symbolic transfer of meaning from an original to a substitute object.[20] Similarly psychoanalytic readings, like Richard Wheeler's, Meredith Skura's, or Marc Shell's, tend to dissolve the differences among individuals and between actuality and fantasy, freeing them to occupy one another's places. ("Whereas the Duke is Angelo's surrogate and Mariana Isabella's surrogate," claims Rupin Desai, for instance, in *The Psychoanalytic Review,* "the definite marriage of Angelo and Mariana and the probable marriage of the Duke and Isabella are, in fact, a marriage between Angelo and Isabella by double proxy."[21]) Recent new historicist readings like Jonathan Dollimore's or Barbara Baines', with their emphasis upon ideological "displacement," likewise register the strange *mobility* of meaning in the play, the difficulty of fixing or specifying significance, priority, or proportion in a world where everything could conceivably be replaced by something else. Vicariousness is raised from a moral axiom (the exercise of mercy), or a fact about audience response, to a principle of semiotic indeterminacy.

For knowing what lessons the viewing of *Measure for Measure* is supposed to convey is difficult, not merely because members of any audience inevitably vary but because the play provides them so little guidance. Assessing "damages" requires some consensually acceptable standard of adequacy, of "fairness." Penalties must "fit" crimes; and even if they are excused in an act of forgiveness, the possibility of punishment must still be adumbrated in order for mercy to register as such. But in the world of *Measure for Measure,* there is little such consensus, no standard of appropriateness. We have already seen how the play's generally jaundiced view of sexuality does not much ease the task of judging sexual "offenses": sexual acts seem to have no natural or plausible valence but can be evaluated in wildly different ways, depending upon one's frame of reference.

The commitment of several characters to a Christian religious vocation further complicates the possibility of establishing some kind of commensurability. Isabella, especially, assumes that spiritual goods like honor and purity are infinitely more important than secular, visible possessions. In her system of values, a promise of ardent prayer constitutes the most potent bribe she can offer Angelo, beside which gold is barren and trivial. The counterintuitive otherworldliness of Isabella's concept of commensurability is central to Christianity, a religion founded upon the spectacularly lopsided substitution of the blameless Christ for sinful humanity in the system of God's justice. But since such religious convictions are not subject to the verification of the senses, they are open to challenge by those more firmly attached to the things of this world—like Claudio, for whom any fate seems better than death. His hierarchy of priorities is different from Isabella's, and so therefore are his conceptions of commensurability.

Measure for Measure seems, then, to make two incompatible assertions. First, human beings differ radically from one another, so that one person's meat is another person's poison, one person's truth another person's falsehood, one person's propriety another person's scandal. Second, human beings are not all that different from one another and can exchange themselves, or be exchanged for one another, quite freely. Shakespeare is not the first Renaissance dramatist to make these contradictory claims simultaneously: as we have already seen, they also inform the theater of Kyd and Marlowe. On the one hand, the lack of transcendent guarantees in the secular theater of the Renaissance seems to open up the prospect of untrammeled individualism, typically figured as "inward" or "unseen." Members of audiences, like characters, can generate an infinite variety of interpretive options. On the other hand, social life seems to demand, despite this individualism, a fund of consensually accepted principles and a sense of shared human lot. In *Measure for Measure* as in *The Spanish Tragedy* the capacity for vicariousness, which holds communities together and which gives theater its purpose, originates in the publicly obvious, universally shared fact of human embodiment. The *mechanism* of empathy, in other words, is aligned with the spectacularly externalized aspects of theatrical performance, and with the conception of an audience as a consensual community. At the same time, in Shakespeare as in Kyd or Marlowe, no particular empathetic attachment can be counted upon to work. So the *consequence* of empathy—the interpretation that a spectator makes of the play—is aligned with invisibility, inwardness, and incalculable idiosyncrasy.

So Shakespeare resembles Jonson in the way he flirts with the possibility of an entirely privatized existence but finds it impossible to do away with the "external" realm. His art is bound up, however uncomfortably, with the values of public exposure and group experience. (Perhaps Milton's indifference to this latter possibility, by contrast, accompanies his preference for nondramatic forms, relatively unaffected by the corporeal exigencies of performance.) For both playwrights, the exterior, interpersonal domain is indispensable despite its manifest inadequacy, or the inadequacy of its manifestation. Thus, too, the ambiguously interiorized domain of sexual experience figures for Jonson and Shakespeare as both threat and promise, fraught with many of the same contradictions as theater itself.

The end of *Measure for Measure,* which so many have found troubling or unsatisfactory, registers strongly the conflicts of the tradition of which it is a part. Since the play cannot reach closure if its contradictions are simply left radically unreconciled, the drastic discrepancies between the various characters' moral and social outlooks are provisionally adjusted by Duke Vincentio, a concealed authority who learns everybody's secrets in the course of the play. . . . English Renaissance writers associate power that takes the form of invisible omniscience not only with God but also with the machiavel who denies God even while appropriating his attributes. Both characterizations have been accorded the Duke by different critics, and each receives some support in the play, which opens with a scene of deputation familiar to readers of *The Prince* and concludes with Angelo's comparison of Vincentio to "providence divine." Given the structural similarity between machiavel and deity, these alternatives may not be as starkly opposed as they seem.[22]

Perhaps, given the dilemmas in which *Measure for Measure* implicates itself, the Duke ought to be seen as Shakespeare's rather desperate contrivance to mediate between the characters' secret, subjective worlds and the external domain of publicly administered law. By act 3, the play's problems can only be solved by someone who can obtain access to motives and intentions, a privilege usually reserved for a confessor. At the same time, unlike a clergyman, he must retain the secular ruler's ability to mandate changes in behavior in order to bring matters to a satisfactory conclusion. In the real world such a combination would approach tyranny. Thus even in Shakespeare's England, in which the functions of church and state were closely intertwined and in which the king called himself the church's Supreme Governor, the sovereign's actual power to interfere in ecclesiastical affairs was quite restricted.[23] In *Measure for Measure,* however, a prince disguised as a friar is able to bridge, however unsteadily, the gap between power and knowledge, outside and inside, in order to enjoin a resolution.

Although the Duke's unusual means of access to his subjects sometimes—often—seems creepy and presumptuous, he is no villain: Gyges and his descendants give us some context for the way Vincentio chooses to deploy his unusual privileges. Yet he remains an earthly ruler confronting juridical dilemmas that are framed so as to be insoluble by earthly power. The generic anomaly of *Measure for Measure*—what A. P. Rossiter speaks to when he complains of "the imposed quality of the action"[24]—is a direct consequence of the play's contestatory way of imagining the relationship between sexuality and community. For the final marriages, then, can only be achieved by outright coercion, by the enforcement of laws that prevent whoredom, promiscuity, extramarital dalliance, sexual harassment, breach of promise, and the nonsupport of bastard children. Inevitably in this scheme, marriage is inflicted as a form of discipline—as an alternative to capital punishment, in fact; it no longer seems a conduit of pleasure or a flowering of mutual commitment. Richard Wheeler complains of *All's Well That Ends Well* that "the play does little to suggest that the bed trick, which allows the comic plot to be completed, significantly alters the psychological conditions that have made it necessary."[25] The same might be said of *Measure for Measure,* because the Duke does not have the capacity to "alter psychological conditions" by decree. He can manipulate, educate, cajole, and punish, in ways not guaranteed to succeed. He can bring the aggressive, devouring, suicidal impulses associated with sexuality throughout the play under the institutional rubric of marriage; but in order for us to experience the ending as "happy," we have to forget the critique of such disciplinary structures mounted in the earlier acts, overlooking the fact that merely institutional arrangements do not address the fundamental unruliness of sexual desire. The Duke's powers, despite his special capacities, are still conceived as "external" to the subjects he coerces into some semblance of harmonious community. The "internal" renovation of human nature presumably remains the prerogative of a God who can at most only be adumbrated in the theater.

One symptom of the Duke's limitation, and the theater's, is the way that the characters' inwardness, apparently so entirely divulged to his (and our) omniscient, managing vision, recedes almost instantly into unknowability in the midst of what is structured as a scene of revelation and pardon. Isabella, arguing that Angelo ought to be pardoned, makes a distinction between intention and behavior that would have been familiar in a Renaissance courtroom, but that her ascetic scruples would not have permitted her earlier in the play:

> Thoughts are no subjects,
> Intents but merely thoughts.
> (5.1.553–54)

Whether or not this constitutes a good reason for pardoning Angelo, or merely indicates Isabella's moral confusion, has been much debated by critics since Samuel Johnson. What Isabella certainly does describe here is the constraint Shakespeare places both upon the power of his duke and the power of his audience. Angelo never indicates that he prefers the Duke's mercy, and life with Mariana, to the death he had requested. Lucio frankly announces he prefers capital punishment to wedded life with Kate Keepdown, but it is unclear whether he is "serious." Claudio and Julietta are accorded no lines to celebrate their unexpected reunion. Isabella, so eloquent in her plea for Angelo's life, fails to acknowledge Claudio's restoration or to respond to the Duke's proposal. "Unorthodox" readings of *Measure for Measure* have involved "reading in" defiance where previous critics assumed acquiescence: Isabella flees in horror from the Duke. What seems important is not whether such interpretations are likely, or whether they were played on Shakespeare's stage, but that they are possible. The expected expressions of gratitude, wonder, or acceptance are capable of being withheld, and once they are withheld we cannot take them simply for granted. In the final lines of *Measure for Measure* most of the characters resist, even repudiate, our scrutiny. Shakespeare seems deliberately to puncture the illusion of complete revelation, reasserting the problem of unknowable inward truth just at the moment when it might be supposed to disappear.

Notes

1. The problems of selective enforcement, and of difficulty controlling the professional sex trade, were not new: see Richard Wunderli, *London Church Courts and Society on the Eve of the Reformation,* pp. 49–53 and 81–102, for an account of the early sixteenth-century situation.

2. Margaret Scott, " 'Our City's Institutions': Some Further Reflections on the Marriage Contract in *Measure for Measure,*" *ELH* 49 (1982): 794. For a variety of views of the problems of precontract in *Measure for Measure,* see Ernest Schanzer, "The Marriage Contracts in *Measure for Measure,*" *Shakespeare Survey* 13 (1960): 81–89; J. Birje-Patil, "Marriage Contracts in *Measure for Measure,*" *Shakespeare Studies* 5 (1969): 106–11; Harriet Hawkins, "What Kind of Pre-Contract Had Angelo? A Note on Some Non-Problems in Elizabethan Drama," *College English* 36 (1974): 173–79. For the claim that Shakespeare wished to influence James's policy toward sex offenders, see Donald McGin, " 'The Precise Angelo,' " *Joseph Quincy Adams Memorial Studies* ed. James McManaway, Giles Dawson, and Edwin Willoughby (Washington: Folger Shakespeare Library, 1948), pp. 125–39, and Catharine F. Siegel, "Hands Off the Hothouses: Shakespeare's Advice to the King," *Journal of Popular Culture* 20 (1986): 81–88.

3. Richard Wheeler makes a similar point in *Shakespeare's Development and the Problem Comedies: Turn and Counter-Turn* (Berkeley: University of California Press, 1981), p. 102, when he describes the "attitudes that imply an ineradicable tension between moral aspiration and an inherently debasing sexual nature."

4. Barbara Baines, in "Assaying the Power of Chastity in *Measure for Measure,*" *SEL* 30 (1990): 284–98, points out that the social prestige that attaches to chastity in Vienna leads the

morally self-conscious characters—Isabella, Angelo, and the Duke—to make a virtue out of sexual renunciation and to value a reputation for celibacy.

5. Jonathan Dollimore, "Transgression and Surveillance in *Measure for Measure,*" *Political Shakespeare: New Essays in Cultural Materialism* (Manchester: Manchester University Press, 1985), pp. 72–87.

6. Geoffrey Galt Harpham, *The Ascetic Imperative in Culture and Criticism* (Chicago: University of Chicago Press, 1987), p. 27.

7. G. Wilson Knight, "*Measure for Measure* and the Gospels," *The Wheel of Fire: Essays in Interpretation of Shakespeare's Sombre Tragedies* (London: Oxford University Press, 1930), p. 81; Muriel C. Bradbrook, "Authority and Justice in *Measure for Measure,*" *Review of English Studies* 17 (1984): 386.

8. Anne Barton, Introduction to *Measure for Measure* in *The Riverside Shakespeare* (Boston: Houghton Mifflin, 1974), p. 546; Carolyn Brown, "Erotic Religious Flagellation and Shakespeare's *Measure for Measure,*" *ELR* 16 (1986): 162 (Harriet Hawkins makes a similar argument in " 'The Devil's Party: Virtues and Vices in *Measure for Measure,*" *Shakespeare Survey* 31 (1978): 104–14); J. W. Lever, Introduction to the Arden *Measure for Measure* (London: Methuen, 1965), p. lxxix; Arthur Kirsch, "The Integrity of *Measure for Measure,*" *Shakespeare Survey* 28 (1975): 96; Harold C. Goddard, "Power in *Measure for Measure,*" in *The Meaning of Shakespeare* (Chicago: Chicago University Press, 1951); Barbara Baines, "Assaying the Power of Chastity," p. 288.

9. Ignatius Loyola, William Perkins, Thomas Cooper, and many others provide members of the various Christian confessions with methods of meditation designed to ferret out and acknowledge recesses of the self the fallen, self-loving individual would prefer not to acknowledge. The most complete discussion I have encountered on this problem, however, is Daniel Dyke's now relatively little-known *Mystery of self deceiving,* first published in London in 1614. Dyke is interested not only in how and why people can be mistaken about one another, but in why even one's apparently unmediated self-knowledge can be incomplete or uncertain: "Man knoweth his inward thoughts, purposes, and desires, but the frame and disposition of his heart he knows not, nor yet always the qualities of those thoughts, whether they tend, what secret deceit lies, and lurks in them" (p. 312).

10. See, for instance, J. W. Lever, Introduction to the Arden *Measure for Measure,* p. lxxx; Kirsch, "The Integrity of *Measure for Measure,*" p. 97; Hugh Richmond, *Shakespeare's Sexual Comedy: A Mirror for Lovers* (New York: Bobbs Merrill, 1971), p. 155.

11. John Milton, *The Doctrine and Discipline of Divorce,* chapter 3, in *The Works of John Milton* (New York: Columbia University Press, 1931), 3.2:393.

12. For a persuasive account of Milton's antinomian politics in another treatise see Stanley Fish, "Driving from the Letter: Truth and Indeterminacy in Milton's *Areopagitica,*" in *Re-Membering Milton,* ed. Mary Nyquist and Margaret Ferguson (New York: Methuen, 1987), pp. 234–54.

13. I should emphasize that all three writers are more complex than the positions with which I associate them here. What I am calling "Miltonic" is Milton's position in the divorce tracts; his attitude to the body is equivocal in the early poetry and changes fundamentally later in his career . . . as scrupulously charted by James Turner in *One Flesh: Paradisal Marriage and Sexual Relations in the Age of Milton* (Oxford: Oxford University Press, 1987). Likewise, what I am calling "Jonsonian" here is characteristic of Jonson's comedies between *Every Man Out of His Humour* and *Bartholomew Fair:* his attitude in the masques and poems is often quite different. See my "Satiric and Ideal Economies in the Jonsonian Imagination," *English Literary Renaissance* 19 (1989): 42–64, for a fuller account of Jonson's work in other genres. Shakespeare, of course, is an immensely complicated case, and I do not pretend to account for anything except *Measure for Measure.*

14. Many have pointed out the crucial role substitutions, deputations, and exchanges play in the plot of *Measure for Measure.* See, for example, Richard Wheeler, *Shakespeare's Develop-*

ment and the Problem Comedies, pp. 120–38; Meredith Skura, "New Interpretations for Interpretation in *Measure for Measure,*" *Boundary* 27, no. 2 (1979): 39-58; Alexander Leggatt, "Substitution in *Measure for Measure,*" *Shakespeare Quarterly* 39 (1988): 342–59; Marc Shell, *The End of Kinship: "Measure for Measure," Incest, and the Idea of Universal Siblinghood* (Stanford: Stanford University Press, 1988), pp. 97–136.

15. For the claim that there is a significant difference, see Ernest Schanzer; for the claim that there is not, see Harriet Hawkins, "What Kind of Pre-Contract Had Angelo?"

16. David Lloyd Stevenson, "Design and Structure in *Measure for Measure,*" *ELH* 23 (1956): 256–78; Bernice Kliman, "Isabella in *Measure for Measure,*" *Shakespeare Studies* 15 (1982): 137–48.

17. Wheeler, *Shakespeare's Development and the Problem Comedies,* p. 122.

18. Harriet Hawkins, "The Devil's Party," *Shakespeare Survey* 31 (1978): 112. See also Harold C. Goddard, in "Power in *Measure for Measure,*" p. 450: "The vices of the two ends of 'society' turn out under examination to be much alike."

19. Shell, *The End of Kinship,* pp. 92–93.

20. G. Wilson Knight, "*Measure for Measure* and the Gospels"; M. C. Bradbrook, "Authority and Justice in *Measure for Measure,*" *Review of English Studies* 17 (1941): 385–99; Roy Battenhouse, "*Measure for Measure* and the Christian Doctrine of Atonement," *PMLA* 61 (1946): 1029–59.

21. Rupin Desai, "Freudian Undertones in *Measure for Measure,*" *Psychoanalytic Review* 64 (1977): 487–94. A similar claim is made by W. L. Godshalk, "*Measure for Measure:* Freedom and Restraint," *Shakespeare Studies* 6 (1970): 137–73: "Although they remain physically pure, both the duke and Isabella symbolically share the sin of Angelo and Mariana in the illicit bed, as they recapitulate the act of Claudio and Juliet" (p. 146).

22. Certainly some of the complaints about the Duke—usually mounted as objections to a "providentialist" reading of his role—recall traditional skeptical complaints about the Christian God. When Marcia Riefer, in " 'The Instruments of Some More Mightier Member': The Constriction of Female Power in *Measure for Measure,*" *Shakespeare Quarterly* 35 (1984): 160, criticizes the Duke on the grounds that he "is actually setting up Angelo for a fall while protecting himself," she recapitulates the objection Milton's God must deal with in *Paradise Lost* III, that the whole history of man is a setup by a deity who knows in advance that his puppet will fail him, then punishes him for failing, then expects to be worshipped for "redeeming" him.

23. For a short account of the limits placed on the royal supremacy by the Parliament of 1559, see A. G. Dickens, *The English Reformation* (New York: Schocken Books 1964), pp. 294–306; for Elizabeth's ecclesiastical policy, see William Haugaard, *Elizabeth and the English Reformation* (Cambridge: Cambridge University Press, 1968); for a more detailed and technical account of the legal issues involved, see Robert E. Rodes, *Lay Authority and Reformation in the English Church: Edward I to the Civil War* (Notre Dame: University of Notre Dame Press, 1982), pp. 67–243.

24. *Angel with Horns: Fifteen Lectures on Shakespeare,* ed. Graham Storey (London: Longman, 1961), p. 58.

25. Wheeler, *Shakespeare's Development and the Problem Comedies,* p. 55.

Getting Oneself Unmasked: The Duke, the "Friar", and Lucio

HARRY BERGER JR.

When we organize our interpretation of the play around the question of the Duke it becomes evident that speech and discourse are not about sexuality, but rather sexuality and the sins associated with it are about discourses, the discursive evasions that mark the variants of the sinner's discourse in the interplay of self-inculpation and exculpation. . . . [I]f we read the Duke's language and behavior primarily as evidence of the vicissitudes of reflexive self-representation, we discover the signs of a peculiarly morbid version of the discourse, one that reveals its inculpatory force chiefly through the speaker's efforts to evade it. After the Duke acknowledges himself accountable for disorder in Vienna he tries to distance himself from both his express knowledge and the effects of his leniency. After he hints to the Friar that his election of Angelo was partly motivated by the desire to put his seeming virtue to the test, he acts as if this were not the case; he in effect disowns knowledge of his complicity even as he masterminds the dirty tricks that make it hard to disown, since they continue the project of assaying and entrapping Angelo. The outlandishness of his discourse of self-exculpation, the measure of the anxiety against which he defends, is expressed by his decision to ensconce himself in imaginary holy orders. But the divided structure of that role—spiritual advisor vs. intriguer—reflects and reinforces the conflict revealed in 1.3 between the desire to clean up Vienna and the desire to probe for suspected flaws in Angelo. The shift of the Duke's attention and energy from the former desire to the latter correlates with the shift from moralizing to machination, and his effort to cloak that shift in the pious rhetoric he uses to persuade Isabella in 3.1 further diminishes the utility of his disguise as a defense against self-inculpation. The psychomachian result of this crisis is registered in the reactions to Lucio that include the three soliloquies in 3.2 and 4.1. In 5.1, after the Duke reclaims his identity by staging the psychomachia, the edge of bitterness flashed by that contentious exercise continues to glint in the rhetoric

Reprinted from *Making Trifles of Terrors: Redistributing Complicities in Shakespeare* by Harry Berger Jr., Edited, with an Introduction, by Peter Erickson, with the permission of the publishers, Stanford University Press.

of remission through which the happy ending is secured. The speaker who is most active in helping the Duke and others identify the "Friar," and the one who defrocks the "Friar," is his chief heckler and the Duke's admirer, Lucio. Their common antipathy toward the "Friar" draws them together in an unlikely conjunction that the Duke immediately disarticulates ("Thou art the first knave that e'er mad'st a duke," 5.1.354). But from early in the play the Duke has been bound to Lucio by a strange proximity that makes disarticulation both difficult and necessary.

In 3.2, for example, after the "Friar" denounces Pompey and orders him to prison, Lucio enters and does exactly the same thing. Although the Duke's denunciation is in high iambic style and Lucio's is a prosy fusillade, a staccato of jeering rhetorical questions (3.2.43–50), and although the listening Duke's comment on the diatribe is a critical aside that lumps Lucio together with Pompey ("Still thus, and thus; still worse!" 51), the two denunciations are equally contemptuous. And when Lucio responds to Pompey's request for bail with "imprison him" (64), he echoes the instruction given by the "Friar" at 3.2.30, "Take him to prison." As Bradshaw notes, in this scene the Duke finds himself morally supported by—and coupled to—"an embarrassing ally."[1] Lucio's notable inconsistency in this scene, alternately flouting and siding with authority and the law, makes sense chiefly as a pattern of utterances we hear the disguised Duke overhear and respond to from his de facto position as an eavesdropper. Listening with the Duke's ears gives everything Lucio says or does the force of an encroachment, a violation of the Duke's *cordon sanitaire.* First, the Duke hears what must seem to him to be a distorted echo, therefore a parody, of his aggressive treatment of Pompey, which Lucio was not present to witness. Then we hear Lucio criticize his abdication in terms so accurate that many commentators suspect he has inside knowledge, a suspicion that may be usefully directed toward the Duke: can he fail to hear an allusion to his mendicant masquerade in Lucio's "a mad, fantastical trick . . . to steal from the state and usurp the beggary he was never born to" (89–90)? After this, Lucio's misinformed disparagement of Angelo's iciness leads, as if by the logic of rhetorical antithesis, to his misdirected praise of the Duke's "feeling for the sport" (115–16).

In this scene, and also in 4.3 and 5.1, Lucio's slander seems to be aimed chiefly at an auditor he treats as a purse-lipped cleric and probable hypocrite, as if he sees in this "Friar," in any friar, an occupational paradigm or parody of Angelesque precision: a prig who puts his virtue on parade and whose habit sends the generally false message that its "wearer doth rebate and blunt his natural edge / With profits of the mind, study and fast" (1.4.60–61); a potential ally of the deputy, the antitype of the tolerant Duke, an antibody threatening the flow of "use and liberty" (62) through Vienna's venal if not venereal veins. To irritate what he treats as an Angelo-figure, a generically self-styled angel or messenger of God, Lucio belabors the "Friar" with equally parodic, and therefore strategically distorted, representations of the Duke. We know the Duke knows better and can correct both sides of the false antithesis. But what picture would this correction yield? The picture of the lenient ruler turned intriguer and factitious friar, the Duke of dark corners at work on his intertwined Angelesque and angelesque agendas, parading his virtue while hunting down or stirring up secret sins and making pious reparation for his complicity in vice. These are the agendas for which he punishes himself by his campaign to get himself unmasked as the "Friar."

Lucio's utterances in 3.2 thus emerge as if from an imperfectly baffled echo chamber within the Duke's conscience. But before 3.2 ends, this noisy resonator of his conscience who is also the creature of his permissiveness is discredited in a manner that affects both those relations. After Lucio has turned down Pompey's request for bail and aggravated the "Friar" by slandering the Duke, and after the Duke's bitter aside about Lucio's "Back-wounding calumny," Mistress Overdone complains—in the Duke's presence—that she is off to jail because of

> Lucio's information against me, Mistress Kate Keep-down was with child by him in the Duke's time, he promised her marriage. His child is a year and a quarter old come Philip and Jacob. I have kept it myself; and see how he goes about to abuse me.
>
> Esc. That fellow is a fellow of much license. Let him be called before us. Away with her to prison.
>
> (3.2.192–99)

The news about Lucio is divulged by a beleaguered and possibly unreliable source and is embedded in a fragmentary, rapidly paced segment of action that can easily divert attention from it. Nevertheless, it *is* news, and the abrupt, rapid-fire battery of Overdone's three accusatory clauses gives dramatic urgency to what Patricia Parker might call an undilated delation, one that will be verified (as we have seen) by Lucio himself in 4.3 and will provide the substance of the Duke's final action against Lucio in 5.1.[2] Interpretive retrospect thus reads against the grain of the dramaturgical tempo and confers on Overdone's words, her last in the play, the force of a crucial revelation the importance of which is only increased when we take account of its effect on our assessment of Lucio's words and actions up to this point.

First, then, we suddenly learn that he is guilty of the same "crime" as Claudio and of the same "promise-breach" as Angelo, and this double comparison works to his disadvantage, making his betrayal even more perfidious than Angelo's of Mariana. Second, his apparently disinterested service on Claudio's behalf in the earlier scenes now appears motivated by awareness that he is subject to the same penalty and that any success Isabella might have with Angelo could be beneficial to Lucio himself as well as Claudio. Overdone's revelation also brings out the residual self-concern in what was apparently no more than a blustery hyperbole uttered by Lucio earlier in the scene when he contrasted Angelo's rigor to the sympathetic tolerance of the Duke, who, before "he would have hanged a man for the getting a hundred bastards, . . . would have paid for the nursing a thousand" (3.2.113–15).[3] Third, although Lucio shows affection for the Duke and his ways and contempt for the precise deputy, his treatment of Pompey and Overdone contributes to Angelo's cleanup campaign; whether or not he betrays Overdone to the law because he resents her having kept his child, as Bradshaw argues (189), the betrayal may be construed as a kind of preemptive plea bargaining similar in purpose to his support of Claudio and Isabella. There is, however, another line of explanation for Lucio's behavior, different in emphasis but not entirely incompatible with the idea that he is chiefly intent on saving his skin. This is that he alternately appeases and flouts authority as if he respects its power but despises its hypocrisy and wishes to test its limits. There are moments in which he seems unable to resist playing the rogue and asking for trouble.[4] To some extent he is a vice figure who exhibits "the functions and attributes of the Lord of Misrule, the Fool, the Buffoon, and the Jester," the qualities Dover Wilson ascribes to Falstaff.[5] Thus, although Lucio may at first be entertaining, his image worsens as 3.2 proceeds; precisely as it does so this deteriorating figure not only echoes the Duke's judgment but flaunts his intimacy with him. The consequences of the Duke's permissiveness begin to look more serious, and with Overdone's revelation Lucio's perfidy explodes in our faces like a firecracker.[6]

In our faces, and in the Duke's, for he is onstage at the time; it is news to him as well as to us, and if we listen with the Duke's ears, the most telling phrase is "in the Duke's time." Overdone's words link the Duke to Lucio's foul play, presenting him with a pointed contrast between Angelo's treatment of Claudio and the effects of his own negligence. Conceived and carried off on the Duke's watch, itself a child of the Duke's time, Lucio's escapade reinterprets the meaning of corruption in a way that can only cast a darkening shadow over the Duke's complicity. It exemplifies more than the "loose morals" associated with irresponsible sex: the "much license" Escalus refers to includes the triple betrayal of mother, child, and caretaker.[7] Throughout the play the "corruption" overrunning "the stew" has been delineated in terms of Viennese categories that would minimize such a betrayal by redescribing its victims as punk, whoreson, and bawd. These categories repress or occlude a moral standard different from the play's dominant Platonico-Puritan ideology of *misosoma* with its attendant misogyny. It is a standard that locates "corruption" in the failure of community or charity, the duplicity or unreliability of people's dealings with each other, the lack of truth (troth) in their relations. Overdone's speech gives us a glimpse of the moral contraries picked out by this standard. Against Lucio's betrayal we may set the charitable act remarked by Bradshaw: Overdone's caring for Lucio's bastard is the play's "one conspicuously disinterested act of human kindness," and it "occurs in the lower depths and makes little or no impression on the Duke" (192). The act and the standard it imports are indeed recessive, and they surface only in a passing reference by a speaker who may herself have an interest in mentioning the act. Yet I think the abrupt and anomalous character of the mention, along with its transformative effect on our reading of previous events, *does* make the act, the standard, and its recessiveness conspicuous. And I'm not sure Overdone's disclosure makes little or no impression on the Duke.

The redescription of Lucio's victims as punk, whoreson, and bawd reduces them to positions or players in Vienna's sex trade and makes them fair game for both lawful prosecutions and lawless persecutions. By treating them and Pompey in this manner Lucio participates in both kinds of action: refusing to bail Pompey and informing on Overdone, he contributes to the program of reform devised by the Duke and delegated to Angelo; at the same time, this aggression is directed toward those whose occupations he and the Duke, in their different ways, supported. Thus his two-sided relation to the sex trade imitates the Duke's and represents a nasty parody of it. Overdone's disclosure offers a brief abstract of pernicious "bringings-forth" that might be laid to his own regime and that are now melodramatically condensed for the Duke in the figure of Lucio. That he registers Lucio's acts and claims of alliance is indicated by his utterances during the remainder of 3.2, for as we have seen, they exhibit an intensified form of the movement of recoil and decontamination, of self-exculpation, that first marked his dialogue with the "Friar" in 1.3. This is evident, for example, when he tells Escalus he is "Not of this country" but "from the See / In special business from his Holiness" (3.2.211–14). His sense of the deeper corruption is directly expressed in the complaint that "There is scarce truth enough alive to make societies secure; but security enough to make fellowships accurst" (220–21). The arch question he appends to his diatribe, "of what disposition was the Duke?," continues the effort of self-exculpation that reaches a climax in the concluding "sword of heaven" soliloquy.

"Sir, your company is fairer than honest; rest you well": so, at the end of 4.3, the "Friar" tries to make his getaway after being subjected to Lucio's "pretty tales of the Duke." But his valedictory hint is ignored: "I'll go with thee to the lane's end. If bawdy talk offend you, we'll have very little of it. Nay, friar, I am a kind of burr, I shall stick" (4.3.173–77). Sticking to the Duke as well as the "Friar," Lucio as burr dramatically figures, and his persistence ironically mocks, the Duke's inability to distance himself from the behavior for which, in 1.3, he had held himself accountable. Lucio perversely exhibits the Vienna-problem in its worst light when he himself confirms Overdone's report of his mistreatment of Kate Keep-down and boasts of having lied about it to the Duke (4.3.167–72). Whatever we imagine Lucio to intend, we and the Duke watch him perform his knavery in the "Friar's" face and frustrate Vincentio's desire for the moral advantage and insulation he sought from his disguise.

It makes sense, then, that the burr who unwittingly pricks the Duke's conscience while trying to make the "Friar" prickle turns out to be the Duke's principal auxiliary in his campaign to get himself exposed. Lucio externalizes the Duke's anger when he strips off the mask of pious hypocrisy. The embodiment of all that was wrong in the Duke's style of government presents himself as an agent, if not an allegory, of the Duke's conscience. The strangest moment in this strange event occurs during the interchange at 5.1.324–53, when Lucio claims that it was the "Friar," not he, who had earlier slandered the Duke. Superficially, the motive here is obvious: Lucio is joining the others in following the Duke's lead and ganging up on the "Friar." Since the "Friar" has been discredited, Lucio can safely taunt him: "You and I both know that what I say you said about the Duke is actually what I said about the Duke. So what are you going to do about it?" Lucio is being just as bad as he can be. But if we recall the content of those slanders, some of which may have struck home more than others, we could well expect the Duke to hear another message in this patent misattribution: "I don't really believe what I said about the Duke's lechery. That was no truer than what I'm saying now, no less patent a misattribution. Had the Duke been present he would have known that my slander was actually a hyperbolic or metonymic way of expressing grateful admiration for his discreet and tolerant method of government, and especially for the license he allowed us." The sentiment behind this message may be phrased in words borrowed from Pompey, "I hope here be truths" (2.1.126, 132); replacing *hope* with *fear* would give us the Duke's probable reaction.

Their common aggression against the "Friar" in 5.1 draws the Duke and his burr together more closely than the Duke would like. But since after his exposure the Duke perversely clings to the "Friar's" moral authority, it also makes sense that he would try to extricate the burr and throw it away. Thus his last official act in the play is directed against the brazen embodiment of his Vienna-problem, whom he singles out as unworthy of the "apt remission" he has just granted to Barnardine, Claudio, and Angelo in rapid order: "And yet here's one in place I cannot pardon" (5.1.497). What would it have meant for him to implement this refusal, to seal Lucio's fate by sending an abhorred child of ducal lenity to Abhorson on the grounds of "Slandering a prince" (522)? It would have sealed his own commitment to the discourse of self-exculpation. The play would have ended leaving "more behind that is . . . [less] gratulate" and more than is "meet you all should know." So, as with the others, the Duke backs off and finds an inept remission. The series of moves in this episode is zany enough to deserve a closer look.

In response to the Duke's asking why he was vilified, Lucio apologetically ("I spoke it but according to the trick") tries to preempt the judgment and limit his punishment: "if you will hang me for it, you may: but I had rather it would please you I might be whipped" (5.1.502–4). After the Duke wins this round by taking both suggestions—"Whipp'd, first, sir, and hang'd after" (505)—he goes on to pay Lucio back for the "pretty tale(s)" he had told at the Duke's expense in 4.3 (163–74), and although the Duke had in fact learned about Kate Keep-down in 3.2, he rubs it in by alluding to the anecdote in which Lucio boastfully informed on himself. He tells the Provost to proclaim

> round about the city,
> If any woman wrong'd by this lewd fellow,
> —As I have heard him swear himself there's one
> Whom he begot with child—let her appear,
> And he shall marry her. The nuptial finish'd,
> Let him be whipp'd and hang'd.
>
> LUCIO I beseech your Highness, do not marry me to a whore. Your Highness said even now, I made you a duke; good my lord, do not recompense me in making me a cuckold.
>
> DUKE Upon mine honor, thou shalt marry her.
> Thy slanders I forgive, and therewithal
> Remit thy other forfeits.—Take him to prison,
> And see our pleasure herein executed.
>
> LUCIO Marrying a punk, my lord, is pressing to death,
> Whipping, and hanging.
>
> DUKE Slandering a prince deserves it.
>
> (5.1.506–21)

By this time in the fifth act the prefatory "here's one . . . I cannot pardon" flags an imminent act of pardon, and although the Duke appears once again to have planned this maneuver, it zigzags through changes of emphasis to a conclusion that all but throws it off course: let Lucio be whipped and hanged for slandering a prince; let him be married for wronging a woman, then whipped and hanged; let the slanders be forgiven and their "forfeits" remitted, but let the other penalty stand; let him be taken to prison so that the Duke's "pleasure herein" may be executed; let him suffer the unpleasure of marriage "to a whore" for slandering a prince.

Not unlike Angelo, who welcomed death but was silent about his compulsory marriage, Lucio protests only the sentence of marriage. The logic of his complaint is that since he is forced to marry not only a woman he wronged but also a sex worker he is doomed to a shameful life of what may be called occupational cuckoldry. This seems to satisfy the Duke who, by now, has his pardons and remissions at the ready and whose cancellation of the death penalty indicates that letting Lucio linger on in living shame will be sweeter revenge. But why, if the execution of the Duke's pleasure consists in seeing Lucio unhappily married to a woman he wronged, does he order him to be taken to prison? "Take him to prison, / And see our pleasure herein executed": the only circumstantial explanation of the first clause—that the bride has been incarcerated with the other sex workers, so the marriage must take place in prison—does not register clearly because the Duke's prior instruction to the Provost culminating in "let her appear" (506–10) diverts attention from it. But in any event, the explanation would not fully account for the touch of incoherence in this angry and abrupt imperative. What, precisely, does *herein*—"in this matter"—gesture toward? Lucio's marriage is the obvious referent, yet the energy of the utterance strangely and contradictorily veers toward the punitive contents of the "other forfeits," as if the Duke momentarily forgets the pardon he has just pronounced and reinstates his original sentence.

This ghostly gesture adds interest to the term *executed.* Of its two senses, "accomplished" or "performed" and "put to death," the first is the one the context obviously selects. Yet of the twelve other variants of *execute* in the play—I exclude the two occurrences of the occupationally specific term *executioner*—all but the first (at 1.1.59) denote the second more specific sense, and eight of these are found in the relatively recent action of 4.2 and 4.3.[8] Their influence on the present usage generates the wild reading "See our pleasure herein put to death," which destabilizes the simple, patently ceremonial intent of the phrase and provokes the search for other possibilities. The reading puts pressure on the royal plural pronoun: in loosening the ceremonial constraint, it opens up a space for another referent to creep in, "Lucio's pleasure as well as mine," and this in turn offers resistance to the ceremonial reduction of "our pleasure" to a euphemism expressing royal prerogative. The wild reading begins to make a comprehensive kind of sense, for the coupling of the Duke's pleasure with Lucio's is the theme of Lucio's slander, which, behind its distortions, comments on the Duke's voyeuristic pleasure in the sinful pleasures of others. It is this *curiositas* that he tried to atone for by playing "Friar" and that now bears the burden of Lucio's vicious pleasure. The sentence of marriage that will kill Lucio's pleasure will thus pronounce the death of the *curiositas* it is coupled to.

"Take him to prison, / And see our pleasure herein executed." Because this is the last of a string of carceral imperatives, several of them uttered by the Duke, it has a punitive ring that exceeds its circumstantial function. In 5.1 alone it is preceded by "To prison with her!" (Isabella), "Lay hold on him" (Lucio), and "Away with him" (Angelo), not to mention Escalus's rabid repetition of "Away with him [the 'Friar'] to prison" (5.1.124, 357, 414, 342–46). "Take him to prison" repeats the words used by the Duke as "Friar" at 3.2.30 after denouncing Pompey for his "filthy vice," and the echo sharpens the sense that at play's end the Duke is still trying to distance himself, decontaminate himself, from the agents, argot, and institutions promoting Vienna's vicious pleasures, all of which have now been compacted into the irrepressibly loose-tongued nose-plucking figure of Lucio, the final icon of the Vienna-problem. The carceral imperative has become the problem-solving reflex, the tactic of decontamination, the speech act by which the Duke reappropriates and demonstrates his politico-legal authority. It gestures peremptorily toward a fantasy of imprisonment and execution that Lucio, impudently playing the moral odds, goads or dares him to actualize. The utterance is too conspicuously not saying "Take him to prison and put him to death" to prevent that wish from leaking into the nobler forbearance he tries to display: "In spite of all he has done to me I am not going to put him to death."

This wish disrupts the Duke's endgame since, as we have seen, the carceral imperative is a strategic feint enabling him to reappropriate and demonstrate moral authority by exercising the power of pardon. To succumb to the wish to decontaminate himself by killing Lucio for misdeeds attributable to the ruler's permissive pass would be to inculpate himself. The Duke therefore plans to terminate Lucio's pleasure rather than Lucio, and the intent of the command is to associate compulsory marriage with incarceration: "Take him to prison, that is, to marriage, and see our (his and my) pleasure therein executed." Forcing Lucio to marry the prostitute he wronged is a just and reasonable application of the principle of measure for measure, and one might expect him to leave it at that, since it would enable him to retaliate against his slanderer under the cover of a more disinterested judgment. Yet at the last moment he swerves again, and applies the principle illogically: compulsory marriage is Lucio's just desert for slandering a prince. I can imagine the Duke's final retort delivered as a smart but offhanded putdown by a speaker well in control of the situation and eager to wind things up. He catches Lucio's plaintive hyperbole, "Marrying a punk . . . is . . . / Whipping and hanging," tosses it back at him, and thus reinstates the original sentence as a "death" penalty. But I prefer to hear something more in the Duke's voicing of the retort, the touch of anger confused by its bidirectional vector—anger at Lucio and at himself—that gives the Duke's utterances in this scene their distinctive timbre. However flippant, the retort is enriched and blurred by overtones of the wish to execute Lucio, cast off the burr who sticks to him, and get rid of the ducal complicity the burr brazenly represents. This makes the gesture of remission ring a little hollow, especially since the wish fuses with the Duke's desire to seek revenge for the affronts to his princely dignity and personal probity. To hear it this way is to recall his reactions to Lucio in 3.2—the interplay in his language between the appeal to the discourse of injured merit and the refractions of self-accusation the appeal fends off.

"Slandering a prince deserves it. / She, Claudio, that you wrong'd, look you restore" (5.1.521–22). Presumably the speaker pauses between these two lines and gathers himself for his happy-ending speech. But the pause doesn't provide insulation; it is a kind of relay, the site of a kinetic transfer. The strains of anger and self-justification pulsing through the relay make "look you restore" sound more peremptory and curt. Coming only twelve lines after his command to the Provost, "If any woman wrong'd by this lewd fellow, . . . he shall marry her" (506–10), the Duke's exhortation to Claudio takes on the weight of a warning, a quasi-command, that assimilates Claudio's wrong to

Lucio's. It is as if the Duke recognizes that his attempt to deal impartial justice to Lucio has been thrown off and now tries to regain his balance; lingering anxiety about the aptness of the remission he grants Lucio leads him to replay it and get it right in his address to Claudio. But the exhortation at line 522 fits Lucio better than Claudio, of whom it is misleading to suggest that he "wrong'd" Juliet in the same way Lucio wronged his child and its mother. Sandwiched between assertions to Lucio and Angelo, the warning to Claudio falsely assimilates his impending nuptials to the shotgun weddings the Duke has just godfathered.

The saccadic tempo of the exit speech, with its succession of terse addresses, its promissory hints and deferred disclosures, makes the obligatory business of happy ending seem a little jumpy and impatient. In moving from Lucio to Claudio to Mariana and Angelo, the Duke begins the speech with a comedic flourish that proclaims his power, justice, and good works as a matchmaker; he announces the attainment of the ends that justify his duplicitous means before going on to thank the two confederates who made his masquerade and dirty tricks possible. The oddest feature of this performance is that although Claudio's sentence and the efforts to circumvent it drive the play's plot and narrative action, the Duke's address to Claudio is not merely the first but also the shortest in the exit speech.[9] His first and only words to Claudio since 3.1 are thus anteclimactic, as if Claudio is no more than a bridge to be passed quickly over on the way from Lucio to the other recipients of ducal attention. This oddity seems to have some connection with the fact that his last and longest address is reserved for Isabella, whom he had so blithely and energetically kept in the dark about her brother's escape from death. But what is the connection? Does his cursory treatment of Claudio, and his separation of the two addresses, reflect his embarrassment in the presence of Isabella? Does he recognize that she reconciled herself almost too quickly and willingly to Claudio's death, and may herself be embarrassed by Claudio's presence? Just before he addresses Isabella, the Duke makes his first and only public mention of the head trick in a comment to Angelo that has, as I noted above, the effect of a final affront to his defeated rival. But what effect does it have on Isabella, who can't be presumed to have known about the head trick before this reference to it? For the first time she is able to comprehend not only his role in saving Claudio but also the extent to which, the deliberateness with which, he has deceived her from 4.3 to this moment. Does the Duke mention the head trick for her benefit as well as Angelo's? Is the possible ambivalence of the effect of the mention on Isabella something the Duke—given what we know he knows—may be imagined to desire?[10]

What kind of spin do these questions put on the intentions represented by the words with which the Duke edges into his proposal, "I have a motion much imports your good," and by the conditional clause that politely qualifies it, "Whereto if you'll a willing ear incline"?[11] Is the gesture of proposal muddied by the possibility that it constitutes the last move in the Duke's successful campaign against Angelo? For those who may detect in the conditional qualifier a distant echo of the annunciation motif parodically introduced by Lucio's "Hail, virgin, if you be" (1.4.16), the Duke's appeal might well seem to register an aspiration to the semblance of "power divine"—to the purity no less than the power of the messenger bearing "heavenly comforts." But how could such a gesture of angelic donation avoid being contaminated by the "doubling or counterfeiting [of] Angelo's desire" that the proposal represents?[12] The triumphant closure the Duke's exit speech tries to perform is perforated by too many questions, lends itself to too many competing interpretations, to fulfill its function. The noise or static they generate is sustained by the conspicuous openness of the silences that greet the Duke's parade of pardons and by the tonal dissonance of the exit speech. Its strains of anger and self-justification bear the burden of the ruler who carries the torch of his *curiositas* into every dark corner in search of the exculpation that will ensconce him in seeming knowledge and free him from the swinges of his burning throne.

I hope here be truths

Notes

1. Graham Bradshaw, *Shakespeare's Scepticism* (New York: St. Martin's Press, 1987), 193.
2. See, for example, Patricia Parker, "Shakespeare and Rhetoric: 'Dilation' and 'Delation' in *Othello,*" in *Shakespeare and the Question of Theory,* ed. Patricia Parker and Geoffrey Hartman (New York: Methuen, 1985), 54–74.
3. This disclosure also throws a revisionary line back to Lucio's earlier statement to Claudio that he hopes Isabella succeeds with Angelo "for the encouragement of the like, which else would stand under grievous imposition" (1.2.177–79).
4. See, for example, his all but daring the "Friar" to report him to the Duke at 3.2.155–63, and his back talk to the Duke in the early moments of 5.1.
5. J. Dover Wilson, *The Fortunes of Falstaff* (Cambridge: Cambridge University Press, 1961), 20.
6. Lever remarks on the "progressive denigration" Lucio's character undergoes in this scene (Arden ed. xcvi).
7. Overdone's representation of herself as unappreciated and abused echoes the Duke's self-pitying aside at 3.2.179–83.
8. The references in question are at 1.1.59; 1.4.74; 2.1.34; 2.2.11; 4.2.23, 121, 128, 133, 151, 157, 174; and 4.3.33.
9. On the odd diminution of Claudio, see Jonathan Goldberg, "Shakespearean Inscriptions: The Voicing of Power," in Parker and Hartman (eds.), *Shakespeare and the Question of Theory,* 125–27.
10. We know, for example, that he has overheard Isabella's virulent condemnation of Claudio in 3.1.

11. Strictly speaking, these words constitute not a proposal but a pre-proposal, a proposal to propose.

12. The phrase is Julia Lupton's, cited from her stimulating chapter on *Measure for Measure,* "Saints on Trial: The Genre of *Measure for Measure,*" in *Afterlife of the Saints: Hagiography, Typology, and Renaissance Literature* (Stanford: Stanford University Press, 1996). I'm very grateful to Professor Lupton for letting me read and benefit from her account of the play in advance of publication.

Index

The Volume Editor

Richard P. Wheeler, Professor of English at the University of Illinois at Urbana-Champaign, has a B.A. from Cornell College (Iowa) and an M.A. and Ph.D. from the State University of New York at Buffalo. He is the author of *Shakespeare's Development and the Problem Comedies: Turn and Counter-Turn;* co-author, with C. L. Barber, of *The Whole Journey: Shakespeare's Power of Development;* and editor of Barber's *Creating Elizabethan Tragedy: The Theater of Marlowe and Kyd.* He has published essays and reviews on Shakespeare, Renaissance drama, W. B. Yeats, and D. H. Lawrence.

The General Editor

♦

Zack Bowen is Professor of English at the University of Miami. He holds degrees from the University of Pennsylvania (B.A.), Temple University (M.A.), and the State University of New York at Buffalo (Ph.D.). In addition to being general editor of this G. K. Hall series, he is editor of the James Joyce series for the University of Florida Press and the *James Joyce Literary Supplement.* He is author and editor of numerous books on modern British, Irish, and American literature. He has also published more than one hundred monographs, essays, scholarly reviews, and recordings related to literature. He is past president of the James Joyce Society (1977–1986), former chair of the Modern Language Association Lowell Prize Committee, and current president of the International James Joyce Foundation.